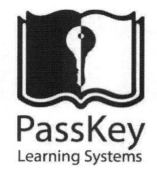

PassKey
Learning Systems

EA Review
Part 1 Individuals
Enrolled Agent Study Guide

July 1, 2019-February 29, 2020
Testing Cycle

Joel Busch, CPA, JD
Christy Pinheiro, EA, ABA®
Kolleen Wells, EA
Richard Gramkow, EA

Editor: Joel Busch, CPA, JD

Title: PassKey Learning Systems EA Review Part 1 Individuals; Enrolled Agent Study Guide, July 1, 2019-February 29, 2020 Testing Cycle

ISBN-13: 9781935664581

First Printing, March 2019.

PassKey EA Review® is a U.S. Registered Trademark

Official website: *www.PassKeyPublications.com*

This study guide is designed for exam candidates who will take their exams in the July 1, 2019, to February 29, 2020 testing cycle.

IMPORTANT INFORMATION REGARDING THE ENROLLED AGENT SPECIAL ENROLLMENT EXAMINATION
The government shutdown has delayed the annual revision of the Special Enrollment Examination. The examination administered between May 1, 2019 and June 30, 2019 will be based on tax law for the calendar year 2017. A revised examination will be released on July 1, 2019, and will be based on tax law for the calendar year 2018.

Table of Contents

Recent Praise for the PassKey EA Review Series

(Real customers, real names, public testimonials)

I passed with Passkey!
Raenelle Dennis Sellers, EA

I passed with Passkey! Thank you for all the resources you make available. It was invaluable!

Thank you!
Laura Southerland, EA

Thank you for having this course available. I was able to pass each part on the first try by using the online course, study books, my work knowledge, as well as my Bachelor's in Accounting. [PassKey's] practice questions were very similar to the actual EA exam.

I passed all three parts.
Robbie Cantoron

I passed all three parts of the EA exam using this book, which is why I'll give it five stars...There are many tax laws I've learned about by studying this book that I haven't encountered yet preparing returns, so I did end up learning a lot. The trick is to focus (after reading the material) on the multiple-choice questions at the end of each chapter and their solutions: this is how you'll apply and practice what you've learned and really learn the details.

This is the only book you need.
Suika Yutaka

I prefer self-study over any type of course, and I loved this book. Plus, I have a very demanding job, and this made me greatly appreciate the concise style of this book. Also note that this is the most reasonably priced full EA review I know of (i.e., covering all three parts of the exam). Greatest praise!

You can pass using just this book.
Vishnu Kali Osirion

I really rushed studying for this section. These authors make tax law relevant to your day-to-day experiences and understandable. You can pass the exam with just this as a resource. I do recommend purchasing the workbook as well just for question exposure. The questions in the book and in the workbook are pretty indicative of what's on the exam. This is a must buy. Cheers.

PassKey is the way to go!
Alaina Crowell

I passed all three SEEs on the first try in ten weeks! Each unit is explained so clearly, and I was completely prepared for each SEE. Wonderful books.

This review is the best on the market.
Yaw Asiante-Asamoah

I passed on all three parts on one attempt. The questions in the Review and Workbook are similar to the real exams. I got a big raise and my bonus went up at my seasonal job. It's worth the money, trust me.

This book helped me pass.
Kenichi Mochizukion

I used the PassKey workbook after studying the PassKey textbook. The example questions cover all the topics and require good understanding to answer, so it was very helpful to reveal my weak areas prior to the exam.

Wonderful!
Ana Lavallee

PassKey was all I needed to pass the three tests to become an EA in just three months. The books are easy to read and understand. Thank you!

Outstanding!
Derrell L. Chastain

Outstanding! Helped me pass the EA exam...I used all three books!

Highly recommend these materials
Tosha H. Knelangeon

Using only this book and the workbook, I passed all three EA exams on my first try. I highly recommend these materials. As long as you put in the time to read and study all the information provided, you should be well-prepared.

Very useful, I passed 1st and 2nd exams by reading only PassKey!
Shixiong Feng

Very useful; I passed the 1st and 2nd exams by only reading the PassKey EA Review. If you are willing to spend some time to read the whole book thoroughly, then this book is the only thing you need to pass the EA exams.

Amazing!
Sopio Svanishvilion

PassKey helped me pass all three parts of the Enrolled Agent exam. They are a "must have" if you want to pass your EA exams.

Perfect!
Charles Farmer, Jr.

Awesome! Passed my first test the first time!

Introduction

Congratulations on taking the first step toward becoming an enrolled agent, a widely respected professional tax designation. The Internal Revenue Service licenses enrolled agents, known as EAs, after candidates pass a competency exam testing their knowledge of federal tax law. As an enrolled agent, you will have the same representation rights as a CPA, with the ability to represent taxpayers in IRS audits and appeals—an EA's rights are unlimited before all levels and offices of the IRS.

The PassKey study guide series is designed to help you study for the EA exam, which is formally called the *IRS Special Enrollment Examination* or *"SEE."*

EA Exam Basics

The EA exam consists of three parts, which candidates may schedule separately and take in any order they wish. The computerized exam covers all aspects of federal tax law, with Part 1 testing the taxation of individuals; Part 2 testing the taxation of businesses; and Part 3 testing representation, practice, and procedures.

Each part of the EA exam features 100 multiple choice questions, with no written answers required. The exam may include some experimental questions that are not scored. You will not know which of the questions count toward your score and which do not.

Computerized EA Exam Format
Part 1: Individual Taxation–100 questions
Part 2: Business Taxation–100 questions
Part 3: Representation, Practice, and Procedures–100 questions

You will have 3.5 hours to complete each part of the exam. The actual seat time is four hours, which allows time for a pre-exam tutorial and a post-exam survey. An on-screen timer counts down the amount of time you have to finish.

The testing company Prometric exclusively administers the EA exam at thousands of testing centers across the United States and in certain other countries. You can find valuable information and register online at *www.prometric.com/SEE*.

Prometric Testing Center Procedures

The testing center is designed to be a secure environment. The following are procedures you will need to follow on test day:

1. Check in about a half-hour before your appointment time, and bring a current, government-issued ID with a photo and signature. If you do not have a valid ID, you will be turned away and will have to pay for a new exam appointment. Refunds will not be issued by Prometric if you forget to bring proper ID with you.

2. The EA exam is a closed-book test, so you are not allowed to bring any notes or reference materials into the testing room. The center supplies sound-blocking headphones if you want to use them.

3. No food, water, or other beverages are allowed in the testing room.

4. You will be given scratch paper and a pencil to use, which will be collected after the exam.

5. You will be able to use an onscreen calculator during the exam, or Prometric will provide you with a handheld calculator. You cannot bring your own calculator into the examination room.

6. Before entering the testing room, you will be scanned with a metal detector wand.

7. You will need to sign in and out every time you leave the testing room. Bathroom breaks are permitted, but the test timer will continue to count down.

8. You are not allowed to talk or communicate with other test-takers in the exam room. Prometric continuously monitors the testing via video, physical walk-throughs, and an observation window.

Important Note: Violation of any of these procedures may result in the disqualification of your exam. In cases of cheating, the IRS says candidates are subject to consequences that include civil and criminal penalties.

Exam-takers who require special accommodations under the Americans with Disabilities Act (ADA) must contact Prometric directly at 1-800-967-1139 to obtain an accommodation request. The test is administered in English; a language barrier is not considered a disability.

Exam Content

Each May, using questions based on the prior calendar year's tax law, the IRS introduces multiple new versions of each part of the EA exam. If you fail a particular part of the exam and need to retake it, do not expect to see the identical questions the next time.

Prometric's website includes broad content outlines for each exam part. When you study, make sure you are familiar with the items listed, which are covered in detail in your PassKey guides.

Questions from older exams are available on the IRS website for review. Be aware that tax law changes every year, so be familiar with recent updates and do not rely too heavily on these earlier questions and answers.

Your PassKey study guides present an overview of all the major areas of federal taxation that enrolled agents typically encounter in their practices and are likely to appear on the exam. Although our guides are designed to be comprehensive, we suggest you also review IRS publications and try to learn as much as you can about tax law in general, so you are well-equipped to take the exam.

In addition to this study guide, we highly recommend that all exam candidates read:

- **Publication 17**, *Your Federal Income Tax* (for Part 1 of the exam), and
- **Circular 230**, *Regulations Governing the Practice of Attorneys, Certified Public Accountants, Enrolled Agents, Enrolled Actuaries, and Appraisers before the Internal Revenue Service* (for Part 3 of the exam)

You may download these publications for free from the IRS website.

> **Note:** Some exam candidates take *Part 3: Representation, Practice, and Procedures* first rather than taking the tests in order, since the material in Part 3 is considered less complicated. However, test-takers should know that several questions pertaining to taxation of *Individuals* (Part 1) and *Businesses* (Part 2) are often included on the Part 3 exam.

Exam Strategy

Each multiple-choice question has four answer choices. There are several different question formats, and examples of each format are featured in your PassKey study guides. During the exam, you should read each question thoroughly to understand precisely what is being asked. Be particularly careful when the question uses language such as "not" or "except."

Format One–Direct Question
Which of the following entities are required to file Form 709, *United States Gift Tax Return*? A. An individual B. An estate or trust C. A corporation D. All of the above
Format Two–Incomplete Sentence
Supplemental wages do not include payments for: A. Accumulated sick leave B. Nondeductible moving expenses C. Vacation pay D. Travel reimbursements paid at the federal government's per diem rate
Format Three–All of the Following Except
There are five tests which must be met for you to claim an exemption for a dependent. Which of the following is not a requirement? A. Citizen or Resident Test B. Member of Household or Relationship Test C. Disability Test D. Joint Return Test

If you are unsure of an answer, you may mark it for review and return to it later. Try to eliminate clearly wrong answers from the four possible choices to narrow your odds of selecting the right answer. But be sure to answer every question, even if you have to guess, because all answers left incomplete will be marked as incorrect. Each question is weighted equally.

There may also be a limited number of questions that have four choices, with three incorrect statements or facts and only one with a correct statement or fact, which you would select as the right answer.

With 3.5 hours allotted for each part of the exam, you have slightly more than two minutes per question. Try to answer the questions you are sure about quickly, so you can devote more time to those that include calculations or that you are unsure about. Remember, the clock does not stop for bathroom breaks, so allocate your time wisely.

To familiarize yourself with the computerized testing format, you may take a tutorial on the Prometric website. However, the tutorial only illustrates what the test screens look like; it does not allow you to revisit questions you have left open or marked for review, as you can do during the actual exam.

Scoring Methods

The EA exam is not graded on a curve, and the IRS does not reveal either a percentage of correct answers needed to pass or a predetermined pass rate. Each question on the exam is worth one point. The IRS determines scaled scores by calculating the number of questions answered correctly from the total number of questions in the exam and converting to a scale that ranges from 40 to 130. The IRS has set the scaled passing score at 105, which corresponds to the minimum level of knowledge deemed acceptable for EAs.

After you finish your exam and submit your answers, you will exit the testing room, and a Prometric staff member will print results showing whether you passed or failed. Test results are automatically shared with the IRS, so you do not need to submit them yourself. Test scores are confidential and will be revealed only to you and the IRS. If you pass, your printed results will show a passing designation but not your actual score. The printout also will not indicate which specific questions you answered correctly or incorrectly.

If you fail, you will receive a scaled score, so you will be able to see how close you are to the minimum score of 105. You will also receive the following diagnostic information to help you know which subject areas to concentrate on when studying to retake the exam:

- *Level 1: Area of weakness where additional study is necessary. It is essential for you to focus on this domain as you prepare to retake the test. You may want to consider taking a course or participating actively in a study group on this topic.*

- *Level 2: Might need additional study.*

- *Level 3: Clearly demonstrated an understanding of the subject area.*

These diagnostic indicators correspond to various sections of each part of the exam.

If necessary, you may take each part of the exam up to four times during the current testing window. You will need to reregister with Prometric and pay fees each new time you take an exam part.

You may carry over passing scores for individual parts of the exam up to two years from the date you took them.

Pass Rates

The yearly pass rates for the SEE vary by exam. In the prior year testing period, the highest pass rate was for Part 3, with a nearly 90% success rate. Just over 80% of test-takers passed Part 1.

The pass rate for Part 2 was much lower, averaging only about 40%. Prometric notes that it can be misleading to compare pass rates for the various exams because the same individuals do not take each one. The number of candidates who take Part 1 is nearly double the number of candidates taking either Part 2 or Part 3.

Applying for Enrollment

Once you have passed all three parts of the EA exam, you can apply to become an enrolled agent. The process includes an IRS review of your tax compliance history. Failure to timely file or pay personal income taxes can be grounds for denial of enrollment. The IRS' Return Preparer Office will review the circumstances of each case and make determinations on an individual basis. You may not practice as an EA until the IRS approves your application and issues you an enrollment card, a process that takes up to 60 days or more.

Successfully passing the EA exam can launch you into a fulfilling and lucrative new career. The exam requires intense preparation and diligence, but with the help of PassKey's comprehensive *EA Review*, you will have the tools you need to learn how to become an enrolled agent.

We wish you much success.

This page intentionally left blank.

Ten Steps for the EA Exam

STEP 1: Learn

Learn more about the enrolled agent designation, and explore the career opportunities that await you after passing your EA exam. In addition to preparing income tax returns for clients, EAs can represent individuals and businesses before the IRS, just as attorneys and CPAs do. A college degree or professional tax background is not required to take the EA exam. Many people who use the PassKey study guides have had no prior experience preparing tax returns, but go on to rewarding new professional careers.

STEP 2: Gather Information

Gather more information before you launch into your studies. The IRS publishes necessary information about becoming an EA on its website (www.irs.gov/Tax-Professionals/Enrolled-Agents). You will also find valuable information about the exam itself on the Prometric testing website at www.prometric.com/see. Be sure to download the Candidate Information Bulletin, which takes you step-by-step through the registration and testing process.

STEP 3: Obtain a PTIN

PTIN stands for "Preparer Tax Identification Number". Before you can register for your EA exam, you must obtain a PTIN from the IRS. The PTIN sign-up system can be found at www.irs.gov/ptin. You will need to create an account and provide personal information. Starting in 2017, there is no longer a fee for obtaining or renewing a PTIN. Foreign-based candidates without a Social Security number are also required to have a PTIN in order to register to take the exam; they will need to submit additional paperwork with their Form W-12.

STEP 4: Register with Prometric

Once you have your PTIN, you may register for your exam on the Prometric website by creating an account to set up your user ID and password. You must also complete Form 2587, Application for Special Enrollment Examination.

STEP 5: Schedule Your Test

After creating an account, you can complete the registration process by clicking on "Scheduling." Your exam appointment must be scheduled within one year from the date of registration. You can choose a test site, time, and date that are convenient for you. Prometric has test centers in most major metropolitan areas of the United States, as well as in many other countries.

You may schedule as little as two days in advance—space permitting—through the website or by calling 800-306-3926 Monday through Friday. Be aware that the website and the phone line show different available times and dates, so you may want to check both for your preferred testing dates. The testing fee is nonrefundable. Once you've scheduled, you'll receive a confirmation number. Keep it for your records because you will need it to reschedule, cancel, or change your appointment.

STEP 6: Adopt a Study Plan

Focus on one exam part at a time, and adopt a study plan that covers each unit of your PassKey guides. You'll need to develop your own individualized study program. The period of time you'll need to prepare for each exam is truly unique to you, based on how much prior tax preparation experience you have and your current level of tax knowledge, how well you understand and retain the information you read, and how much time you have to study for each test. For those without prior tax experience, a good rule of thumb is to study at least 60 hours for each of the three exam sections. Part 2: Businesses may require additional study preparation, as evidenced by the lower pass rates. One thing is true for all candidates: for each of the tests, start studying well in advance of your scheduled exam date.

STEP 7: Get Plenty of Rest and Good Nutrition

Get plenty of rest, exercise, and good nutrition prior to the EA exam. You'll want to be at your best on exam day.

STEP 8: Test Day

Be sure to arrive early at the test site. Prometric advises arriving at least 30 minutes before your scheduled exam time. If you miss your appointment and are not allowed to take the test, you'll forfeit your fee and have to pay for a new appointment. Remember to bring a government-issued ID with your name, photo, and signature. Your first and last name must exactly match the first and last name you used to register for the exam.

STEP 9: During the Exam

This is when your hard work finally pays off. Focus and don't worry if you don't know the answer to every question, but make sure you use your time well. Give your best answer to every question. All questions left blank will be marked as wrong.

STEP 10: Congratulations. You Passed!

After celebrating your success, you need to apply for your EA designation. The quickest way is by filling out Form 23, Application for Enrollment to Practice Before the Internal Revenue Service, on the IRS website. You may also pay online. Once your application is approved, you'll be issued an enrollment card, and you'll officially be a brand new enrolled agent!

PART 1: INDIVIDUALS

Essential Tax Law Figures for Individuals

Here is a quick summary of some of the essential tax figures for the enrolled agent exam cycle that runs from July 1, 2019, to February 29, 2020:

> **Note:** The *Tax Cuts and Jobs Act* (TCJA) became law on December 22, 2017. This sweeping legislation represents the broadest reform of U.S. tax law in over thirty years and will affect individuals and businesses across the country. Most of the provisions in the TCJA became effective in the 2018 tax year.

Income Tax Return Filing Deadline: April 15, 2019 (extended due date: October 15, 2019) Residents of Maine and Massachusetts have until April 17, 2019, to file because April 15, 2019, is Patriots' Day in those states and April 16, 2019, is Emancipation Day in Washington D.C. Extension Deadline: October 15, 2019

2018 Personal and Dependency Exemptions: The personal exemption is eliminated for tax years 2018 through 2025 by the Tax Cuts and Jobs Act. Although the exemption amount is zero, the ability to claim an exemption may make taxpayers eligible for other tax benefits. For 2018 tax year filings, taxpayers can determine a dependent's eligibility by using the "deemed exemption" amount of $4,150. [1]

2018 Standard Deduction Amounts (by Filing Status):
- MFJ or Qualifying Widow(er) $24,000; Additional Age 65 or Older or Blind:$1,300
- MFS: $12,000; Additional Age 65 or Older or Blind: $1,300
- HOH: $18,000: Additional Age 65 or Older or Blind: $1,600
- Single: $12,000; Additional Age 65 or Older or Blind: $1,600
- Dependent of another taxpayer; the lesser of:
  - The greater of $1,050 or Earned Income + $350
  - or $12,000

2018 Gross Income Filing Thresholds for U.S. Citizens and U.S. Residents:

- Single: $12,000 (65 or older: $13,600)
- Head of household: $18,000 (65 or older: $19,600)
- Married filing jointly: $24,000
  - 65 or older (one spouse): $25,300
  - 65 or older (both spouses): $26,600
- Married filing separately (of any age): $5 (this is not a typo, it really is $5)
- Qualifying widow(er) with dependent child: $24,000 (65 or older $25,300)

---

[1] In 2018, a "deemed personal exemption" amount of $4,150 is used for purposes of determining who is a "qualifying relative" under IRC Sec. 152(d)(1)(B).

Other Situations When a Taxpayer Must File a 2018 Return

- Any taxpayer with self-employment income of $400 or more in 2018 must file a return.
- Any taxpayer who received HSA, Archer MSA, or Medicare Advantage MSA distributions.
- Any taxpayer who earned wages of $108.28 or more from a church or qualified church-controlled organization that is exempt from employer Social Security and Medicare taxes.
- Any taxpayer who received advance payments of the Premium Tax Credit from insurance coverage through the Health Insurance Marketplace. The taxpayer should receive Forms 1095-A showing the amount of the advance payments, if any.
- Any taxpayer that owes household employment taxes. If a taxpayer is filing a return only because they owe this tax, the taxpayer can file Schedule H by itself.
- Any taxpayer that owes additional tax on a qualified plan, including an individual retirement arrangement (IRA), or another tax-favored account. However, if a taxpayer is filing a return only because this tax is owed, the taxpayer can file Form 5329 by itself

2018 Contribution Limits - Traditional and Roth IRAs

- Roth and traditional IRAs: $5,500, (catch-up contribution of $1,000 for taxpayers age 50 or older)[2] Roth IRA contribution limit phaseout (MAGI): $189,000 to $199,000 (MFJ); $120,000 to $135,000 (Single and HOH); $0 to $10,000 (MFS).[3]
- 401(k), 403(b): $18,500, (additional catch-up contribution of $6,000 for taxpayers age 50 or older)
- SIMPLE IRA plans: $12,500 (allowable catch-up contribution of $3,000 for taxpayers age 50 or older)
- SIMPLE IRA Contribution Limits: $12,500 Limit for Keogh plans and SEP-IRAs: $55,000

> **Note:** IRA *conversions* from traditional IRAs to Roth IRAs are allowed after enactment of the Tax Cuts and Jobs Act, however, later *recharacterizations* are no longer allowed after December 31, 2017.[4] The new law also prohibits recharacterizing amounts that were rolled over to a Roth IRA from other types of retirement plans, such as 401(k) or 403(b) plans.

---

[2] The 2018 Traditional and Roth IRA Contribution Deadline is April 15, 2019.

[3] With regards to the Roth contribution limit, if the taxpayer is "married filing separately" but did not live with their spouse at any time during the year, the taxpayer may use the higher phaseout threshold for single taxpayers.

[4] An IRA "recharacterization" is a reversal of a previous conversion. For example, if a taxpayer converts to a Roth IRA and then later changes his mind, he would use a process known as "recharacterization" to convert the funds *back* to his traditional IRA.

2018 Estate and Trust *Exemption* Amounts[5]

- Estate Exemption Amount: $600
- Simple Trust: $300
- Complex Trust: $100

2018 Estate and Gift Tax *Exclusion* Amounts

- 2018 Annual Exclusion for Gifts: $15,000
- Lifetime noncitizen marital threshold for gift tax: [6] $152,000
- Estate and Gift Tax Exclusion: $11,180,000
- Applicable Credit: $4,417,800
- Generation-Skipping Transfer Tax Exemption: $11,180,000

2018 Maximum Compensation Subject to FICA

- OASDI maximum wage base: $128,400 (2018 tax rate: 12.4% self-employed, 6.2% employees). The maximum OASDI tax is $15,921.60 in 2018 (for self-employed individuals and the combined employer-employee contributions).
- Medicare Tax: no ceiling on Medicare tax (2018 tax rate: 2.9% self-employed, 1.45% employees).
- *Additional* Medicare Tax of 0.9% tax is imposed on earned income for higher-income taxpayers (income of more than $250,000 for MFJ[7]; $125,000 for MFS, and $200,000 for Single, HOH, or Qualifying Widow(er)

2018 Net Investment Income Tax (NIIT): The tax is the *lesser* of: 3.8% of net investment income or the amount of modified adjusted gross income (MAGI) over the following thresholds:

- Single and HOH: $200,000
- MFJ and qualifying widow(er): $250,000
- MFS: $125,000
- Estates and trusts: $12,500

2018 Standard Mileage Rates:

- Business: 54.5¢ per mile[8]
- Charitable purposes: 14¢ per mile
- Medical and moving: 18¢ per mile[9]

---

[5] For estates and trusts, the exemption amount is not allowed in the entity's final tax year (the year of dissolution).

[6] There is no limit on the amount that a U.S. citizen can transfer to another U.S. citizen spouse in a calendar year. This limitation only applies to noncitizen spouses.

[7] Earned income of spouses is combined towards this Additional Medicare Tax threshold for MFJ returns.

[8] Starting in 2018, business mileage is no longer deductible as an unreimbursed employee business expense, except for U.S. armed forces reservists, state or local government officials paid on a fee basis, and certain performing artists.

[9] Starting in 2018, moving mileage is deductible only by U.S. armed forces members on active duty who move pursuant to a military order and incident to a permanent change of station.

2018 Long-Term Care Premiums Maximum premiums (per person): For 2018, the maximum amount of qualified long-term care premiums includible as medical expenses has increased. The limit on premiums is for each taxpayer (not per return). Qualified long-term care premiums up to the amounts shown below can be included as medical expenses on Schedule A.

- Age 40 or under: $420
- Age 41 to 50: $780
- Age 51 to 60: $1,560
- Age 61 to 70: $4,160
- Age 71 or over: $5,200

2018 Credits and Exclusions

- Child Tax Credit: $2,000 per qualifying child. Maximum Refundable Portion: $1,400. The credit phases out $50 for each $1,000 of MAGI over $400,000 (MFJ), $200,000 (all other taxpayers).
- "Other Dependent Credit": $500. There is no refundable portion.
- Foreign Income Exclusion: $103,900
- Adoption Credit: $13,810 Phaseout range: MAGI between $ 207,140 - $247,140
- Credit for Child and Dependent Care Expenses: $3,000 maximum qualifying expenses (one child); $6,000 (two or more children)

2018 Tax Rates for Capital Gains and Dividends[10]

Short-term capital gains and ordinary dividends are taxed at ordinary income rates. The top rates for qualified dividends and long-term capitals gains in 2018 are as follows:

Tax Rate	Single/MFS	MFJ	HOH	Estates & Trusts
0%	$0 - $38,600	$0 - $77,200	$0 - $51,700	$0-$2,600
15%	$38,601 - $425,800	$77,201 - $479,000	$51,701 - $452,400	$2,601 to $12,700
20%	$425,801 or more	$479,001 or more	$452,401 or more	$12,701 or more

2018 "Nanny Tax" on Household Employees: The nanny tax threshold is $2,100 in 2018. A household employer is normally obligated to withhold and pay federal FICA (Social Security and Medicare) taxes for any household employee they paid $2,100 or more during the year. A household employer is required to pay FUTA taxes if they paid a household employee $1,000 or more in a calendar quarter in the current or prior year. These thresholds are on a *per employee* basis.

2018 "Kiddie Tax" Threshold: The "Kiddie Tax" age limit is up to 18 and certain dependents under 24. The unearned income limitation is $2,100. Starting in 2018, the kiddie tax will be based on trust and estate tax rates.

---

[10] The Individual tax rates on capital gains and the 3.8% net investment income tax (NIIT) in 2018 are unchanged by the TCJA.

2018 Earned Income Tax Credit (EITC):[11] The maximum amount of the EITC for the year is:

- $6,431 with three or more qualifying children
- $5,716 with two qualifying children
- $3,461 with one qualifying child
- $519 with no qualifying children

To be eligible for the EITC, the taxpayer must have earned income of at least $1 but less than:

- $49,194 ($54,884 if Married Filing Jointly) with three or more qualifying children
- $45,802 ($51,492 if Married Filing Jointly) with two qualifying children
- $40,320 ($46,010 if Married Filing Jointly) with one qualifying child
- $15,270 ($20,950 if Married Filing Jointly) with no qualifying child
- Investment income must also be $3,500 <u>or less</u> for the year to be eligible for EITC.

2018 Alternative Minimum Tax Exemptions:

- Unmarried taxpayers: $70,300
- Married Filing Jointly: $109,400
- Married Filing Separately: $ 54,700

2018 Alternative Minimum Tax Exemption Phaseout Thresholds:

- Unmarried taxpayers: $500,000 to $781,200
- Married Filing Jointly: $1,000,000 to $1,437,600
- Married Filing Separate: $500,000 to $718,800

2018 Section 179 Expense: Maximum amount: $1,000,000; Beginning phase-out limitation (for Section 179-eligible assets placed in service during the year: $2,500,000. Assets eligible for Section 179 now include:

- Furnishings used in lodging
- Qualified improvement property (QIP)
- Nonresidential improvements to real property, including: HVAC (air conditioning and heating systems), fire and security systems, plumbing, and flooring.

2018 Bonus Depreciation: 100% additional first-year depreciation is available for qualified property *acquired* and *placed in service* after September 27, 2017. Bonus

---

[11] The IRS cannot issue refunds claiming the Earned Income Tax Credit (EITC) and the Additional Child Tax Credit (ACTC) before February 15, 2019. This is a congressional provision in the *Protecting Americans from Tax Hikes (PATH) Act.*

depreciation now applies to used property. Assets that qualify for bonus depreciation include:

- MACRS property with a recovery period of 20 years or less
- Computer software
- Water utility property
- Qualified film or television production (does not include pornographic films)
- Qualified live theatrical production, as defined in section 181(e)
- Fruit and nut bearing trees[12]

> **Note:** One of the most significant differences between Section 179 and bonus depreciation is that Section 179 is limited by taxable business income, while bonus depreciation can create a net operating loss (NOL). We will cover more on this topic later.

2018 HSA and HDHP Limits:

2018 HSA Contribution Limits	
HSA Contribution Limits	Individual: $3,450 Family: $6,850
Minimum Deductible for HDHPs	Individual: $1,350 Family: $2,700
Maximum Out-of-Pocket Expenses	Individual: $6,650 Family: $13,300[13]

2018 Retirement Savings Contribution Credit (Saver's Credit)[14] Income Limits Increased: The maximum amount of credit-qualifying contributions is $2,000 ($4,000 if married filing jointly). Beginning in 2018, the Saver's Credit can be taken for contributions to an ABLE account if the taxpayer is the designated beneficiary of the ABLE account. The income limitations are as follows:

Credit amount	Single AGI Limits	HOH AGI Limits	MFJ AGI Limits
50%	$19,000 or less	$28,500 or less	$38,000 or less
20%	$19,001-$20,500	$28,501-$30,750	$38,001-$41,000
10%	$20,501-$31,500	$30,751-$47,250	$41,001-$63,000

---

[12] This includes grapevines, orange trees, almonds and olive orchards, etc. In the past, fruit and nut bearing trees would not be "placed in service" for several years, because the trees would not be "placed in service" until they bear fruit. Now, farmers are allowed to take bonus depreciation at the time of planting. This is an election for bonus depreciation only. These plants and trees would not be eligible for Section 179 in their pre-productive period. A farmer may also choose to wait, and when the trees begin bearing fruit or nuts, then the farmer may claim section 179 or MACRS depreciation.

[13] An HSA can be combined with a qualified high-deductible health plan and offers the opportunity to save for health care on a pre-tax basis. Another name for an HDHP is an "HSA-Eligible" Plan.

[14] The IRS uses two different names for this particular credit: the "Saver's Credit" and the "Retirement Savings Contribution Credit." However, they are the same credit.

2018 Educational Savings Bond Expense Exclusion: The savings bond education tax exclusion allows taxpayers to exclude interest income upon the redemption of eligible Series EE and I Bonds when the bond owner pays qualified higher education expenses at an eligible institution. This exclusion is subject to the following income limitations. Modified adjusted gross income phase-out range:

- MFJ: $119,300 - $149,300
- All other filing status: $79,550 - $94,550

2018 Education Credits and Deductions:

- **American Opportunity Credit**: up to $2,500 per student for the first four years of higher education expenses paid. The credit phases out for single taxpayers with MAGIs between $80,000 and $90,000 ($160,000 and $180,000 for MFJ).

- **Lifetime Learning Credit**: 20% of tuition paid up to a credit of $2,000 per return. The credit phases out between $57,000 and $67,000 of MAGI for single filers ($114,000 to $134,000 for MFJ).

- **Coverdell Education Savings Accounts (Also called an "Education IRA"):** Contribution limit is $2,000 in 2018. The income limit for making a maximum contribution to a Coverdell is $190,000-$220,000 of MAGI for MFJ tax returns. For any taxpayers not filing a joint return, the contribution limit range is $95,000-$110,000 of AGI.

- **Section 529 Plans (Qualified Tuition Programs):** 529 plans now allow distributions of up to $10,000 for educational expenses in connection with the enrollment at a public, private, or religious elementary or secondary school. The IRS doesn't specify a specific dollar amount for annual contribution limits to 529 college savings plans, but contributions are considered gifts for tax purposes and subject to the gift tax limits. In 2018, gifts totaling up to $15,000 per individual will qualify for the annual exclusion. In 2018, donors can elect to treat up to $75,000 of the contribution for the year as if it had been made ratably over a 5-year period.

- **Student loan interest deduction:** $2,500 (maximum per tax return) This deduction is subject to income limitations, and begins to phase out for taxpayers with MAGI in excess of $65,000 ($135,000 for joint returns) and is completely phased out for taxpayers with MAGI of $80,000 or more ($165,000 or more for joint returns). There is no change in the phase-outs from the prior year.

Essential Tax Law Updates for Individuals

New Form 1040: This new design is a shorter form for the 2019 filing season. Form 1040A and Form 1040EZ will not be available for filing 2018 tax returns. The new Form 1040 uses a "building block" approach, which can be supplemented with additional schedules if needed. New schedules (Schedule 1 through 6) have been created for instances where additional information needs to be included beyond those items listed on the face of Form 1040.

Backup Withholding Rate Lowered: The Tax Cuts and Jobs Act reduced the backup withholding tax rate from 28% to 24% in 2018.

NOL Carrybacks Disallowed: Before the Tax Cuts and Jobs Act, most taxpayers could carryback a net operating loss for two years and carry it forward up to 20 years. The TCJA repealed the two-year carryback period and grants an indefinite carryforward period to most businesses. NOL deductions are now limited to 80% of the business' taxable income. Farming businesses are still allowed to carry back losses for two years.

Student Loan Discharges: In 2018, a discharge of student debt due to death or total and permanent disability (TPD) is no longer treated as taxable income.

Miscellaneous Itemized Deductions: All miscellaneous itemized deductions subject to the 2%-of-AGI floor under prior law are repealed through 2025. This means that no miscellaneous itemized deductions will be allowed for job expenses and other miscellaneous deductions subject to the 2% limitation. This does not affect other miscellaneous deductions NOT subject to the 2% limitation (explained later).

Pease Limitation: In 2018, the "Pease Limitation" has been temporarily repealed. The limitation on itemized deductions for higher-income taxpayers has been suspended for tax years 2018 through 2025.

2018 SALT Cap: The deduction for state and local income or property taxes is now capped at $10,000 ($5,000 for MFS filers). An amount paid before January 1, 2018, for state or local income tax will be treated as paid on the last day of the tax year for which it was imposed.

Foreign Real Property Taxes: The TCJA eliminates the deduction for foreign real property taxes unless they are paid or accrued in carrying on a trade or business or in an activity engaged in for profit.

Moving expenses: Moving expenses are no longer deductible for most taxpayers, except for members of the armed forces on active duty who move pursuant to a military order and incident to a permanent change of station. Moving expenses that are reimbursed or paid by an employer must be included in the employee's taxable income as wages.

Personal Casualty Losses: Personal casualty losses are no longer deductible on Schedule A unless the loss is attributable to a federally declared disaster area.

New Credit for Other Dependents or "Family Credit": Under the TCJA, there is a new $500 nonrefundable credit called the Credit for Other Dependents. These include dependent children over the age of 16 and qualifying relatives under Sec. 152(d). The dependent must meet a gross income test that is still tied to the "deemed exemption" amount which is $4,150 in 2018[15].

Kiddie Tax Changes: Under the TCJA, a child's net unearned income is now taxed at the rates applicable to trusts and estates, rather than the parent's tax rates. In previous years, a child's net unearned income was taxed at a parent's top marginal rate. The determination of which children are subject to the kiddie tax remains the same. "Unearned income" also includes income from a trust unless it is a qualified disability trust.

Sec. 199A QBI deduction: This new deduction is up to 20% of a taxpayer's "qualified business income" (QBI). The deduction applies to taxable income derived from sole proprietorships, partnerships, S corporations, trusts, and estates. Only individuals, estates and trusts can claim the QBI deduction. The deduction only applies to domestic business activity (U.S.-only). The calculations on Schedule C, Schedule F, and Schedule SE are not affected by the QBI deduction. Taxable income cannot be reduced below zero by the deduction (i.e., it cannot be used to generate an NOL). The deduction is limited for higher-income taxpayers and for specified service trades or businesses.

Accounting method changes: The TCJA provides that businesses with less than $25 million in gross receipts can now choose to use the cash method of accounting instead of accrual. Under prior law, the availability of the cash method of accounting was limited only to small businesses. Businesses planning to convert from the accrual to the cash method based on the new TCJA rules must request a change in accounting method by filing Form 3115 no later than the last day of the tax year in which the taxpayer wishes to implement the change.[16]

Charitable contributions: Effective for 2018, the AGI limitation on cash contributions is increased from 50% to 60% of AGI. The 30%-of-AGI limitation on most contributions of appreciated assets still applies. Donors age 70 ½ or older may also donate up to $100,000 per tax year directly from an IRA, in lieu of taking an annual required minimum distribution (RMD). Excess contributions that exceed the limits may be deducted over a 5-year carryover period. Carryovers retain their same percentage limit classifications. These same rules apply to the new 60% limit on cash charitable contributions made to qualified organizations. In 2018, no deduction is allowed for any amount paid for the right to purchase tickets for seating at a collegiate athletic event.

---

[15] The deduction for personal exemptions is suspended (reduced to $0) for tax years 2018 through 2025 by the Tax Cuts and Jobs Act. However, the ability to claim an exemption may make taxpayers eligible for other tax benefits.

[16] On August 3, 2018, the IRS issued Revenue Procedure 2018-40. The notice contains guidance for adopting the small taxpayer accounting methods newly allowable under the TCJA changes.

Mortgage Interest Limitation: For mortgages taken out in 2018, only the mortgage interest paid on the first $750,000 ($375,000 if MFS) of mortgage debt is deductible. The previous $1,000,000 ($500,000 for MFS) acquisition indebtedness limit will continue to apply for future tax years for any mortgages incurred *before* December 15, 2017.[17] A taxpayer who entered into a binding written contract before December 15, 2017, to close on a purchase of a principal residence before January 1, 2018, and who purchases the home before April 1, 2018, shall be considered to have incurred acquisition indebtedness prior to December 15, 2017.

Home Equity Loans: The deduction for interest on home equity indebtedness (a home equity loan or line of credit) is eliminated, unless the loan was used to "acquire or improve" the property.

2018 Affordable Care Act (Obamacare) Penalty: For tax year 2018, the ACA penalty is 2.5% of total household adjusted gross income, or $695 per adult and $347.50 per child, up to a maximum of $2,085 per family.[18]

Meal and Entertainment expenses: Starting in 2018, deductions for most entertainment expenses are disallowed. Most meals are still 50% deductible.[19]

Employee Fringe Benefit Changes: The deduction for transportation fringe benefits is no longer available to employers, but the exclusion from income for transportation benefits for employees is still available. This includes parking passes, transit passes, and similar reimbursements. However, bicycle commuting reimbursements are deductible by the employer but taxable to the employee.

Tax Rates and Brackets: There are still seven tax brackets for individuals, but the percentages and income range for each bracket have changed. The TCJA lowers the highest marginal tax rate from 39.6% to 37%. The following seven tax brackets apply for individuals: 10%, 12%, 22%, 24%, 32%, 35% and 37%.

Gambling losses: The TCJA modifies the gambling loss deduction, beginning in 2018. The new definition of "gambling losses" has been expanded to include other expenses incurred in wagering activities, such as travel back-and-forth to a casino. All deductions for expenses incurred in carrying out any type of wagering transactions, (not just gambling losses), are deductible only to the extent of gambling winnings.

2018 Divorce and Alimony Changes: The TCJA eliminates the deduction for payments required under divorce or separation decrees that are executed <u>after</u> December 31, 2018. This new rule also applies to divorce and separation agreements executed prior to 2019,

---

[17] Binding Contract Exception: A taxpayer who has entered into a written binding contract before December 15, 2017 to close on the purchase of a principal residence before January 1, 2018, and who purchases such residence *before* April 1, 2018, can apply the previous $1,000,000 limitation of acquisition indebtedness.

[18] The TCJA includes the repeal of the Affordable Care Act's individual mandate, but this repeal will not go into effect until 2019. In 2018, taxpayers are still subject to a fine for not having health insurance coverage (unless they qualify for an exemption).

[19] Some exceptions exist for employers who operate eating facilities or cafeterias for their employees. Team-building and company activities, such as: holiday parties, company picnics, etc. are also still 100% deductible. These exceptions are covered more extensively in Part 2, Businesses.

but only if they have been substantially modified after 2018. For any divorce or separation decrees executed after December 31, 2018, alimony and separate maintenance payments are no longer included in income by the recipient of the payments.

Retroactive Combat Exemptions on Military Pay: U.S. Armed Forces members who served in the Sinai Peninsula of Egypt may qualify for combat zone tax benefits retroactive to June 2015.

Deductible Medical Expense Threshold: For 2018, the deduction for medical expenses is allowed to the extent that the costs exceed 7.5% of adjusted gross income (AGI). After tax year 2018, the medical expense AGI limitation reverts to 10%.

Virtual Currency/Cryptocurrency: The IRS announced that virtual currencies, such as Bitcoin or Litecoin, would be treated as property and not as currency, thus creating immediate tax consequences for those using virtual currency to pay for goods and services.

ITIN Expiration: ITINs will continue to expire. ITINs that have not been used on a federal tax return at least once in the last three consecutive years will expire. ITINs with middle digits 73, 74, 75, 76, 77, 81 or 82 also expired in 2018. Affected taxpayers must submit a renewal application if they are required to file in 2019.

ABLE Account Contribution Limits: The TCJA increases the contribution limitation to Achieving a Better Life Experience (ABLE) accounts. ABLE Accounts are tax-advantaged savings accounts that are similar to 529 education savings plans, but ABLE accounts are specifically designed for individuals with disabilities without jeopardizing public benefits. For the 2018 tax year, the annual contribution limit is set at $15,000. Designated beneficiaries of ABLE accounts may now claim a Retirement Savings Contributions Credit (Saver's Credit) for contributions they make to their ABLE account for tax years 2018-2025.

Estimated Tax Penalties: On January 16, 2019, the IRS released IR-2019-03, announcing that it is waiving the underestimated tax penalty for many taxpayers whose 2018 federal income tax withholding and estimated tax payments fell short of their total tax liability for the year. For the 2018 tax year only, the IRS is waiving the penalty for any taxpayer who paid at least 85% of their total tax liability during the year through federal income tax withholding, quarterly estimated tax payments, or a combination of the two. The usual percentage threshold is 90% to avoid an underestimated tax penalty.

Estimated Tax for Farmers: The Internal Revenue Service will waive the estimated tax penalty for any qualifying farmer or fisherman who files his or her 2018 federal income tax return and pays any tax due by Monday, April 15, 2019. The deadline is Wednesday, April 17, 2019, for taxpayers residing in Maine or Massachusetts. To be eligible for the waiver, qualifying farmers or fishermen must attach Form 2210-F, to their 2018 income tax return.

Like-Kind Exchanges (Section 1031 Exchanges): In 2018, like-kind exchanges are still allowed for real estate, but repealed for exchanges of personal property. Only real property is permitted to be exchanged under Section 1031.

Deduction for investment expenses suspended: The TCJA suspended miscellaneous itemized deductions subject to the 2%-of-AGI floor, which includes the deduction for many items, such as investment expenses, safe deposit fees, trustee fees, union dues, and investment advisor fees. The TCJA did *not* repeal the deduction for investment *interest* expense. Investment *interest* expense is any interest incurred on loans used to purchase taxable investments.

Sexual Harassment Nondisclosure Agreements: Starting in 2018, taxpayers can no longer deduct any settlement or payment related to sexual harassment or sexual abuse if the settlement is subject to a nondisclosure agreement. In addition, businesses also can no longer deduct attorney fees related to such a settlement or payment.

Important Expired Legislation: The following were commonly-tested provisions of the SEE, but are now expired:

- Exclusion of canceled debt from a primary residence (qualified principal residence indebtedness)
- Mortgage insurance premiums deductible (PMI) as qualified residence interest.
- Tuition and Fees Deduction.
- Credit for nonbusiness energy property (residential energy credit).

Unit 1: Preliminary Work with Taxpayer Data

> **More Reading:**
> Publication 5307, *Tax Reform Basics for Individuals*
> Publication 17, *Your Federal Income Tax*
> Publication 519, *U.S. Tax Guide for Aliens*
> Publication 54, *Tax Guide for U.S. Citizens and Resident Aliens Abroad*

For Part 1 of the enrolled agent exam, you will be expected to know a broad range of information about preparing tax returns for individual taxpayers. This information includes the basics of filing status, requirements, and due dates; taxable and nontaxable income; deductions, credits, adjustments to income; determining the basis of property; figuring capital gains and losses; rental income; retirement income; estate and gift taxes, and much more. We begin with the preliminary work that tax return preparers are expected to do to prepare accurate tax returns for their individual clients.

For the current exam cycle, Part 1 of the exam is broken down into the following sections and corresponding percentages of questions:

1. Preliminary Work with Taxpayer Data – 17 questions
2. Income and Assets – 21 questions
3. Deductions and Credits – 21 questions
4. Taxation and Advice – 14 questions
5. Specialized Returns for Individuals – 12 questions[20]

We will cover preliminary work with taxpayer data, as well as the importance of a taxpayer's biographical information in this unit.

> **Important:** For exams taken between July 1, 2019 and February 29, 2020, all the EA exam questions and topics relate to the 2018 tax year. Questions that contain the term 'current tax year' also refer to the 2018 tax year.

Use of Prior Year Returns

When enrolled agents and other tax professionals prepare tax returns for clients, they are expected to perform due diligence in collecting, verifying, and gathering taxpayer data. A preparer is also expected to review prior year tax returns for compliance, accuracy, and completeness.

A preparer is required by law to notify a taxpayer of an error or omission if discovered on a prior year tax return, and the consequences of not correcting the error or omission. However, a preparer is not required to correct the error.

The use of prior year returns can help prevent major mathematical errors and alert a preparer to specific issues that might affect the taxpayer.

---

[20] The current exam specifications are listed in the official Enrolled Agent Special Enrollment Examination Candidate Information Bulletin, which is available for download on the official Prometric website.

In reviewing prior year tax returns, a preparer needs to determine whether there are items that affect the current year's return, including the following:

- Carryovers

- Net operating losses

- Credit for prior year minimum tax (Form 8801, *Credit for Prior Year Minimum Tax-Individuals, Estates, and Trusts*)

- Depreciation

Taxpayer Biographical Information

When filing tax returns, certain biographical information of the client is required. A tax professional must collect this information from the taxpayer in order to prepare an accurate tax return:

- Legal name, date of birth, and marital status

- Residency status and/or citizenship

- Dependents

- Taxpayer identification number

To prevent filing returns with stolen identities, a tax preparer should ask taxpayers to provide two forms of identification (picture IDs are preferable) that include the taxpayer's name and current address. Also, seeing Social Security cards, ITIN letters and other documents avoids including incorrect TINs for taxpayers, spouses, and dependents on returns. Tax preparers should take care to ensure that they transcribe all TINs correctly.[21]

The IRS requires each individual listed on a federal income tax return to have a valid taxpayer identification number (TIN). That includes the taxpayer, his or her spouse (if married), and any dependents. The types of TINs are:

- Social Security number (SSN)

- Individual taxpayer identification number (ITIN)

- Adoption taxpayer identification number (ATIN)[22]

Note: A taxpayer's personal information is considered highly sensitive and confidential. A preparer who wrongfully discloses a taxpayer's information could face civil and criminal charges.

A taxpayer who cannot obtain an SSN must apply for an ITIN or an ATIN if he files a U.S. tax return or is listed on a tax return as a spouse or dependent.

ITIN Applications and Renewals

Taxpayers who are ineligible for a Social Security number must request an ITIN. Nonresident aliens with a U.S. tax liability generally have ITINs, although not always. For example, an ITIN would be required when a soldier marries a foreign spouse and wishes to file

---

[21] Incorrect taxpayer identification numbers are one of the most common causes of rejected tax returns. Due diligence requirements with regards to taxpayer data are covered more extensively in the EA review for Part 3, *Representation.*
[22] A special form is used for ATIN requests: Form W-7A, *Application for Taxpayer Identification Number for Pending U.S. Adoptions.* This form is used to apply for an ATIN for child who is placed in the taxpayer's home for legal adoption.

jointly. In order to file a joint return, the couple would need to request an ITIN for the foreign spouse. People who do not have lawful status in the United States may obtain an ITIN for tax reporting purposes only.

> **Example:** Umberto is an Italian citizen who has never been to the United States. In January 2018, he inherits a rental property from his deceased aunt, Giuseppina, who was a green-card holder living in the U.S. On the advice of his accountant, Umberto decides to keep the rental property. He hires a management company to receive the rents and manage the property in his absence. Umberto requests an ITIN for tax reporting purposes. He will report his U.S. rental income on Form 1040NR.

In order to request an ITIN, taxpayers must file Form W-7, *Application for IRS Individual Taxpayer Identification Number*, and supply documentation that establishes their foreign status and true identity. There are three ways to apply for an ITIN.

- Using Form W-7
- Using an IRS-authorized Certified Acceptance Agent or
- In person at a designated IRS Taxpayer Assistance Center

All ITINs will now expire, unless they are renewed. New ITIN procedures include:

- Enhanced documentation for new Individual Taxpayer Identification Numbers (ITINs)
- Older ITINs will expire if not renewed.
- Newer ITINs will expire if not used within three years.
- The IRS will no longer accept passports of dependents as stand-alone documents that lack a date of entry into the United States.

ITIN Application Procedures

When a taxpayer applies for an ITIN, his Form W-7 must include original documentation such as: passports and birth certificates, or certified copies of these documents from the issuing agency. Notarized copies are no longer accepted. A taxpayer can also employ the services of a CAA, or Certified Acceptance Agent, to request an ITIN.

CAAs can authenticate a passport and/or birth certificate for taxpayers who want to request an ITIN, but do not wish to mail their original documents to the IRS.

> **Example:** Adriana is a U.S. citizen with a Social Security number. Adriana lives and works in Mexico for an international U.S. company. Later in the year, she marries Carlos, a citizen of Mexico, who has a daughter from a prior marriage. Adriana decides to file jointly with her new husband, Carlos, and claim her stepdaughter as a dependent. In order to do so, they must request ITINs for Carlos and his daughter.

> **Note:** The issuance of an ITIN does not affect an individual's immigration status or give the taxpayer the right to work in the United States. A taxpayer with an ITIN is not eligible to receive Social Security benefits or the Child Tax Credit or Earned Income Tax Credit. ITINs are for federal tax reporting only and are not intended to serve any other purpose.

Adoption Taxpayer Identification Number (ATIN)

ATINs are specifically designed for adopted children who are not yet eligible for a Social Security number. For an adopted child who does not yet have an SSN, a taxpayer may request an ATIN if:

- The child is placed in the taxpayer's home for legal adoption
- The adoption is a domestic adoption, or the adoption is a foreign legal adoption and the child has a permanent resident alien card or certificate of citizenship
- The taxpayer cannot obtain the child's existing SSN, even though he has made a reasonable attempt to obtain it from the birth parents, the placement agency, and other persons
- The taxpayer cannot obtain an SSN for other reasons, such as the adoption not yet being final

An ATIN cannot be used to obtain the Earned Income Tax Credit, the Child Tax Credit, or the American Opportunity Credit.

Special Rule for a Deceased Child

If a child is born and dies within the same tax year and is not granted an SSN, the taxpayer may still claim that child as a dependent.

> **Example:** Camilla gave birth to a son on October 1, 2018. The baby had health problems and died a week later. He was issued a birth certificate and a death certificate, but not an SSN. Camilla can claim her son as a qualifying child in 2018. Camilla must paper-file her return to claim her deceased son as a dependent. Her son will be considered a "qualifying child" for tax purposes, even though the child only lived a short time.

The tax return must be filed on paper with a copy of the birth certificate or a hospital medical record attached. The birth certificate must show that the child was born alive; a stillborn infant does not qualify. The taxpayer would enter "DIED" in the space for the dependent's Social Security number on the tax return.

Recordkeeping Requirements for Individuals

Whether a paid tax return preparer is involved or not, a taxpayer is responsible for keeping copies of tax returns and maintaining other records, for as long as they may be needed for the administration of any provision of the Internal Revenue Code.

Generally, a taxpayer should keep copies of tax returns and supporting documentation for at least three years from the date the returns were filed or the date they were due, whichever is later. The IRS does not require taxpayers to keep records in any particular way, but it says individuals need good records for the following purposes:

- **Identify sources of income:** Taxpayers receive money or property from a variety of sources. Individuals need this information to separate business from nonbusiness income and taxable from nontaxable income.
- **Keep track of expenses:** Tracking expenses as they occur helps taxpayers identify expenses that can be used to claim deductions.

- **Keep track of the basis of property:** Taxpayers need to retain records showing the original cost or other basis of property they own and any improvements made to them.

- **Support items reported on tax returns:** If the IRS has questions about items on a return, a taxpayer should have records to substantiate those items. In an IRS audit, the burden of proof is on the taxpayer to prove their expenses in order to deduct them.[23]

- **Prepare tax returns:** Good records help taxpayers (and their preparers) file accurate returns more quickly.

> **Note:** Even if a tax professional prepares and signs an individual's tax return, the taxpayer is ultimately responsible for the accuracy of its contents.

The IRS allows taxpayers to maintain records in any way that will help determine the correct tax. Electronic records are acceptable, as long as a taxpayer can reproduce the records in a legible and readable format. Basic records that all taxpayers should keep include items related to:

- **Income:** Forms W-2, Forms 1099, bank statements, pay stubs, brokerage statements, Schedules K-1

- **Expenses:** Sales slips, invoices, receipts, credit card statements, canceled checks or other proof of payments, written communications from qualified charities, Forms 1098 to support mortgage interest and potentially real estate taxes paid (if the taxes are paid through an impound account)

- **Home purchase and sale:** Closing statements, HUD statements, purchase and sales invoices, proof of payment, insurance records, receipts for improvement costs

- **Investments:** Brokerage statements, mutual fund statements, Forms 1099-DIV, Forms 2439

Basic Tax Forms for Individuals

Along with tax reform changes from the Tax Cuts and Jobs Act, taxpayers also have a new Form 1040. The new Form 1040 is half the size of the old one, and is designed to look more like a "postcard-sized" return. The IRS also created six new numbered schedules for Form 1040. Forms 1040A and 1040-EZ are no longer available.

Form 1040: The Form 1040 now uses a "building block" approach, which can be supplemented with the additional schedules if needed. New schedules (Schedule 1 through 6) have been created for instances where additional information needs to be carried over to the face of Form 1040. The new Form 1040 schedules are:

- **Schedule 1,** Additional Income and Adjustments to Income
- **Schedule 2,** Tax
- **Schedule 3,** Nonrefundable Credits
- **Schedule 4,** Other Taxes

---

[23] The responsibility to prove entries, deductions, and statements made on a taxpayer's tax return is known as the "burden of proof". Generally, taxpayers must meet their burden of proof by having the information and receipts (where needed) for the expenses and deductions claimed on their return. However, in tax-related criminal cases and civil fraud cases, the burden of proof is on the government.

- **Schedule 5,** Other Payments and Refundable Credits
- **Schedule 6,** Foreign Address and Third Party Designee

Form 1040NR: Form 1040NR is used by nonresident aliens to report their U.S. source income. The 1040NR is *never* used by U.S. citizens or U.S. residents. The IRS defines an alien as any individual who is not a U.S. citizen or U.S. national. A nonresident alien is an alien who has not passed the green card test or the substantial presence test. Form 1040NR is used by investors overseas, as well as nonresident taxpayers who earn money while in the U.S.

> **Example:** Reynaldo is a worldwide boxing champion and a legal citizen of the Philippines. Reynaldo receives a nonimmigrant visa to fight in a boxing match in the U.S., where he earns $500,000 for the fight. He only remains in the U.S. for six days. After his boxing appearance, he returns to the Philippines. Reynaldo is not eligible for an SSN and must request an ITIN to report his U.S. income. Without the ITIN, he would be subject to automatic backup withholding on his U.S. earnings. Reynaldo's tax accountant correctly reports his income and tax on Form 1040NR. Reynaldo does not have to report his worldwide income on his Form 1040NR, only the income he earned in the United States.

Form 1040X, *Amended U.S. Individual Income Tax Return*: This form is used to correct a previously filed Form 1040 or 1040NR. It is also used to change amounts previously adjusted by the IRS, make a claim for a carryback due to a loss or unused credit, correct a liability for the Additional Medicare Tax, or make certain elections after the prescribed deadline. Amended returns cannot be filed electronically.

Federal Income Tax Rates

An individual's federal taxable income is taxed at progressive rates in the United States. The more taxable income a taxpayer has, the higher the percentage of that income he pays in taxes. The IRS groups individuals by ranges of their taxable income level, or *brackets*, and applies increasing tax rates at each successive level.

For tax year 2018, there are still seven tax brackets for individuals: 10%, 12%, 22%, 24%, 32%, 35%, and 37%. However, because of changes in the Tax Cuts and Jobs Act, most of the brackets have been adjusted down, including the top marginal rate, which fell from 39.6% to 37%.

For example, in 2018, a single taxpayer with $9,525 of taxable income would be in the 10% tax bracket. If he had $50,000 of taxable income, he would be in the 22% tax bracket, while a taxpayer with more than $500,000 of taxable income would be in the highest tax bracket of 37%. The bottom rate remains at 10%.

The applicable tax rate for each successive bracket applies only to the additional amounts of taxable income that fall within that bracket.

> **Example:** Alexa is single and earned $38,000 in wages during 2018. For the first $9,525, she is taxed at a 10% rate. For the next segment of her taxable income, from $9,525 to $38,000 she is taxed at a 12% rate.

In addition to the regular tax in the United States, there is a parallel tax called the alternative minimum tax (AMT). A taxpayer must pay either the regular tax or the AMT, depending on whichever amounts to the greater tax. The AMT is covered in detail later.

2018 Federal Income Tax Rates By Filing Status				
Tax Rate	MFJ & QW	Single	HOH	MFS
10%	Up to $19,050	Up to $9,525	Up to $13,600	Up to $9,525
12%	$19,051 to $77,400	$9,526 to $38,700	$13,601 to $51,800	$9,526 to $38,700
22%	$77,401 to $165,000	$38,701 to $82,500	$51,801 to $82,500	$38,701 to $82,500
24%	$165,001 to $315,000	$82,501 to $157,500	$82,501 to $157,500	$82,501 to $157,500
32%	$315,001 to $400,000	$157,501 to $200,000	$157,501 to $200,000	$157,501 to $200,000
35%	$400,001 to $600,000	$200,001 to $500,000	$200,001 to $500,000	$200,001 to $500,000
37%	over $600,000	over $500,000	over $500,000	Over $300,000

Tax Return Due Dates and Extensions

The normal due date for individual tax returns is April 15; if April 15 falls on a Saturday, Sunday, or legal holiday, the due date is extended until the next business day. Residents of Maine and Massachusetts have until April 17, 2019, to file their federal returns because April 15, 2019, is Patriots' Day in those states and April 16, 2019, is Emancipation Day in Washington, D.C.

The IRS will accept a postmark as proof of a timely-filed return. For example, if a tax return is postmarked on April 15, 2019, but does not arrive at an IRS service center until April 30, the IRS will accept the tax return as having been filed on time. In cases where a tax return is filed close to the deadline, it is advisable for a taxpayer to pay for proof of mailing or certified mail. This is also called the "mailbox rule." E-filed tax returns are given an "electronic postmark" to indicate the day they are accepted and transmitted to the IRS.

If a taxpayer cannot file his tax return by the due date, he may request an extension by filing Form 4868, *Application for Automatic Extension of Time to File*, which may be filed electronically. An extension grants an additional six months to file a tax return.

Note: Although an extension gives a taxpayer extra time to *file* his return, it does not extend the time to *pay* any tax due. A taxpayer will owe interest on any amount that is not paid by the regular filing deadline, plus a late payment penalty. Taxpayers are expected to estimate and pay the amount of tax due by the filing deadline.

Filing Deadline Exceptions

Federal Disaster Areas: Taxpayers in federally declared disaster areas are often granted extensions to file and pay their income taxes and to make estimated tax payments. The IRS may also abate interest and any late filing or late payment penalties that apply to taxpayers in these disaster areas. This type of tax relief generally includes:

- Individuals and businesses located in a disaster area,
- Those whose tax records are located in a disaster area, and
- Relief workers who are working in the disaster area.

Note: A taxpayer does not have to be physically located in a federally declared disaster area to qualify as an "affected taxpayer." Taxpayers are also considered "affected" if the records necessary to meet a filing or payment deadline postponed during the relief period are located in a covered disaster area. Therefore, disaster relief also applies to tax preparers (and their clients) who are unable to file returns or make payments on behalf of their clients because of a disaster.

Example: Danny owns a 30% interest in a partnership that is located in a federally declared disaster area. However, Danny himself does not live in the disaster zone. Since Danny must rely on information (Schedule K-1) from the partnership in order to file his individual tax return, he qualifies as an "affected taxpayer" for purposes of receiving filing and payment relief. Danny's filing and payment deadlines are suspended until the end of the postponement period, just like the affected partnership.

June 15 Deadlines (Automatic Two-Month Extension)

Three groups of taxpayers are granted an automatic two-month extension to file and pay any tax due:

- Nonresident aliens who have income that is not subject to U.S. withholding
- U.S. citizens or legal U.S. residents who are living outside the United States or Puerto Rico and their main place of business is outside the U.S. or Puerto Rico
- Taxpayers on active military service duty outside the U.S.

A citizen or resident alien living abroad must attach a statement to his tax return explaining which situation qualifies him for the special two-month extension. Even if he is allowed an extension, the taxpayer will have to pay interest on any tax not paid by the regular tax deadline of April 15, 2019.

Taxpayers Outside of the Country: A taxpayer who is out of the country can request an additional discretionary two-month extension of time to file his tax return, beyond the regular six-month extension of October 15. For calendar-year taxpayers, the "additional" extension date would be December 15.

To request this extension, a taxpayer must send the IRS a letter explaining the reason why he needs the additional two-month period of time to file.[24] Unless the request is denied, the taxpayer will not receive a response from the IRS.

Special Extension to Qualify for the Foreign Earned Income Exclusion: A taxpayer can get an extension of more than six months to file their tax return, if they need the additional time to meet either the bona fide residence test or the physical presence test, to qualify for either the Foreign Earned Income Exclusion or the Foreign Housing Exclusion. To obtain this extension, the taxpayer must file Form 2350, *Application for Extension of Time to File U.S. Income Tax Return.*[25]

---

[24] See IRS Publication 54, *Tax Guide for U.S. Citizens and Resident Aliens Abroad*, for more information about extended deadlines. Publication 54 discusses four extensions: an automatic two-month extension, an automatic six-month extension, an additional extension for taxpayers out of the country, and an extension of time to meet certain tests.
[25] Generally, if a taxpayer is granted an extension with Form 2350, it will be thirty days beyond the date on which the taxpayer can expect to qualify under either the bona fide residence test or the physical presence test.

Special Exception for Combat Zones: The deadline for filing a tax return, claim for a refund, and the deadline for payment of tax owed, are automatically extended for any service member, Red Cross personnel, accredited correspondent, or contracted civilian serving in a combat zone.

These taxpayers have their tax deadlines suspended from the day they started serving in the combat zone until 180 days after they leave the combat zone. These deadline extensions also apply to the spouses of armed services members serving in combat zones.

> **Example:** Cesar is a U.S. Marine who has served in a combat zone since March 1, so he is entitled extra time to file and pay his taxes. The forty-six days between the date he entered the combat zone and the April 15 filing deadline are added to the normal extension period of 180 days, so he has a 226-day extension period after he leaves the combat zone. IRS deadlines for assessment and collection are also suspended during any period that a U.S. service member is in a combat zone.

Penalties and Interest

The IRS can assess a penalty on individual taxpayers who fail to file, fail to pay, or both. The failure-to-file penalty is generally greater than the failure-to-pay penalty. If someone is unable to pay all the taxes he owes, he is better off filing on time and paying as much as he can. The IRS will consider payment options to individual taxpayers. These penalties can be abated if the taxpayer can establish that there was a reasonable cause for not paying or filing on time.

Failure-to-File Penalty: The penalty for filing late is usually 5% of the unpaid taxes for each month or part of a month that a return is late. The penalty is based on the tax that is not paid by the due date, without regard to extensions. The penalty will not exceed 25% of a taxpayer's unpaid taxes.

If both the failure-to-file penalty and the failure-to-pay penalty apply in any month, the 5% failure-to-file penalty is reduced by the failure-to-pay penalty. If a taxpayer is owed a tax refund, he will not be assessed a failure-to-file penalty. For the tax year 2018, the minimum failure-to-file penalty is $210 or 100% of the unpaid tax (whichever is less) for a taxpayer who files his return more than 60 days late.

Failure-to-Pay Penalty: If a taxpayer does not pay his taxes by the original due date (determined without regards to any extension), he could be subject to a failure-to-pay penalty of ½ of 1% (0.5%) of unpaid taxes for each month or part of a month after the due date that the taxes are not paid.

This penalty can be as much as 25% of a taxpayer's unpaid taxes. The failure-to-pay penalty rate increases to a full 1% per month for any tax that remains unpaid the day after demand for immediate payment is issued, or ten days after notice of intent to levy certain assets is issued.

> **Note:** A taxpayer may request penalty abatement due to "reasonable cause." Acceptable reasons for abatement include: fire, casualty, natural disaster or other disturbances, inability to obtain records due to a casualty or a disaster, death, serious illness, incapacitation or unavoidable absence of the taxpayer or a member of the taxpayer's immediate family.

Interest on the Amount Due: In addition to filing penalties, the taxpayer will also be charged interest on the amount due. Generally, interest accrues on any unpaid tax from the due date of the return until the date of payment in full.

The interest rate is determined quarterly and is the federal short-term rate plus 3%. Interest compounds daily. Unlike penalties, interest cannot be abated for reasonable cause.

> **Example:** Nicoletta died two years ago. She had a filing requirement when she passed away. However, Nicoletta died without a will, and an executor was not named by the court until November 10, 2018. Nicoletta's brother, Silvio, was named the executor. Silvio filed two years of delinquent tax returns on behalf of his deceased sister, and also requested a penalty abatement for filing Nicoletta's final tax returns late. The IRS granted the penalty abatement, although the interest on the amount due was not abated, and still had to be paid by the executor.

Relief from Joint Tax Liability

In certain cases, a spouse can be relieved of the tax, interest, and penalties on a joint return. When spouses file a joint return, they are both legally responsible for the entire tax liability. However, a taxpayer can file a claim for spousal relief under three different grounds:

- **Innocent Spouse Relief**
- **Separation of Liability Relief**
- **Equitable Relief**

Innocent Spouse Relief: This is when a joint return has understated tax liability due to erroneous items attributable to a taxpayer's spouse or former spouse. Erroneous items include income received by a spouse that is omitted from the return. Deductions, credits, and property basis are also erroneous items if they are incorrectly reported on the joint return. To be considered an innocent spouse, the taxpayer must establish that he or she did not know (or have reason to know) that there was an understated tax liability at the time of signing the joint return. The taxpayer must request relief within two years after the date on which the IRS begins collection activity.

Separation of Liability Relief: The above restrictions also apply to separation of liability relief. In this case, however, the taxpayer must no longer be married to, or must be legally separated from, his or her spouse, or must be widowed or have lived apart for at least twelve months from the spouse with whom the joint return was filed.

The understated tax, plus interest and penalties, would be allocated to the taxpayer based on the amount for which he or she is responsible.

Equitable Relief: If a taxpayer does not qualify for the first two types of relief, he or she may be eligible for equitable relief. The IRS will review the facts and circumstances of the taxpayer's case and determine whether it would be unfair to hold the taxpayer liable for the understated tax. Unlike the other two forms of relief, equitable relief may also be granted for an underpaid tax, meaning it was properly reported on a tax return but not paid. Further, in some cases, the spouse requesting relief may have known about the understated or underpaid tax but did not challenge the treatment for fear of his or her spouse's retaliation.

> **Example:** Margot is a victim of domestic violence who now lives apart from her husband. When she signed her joint return, she knew her husband was underreporting income from his business but was afraid of what would happen if she refused to sign. After the IRS discovered the understated tax, Margot filed for equitable relief and was able to document her history of spousal abuse using affidavits from family members and other legal proof. The IRS granted her request for relief of her portion of the understated tax, penalties, and interest.

The taxpayer has up to ten years to request equitable relief under certain circumstances. Form 8857, *Request for Innocent Spouse Relief*, is used to request all three types of relief.

Injured Spouse Claims

An "injured spouse" claim and "innocent spouse" relief have similar-sounding names, but they are completely different. To be considered an injured spouse, a taxpayer must meet all of the following criteria:

- Have filed a joint return
- Have paid federal income tax or claimed a refundable tax credit
- All or part of the taxpayer's refund was, or is expected to be, applied to his or her spouse's past financial obligations, and
- Not be responsible for the debt

A spouse who believes that he is entitled to a portion of the refund on a joint return can file Form 8379, *Injured Spouse Allocation.*

> **Example:** Alonzo filed a joint return with his wife, Kimberly, who has delinquent student loans. Kimberly incurred the student loan debt before she was married. Alonzo files Form 8379 to request his portion of their tax refund as an injured spouse. The IRS will retain Kimberly's portion of the couple's tax refund to offset her debt but will allow Alonzo to obtain his portion of the refund.

Refund Claims and Amended Returns

To claim a refund, a taxpayer must generally file an amended tax return (Form 1040X) within three years from the date the return was originally due, or two years from the date the tax was paid, whichever is later.[26]

If a claim is not filed within the applicable period, a taxpayer generally will not be entitled to a refund. However, if the taxpayer files an extension and files his original return prior to the October 15 extension deadline, the three-year period begins on the date that the taxpayer originally filed his return.

Amended returns (Form 1040X) cannot be filed electronically. They must be filed on paper. If a taxpayer is entitled to a refund, he cannot request a direct deposit on Form 1040X.

---

[26] If the taxpayer had an extension to file (for example, until October 15), but the taxpayer filed earlier and the IRS received it July 1, the return is considered *filed on* July 1 (Form 1040X instructions).

Example: Jenny prepared her own 2015 tax return and filed it after the deadline, on May 1, 2016. She did not request an extension, so the return was delinquent when she filed it. She later discovered that she had forgotten to claim the Earned Income Tax Credit. Approximately three years later, she files an amended return on May 5, 2019. Jenny's refund claim is denied because she filed her original return past the due date *without* a valid extension. Therefore, her amended return was not filed timely, and her refund is forfeited.

Example: Jiao has not filed a tax return for a long time, and now he wants to file several years of delinquent tax returns: 2013 through 2018. Jiao files the returns and realizes that he was entitled to refunds for each year. If he files all the back-tax returns by April 15, 2019, he will receive refunds for his 2015-2018 tax returns. His refunds for 2013 and 2014, however, have expired. He will not receive a refund for those years.

Example: Michael made estimated tax payments of $1,000 and requested an extension to file his 2015 income tax return. He filed his 2015 return timely, before the extended due date of October 15, 2016. When he filed his return on September 7, 2016, he paid an additional $200 tax due. Michael later finds an error on the return. He files an amended return on September 7, 2019, three years after the extended due date, and claims and receives a refund of $700.

Extended Statute for Filing Late and Claiming Refunds

In some cases, a request for a late tax return and claiming a tax refund beyond the deadline will be honored. The IRS will consider any sound reason for failing to file a tax return, make a deposit, or pay tax when due. Sound reasons, if established, include:

- Fire, casualty, natural disaster or other disturbances
- Inability to obtain records
- Death, serious illness, incapacitation or unavoidable absence of the taxpayer or a member of the taxpayer's immediate family

Note: A lack of funds, in and of itself, is not considered "reasonable cause" for failure to file or pay taxes on time.

There are also special scenarios which allow a taxpayer to request a refund beyond the normal deadline. These special scenarios involve:

- A bad debt from worthless securities (up to seven years prior)
- A payment or accrual of foreign tax
- A net operating loss carryback[27]
- A carryback of certain tax credits
- Exceptions for military personnel
- Taxpayers in federally declared disaster areas
- Taxpayers who have been affected by a terroristic or military action

---

[27] Under the TCJA, the rules for NOL carrybacks and carryforwards has changed. In general, taxpayers must carry forward an NOL indefinitely, rather than carry it back. However, NOLs generated from farming losses are still allowed to be carried back up to two years.

Time periods for claiming a refund are also extended when a taxpayer is "financially disabled." This usually requires that the taxpayer be mentally or physically disabled to the point that he is unable to manage his financial affairs.

> **Example:** Renaldo has been helping his elderly mother, Evita; file her tax returns for the last several years. Over time, she has become forgetful of things. In 2018, Renaldo discovers a large file in his mother's home filled with old brokerage statements. Several of the brokerage statements show losses from worthless securities, dating back many years. Evita had been putting the statements away because she believed that they were unimportant. Evita's Form 1099-B from 2012 shows a significant loss from worthless stock (over $18,000 in losses that were never reported). Even though the brokerage statement is six years old, Evita is still allowed to amend her 2012 tax return to claim the stock losses. That is because the IRS allows up to seven years to amend a tax return for losses from worthless securities. Evita can file a Form 1040X to claim the losses and still receive a refund under this extended statute of limitations.

The Statute of Limitations for IRS Assessment and Collection

The IRS is generally required to assess tax or audit a taxpayer's return within three years after the return is filed or, if filed early, the due date of the return. If a taxpayer files his tax return late, the IRS has three years from the later of:

- The due date of the return, or
- The date the return was actually filed.

If a taxpayer *never* files a return, there is no deadline for an assessment of tax. If the taxpayer files a fraudulent tax return, there is no deadline for IRS assessment or collection.

The statute of limitations for IRS collection is ten years from the date tax is assessed, (as long as there is no evidence of fraud). This is also called the Collection Statute Expiration Date (CSED). This ten-year period begins to run on the date of the tax assessment, not on the date of filing. So, for example, if the taxpayer owes when they file their tax return, the IRS will send a bill. The bill is the assessment. The IRS can attempt to collect unpaid taxes for up to ten years from the date the taxes are *assessed*.

The IRS assigns a collection statute expiration date, or "CSED," to every delinquent taxpayer account. Once the CSED expires, the IRS loses its right to seize assets or make payment demands. Certain events can extend the amount of time the IRS has to collect. The IRS has six years to assess tax on a return if a "substantial understatement" is identified, meaning that gross income was understated by more than 25%.

> **Example:** Dalila filed her 2015 tax return on February 27, 2016. Since she filed her return before the actual due date, the three-year statute period for audit began April 15, 2016, and ends on April 15, 2019. After that date, the IRS must be able to prove fraud or a substantial understatement of gross income to audit and assess additional tax on Dalila's tax return.

Example: Franco has always filed his tax returns in a timely manner. Five years ago, Franco was self-employed and did not understand how to manage his money or pay estimated taxes. He had a large tax bill from that year. Franco still filed his tax return on time and correctly reported the amount due, with the intention of making monthly payments. The IRS issued its assessment and sent Franco a bill for $24,000 (the amount that Franco owes, plus penalties and interest). Franco requested an installment agreement and began making monthly payments toward his tax debt. Shortly thereafter, Franco had a terrible car accident and became completely disabled. He no longer has the means to work or pay the bill. The IRS has five years left to collect on the debt, and after that, the statute for collection expires. Although the interest and penalties will continue to accrue, if Franco does not have any assets or any means to pay the bill, the debt will likely be deemed "uncollectible."

Estimated Taxes for Individuals

The federal income tax is a "pay-as-you-go" tax, meaning a taxpayer must pay taxes as he earns or receives income throughout the year. If a taxpayer earns income that is not subject to withholding, such as self-employment income, rents, and alimony; or if his taxes withheld are insufficient to cover his tax liability, he may be required to make quarterly estimated tax payments.

Estimated tax is used to pay income tax as well as self-employment tax and alternative minimum tax.

Safe Harbor Rule: Taxpayers can avoid making estimated tax payments by ensuring they have enough tax withheld from their income. A taxpayer must generally make estimated tax payments if:

- He expects to owe at least $1,000 in tax (after subtracting withholding and tax credits)
- He expects the total amount of withholding and tax credits to be less than the *smaller* of:
  - 100% of the tax liability on his prior year return
  - 90% of the tax liability on his current year return

A taxpayer will not face an underpayment penalty if the total tax liability on his return (minus the amounts of tax credits or paid through withholding) is under $1,000.

Example: Jane is a full-time secretary. She also earns money part-time as a self-employed manicurist. In 2018, she did not make any estimated payments. However, Jane made sure to increase her withholding at her regular job to cover any amounts that she would have to pay on her self-employment earnings. When she files her tax return, she discovers that she still owes $750. Although she is responsible for paying the additional tax that is owed, she will not owe an underpayment penalty because her total tax liability, after withholding, is still less than $1,000.

Example: Greg earned $95,000 in 2018 and paid $8,200 in tax. Although he expects his income to increase in 2019, he will not be assessed a penalty for underpayment of estimated taxes, provided he pays at least $8,200 in estimated tax during the year (100% of the tax liability on his prior year return).

A U.S. citizen or U.S. resident is not required to make estimated tax payments if he had zero tax liability in the prior year.

> **Example**: Jacob, age twenty-five and single, earned $2,700 before he was laid off in the prior year. He received $3,500 in unemployment compensation after the layoff. He did not file a return or pay any income tax that year because his gross income was less than the filing requirement. In 2018, Jacob began working as a self-employed programmer but made no estimated tax payments during the year. Even though he owed $5,000 in tax at the end of 2018, Jacob does not owe the underpayment penalty because he had zero tax liability in the prior year.

If a taxpayer wishes to change his withholding amounts from his wages, he must use Form W-4, *Employee's Withholding Allowance Certificate*, and submits the form to his employer. The Form W-4 is not submitted to the IRS.

Safe Harbor Rule for Higher-Income Taxpayers: If the taxpayer's adjusted gross income was more than $150,000 ($75,000 if MFS), the taxpayer must pay the *smaller of* 90% of their expected tax for 2019 or *110%* (instead of the normal 100%) of the tax shown on their 2018 return to avoid an estimated tax penalty.

> **Example:** Massimo earned $200,000 in 2018. After applying all of his credits, he had a $30,000 tax liability for the year. In 2019, he expects to earn closer to $450,000. As long as he pays at least 110% of his tax liability in 2018 (110% x $30,000 =$33,000), he will not owe an estimated tax penalty, regardless of how much he owes when he files his return.

Estimated Tax Due Dates for Most Individuals

The year is divided into four payment periods for estimated taxes, each with a specific payment due date. If the due date falls on a Saturday, Sunday, or legal holiday, the due date is the next business day. A taxpayer must complete Form 1040-ES, *Estimated Tax for Individuals*, to pay his estimated tax.

If a payment is mailed, the date of the U.S. postmark is considered the date of payment.

First Payment Due: April 15
Second Payment Due: June 15
Third Payment Due: September 15
Fourth Payment Due: January 15 (of the following year)

Estimated Taxes for Farmers and Fishermen

Special rules apply to the payment of estimated tax by qualified farmers and fishermen (those who file on Schedule F). If at least two-thirds of the taxpayer's gross income in the current year comes from (or in the prior year came from) farming or fishing activities, the following rules apply:

- The taxpayer does not have to pay estimated tax if he files his return and pays all tax owed by the first day of the third month after the end of his tax year (generally this is March 1).

- The taxpayer does not have to pay estimated tax if his current year income tax withholding is at least two-thirds (.6667) of the total tax liability on his current tax return or 100% of the total tax liability on his prior year return.

- If the taxpayer must pay estimated tax, he is required to make only one estimated tax payment (called the "required annual payment") by the fifteenth day after the end of his tax year (for individuals, this is usually January 15).

For this special tax treatment, qualified farming income includes gross farming income on Schedule F, gross farming rental income, gains from the sale of livestock, and crop shares for the use of a farmer's land. This rule also applies to qualified fishermen.

Note: This special estimated tax rule also applies to a person's share of gross income from partnerships and S corporations, where the majority of its income is derived from farming or fishing. This safe harbor for estimated payments does not apply to C corporations, however, regardless of the type of business activity.

Example: Nicholas is a self-employed owner of a commercial fishing vessel. He reports his income and loss on Schedule F. All of his income is from commercial fishing, so he is not required to pay quarterly estimated taxes. Nicholas's records are incomplete, so he asks his tax accountant to file an extension on his behalf. Since Nicholas will be unable to file his 2018 tax return by March 1, 2019, his accountant notifies Nicholas that he is required to make a single payment of estimated taxes by January 15, 2019.

Note: If a qualified farmer (or fisherman) files their 2018 Form 1040 by March 1, 2019, and pays all the tax they owe at that time, they do not need to make <u>any</u> estimated tax payments during the year. This rule does not apply to any other type of business activity—it only applies to farmers and fishermen. [28]

Example: Naomi earns 100% of her income from growing organic strawberries. She is a qualified farmer and reports all her business income on Schedule F. She is not required to pay quarterly estimated taxes. Naomi filed her 2018 tax return on February 20, 2019, and enclosed a check for her entire balance of $4,900. Since she filed before the March 1, 2019 deadline, she will not be subject to any estimated tax penalties.

Backup Withholding

There are times an entity is required to withhold certain amounts from a payment and remit the amounts to the IRS. For example, the IRS requires backup withholding if a taxpayer's name and Social Security number on Form W-9, *Request for Taxpayer Identification Number and Certification*, does not match its records.

The IRS will sometimes require backup withholding if a taxpayer has a delinquent tax debt, or if he fails to report all his interest, dividends, and other income. Payments that are subject to

---

[28] On March 1, 2019, the Internal Revenue Service announced that it will waive the estimated tax penalty for any qualifying farmer or fisherman who files his or her 2018 federal income tax return and pays any tax due by Monday, April 15, 2019. To be eligible for the waiver, qualifying farmers and fishermen must attach Form 2210-F, *Underpayment of Estimated Tax By Farmers and Fishermen*, to their 2018 income tax return. This waiver was announced in 2019, so if you are tested on the estimated tax rules for farmers and fishermen, you will be asked about the general rules, not this special waiver.

backup withholding may include wages, interest, dividends, rents, royalties, and payments to independent contractors for services on Form 1099-MISC.

Backup withholding also applies, following notification by the IRS, where a taxpayer underreported interest or dividend income on their federal income tax return. To *stop* backup withholding, the payee must correct any issues that caused it. They may need to give the correct TIN to the payer, resolve the underreported income and pay the amount owed, or file a missing return.

Note: The new backup withholding rate in 2018 is 24% for all U.S. citizens and legal U.S. residents. Generally, backup withholding applies only to U.S. citizens, resident aliens and not to nonresident aliens. However, a nonresident alien may be subject to withholding, as well. Nonresident aliens are subject to U.S. tax withholding on "fixed or determinable, annual, or periodic" (FDAP) income. Most types of U.S. source income received by a foreign person are subject to withholding of 30% (unless an exemption or tax treaty applies).

Example: Randy is a U.S. citizen. He owns a number of investments through ABC Financial Advisors, Inc. In 2018, the IRS notifies ABC Financial Advisors that Randy's Social Security number is incorrect. ABC Financial Advisors notifies Randy by mail that the company needs his correct Social Security number, or it will have to start backup withholding on his investment income. Randy ignores the notice and never bothers to update his SSN. ABC Financial Advisors must begin backup withholding on Randy's investment income.

Example: Federico is a citizen of Spain. He does not live in the U.S., but he owns several U.S. investments, including stock in several U.S. companies and U.S. Treasury bonds. He is required to provide an ITIN to his investment firm. If he does not provide a tax identification number, the investment firm will be required to automatically withhold taxes from his U.S.-source income.

Under backup withholding rules, a business, financial institution, or bank must withhold taxes from a payment if:

- The individual did not provide the payor with a valid taxpayer identification number
- The IRS notified the payer that the TIN or SSN is incorrect
- The IRS notified the payor to start withholding on interest and dividends because the payee failed to report income in prior years
- The payee failed to certify that he was not subject to backup withholding for underreporting of interest and dividends

(Test yourself first; then check the correct answers at the end of this quiz.)

1. Ricky files his 2018 tax return on February 25, 2019. He has a balance due of $800 on the return. How long can he wait to pay the amount owed and not incur a late payment penalty?

A. He will owe a late payment penalty unless he pays his tax liability when he files his return.
B. He has until the due date of the return (not including extensions) to pay the amount owed and not owe a penalty.
C. He has until the due date of the return (including extensions) to pay the amount owed and not owe a penalty.
D. He does not have to pay the amount due by a certain date because it is less than the safe harbor amount of $1,000.

2. Catherine files an extension request (Form 4868), which allows her an additional six months to file her tax return. When she finally prepares her return, she realizes that she owes a substantial amount of tax. She pays the tax when she files the return, which she does before the extended due date. Which penalties, if any, will Catherine be likely to owe?

A. She will owe interest on the amount owed and a late payment penalty.
B. She will owe interest on the amount owed and a late filing penalty.
C. She will owe interest on the amount owed, a late payment penalty, and a late filing penalty.
D. She will not owe any penalties because she filed before the extended due date and paid the taxes owed with the return.

3. Cynthia is divorced, files as head of household, and has two dependents. Cynthia is a citizen of Canada and a legal U.S. resident (green card holder). She lived in Canada for the entire tax year. She earned $43,000 in 2018 and plans to itemize her deductions. Which tax form should Cynthia use?

A. Form 1040
B. Form W-7
C. Form 1040X
D. Form 1040NR

4. The 2018 backup withholding rate for U.S. taxpayers is:

A. 10%
B. 30%
C. 25%
D. 24%

5. Isabella files as single and has no refundable credits. She is not self-employed. Based on the figures below, is she required to pay estimated tax in the current year?

AGI for prior tax year	$73,700
Total tax on prior year return	9,224
Anticipated AGI for the current year	82,800
Total current year estimated tax liability	11,270
Tax expected to be withheld in the current year	$10,250

A. Yes; she is required to make estimated tax payments.
B. No; she is not required to make estimated tax payments.
C. She is not required to make estimated tax payments because she does not have self-employment income.
D. None of the above is correct.

6. Generally, how long should taxpayers keep the supporting documentation for their tax returns?

A. Four years from the date the return was filed, or the return was due, whichever is later
B. Three years from the date the return was filed, or the return was due, whichever is later
C. Two years from the date the return was filed, or the return was due, whichever is later
D. Ten years from the date the return was filed, or the return was due, whichever is later

7. Which of the following taxpayers is required to have an individual taxpayer identification number (ITIN)?

A. A nonresident alien with a Social Security number which moves outside the U.S.
B. Anyone who does not have a Social Security number
C. A nonresident alien who must file a return and is not eligible for a valid Social Security number
D. All nonresident aliens and resident aliens that are physically present in the U.S.

8. Clark's 2015 tax return was due April 15, 2016. He filed it on time, on March 2, 2016. Later, Clark discovered that he is eligible for an education credit that will result in a refund. He neglected to take this credit on his 2015 return. What is the latest date that Clark can amend his 2015 tax return in order to receive a refund?

A. April 15, 2018
B. April 15, 2019
C. March 2, 2018
D. March 2, 2020

9. Cristiano is single and earned $350,000 as a self-employed software developer during the current year. Under the estimated tax safe harbor rules for high-income taxpayers, he can avoid an underpayment penalty if he pays what percentage of his prior year tax liability?

A. 50%
B. 90%
C. 100%
D. 110%

10. Rochelle is a U.S. citizen who lives in England the entire tax year. She owes $4,500 of tax for 2018. Which of the following statements is correct regarding her filing and payment requirements?

A. She must file and pay her taxes by April 15.
B. She must remit her taxes by April 15, but she does not have to file until October 15.
C. She is allowed an automatic two-month extension to file and pay her taxes, but she must attach a statement to her return explaining why she qualifies for the extension.
D. Since she is an expat, she will not owe any additional interest on her tax liability.

11. Which of the following is not an acceptable reason for extending the statute of limitations for claiming a refund past the normal deadline?

A. A bad debt from a worthless security
B. Living in a federally declared disaster area
C. Exceptions for military personnel
D. Living outside the country for three years

12. If a taxpayer files his tax return more than 60 days after the due date or extended due date, what is the minimum penalty he will face?

A. A minimum of 25% of his unpaid taxes
B. A minimum of 5% of his unpaid taxes
C. The smaller of $210 or 100% of the unpaid tax
D. The greater of $135 or 100% of the unpaid tax

13. Which of the following documents will be accepted as a valid means of identification for a taxpayer applying for an ITIN?

A. Notarized copies of birth certificates and passports
B. Original or certified copies of birth certificates and passports
C. Color copies of birth certificates and passports
D. Photocopies of birth certificates and passports

14. Dottie is a U.S. resident who paid estimated tax in 2018 totaling $2,500. In 2019, she closed her business as a self-employed florist and is now unemployed. Dottie expects to have zero tax liability in 2019. Which of the following statements is correct?

A. She is still required to make estimated tax payments in 2019.
B. She is not required to make any estimated tax payments in 2019.
C. She must pay a minimum of $2,500 in estimated tax payments in 2019, or she will be subject to a failure-to-pay penalty.
D. She must make a minimum of $2,250 (90% × $2,500) in estimated tax payments in 2019, or she will be subject to an underpayment penalty.

15. What is the statute of limitations for an IRS assessment on a tax return from which more than 25% of the taxpayer's gross income was omitted?

A. There is no statute of limitations on a return in which gross income was omitted
B. Three years from the date the return was filed, or the return was due, whichever is later
C. Six years from the date the return was filed
D. Ten years from the date the return was filed

16. All of the statements about estimated tax payments are correct *except*:

A. An individual whose only income is from self-employment will generally have to pay estimated payments.
B. If insufficient tax is paid through withholding, estimated payments may be necessary.
C. Estimated tax payments are required when the amount of taxes withheld is greater than the overall tax liability.
D. Estimated tax is used to pay not only income tax, but self-employment tax and alternative minimum tax as well.

17. Sally and Albert file a joint return. Their tax refund will be applied toward Albert's unpaid child support obligations from an earlier relationship. To request her portion of their refund, Sally should file:

A. As an innocent spouse
B. As a damaged spouse
C. As an injured spouse
D. For equitable relief

1. The answer is B. Ricky has until the original due date of the return (not including extensions) to pay the amount owed and not incur a late payment penalty. Taxpayers should submit their payment of taxes due on or before April 15 (or the next business day if April 15 falls on a Saturday, a Sunday, or a legal holiday). For the 2018 tax year, the taxpayer has until April 15, 2019, to pay the amount he owes.

2. The answer is A. Even though she files Form 4868, Catherine may owe interest and a late payment penalty on the amount owed if she does not pay the tax due by the regular due date. However, she will not be assessed a late filing penalty (failure-to-file) because she filed her tax return before the extended due date.

3. The answer is A. Since Cynthia plans to itemize her deductions, she must file Form 1040. Form 1040NR is only for nonresident taxpayers. With few exceptions, green card holders are taxed as U.S. citizens and do not file Form 1040NR, regardless of where they live.

4. The answer is D. The 2018 backup withholding rate is 24%.[29] The IRS may require backup withholding if a taxpayer has a delinquent tax debt; if he fails to report all his interest, dividends, and other income; or if his Social Security number does not match records provided to the IRS.

5. The answer is B. Isabella does not need to pay estimated tax because she expects her income tax withholding in the current year ($10,250) to be greater than both—90% of the tax to be shown on her current year return ($11,270 × 90% = $10,143) and 100% of her prior year tax liability ($9,224). Therefore, Isabella qualifies for the safe harbor rule and is not required to make estimated tax payments. A taxpayer is not required to pay estimated tax if:
- The taxpayer had no tax liability in the prior year
- The taxpayer was a U.S. citizen or resident alien and had no tax liability in the prior year, and
- The prior tax year covered a twelve-month period

A taxpayer also does not have to pay estimated tax if she pays enough through withholding so that the tax due on the return is less than $1,000. In most cases, a taxpayer must pay estimated tax if she expects withholding (plus any refundable credits) to be less than the smaller of:
- 90% of the tax to be shown on the current year tax return, or
- 100% of the tax shown on the prior year tax return

6. The answer is B. Taxpayers should keep the supporting documentation for their tax returns for at least three years from the date the return was filed, or three years from the date the return was due, whichever is later. This includes applicable worksheets, receipts, and other forms.

7. The answer is C. If a taxpayer must file a U.S. tax return or is listed on a tax return as a spouse or dependent and is not eligible for a Social Security number, he must apply for an ITIN.

8. The answer is B. If Clark has his amended 2015 return postmarked *on or before* April 15, 2019, it will be within the three-year limit, and the return will be accepted. If the amended return is postmarked after that date, it will fall outside the three-year statute of limitations, and he will not receive the refund.

---

[29] Due to the TCJA, for payments made on or after January 1, 2018, the backup withholding rate has been reduced to 24% for U.S. citizens and U.S. resident aliens.

To claim a refund, the amended return must be filed by the later of three years from the date the return was due (or two years from the date the tax was paid).

9. The answer is D. To avoid an underpayment penalty, Cristiano must pay the <u>smaller of</u>:

- 110% of his *prior year* tax liability or
- 90% of his expected tax for the current year.

This estimated tax safe harbor rule applies to higher-income taxpayers with adjusted gross income of more than $150,000 ($75,000 if filing an MFS return).

10. The answer is C. Rochelle is allowed an automatic two-month extension to file and pay her taxes, but she must attach a statement to her tax return explaining why she qualifies for the extension. A U.S. citizen or resident alien living outside the United States has an automatic two-month extension to file and pay her taxes. The same is true for members of the military who are serving outside the United States. She will still owe interest on the tax that was due before the normal filing deadline, if she does not pay the amount due by that date.

11. The answer is D. Living outside the country is not a valid reason to extend the statute of limitations for claiming a refund. In some cases, a request for a tax refund will be honored past the normal three-year deadline. Exceptions exist for military personnel, individuals who are financially disabled, taxpayers who live in federally-declared disaster areas, and taxpayers who have bad debts from worthless securities.

12. The answer is C. For the tax year 2018, the failure-to-file penalty is the lesser of $210 or 100% of the amount of tax owed for a taxpayer who files his return more than 60 days late.

13. The answer is B. Only original documents of birth certificates and passports are accepted, or documents that have been "certified" by the original issuing agency. Notarized copies are no longer accepted.

14. The answer is B. Dottie is not required to pay estimated tax if she expects to have zero tax liability for the current tax year.

15. The answer is C. If a taxpayer omitted more than 25% of his gross income on his return, the IRS has up to six years to assess a deficiency.

16. The answer is C. If a taxpayer's withholding exceeds his tax liability, no estimated payments would be required. The taxpayer would receive a refund of the overpaid tax when he files his tax return.

17. The answer is C. Sally should file a claim as an *injured* spouse to request her portion of their tax refund. She would do so by filing Form 8379, *Injured Spouse Allocation.* If the request is granted, the IRS will retain her husband's portion of their tax refund to offset his unpaid child support but will allow Sally to obtain her portion of the refund. In contrast, innocent spouse relief is when tax has been incorrectly reported on a joint return, and one spouse is relieved of the obligation to pay the other spouse's portion of the tax liability.

Unit 2: Filing Status and Residency

> **For additional information read:**
> Publication 17, *Your Federal Income Tax*
> Publication 501, *Dependents, Standard Deduction, and Filing Information*
> Publication 54, *Tax Guide for U.S. Citizens and Resident Aliens Abroad*
> Publication 519, *U.S. Tax Guide for Aliens*

The IRS uses a taxpayer's filing status to determine filing requirements, standard deductions, eligibility for certain credits, and the amounts of tax owed. There are five filing statuses, with rules governing each, including special rules for annulled marriages and widow(er)s with dependent children.

In general, a taxpayer's filing status depends first on whether he or she is married or unmarried as of the last day of the year. For federal tax purposes, "marriage" was traditionally defined as a legal union between a man and a woman as husband and wife. For tax years 2013 and beyond, a marriage between same-sex spouses is also recognized as a legal union, as long as the marriage was performed in a domestic or foreign jurisdiction that recognizes the validity of same-sex marriage.[30]

Study Alert: Expect to be tested on the concept of same-sex marriage on the EA Exam. Remember that registered domestic partners or those in civil unions are NOT considered "married" for federal tax purposes, and you may see a question on the exam regarding this tax law issue as it relates to filing status.

Single

A taxpayer is single for the entire tax year if, on the last day of the tax year, he or she was:

- Unmarried,

- Legally separated or divorced, or

- Widowed (and not remarried during the year). However, special rules apply to widowed taxpayers. We will cover those rules later.

Example: Rey and Natasha legally divorced on December 28, 2018. They do not have any dependents. They cannot file either as married filing jointly or married filing separately for 2018. Instead, each must file as "single" for 2018. It doesn't matter that they were legally married for almost the entire year. The fact that the divorce became final at the end of the year means that they are legally unmarried for tax purposes.

Married Filing Jointly (MFJ)

The married filing jointly status typically provides more tax benefits than filing a separate return. On a joint return, spouses report all of their combined income, allowable expenses,

---

[30] On September 2, 2016, the IRS issued final regulations (T.D. 9785) to reflect the holdings of the landmark Supreme Court cases *Obergefell v. Hodges* and *United States v. Windsor*. The final regulations defined (for federal tax purposes) that a marriage of two individuals would be recognized if the marriage is recognized by the state, possession, or territory of the United States in which the marriage is entered into, regardless of the married couple's place of domicile. Legal marriages performed in foreign countries are also recognized.

exemptions, and deductions. Spouses can file a joint return even if only one spouse had income. Both spouses must agree to sign the return, and both are responsible for any tax owed, even if all the income was earned by only one spouse. A subsequent divorce usually does not relieve either spouse of the liability associated with the original joint return (see exceptions related to innocent spouse relief, covered earlier).

Taxpayers can file jointly if they are married as of December 31 and:

- Live together as husband and wife or as a legally married same-sex couple,
- Live together in a common law marriage recognized in the state where they now reside or in the state where the common law marriage began,
- Live apart but are not legally separated or divorced,[31] or
- Are separated under an interlocutory (not final) divorce decree.

In addition, a widowed taxpayer may use the married filing jointly status and file jointly with his deceased spouse, if his spouse died during the year and he or she has not remarried as of the end of the year. A U.S. resident or U.S. citizen who is married to a nonresident alien can elect to file a joint return as long as both spouses agree to be taxed on their worldwide income.

> **Example:** Patricia is a U.S. citizen living in Indonesia. She is married to Vikal, a nonresident alien and citizen of Indonesia. The spouses elect to treat Vikal as a U.S. resident (for tax purposes) by attaching a statement to their joint return. Patricia and Vikal must request an ITIN for Vikal and report their worldwide income for the year they make the choice and for all later years unless the election is ended or suspended. Although Patricia and Vikal must file a joint return for the year they make the election, as long as one spouse is a U.S. citizen or U.S. resident, they can file either joint or separate returns for later years.

> **Note:** Federal law does not allow Registered Domestic Partners to file a joint return. This rule also applies to civil unions.[32] However, the IRS *does* recognize common-law marriages. Currently, the only states that recognize common law marriage are the District of Columbia, Colorado, Iowa, Kansas, Montana, Oklahoma, Rhode Island, South Carolina, Texas, and Utah. Common-law marriage laws vary from state to state, and cohabitation alone does not constitute a common law marriage. Same-sex relationships or marriages are never recognized as common law.

Married Filing Separately (MFS)

The MFS status is for taxpayers who are married and either:

- Choose to file separate returns, or
- Do not agree to file a joint return.

If one spouse chooses to file MFS, the other is forced to do the same, since a joint return must be signed by both spouses.

---

[31] State law governs whether a taxpayer is married or legally separated under a divorce or separate maintenance decree. Single filing status generally applies if the taxpayer is not married, divorced, or legally separated according to state law. Marital laws differ from state to state.
[32] See Revenue Ruling 2013-17.

The MFS filing status means the two spouses report their own income, exemptions, credits, and deductions on separate returns, even if one spouse had no income. This filing status may benefit a taxpayer who wants to be responsible only for his own tax, or if it results in less tax than filing a joint return.

Typically, a married couple will pay more tax on a combined basis when filing separately, than they would by filing jointly.

> **Example:** Darren and Edna have always filed jointly in the past. However, Edna has chosen to separate her finances from her husband this year, even though they are living together. Darren wants to file jointly with Edna, but she has refused. Edna files her tax return using married filing separately as her filing status; therefore, Darren is forced to file MFS as well.

Specific features of the MFS filing status include the following:

- The tax rates are generally higher at the same levels of taxable income than those applicable to MFJ.
- The exemption amount for the alternative minimum tax is half that which is allowed on a joint return.
- Various credits, including the Earned Income Tax Credit, the Premium Tax Credit, and those for child care, education, adoption, and retirement savings, are either not allowed or are much more limited than on a joint return.
- The capital loss deduction is limited to $1,500, half of what is allowable on a joint return.
- The standard deduction is half the amount allowed on a joint return and cannot be claimed if the taxpayer's spouse itemizes deductions.

> **Example:** Fred and Gina keep their finances separate and choose to file MFS. Fred plans to itemize his casualty losses, so Gina is forced to either itemize her deductions or claim a standard deduction of zero.

Married taxpayers sometimes choose to file separate returns when one spouse does not want to be responsible for the other spouse's tax obligations, or because filing separately may result in a lower total tax. For example, if one spouse has high medical expenses or a large casualty loss, separate returns may result in a lower total tax liability because a lower adjusted gross income allows more expenses or losses to be deducted.

Another common reason a taxpayer may choose the MFS filing status is to avoid a refund offset against the other spouse's outstanding prior debt. This might include delinquent child support or student loans, or a tax liability one spouse incurred before the marriage.

> **Example:** Hector and Imelda were married in 2018. Hector owes delinquent back taxes. Imelda chooses to file separately from Hector, so her refund will not be offset by his overdue debts. If they were to file jointly, their entire refund might be retained in order to pay the debt.

Amending Filing Status from MFS

There are rules for when married taxpayers are allowed to change their filing status. Although it is possible to amend a person's filing status, there are strict rules for doing so.

Taxpayers generally cannot change from a joint return to a separate return *after the due date* of the return. For example, if a married couple files jointly on March 13, 2019, and subsequently decide they wanted to file separately instead, they would have only until April 15, 2019 (the due date of the original return) to file amended returns using the MFS filing status.

An exception allows a personal representative for a deceased taxpayer to change from a joint return, elected by the surviving spouse, to a separate return for the decedent for up to a year after the filing deadline.

> **Example:** Alexander and Bianca have always filed jointly. Bianca dies suddenly in 2018, and her last will names Laura, her daughter from a previous marriage, as the executor of her estate. Alexander files a joint return with Bianca for tax year 2018, but Laura, as the executor, decides that it would be better for her deceased mother's estate if Bianca's final tax return were filed as MFS. Laura files an amended return claiming MFS status for Bianca and signs the return as the executor.

To change from separate returns to a joint return, taxpayers must file an amended return using Form 1040X, and may do so at any time within three years from the due date of the separate returns (not including extensions).

Same-Sex Spouses

Same-sex spouses, who are legally married, must file as either married filing jointly or married filing separately. They do not have the choice to file as single. However, be aware that civil unions and registered domestic partnerships are not legally considered "marriages" for IRS purposes. Registered domestic partners (or partners in a civil union) may not file joint federal returns, because these taxpayers are not legally married for federal tax purposes.

> **Example:** Larry and Noah are registered domestic partners in the state of California. They consult Elsa, an EA, who prepares their tax returns. Larry and Noah wish to file jointly. However, registered domestic partners are not considered married under federal law. Therefore, they must file as single for federal tax purposes.

Head of Household (HOH)

A taxpayer who qualifies to file as head of household will usually have a lower tax rate than a single or MFS taxpayer and will receive a higher standard deduction. The head of household status is available to taxpayers who meet all of the following requirements:

- The taxpayer must be single, divorced, legally separated, or "considered unmarried" on the last day of the year.

- The taxpayer must have paid more than half the cost of keeping up a home for the year.

- The taxpayer must have had a qualifying person living in his home for more than half the year. There are exceptions for temporary absences,[33] or for a qualifying parent, who does not have to live with the taxpayer. This would include hospitalization and stays in a nursing home.

---

[33] For IRS purposes, "temporary absences" include time away from home going to college, vacation, business, medical care, hospitalization, military service, summer camp, and detention in a juvenile facility.

> **Example:** Rhonda is unmarried. Her son, Theodore, was eighteen years old at the end of the year. Theodore lived away from his mother all year because he was going to college. He lived in the campus dorms and returned home only on the holidays. Theo does not work and does not provide any of his own support. Since his time away from home to attend school is considered a "temporary absence," Rhonda may claim head of household filing status, and claim Theodore as her dependent.

"Considered Unmarried" for HOH Status

There are some instances where a taxpayer can be considered unmarried (for tax purposes only). To be "considered unmarried" on the last day of the tax year, a taxpayer must meet all of the following conditions:

- File a separate return from the other spouse.
- Pay more than half the cost of keeping up a home for the tax year.
- Not live with a spouse in the home during the last six months of the tax year.
- Maintain the home as the main residence of a qualifying child, stepchild, or foster child for more than half the year.
- Be able to claim an exemption for the child (although there is an exception for divorced parents, explained later).

For the purpose of determining this filing status, valid household expenses used to calculate whether a taxpayer is paying more than half the cost of maintaining a home include:

- Rent, mortgage interest, property taxes
- Home insurance, repairs, utilities
- Food eaten in the home

Valid expenses do not include clothing, education, medical treatment, vacations, life insurance, or transportation. Welfare payments are not considered amounts that the taxpayer provides to maintain a home. The qualifying person for HOH filing status must generally be related to the taxpayer either by blood, adoption, or marriage. However, a foster child also qualifies if the child was legally placed in the home by a government agency. For purposes of the head of household status, a "qualifying person" is defined as:

- A qualifying child
- A married child who can be claimed as a dependent, or
- A dependent parent

A taxpayer's qualifying person may include: the taxpayer's child or stepchild, sibling or stepsibling, or a descendant of any of these. For example, a niece or nephew, stepbrother or stepsister, or grandchild may all be eligible as qualifying persons for the HOH filing status.[34]

---

[34] A taxpayer cannot file as head of household if the taxpayer's only dependent is his or her Registered Domestic Partner.

Example: Leo's unmarried grandchild, Mary, lived with him the entire year. Mary turned 19 at the end of the year. She does not have a job, did not provide any of her own support, and cannot be claimed as a dependent by anyone else. As a result, Mary is Leo's qualifying child. Leo may use the HOH filing status.

An unrelated individual may still be considered a "qualifying relative" for dependency purposes but will not be a qualifying person for the HOH filing status.[35]

Special Rules for HOH Status

Divorced or Noncustodial Parents: A taxpayer can file as HOH and not claim the qualifying child as their dependent. This happens most often with divorced parents. This is because the head of household filing status applies to the taxpayer who maintains the main home of a qualifying child. However, a custodial parent may choose to release the dependency exemption to a noncustodial parent. In this scenario, the custodial parent would claim head of household filing status, while the noncustodial parent would claim the dependency exemption.

Example: Nicolas and Lora have been divorced for five years. They have a twelve-year-old daughter named Cristina who lives with her mother during the week and only sees her father on weekends. Therefore, Lora is considered the custodial parent. The parents agree, however, to allow Nicolas to claim the dependency exemption for Cristina on his tax return. In 2018, Nicolas correctly files as "single" and claims Cristina as his dependent. Lora may still file as HOH if she otherwise qualifies, but she will not claim the dependency exemption for Cristina.

The "considered unmarried" rules apply in determining who can claim a child for dependency and HOH purposes. A couple, even if not formally separated or divorced, must live apart for *more than half the year* for either spouse to claim HOH status.

Example: Darya and Craig separated on July 10, 2018, but were not yet divorced at the end of the year. They have one minor child, Krissy, age eight. Even though Darya lived with Krissy and supported her for the remainder of the year, Darya does not qualify for HOH filing status because she and Craig did not live apart for the last six months of the year.

Example: Austin and Cayla physically separated in February 2018 and lived apart for the rest of the year. They do not have a written separation agreement and are not yet divorced. Their six-year-old daughter, Brigid, lived with her father all year, and Austin paid more than half the cost of keeping up the home. Austin files a separate tax return and claims Brigid as a dependent because he is the custodial parent. Austin can also claim head of household status for 2018. Although Austin is still legally married, he can file as HOH because he meets all the requirements to be "considered unmarried."

Death or Birth during the Year: A taxpayer may still file as head of household if the qualifying child is born or dies during the year. The taxpayer must have provided more than half of the cost of keeping up a home that was the child's main home while he was alive.

---

[35] The rules for qualifying children and relatives will be covered in detail in the next unit, *Personal and Dependency Exemptions.*

Example: Eleonore gives birth to a son in September 2018 who dies within two weeks of his birth. She can claim him on her tax return as a qualifying child even though he only lived a short while. Assuming she qualifies, the child would be a qualifying child for the Child Tax Credit and the Earned Income Tax Credit, even if she was unable to obtain a Social Security number for the child.[36]

Dependent Parents: If a taxpayer's qualifying person is a dependent parent, the taxpayer can file as HOH even if the parent does not live with the taxpayer. The taxpayer must pay more than half the cost of keeping up a home that was the parent's main home for the entire year. This rule also applies to a parent in a rest home. A qualifying "parent" may be a stepparent, in-law, or grandparent who is related to the taxpayer by blood, marriage, or adoption.

Example: Greta is 54 years old and single. She pays the monthly bill for Shasta Pines Nursing Home, where her 78-year-old mother lives. Greta's mother has lived at Shasta Pines for two years and has no income. Since Greta pays more than half of the cost of her mother's living expenses, Greta qualifies for head of household filing status, even though her mother lives in a retirement home.

Example: Janie is single and fully financially supports her mother, Leona, who lives in her own apartment. Leona dies suddenly on May 2, 2018. Janie can claim her mother as a dependent and file as HOH for 2018, even though Leona was not alive for the whole year.

Nonresident Alien Spouses: A taxpayer who is married to a nonresident alien spouse may elect to file as HOH by "disregarding" the nonresident alien spouse. This is a unique rule that only applies to taxpayers who are married to nonresidents.

This is true even if both spouses lived together throughout the year. The taxpayer must not elect to treat the spouse as a resident, and the taxpayer must have a qualifying child (or another qualifying dependent, such as a parent) to qualify for the HOH status. The taxpayer's nonresident alien spouse is not a qualifying person for head of household purposes. The taxpayer must have another qualifying person and meet the other tests to be eligible to file as a head of household.

Example: Two years ago, Marcus, a U.S. citizen, met and married Dorthea, a nonresident alien who is a citizen and resident of Greenland. The couple lived together in Greenland while Marcus was on sabbatical from his university teaching position. They have a son who was born in 2018. Dorthea does not wish to file jointly with Marcus and does not wish to make the election to be treated as a U.S. resident, because she does not want to pay tax on her worldwide income, as she would be required to do if she filed jointly with Marcus. Marcus can file as head of household and claim his son as a dependent, even though he and Dorthea lived together all year, and Dorthea is a nonresident alien.

---

[36] If a child was born and died in the same year and was not issued an SSN, the taxpayer may enter "DIED" on the Form 1040, and attach a copy of the child's birth certificate. The tax return must be filed on paper.

Annulments

Annulment is a legal procedure for declaring a marriage null and void. If a taxpayer obtains a court decree of annulment that holds no valid marriage ever existed, the couple is considered *unmarried* even if they filed joint returns for earlier years.

Unlike divorce, an annulment is retroactive. Taxpayers who have annulled their marriage must file amended returns (Form 1040X), claiming single (or head of household status, if applicable) for all the tax years affected by the annulment that are not closed by the statute of limitations.

> **Example:** Nora and Enzo were granted an annulment on October 31, 2018. They were married for two years. Enzo has sole custody of one son from a prior relationship. For 2018, Nora must file as single and must amend the prior two years' tax returns to single as well. Enzo must also amend his joint returns. If he otherwise qualifies, Enzo can amend his returns to head of household filing status.

Qualifying Widow(er) With a Dependent Child

Qualifying widow(er) with a dependent child is the least common filing status. A qualifying widow(er) receives the same standard deduction as married taxpayers who file jointly. In the year of the spouse's death, a taxpayer can generally file a joint return. However, if a surviving spouse remarries before the end of the year, the married filing separately status must be used for the decedent's final return.

> **Example:** Sally and her husband, Vince, have an infant son. Vince dies suddenly of a heart attack on February 1, 2018. Sally remarries on December 10, 2018. Since she remarried in the same year her former husband died, she no longer qualifies for the joint return filing status with her deceased husband. However, Sally does qualify to file jointly with her new spouse. Therefore, Vince's filing status for his final tax return must be MFS. The executor of Vince's estate would be responsible for filing his final return.

For each of the two years following the year of the spouse's death, the surviving spouse can use the qualifying widow(er) filing status if he has a qualifying dependent and does not remarry. After two years, the taxpayer's filing status converts to single or HOH, depending upon which status applies.

For example, if a taxpayer's spouse died in 2016 and he did not remarry, the taxpayer could use the qualifying widow(er) filing status for tax year 2017 *and* 2018 if he has a qualifying dependent.

> **Example:** Sophia's husband died on July 3, 2017. Sophia has one dependent child who is ten years old. Sophia does not remarry. Therefore, Sophia's filing status for 2017 was MFJ (the last year her husband was alive). For 2018 and 2019, she can file as a "qualifying widow with a dependent child," which is a more favorable filing status than single or HOH. For 2020, she would file as HOH, assuming she remains single and does not remarry.

To be eligible for the qualifying widow(er) filing status, the taxpayer normally must:

- Not have remarried before the end of the year

- Have been eligible to file a joint return for the year the spouse died; it does not matter if a joint return was actually filed

- Have a qualifying child for the year. A qualifying child can be a child or stepchild but does not include a foster child for the purposes of this filing status.

- Have furnished over half the cost of keeping up the qualifying child's home for the entire year

Note: The federal requirements for the Qualifying Widow(er) filing status recently changed. While the taxpayer still needs a qualifying child that meets certain qualifications, the child *does not* have to be claimed as a dependent on the tax return. The taxpayer must only provide the child's name on the return.

Note: A taxpayer's marital status on the last day of the year (December 31) determines their marital status for the entire year, for tax purposes.

Determining Residency for Tax Purposes

To file an accurate tax return, a taxpayer must determine whether he is considered a *resident* or a *nonresident*. There are multiple types of tax residency. For IRS purposes, an "alien" is an individual who is not a U.S. citizen. Aliens are further classified as "nonresident" aliens and "resident" aliens. Residency status is important because these taxpayers are taxed in different ways:

- **Resident aliens** are generally taxed on their worldwide income, the same as U.S. citizens.

- **Nonresident aliens** are taxed only on their income from sources within the United States and on certain income connected with the conduct of a trade or business in the U.S.

- **Dual-status aliens** are both nonresident and resident aliens during the same tax year. Different rules apply for the part of the year a taxpayer is a U.S. resident and the part of the year he is a nonresident.

Residency for IRS purposes is not the same as legal immigration status. An individual may be considered a U.S. resident for tax purposes, based upon the time he spends in the United States, regardless of immigration status. A nonresident alien could be someone who lives outside the U.S., and simply invests in U.S. property or stocks, and is therefore required to file a tax return to correctly report his earnings.

Tax Residency Tests

Certain rules exist for determining the residency for aliens. If a taxpayer is an alien (not a U.S. citizen), he is considered a nonresident alien for tax purposes unless he meets at least one of two tests: the *green card* test or the *substantial presence* test.

Green Card Test

An alien taxpayer is automatically considered a U.S. resident if he is a "lawful permanent resident" of the United States at any time during the tax year. A taxpayer generally has this status if he is a lawful immigrant and has been issued an alien registration card, also known as a "green card."[37]

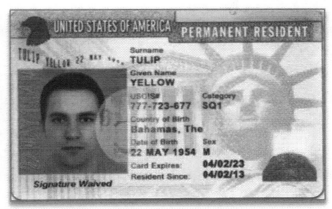

An alien who has been present in the U.S. any time during a calendar year as a lawful permanent resident may opt to be treated as a resident alien for the entire calendar year.

Example: Masha is a citizen of Russia. She arrived in the United States on January 4, 2018 as a student on an F-1 visa. On December 12, 2018, she married Gaston, a U.S. citizen. Masha immediately petitioned USCIS for a change in immigration status to that of lawful permanent resident based upon her marriage Gaston. USCIS approved her petition to become a lawful permanent resident of the United States, and issued her a green card on June 1, 2019. Masha passes the Green Card Test on June 1, 2019. Masha could also elect to be taxed as a U.S. resident in 2018 by filing jointly with her U.S. citizen spouse, Gaston.

Substantial Presence Test

An alien taxpayer without a green card is considered a U.S. resident for tax purposes only if he meets the substantial presence test for the calendar year. To meet this test, he must be physically present in the United States for at least:

- 31 days during the current tax year (2018), and
- 183 days during the three-year period, which includes the current year (2018) and the two years immediately preceding the current year (2017 and 2016).

For purposes of the 183-day requirement, all the days present in the current year are counted, along with:

- 1/3 of the days present in the previous year (i.e., 2017), and
- 1/6 of the days present in the second year before the current year (i.e., 2016).

Note: If an individual meets the requirements of the "substantial presence" test, he is considered for federal tax purposes a resident alien of the United States, even though he may not have legal residency in the United States.

---

[37] Image provided by Department of Homeland Security, U.S. Citizenship and Immigration Services Verification Division.

Tax Residency through Marriage

A nonresident alien who does not meet the substantial presence test, and does not have a green card, may still elect to be treated as a resident for tax purposes if he is married to a U.S. citizen or resident. This election can be made only if:

- At the end of the year, one spouse is a nonresident alien, and the other is a U.S. citizen or resident, and
- Both spouses agree to file a joint return and treat the nonresident alien as a resident alien for the entire tax year.

Example: Veronica and Sergio are married, and both are nonresident aliens at the beginning of the year. In February, Sergio becomes a legal U.S. resident alien and obtains a green card and a Social Security number. Veronica and Sergio may both choose to be treated as resident aliens for tax purposes by attaching a statement to their joint return. Veronica is not eligible for a Social Security number yet, so she must apply for an ITIN. Veronica and Sergio must file a joint return for the year they make the election, but they can file either joint or separate returns for later years.

Exempt Individuals

Numerous exceptions are considered when counting days for the substantial presence test. Days in the United States are not counted if the alien taxpayer:

- Regularly commutes to work in the U.S. from a residence in Canada or Mexico, generally more than 75% of the workdays during the applicable working period (this is deemed a "closer connection to home country")
- Is present in the U.S. as a crew member of a foreign vessel
- Is unable to leave because of a medical condition that arose while in the United States
- Is a professional athlete in the U.S. to compete in a charitable sports event. These athletes exclude only the days in which they actually competed in the sports event, but do not exclude days used for practice, travel, or promotional events.
- Is an exempt individual. Exempt individuals include aliens who are:
  - Foreign government-related individuals in the U.S. temporarily, (such as foreign diplomats)
  - Teachers on temporary visas
  - Visiting Scholars or researchers. Scholars are exempt for two years.
  - Students on temporary visas who do not intend to reside permanently in the U.S. Students are exempt from the substantial presence test for five years.

If the taxpayer does not meet either the green card test or the substantial presence test, he is considered a nonresident alien for tax purposes and is subject to U.S. income tax only on his U.S. source income. A foreign alien who cannot satisfy these two tests is considered a nonresident alien.

Study Tip: You should memorize details of the substantial presence test for the EA exam, including the 183-day requirement and exceptions to the rule.

Example: Marisela is a Brazilian citizen who was physically present in the United States for fifteen days in each of the years 2016, 2017, and 2018. She is not a green card holder. Marisela earned $32,000 in 2018 as a Portuguese translator for a famous musician who was traveling to the U.S. to perform a concert. Since the total days she was present in the U.S. for the three-year period do not meet the substantial presence test, Marisela is not considered a U.S. resident for tax purposes for 2018, and her earnings are taxed as a nonresident. Marisela is required to file Form 1040NR, *U.S. Nonresident Alien Income Tax Return*.

Example: Susanna is a folk singer and a popular recording artist in her home country of Australia. Susanna comes to the U.S. on tour, playing a variety of different venues during the month of April. Afterward, she returns to her home country. Susanna is not a U.S. resident for tax purposes, although she entered the U.S. legally on a P-2 Visa.[38] She is required to report her U.S. source income. Susanna's accountant files a Form 1040NR to report the income that she earned while she was touring in the U.S. She will only report and be taxed on her U.S. source income.

International Students

Most international students and scholars fall under the status of nonresident aliens. An international student is anyone who is temporarily in the U.S. on an F, J, M, or Q visa. Immediate family members of a student, including spouses and unmarried children under age twenty-one who reside with the student, are also considered students for tax purposes. International students holding an F-1 or J-1 visa are exempt from the substantial presence test for the first five calendar years they are in the U.S.

The five calendar years need not be consecutive. Any part of a calendar year in which the student is present in the U.S. counts as a full year.

Example: Myung-soon, a citizen of South Korea, is in the U.S. as a graduate student on F-1 visa status. She has resided continuously in the U.S. since arriving on February 15, 2013. She was in the U.S. all of 2018. Because international students are exempt from the substantial presence test for five years, Myung-soon became a resident alien for federal income tax purposes in 2018. Myung-soon is married to Quim, who lives in South Korea and is a nonresident alien. Beginning in the 2018 tax year, Myung-soon and Quim can both elect to be treated as U.S. residents for tax purposes on a jointly filed return.

Example: The first time Shaniya came to the U.S. was in 2011, when she arrived as a foreign student on an F-1 student visa from her home country of India. She studied at Stanford University in the U.S. until the end of 2013 and then returned home. She re-entered the U.S. on a J-1 student visa in 2018 to attend graduate school. She is allowed to legally work for the university as a graduate teaching assistant on a J-1 student visa. For federal income tax purposes, Shaniya is still taxed as a nonresident alien because she has been in the U.S. for less than five years as a student. She will report her earnings from her on-campus job by filing Form 1040NR. This is true even if she remains in the U.S. the entire year.

---

[38] This is a type of temporary visa issued to individual performers, artists or entertainers.

Dual Status Aliens: A taxpayer is considered a dual-status alien when he has been both a resident alien and a nonresident alien in the same tax year. The most common dual-status tax years are the years of arrival and departure.

A taxpayer's status on the last day of the year determines whether he is a resident alien or a nonresident alien for the tax year. For the part of each year the taxpayer is a *nonresident* alien, he is taxed only on his U.S. source income. For the part of each year the taxpayer is a *U.S. resident alien*, he is taxed on his worldwide income. This applies even if the income was earned earlier in the year while the taxpayer was a nonresident alien but was received after he became a resident for tax purposes.

> **Example:** Ismael legally became a U.S. resident for tax purposes on January 1, 2018. On January 15, 2018, he received $2,000 of income for contract work he did the previous year. Even though the income was earned while he was a nonresident alien, it was received *after* he became a U.S. resident. His income is reported and taxed on Form 1040, not on Form 1040NR.

Tax Treaties

The United States has income tax treaties with a number of foreign countries. Under these treaties, residents of foreign countries may be taxed at reduced rates or be exempt from U.S. income taxes on certain items of income they receive from U.S. source income. These reduced rates and exemptions vary among countries and specific items of income. Treaty provisions are generally reciprocal.

Therefore, a U.S. citizen or resident who receives income from a treaty country and who is subject to taxes imposed by foreign countries may be entitled to certain credits, deductions, exemptions, and reductions in the rate of taxes of those foreign countries. Income received by a nonresident alien that is effectively connected with a trade or business in the United States is, after allowable deductions, taxed at the rates that apply to U.S. citizens and residents. Withholding would be made at the highest applicable rate.

> **Note:** For nonresident aliens, income or gains from U.S. sources is generally subject to backup **withholding at 30%**, unless a lower treaty rate applies. The normal backup withholding rate for U.S. citizens and U.S. residents in 2018 is a flat 24% rate.

2018 Gross Income Filing Thresholds

Not every person is required to file a tax return. Whether a taxpayer is required to file a 2018 federal income tax return depends on several factors. The IRS defines gross income as <u>all income</u> a taxpayer received in the form of money, goods, property, and services that are not exempt from tax. Sometimes, a taxpayer is required to file a tax return even though none of his income is taxable.

> **Note:** "**Earned income**" includes all the taxable income a taxpayer receives from working, such as wages, salaries, tips, and other employee compensation. Earned income also includes self-employment earnings that a taxpayer earns by owning a business or farm. Most other types of income are considered **unearned income**, including interest income, dividends, capital gains, retirement income, inheritances, and prizes.

The 2018 filing requirement thresholds, expressed as levels of gross income, are as follows:

- Single: $12,000 (65 or older: $13,600)
- Head of household: $18,000 (65 or older $19,600)
- Married filing jointly: $24,000
    - 65 or older (one spouse): $25,300
    - 65 or older (both spouses): $26,600
- Married filing separately (of any age): $5 (this is *not a typo*, it really is $5)
- Qualifying widow(er) with dependent child: $24,000 (65 or older $25,300)
- Any taxpayer with self-employment income of $400 or more in any taxable year must file a tax return.

Example: Stephanie and Kipling are married and plan to file jointly. Stephanie is 66 and had gross income of $12,225 for the year. Kipling is 68 and had gross income of $7,500 for the year. Since their combined gross income was $19,725, they are not required to file a tax return in 2018. The filing requirement threshold for joint filers when both spouses are 65 or older is $26,600 in 2018.

Example: Lucy is 36, single, and earned wages of $17,500 last year. She does not have any children. She is required to file a tax return since her income was more than $12,000 in 2018. She will use the single filing status.

Example: Andrea is 70, married, and had $1,500 of wage income in 2018. Her husband, Ricardo, also 70, had $22,700 in wage income. They have no dependents. Normally, Ricardo and Andrea would not have a filing requirement because their gross income is under the filing threshold for joint filers age 65 and over. However, Andrea wants to file separately from her husband. She is therefore required to file a tax return because the filing threshold for MFS taxpayers of any age is $5 in 2018. Ricardo must also file a tax return because his filing status is MFS by default. Ricardo cannot choose to file jointly with his wife unless she agrees, since both spouses are required to sign a joint return.

Filing Requirements for Dependents

Sometimes dependent children are also required to file their own tax return. The filing thresholds are different depending on whether the child has "earned income" or "unearned income." The filing threshold is much lower for those with "unearned" income. *Earned* income includes: wages, tips, self-employment income, and taxable scholarships. *Unearned* income includes: interest, dividends, and capital gain distributions. A dependent under 65 must file a return if *any* of the following apply:

- Their "unearned" income was over $1,050
- Their "earned" income was over $12,000
- Their "gross" income was more than the larger of:
    - $1,050 or
    - Their earned income (up to $11,650) plus $350

Example: Fabian is 20, single, and a full-time college student. Fabian's mother claims him on her tax return. He received $200 of dividend income and earned $5,650 of wages from a part-time job. Fabian's total income is below the gross income filing threshold for dependents. His investment income is also below the filing requirement. Fabian is not required to file a tax return in 2018, and his mother can claim him as a dependent on her tax return.

Example: Javier is a 16-year-old high school student who is claimed as a dependent on his parents' tax return. He worked as a pizza delivery boy 5 hours a week and earned $3,200 of wages in 2018. He also had $1,100 of interest income from a certificate of deposit that his grandmother gave him last Christmas. Javier is required to file a tax return because his unearned income exceeds $1,050. If Javier did not have any interest income, he would not be required to file a return. The investment income is what triggers his filing requirement.

Example: Tina is 17 and is claimed as a dependent on her parent's tax return. Working at an ice cream parlor during the school year, Tina earned a total of $12,600 in wages in 2018. She had no other income, and her parents provide more than one-half of her support. Tina must file a tax return because her total earned income is more than $12,000, but her parents can still claim her as a dependent.

Even if a taxpayer is not legally required to file a tax return, the taxpayer should do so if he or she is eligible to receive a refund. A taxpayer should file a tax return if:

- Had income tax withheld from his pay,
- Made estimated tax payments or had prior year overpayments,
- Qualifies for the Earned Income Tax Credit, or
- Qualifies for any other refundable tax credits.

Example: Susie is single, has a young son, and qualifies for HOH filing status. In 2018, she earns $12,000 of wages and $700 of self-employment income from cleaning houses on the weekends. Although Susie makes less than the filing threshold for her filing status, she must file a tax return because her earnings from self-employment exceed $400. Even if Susie did not have self-employment earnings, she should still file a tax return, because she likely qualifies for the Earned Income Tax Credit. The EITC is a refundable credit which could give Susie a refund.

Filing Requirements for Self-Employed Taxpayers

There are different requirements for taxpayers who are self-employed. Generally, a taxpayer is required to file a tax return if he has net self-employment earnings of $400 or more.

Do not confuse the filing threshold amount for self-employed taxpayers with the filing requirement for information returns (most notably, Form 1099-MISC, *Miscellaneous Income*). Form 1099-MISC is used to report a number of different types of payments, but it is most commonly used to report payments to an independent contractor who is paid at least $600 during the year. This $600 "reporting threshold" has nothing to do with the income tax filing requirement for a self-employed person.

Additional Filing Requirements

Sometimes a taxpayer is required to file a tax return even if the gross income threshold is not met, such as in the previous example when a taxpayer has self-employment earnings of $400 or more. Other examples include the following:

- A taxpayer who earned $108.28 or more as a church employee. For the purposes of this rule, a "church employee" is an employee of a church or religious organization that has a certificate, in effect electing an exemption from employer social security and Medicare taxes.[39]

- If the taxpayer owes Social Security tax or Medicare tax on tips not reported to his employer.

- If the taxpayer must pay the alternative minimum tax.

- If the taxpayer owes additional tax in connection with a qualified plan, an IRA, a health savings account, or another tax-favored health plan.

- If the taxpayer received a Medicare Advantage MSA, Archer MSA, or health savings account (HSA) distribution.

- If the taxpayer owes household employment taxes for a household worker, such as a nanny.

- If the taxpayer must recapture an education credit, investment credit, or other credit.

- If the taxpayer received advance payments of the Premium Tax Credit for himself, his spouse, or a dependent who enrolled in coverage through the Health Insurance Marketplace.

> **Example:** William is 28 and single. In 2018, he was unemployed for part of the year. He only earned $9,000 in wages during the year. Normally, he would not have a filing requirement. However, he withdrew $1,200 from his IRA account at the beginning of the year to pay his bills. The IRA withdrawal is subject to a 10% early withdrawal penalty. This triggers a filing requirement for William. He must file a tax return and pay the penalty, even though his income is less than the filing threshold for single filers.

---

[39] For the purposes of this rule, a "church employee" does not include an ordained minister, a member of a religious order (such as a nun or a monk), or a Christian Science practitioner.

Unit 2: Study Questions

(Test yourself first; then check the correct answers at the end of this quiz.)

1. Rosemarie, age 65, and Domenico, age 72, were married on December 26, 2018. They have no dependents. Rosemarie had gross income of $2,000, and Domenico had gross income of $21,000 for the year. Domenico wants to file jointly, but Rosemarie wants to file separately. Which of the following statements is correct?

A. Domenico is required to file a tax return using the MFS status. Rosemarie is not required to file a return.
B. Domenico may claim Rosemarie as a dependent, as long as she does not file her own separate return.
C. Domenico and Rosemarie are both required to file tax returns, and they must both file MFS.
D. Domenico and Rosemarie may both file as single since they were married for less than one month during the taxable year.

2. Dana's husband died on January 14, 2018. She has one dependent son who is eight years old. She did not remarry during the year. What is the most beneficial filing status for Dana to use for 2018?

A. Married filing jointly
B. Single
C. Qualifying widow(er)
D. Head of household

3. Madison and Todd are not married and do not live together, but they have a two-year-old daughter named Amanda. Madison and her daughter lived together all year while Todd lived alone in his own apartment. Todd cares for his daughter on the weekends. Madison earned $13,000 working as a clothing store clerk. Todd earned $48,000 managing a hardware store. Todd paid over half the cost of Madison's apartment for rent and utilities, where his daughter Amanda lives. He also gave Madison child support and extra money for groceries. Todd does not support any other family member. Which of the following statements is correct?

A. Todd can file as head of household.
B. Madison can file as head of household.
C. Todd and Madison can file jointly.
D. Either parent can claim the dependency exemption for the child, but neither Todd nor Madison can claim head of household filing status.

4. Leslie's marriage was annulled on February 25, 2018. She filed jointly with her husband in the previous two years. She has not yet filed her 2018 tax return. Leslie has no dependents. Which of the following statements is correct?

A. She must file amended returns, claiming single filing status for all open years affected by the annulment. She will file single for the current tax year.
B. She is not required to file amended returns. She can file jointly with her husband in 2018 because she was still married to him for part of the year.
C. She is not required to file amended returns. She must file as married filing separately on her 2018 return.
D. She is not required to file amended returns. She must file as single on her 2018 return.

5. Annie's husband, Franco, has neither a green card nor a visa. He was physically present in the United States for 150 days in *each* of the years 2016, 2017, and 2018. Is Franco a resident alien under the substantial presence test?

A. Yes; he is a resident alien for tax purposes, and he may file jointly with Annie.
B. No; he is a nonresident alien for tax purposes. He cannot file jointly with Annie.
C. Franco is a nonresident alien for tax purposes, but he may elect to file as a resident with his spouse.
D. Franco is a nonresident alien for tax purposes, and he should file Form 1040NR.

6. Trinity, age 22, is single and a full-time college student who is claimed as a dependent on her father's tax return. Her father provides the majority of his daughter's support and pays her college tuition. In 2018, Trinity earned $13,000 in wages from her part-time job as an administrative assistant. She had no other income. Is she required to file a tax return?

A. Yes.
B. No.
C. Trinity is only required to file a tax return if she is a full-time student.
D. Trinity should file a return because she will receive a refund, but she is not required to file.

7. In 2018, Clarence took legal custody of his ten-year-old grandson, Bobby. How long must Bobby live in Clarence's home for Clarence to qualify for head of household status?

A. At least three months
B. More than half the year
C. The entire year
D. More than twelve months

8. Zora is a citizen of Russia. Zora is granted a green card and comes to the U.S. to work as an engineer for an American software firm. Zora arrives in the U.S. on November 1, 2018. She earns a total of $16,000 of U.S. wages in November and December. Which of the following statements is correct?

A. She is not required to file a U.S. tax return.
B. She is required to file a U.S. tax return, and she must file using Form 1040NR, since she was a U.S. resident for only two months.
C. She is required to file a U.S. tax return, and she must file her return using Form 1040.
D. She is not required to file a U.S. tax return in 2018, but she will be required to file a return in 2019.

9. When may a taxpayer amend a joint tax return from "married filing jointly" to "married filing separately" *after* the original filing deadline?

A. Never
B. Only within the statute of limitations for filing amended returns
C. Only when a marriage has been annulled
D. An estate's personal representative may amend a joint return elected by the surviving spouse to a separate return for the decedent.

10. Seven years ago, Vladimir and Pablo were legally joined in a civil union in the state of Vermont. They now live in California. What is the correct statement about their filing status for 2018?

A. Vladimir and Pablo must file jointly.
B. A civil union of same-sex spouses in Vermont is recognized under California law, so they must file joint federal returns because both states recognized civil unions.
C. Vladimir and Pablo have the choice to file as single, married filing jointly, or married filing separately.
D. Civil unions are not recognized as legal marriages for IRS purposes. Vladimir and Pablo must file as single for federal tax purposes.

11. A U.S. citizen who is married to a nonresident alien can file a joint return as long as both spouses:

A. Sign the return and agree to be taxed on their worldwide income
B. Are living overseas
C. Have valid Social Security numbers
D. Are physically present in the United States

12. Huang is an international student temporarily in the U.S. on an F-1 Visa. Huang arrived in the U.S. on January 1, 2018, and was present in the U.S. all year. How long is he exempt from the substantial presence test?

A. One year
B. Three years
C. Five years
D. There is no exemption to the substantial presence test.

13. Which of the following statements is correct regarding the HOH filing status?

A. The taxpayer must be unmarried to qualify for head of household filing status.
B. The taxpayer's spouse must live in the home during the tax year.
C. The taxpayer's dependent parent does not have to live with the taxpayer to qualify for head of household filing status.
D. The taxpayer must have paid roughly half of the cost of keeping up the house for the entire year.

14. The married filing separately (MFS) status is for taxpayers who:

A. Are legally divorced on the last day of the year.
B. Are married and choose to file separate returns.
C. Are unmarried but engaged to be married.
D. Are unmarried but have a dependent child.

15. Victor is 39 years old and has lived apart from his wife, Eleanor, since February 1, 2018. Their divorce was not yet final at the end of the year, and they were not legally separated under a separate maintenance decree. They have two minor children, a son, age 15, and a daughter, age 9. After Victor and Eleanor split up, their son lived with Victor. Their daughter lives with Eleanor. Victor provides all of the support for the minor child living with him. Eleanor refuses to file jointly with Victor in 2018. The most beneficial filing status that Victor qualifies for is:

A. Married filing separately
B. Single
C. Head of household
D. Married filing jointly

16. Liza and Stuart were married for nine years. Stuart died on April 3, 2017. Liza did not remarry after her husband's death. Liza has one dependent child, age 5. Which filing status should Liza use for her 2018 tax return?

A. Single
B. Married filing jointly
C. Head of household
D. Qualifying widow with a dependent child

17. Adrienne and Troy are married and lived together all year. Adrienne earned $900 in wages during 2018, and Troy earned $72,000. Adrienne wants to file a joint return, but Troy refuses to file with Adrienne and instead files a separate return on his own. Which of the following statements is correct?

A. Adrienne can file a joint tax return and e-file it if Troy refuses to provide his signature.
B. Adrienne and Troy must both file separate returns.
C. Adrienne can file as single because Troy refuses to sign a joint return.
D. Adrienne does not have a filing requirement because her income is below the filing threshold.

18. Which dependent relative may qualify a taxpayer for head of household filing status?

A. An adult stepdaughter who lives in her own apartment who is supported by the taxpayer
B. A cousin who lives with the taxpayer all year
C. A parent who lives in his own home and not with the taxpayer
D. An adopted child who lived with the taxpayer for five months of the tax year

19. All of the following individuals are required to file an income tax return *except*:

A. A taxpayer who owes household employment tax for a nanny
B. A church employee who is exempt from FICA taxes and who earned $106 of wages in 2018
C. A 67-year-old qualifying widower who earned $18,000 in 2018
D. A single taxpayer who earned $6,500 in 2018 and owes excise tax on withdrawals from a traditional IRA account

20. Lauren is an 18-year-old high school senior in her last year of high school. She worked as a grocery store bagger on weekends and earned $1,400 in wages during 2018. She also received $4,300 for a winning scratch-off lottery ticket. Her parents claim Lauren as a dependent on their joint tax return. Does Lauren have to file her own return?

A. Yes; because of the amount of her unearned income
B. Yes; because of the combined amount of her unearned and earned income
C. No; because her earned income is below the threshold for a dependent
D. No; because it is illegal for a high school student to play the lottery

21. Which of the following dependency relationships would not qualify a taxpayer to claim qualifying widow(er) as their filing status after the death of a spouse?

A. A biological child
B. A foster child
C. An adopted child
D. A stepchild

22. Louisa legally separated from her husband during 2018. They share custody of a 9-year-old son. Which of the following facts would *prevent* Louisa from filing as head of household?

A. Louisa has maintained a separate residence from her husband since February 1, 2018.
B. Her son's principal home is with Louisa.
C. Louisa's parents assisted her with 40% of her household costs.
D. Louisa's son lived with her for exactly six months. He lived with his father for the rest of the year.

23. Carol and Raul were married five years ago and had no children. They split up two years ago but never officially filed for divorce. Although they lived apart all of 2018, they are neither divorced nor legally separated. Which of the following filing statuses can they use?

A. Single or married filing separately
B. Married filing jointly or married filing separately
C. Married filing separately or head of household
D. Single or qualifying widow(er)

24. Alexandra's younger brother, Sebastian, is 18 and a full-time student. Sebastian lived with a friend in January and February of 2018. From March through July, Sebastian moved in with his sister Alexandra. On August 1, 2018, Sebastian moved back in with his friends and stayed with them for the rest of the year. However, since Sebastian did not have a job, Alexandra gave him money every month and provided the majority of his financial support for the entire year. Alexandra has no other dependents. Which of the following statements is correct?

A. Alexandra can file as head of household.
B. Alexandra can file jointly with Sebastian.
C. Alexandra cannot file as head of household.
D. Sebastian can file as head of household.

25. Paola and Marcello are married and file jointly. During 2018, Paola turned 67, and Marcello turned 66. Paola's gross income was $17,600, and Marcello's gross income from self-employment was $520. Marcello had no other income. Based on this information, which of the following statements is correct?

A. Paola and Marcello are not required to file tax returns.
B. Paola and Marcello are required to file tax returns.
C. Only Paola is required to file a tax return.
D. Only Marcello is required to file a tax return.

26. Taxpayers are considered to be married for the entire year if:

A. One spouse dies during the year, and the surviving spouse does not remarry.
B. The spouses are legally separated under a separate maintenance decree.
C. The spouses are divorced on December 31 of the tax year.
D. The spouses had their marriage annulled on December 31 of the tax year.

27. Ezequiel and Angela are married, but they choose to file separate returns for 2018 because the IRS is auditing Ezequiel for a previous tax issue. Ezequiel and Angela file their MFS returns on time. A few months after filing their separate returns, the audit is over, and Ezequiel's previous tax issue has been resolved. He then wishes to file amended returns and file jointly with his wife in order to claim the Earned Income Tax Credit (EITC). Which of the following statements is correct?

A. Taxpayers are prohibited from changing his filing status in order to claim the Earned Income Tax Credit.
B. Ezequiel and Angela can amend their MFS tax returns to MFJ in order to claim the credit.
C. Ezequiel and Angela can amend their MFS tax returns to MFJ, but they cannot claim the credit.
D. Angela cannot file jointly with Ezequiel after she has already filed a separate tax return.

1. The answer is C. Since Domenico and Rosemarie are married, they can file either jointly or separately. If Rosemarie does not agree to file jointly with Domenico, both taxpayers must file MFS. The filing requirement threshold for married filing separately in 2018 is $5, so both spouses have a filing requirement.

2. The answer is A. If a taxpayer's spouse died during the year, the taxpayer is considered married for the whole year and can file as MFJ. Therefore, Dana should file a joint return for 2018.

3. The answer is D. Although Todd provided over half the cost of maintaining a home for Madison and Amanda, he cannot file as head of household since Amanda did not live with him for more than half the year. Madison cannot file as HOH either because she did not provide more than one-half the cost of keeping up the home for her daughter. However, either Todd or Madison may still claim Amanda as a dependent. Generally, a child is the qualifying child of the custodial parent, so Madison would have the right to claim Amanda. But Madison may also choose to release the dependency exemption to Todd (who is the noncustodial parent) by using Form 8332.

4. The answer is A. Leslie must file amended tax returns for the previous two years. She cannot file jointly with her former husband in 2018. If a couple obtains a court decree of annulment, the taxpayer must file amended returns (Form 1040X), claiming single or head of household status for all tax years affected by the annulment that are not closed by the statute of limitations for filing an amended tax return.

5. The answer is A. Franco meets the substantial presence test and is considered a U.S. resident alien for tax purposes. He is considered to have been present in the United States for a total of 225 days. The full 150 days are counted for 2018; 50 days for 2017 (1/3 of 150); and 25 days for 2016 (1/6 of 150).

6. The answer is A. A single dependent whose earned income was more than $12,000 in 2018 must file a return. Her father may still claim Trinity as a dependent and a qualifying child because she is a full-time student and under age 24 at the end of the year, and did not provide more than one-half of her own support.

7. The answer is B. Bobby must live with his grandfather for more than half the year (over six months) in order to qualify as his dependent. There are exceptions for temporary absences.

8. The answer is C. Zora is required to file a U.S. tax return in 2018, and she must file using Form 1040, not Form 1040NR. Zora is a green card holder, and therefore she is treated as a U.S. resident for tax purposes, regardless of how much time she has been present in the United States. As a resident alien, Zora will be taxed on income from worldwide sources, including any income she earned while she was in Russia.

9. The answer is D. An executor for a deceased taxpayer can amend a joint return to an MFS return up to one year *after* the filing deadline. This is the only exception to a rule that generally prevents a taxpayer from amending his married filing jointly return to a married filing separately return past the filing deadline. Answer "C" is incorrect because if a marriage has been annulled, the filing status would be amended to "single" rather than "MFS," because an annulment invalidates the original marriage contract.

10. The answer is D. Same-sex marriage is now legal in all 50 states and the District of Columbia. However, for federal tax purposes, civil unions are not treated as legal marriages. Civil unions offer same-sex couples some of the same benefits of marriage under state law, but they are not recognized as "marriages" for federal tax purposes. The IRS recognizes a marriage of same-sex spouses that was validly entered into a domestic or foreign jurisdiction whose laws recognize same-sex marriage. Therefore, Vladimir and Pablo must file as single.

11. The answer is A. A U.S. citizen (or U.S. resident), who is married to a nonresident alien, can elect to file a joint return as long as both spouses sign the return and agree to be taxed on their worldwide income. A Social Security number is not required, because a nonresident spouse that is ineligible for an SSN may request an ITIN in order to file jointly with a U.S. resident spouse.

12. The answer is C. In determining residency status for tax purposes, students temporarily in the U.S. on an F, J, M, or Q visa are exempt from the substantial presence test for five years. In addition, an individual who is in either of the following categories is temporarily exempt from counting days toward the substantial presence test:

- **Teacher or trainee:** This includes any nonimmigrant temporarily present in the U.S. on a J or Q visa who is not a student. The definition includes physicians, au pairs, short-term scholars, summer camp workers, and cultural exchange visitors temporarily present in the U.S.
- **Closer connection to home country:** This includes individuals who have a tax home in a foreign country and a closer connection to that country than they do the U.S.

13. The answer is C. A dependent parent does not have to live with a taxpayer for the taxpayer to elect the head of household filing status. This special rule applies to parents who are related to the taxpayer by blood, marriage, or adoption if the taxpayer pays more than half of the qualifying parent's household costs. Answer "A" is incorrect because a married person can still qualify for head of household if they are "considered unmarried" for tax purposes. A married person can be "considered unmarried" in certain circumstances if they live apart from their spouse and can file as head of household.

14. The answer is B. The married filing separately (MFS) status is for taxpayers who are married and either:

- Choose to file separate returns, or
- Do not agree to file a joint return.

15. The answer is C. Victor qualifies for head of household filing status because he can be "considered unmarried" for tax purposes. His child lived with him for more than six months, he did not live with his spouse the last half of the year, and he paid more than half the cost of keeping up a home for the year for a qualifying child. Couples who are living apart but not yet divorced or legally separated are allowed to file jointly, but both spouses must agree to do so. Therefore, since Eleanor refuses to file jointly with Victor, the most beneficial filing status for Victor is head of household.

16. The answer is D. In 2018, Liza is eligible for "qualifying widow(er) with dependent child" filing status. Liza and Stuart qualified to file MFJ in the year he died, with Liza signing the tax return as a surviving spouse. The year of death is the last year for which a taxpayer can file MFJ. For each of the two years *following* the year of the spouse's death, the surviving spouse can use the qualifying widow status, if she has a qualifying dependent and does not remarry.

17. The answer is B. Married couples must agree to file jointly. If one spouse does not agree to file jointly, they are individually subject to the MFS filing threshold. In this case, Adrienne and Troy are both required to file separate tax returns because both are above the applicable earnings threshold for MFS.

18. The answer is C. A parent is the only dependent relative who does not have to live with the taxpayer for the taxpayer to claim "head of household" status. In order to file for head of household, the "qualifying person" must be one of the following: a birth child, adopted child, grandchild, stepchild, foster child, brother, sister, half-brother, half-sister, stepbrother, stepsister, or a descendant of any of those. The qualifying person must also live with the taxpayer (unless the absence is temporary). The only exception to the residency test is a parent, who does not have to live with the taxpayer. A cousin does not qualify because they do not meet the relationship test. The adopted child in answer "D" does not qualify because the child lived with the taxpayer for less than one-half of the year.

19. The answer is B. Church employees who are exempt from Social Security and Medicare taxes and have wages of $108.28 or more for the year are required to file a tax return. In answer B, the church employee's wages are below that threshold. In all of the other answers, the taxpayer would be required to file a return.

20. The answer is A. Lauren has to file a tax return because of the amount of her unearned income: i.e., the $4,300 lottery prize. Her *earned* income—$1,400—was not high enough to trigger a filing requirement, but the lottery winnings (unearned income) do trigger a filing requirement. Answer "D" is incorrect because most U.S. states allow 18-year-olds to play the state lottery because they are legal adults.

21. The answer is B. To be eligible for the qualifying widow(er) filing status, the taxpayer normally must have a dependent child. For the purposes of this filing status, a qualifying child can be an adopted child, biological child, or stepchild, but does *not* include a foster child. This special rule for dependents that excludes foster children only pertains to the qualifying widow(er) filing status. Answer "C" is incorrect because legally adopted children are always treated the same as biological children for tax law purposes.

22. The answer is D. For Louisa to file as head of household, her home must have been the main home of her qualifying child for *more* than half the tax year (i.e., *over* six months). Since her son only lived with her for six months, he would not have been in the household sufficient time to qualify her for this filing status.

23. The answer is B. As long as they are married and are neither divorced nor legally separated, Carol and Raul can file a joint return or file separately. They cannot file as single.

24. The answer is C. Alexandra cannot claim head of household status because Sebastian lived with her for only five months, which is less than half the year.

25. The answer is B. Paola and Marcello must both file tax returns. Normally, Paola and Marcello would not be required to file because their combined gross income was less than the filing requirement, and they are both over 65 (this threshold applies if both spouses are 65 or over and they are filing jointly). However, because Marcello's self-employment income exceeds $400, he is required to file a Schedule C. Further, if Paola did not wish to file a joint return with Marcello, she would nevertheless be required to file separately because her income exceeds the applicable threshold of $5 for MFS filers in 2018. Whether they choose to file jointly or separately, both are required to file tax returns for 2018.

26. The answer is A. Taxpayers are considered "married" for the entire year if:
- They were married on the last day of the tax year, or
- One spouse died during the year, and the surviving spouse has not remarried as of the end of the year.

27. The answer is B. Ezequiel and Angela are allowed to amend their separate returns to a joint return in order to claim the credit. If a taxpayer files a separate return, he may elect to amend the filing status to married filing jointly at any time within three years from the due date of the original return (not including any extensions). However, the same does not hold true in reverse. Once a taxpayer files a joint return, he cannot choose to file a separate return for that year after the due date of the return (with a rare exception for deceased taxpayers).

Unit 3: Dependents and the "Deemed Exemption"

For additional information read:
Publication 501, *Dependents, Standard Deduction, and Filing Information*
Publication 504, *Divorced or Separated Individuals*

Due to changes implemented by the Tax Cuts and Jobs Act, personal and dependency exemptions are suspended (reduced to $0) for tax years 2018 through 2025. However, the ability to *claim* a dependent can make taxpayers eligible for other tax benefits, including a new type of credit available to taxpayers who have dependents. For example, the following tax benefits are all associated with a dependent:

- Child Tax Credit (CTC),
- Additional Child Tax Credit (ACTC),
- Earned Income Tax Credit (EITC),
- Child and Dependent Care Credit,
- Head of household filing status (HOH),
- The new "Credit for Other Dependents" (ODC) and other tax benefits.

Although the TCJA eliminated the benefit of the dependency exemption itself, the law remains unchanged on who qualifies as a dependent for tax purposes. For 2018 tax year filings, taxpayers can determine a dependent's eligibility by using the "deemed exemption" amount of $4,150.[40]

Dependents are either a qualifying child or a qualifying relative of the taxpayer. Examples of dependents include a child, stepchild, brother, sister, or parent.

Primary Tests for Dependency

Identifying and determining the correct number of dependents is a critical component of completing a taxpayer's return. In order to determine if a taxpayer can claim a dependent, there are three primary tests:

- Dependent taxpayer test
- Joint return test
- Citizenship or residency test

Test #1: Dependent Taxpayer Test

A taxpayer (or taxpayer's spouse, if filing a joint return) who may be claimed as a dependent by another taxpayer may not claim anyone as a dependent on his or her own tax return. In other words, the dependent taxpayer test specifies that any taxpayer who can be claimed as a dependent cannot claim a dependent themselves.

---

[40] In 2018, a "deemed personal exemption" amount of $4,150 is used for purposes of determining who is a "qualifying relative" under IRC Sec. 152(d)(1)(B).

Example: Jayne is a 19-year-old single mother who has an infant son who is three months old. Jayne lives with her parents and has a part-time job, but she does not make enough money to support herself or her infant son. Jayne is claimed as a dependent by her parents, so she is prohibited from claiming her infant son as a dependent on her own tax return.

Sometimes an individual meets the rules to be a qualifying dependent of more than one person. Regardless, only one person can claim an individual as a dependent on his tax return.

Example: Ian and Joy are unmarried and live together with their daughter, Juliana. Juliana is a qualifying child for both Ian and Joy, but only one of them can claim Juliana as a dependent on their tax return. Although only one parent can claim Juliana as a dependent, the two parents can agree on which parent should claim the child in order to achieve the best tax outcome.

Test #2: Joint Return Test

If a married individual files a joint return, that person normally cannot be claimed as a dependent by another taxpayer. Even if the other dependency tests are met, a taxpayer is generally not allowed to claim a dependent if that person files a joint return with his or her spouse.

Example: Katy is 18 years old and had no income in 2018. Katy lived with her father the majority of the year. Katy got married on December 31, 2018, to Jerry, who is 24 years old. Katy's new husband earned $26,700 during 2018, and they file jointly together. Katy's father supported her the entire year and even paid for her wedding. However, her father cannot claim Katy as his dependent in 2018 because Katy is filing jointly with her new husband.

However, there is one narrow exception to this test. The joint return test *does not apply* if the joint return is filed by the dependent only to claim a refund and neither spouse would have a tax liability, even if they filed separate returns.

Example: Robbie and Rosalie are both 18 years old and married. They both live with Rosalie's mother, Sylvia. In 2018, Robbie earned $2,800 from a part-time job. That was the only income that either Robbie or his wife earned all year. Neither Robbie nor Rosalie are required to file a tax return, but they decide to file a joint return to obtain a refund of the taxes that were withheld from Robbie's wages. Robbie and Rosalie correctly check the box next to "Can anyone claim you as a dependent?" on their joint tax return. As the exception to the joint return test applies, Sylvia can claim both Robbie and Rosalie on her tax return, if all the other tests for dependency are met.

Test #3: Citizenship or Residency Test

A dependent must be a citizen or resident of the United States or a citizen or resident of Canada or Mexico (with an exception for foreign-born adopted children).[41] If a U.S. citizen or U.S. national legally adopts a child who is not a U.S. citizen, U.S. resident alien, or U.S. national,[42] this test is met as long as the child lives with the taxpayer as a member of the household all

---

[41] Foreign exchange students generally are not U.S. residents and do not meet the citizen or resident test, so they cannot be claimed as dependents, even if they live in the taxpayer's home all year.

[42] A "U.S. national" is an individual who, although not a U.S. citizen, owes his or her allegiance to the United States. U.S. nationals include American Samoans and Northern Mariana Islanders who chose to become U.S. nationals instead of U.S. citizens.

year. If all other dependency tests are met, the child can be claimed as a dependent. This also applies if the child was lawfully placed with the taxpayer for legal adoption.

> **Example:** Carmella, who is a U.S. citizen, adopted an infant boy from China who lived with her for the entire tax year. Even though Carmella's child is not yet a U.S. citizen, he meets the citizen or resident test because he was a member of Carmella's household for the entire year.

Dependency Relationships

A dependent may be either a "qualifying child" or a "qualifying relative". Both types of dependents have unique rules, but some requirements are the same for both. Remember, a person must meet the requirements of either a qualifying child or a qualifying relative to be claimed as a dependent. There are very specific tests to identify the difference between the two.

> **Note:** Both "qualifying children" and "qualifying relatives" must meet all of the primary dependency requirements already specified: the dependent taxpayer, joint return, and citizenship or residency tests. If these three tests are met, the person is a dependent. A taxpayer's spouse cannot be claimed as a dependent; however, a taxpayer's registered domestic partner *may* qualify as a dependent, assuming all the tests for dependency are met. A taxpayer cannot file as head of household if the taxpayer's only dependent is his or her registered domestic partner.

Tests for a Qualifying Child

The tests for a "qualifying child" are more stringent than the tests for a "qualifying relative." Having a qualifying child entitles a taxpayer to claim refundable tax credits, including the Earned Income Tax Credit and the Additional Child Tax Credit. Having a qualifying relative, on the other hand, does not qualify a taxpayer for these special credits. There are five tests for a qualifying *child*:

- **Relationship Test**
- **Age Test**
- **Residency Test**
- **Support Test**
- **Tiebreaker Test** (for a qualifying child of more than one person)

Test #1: The Relationship Test

The qualifying child must be related to the taxpayer by blood, marriage, or legal adoption. Qualifying children include:

- A child, stepchild, or adopted child
- A sibling or stepsibling (includes; half-brother, half-sister, stepbrother, stepsister, etc.)
- A descendant of one of the above (such as a grandchild, niece, or nephew)
- An eligible foster child

For the purposes of this test, an adopted child is treated the same as a natural child. This includes a child who was lawfully placed with the taxpayer for legal adoption.

Test #2: The Age Test

In order to be a qualifying child, the dependent must be:

- Under the age of 19 at the end of the tax year, or

- Under the age of 24 at the end of the tax year and a full-time student, or

- Permanently and totally disabled at any time during the year, regardless of age.

A child is considered a full-time student if he attends a qualified educational institution full-time for at least five months during the year.

> **Note:** For the purposes of the age test, to qualify as a student, the taxpayer's child must be enrolled in the number of hours or courses the school considers full-time at least five months of the year.

A child who is claimed as a dependent must be *younger* than the taxpayer who is claiming him, except in the case of dependents who are disabled. For taxpayers filing jointly, the child must be younger than one spouse listed on the return but does not have to be younger than both spouses.

> **Example:** Gordon and Denise are both 23 years old, married, and file jointly. Denise's 24-year-old stepbrother, Casey, is a full-time student and lives with Gordon and Denise, who provide all of his support. Casey is not disabled. Gordon and Denise are both younger than Casey. Therefore, Casey is not their qualifying child, even though he is a full-time student.

> **Example:** Carl, age 34, and Audrey, age 20, are married and file jointly. Audrey's 21-year-old brother, Brayden, is a full-time student, is single, and lives with Carl and Audrey. They provide all of Brayden's support. In this case, Carl and Audrey can claim Brayden as a qualifying child on their joint tax return because he is a full-time student and is younger than Carl.

> **Example:** Arnold is 55 years old and mentally disabled. Crystal, his 37-year-old sister, provides all of Arnold's support and cares for him in her home, where he lives with her full-time. Despite Arnold's age, he is considered a qualifying child and a dependent for tax purposes because he is completely disabled. Crystal can claim Arnold as her qualifying child, and she can also file as head of household.

Test #3: The Residency Test

A qualifying child must live with the taxpayer for more than half the tax year (over six months). The taxpayer's home is any location where they regularly live; it does not need to be a traditional home. For example, a child who lived with the taxpayer for over half the year in a homeless shelter meets the residency test.[43]

In most cases, because of the residency test, a child is automatically the qualifying child of the custodial parent. However, exceptions to the residency test apply for children of divorced parents, kidnapped children, children who were born or died during the year,[44] and temporary absences (such as for summer camp or a missionary trip).

---

[43] See IRS Publication 596, *Earned Income Credit*, for similar examples and scenarios.
[44] A taxpayer cannot claim a stillborn child as a dependent. The child must be born alive, even if he lived only for a short time.

A "temporary absence" includes illness, college, vacation, military service, institutionalized care for a child who is permanently and totally disabled and incarceration in a juvenile facility. It must be reasonable to assume that the child will return to the home after the temporary absence.

Example: Martino is unmarried and lives with his 10-year-old son, Kevin. Martino provides all of Kevin's support. In 2018, Kevin was diagnosed with a rare form of pediatric cancer and was hospitalized for eleven months. Kevin is still considered Martino's qualifying child because the hospitalization counts as a temporary absence from home. Martino can claim Kevin as his qualifying child, and he can also file as head of household.

Example: Cesare, age 23, is a full-time student and lived in the dorms at his university for the entire year. Cesare worked part-time, but did not pay over half of his total support. Instead, his mother Teresa supported him and paid most of his tuition and living expenses. Cesare's time spent in the dorms counts as a "temporary absence". Therefore, Teresa can claim Cesare on her tax return as a qualifying child, because he meets the relationship, age, residency, and support tests.

Example: Ramona's nine-year-old granddaughter, Sandra, lives with her for five months of the year, with her mother for three months, and with her aunt for four months. Sandra is not Ramona's qualifying child because the residency test is not met. However, she may be Ramona's qualifying relative if other tests are met.

Test #4: The Support Test

A qualifying child cannot provide more than one-half of his own support. This test is different from the "support test" for a qualifying relative, and should not be confused as such. State benefits provided to a person in need, such as welfare, food stamps or housing, are generally considered support provided by the state.

However, if a child receives Social Security benefits, and uses them for his or her own support, the benefits are considered to be provided by the child. A full-time student does not take scholarships (whether taxable or nontaxable) into account when calculating the support test.

Example: Stuart and Vanessa file jointly. They have one daughter named Edith, age 26. Edith earned $4,000 in wages before she was laid off in March and moved back in with her parents. Stuart and Vanessa provided the majority of Edith's support for the rest of the year. Edith got a new job in December and moved out. She is not a qualifying child for federal tax purposes. Edith meets the support test as well as the residency test. However, she does not meet the age test.

Example: Ernesto has a 19-year-old daughter named Gladys. Ernesto provided $5,000 toward his daughter's support for the year. Gladys has a part-time job and provided $13,000 of her own support. Therefore, Gladys provided over half of her own support for the year. Gladys does not pass the support test, and consequently, she is not Ernesto's qualifying child. Gladys can file her own tax return as single.

Note: The definition of **support** includes only income that is actually used for living expenses. A person's own funds are not "support" unless they are *actually spent* for support. For example, if a child earns income that is saved in a bank account rather than spent on the child's living expenses, the amounts saved are not included in the support test.

Example: Holly, age 12, had a small role in a television series. She earned $45,000 as a child actor, but her parents put all the money in a trust fund for her. She lived at home with her parents all year. Holly meets the support test since her earnings were not used for her own support. She meets the tests for a qualifying child, so she can be claimed as a dependent by her parents.

Foster parents may be eligible to claim a foster child, provided the child is legally placed in their home by the courts or a government agency. Payments received from a child placement agency for the support of a foster child are considered support provided by the agency, rather than support provided by the child.

Example: Hilda is a foster parent who provided $3,500 toward her 7-year-old foster son's support for the year. The state of Nevada provided $6,000, which was considered support provided by the state, not by the child. Hilda's foster child did not provide more than half of his own support for the year. Therefore, Hilda can claim her foster son as a qualifying child.

Test #5: Tiebreaker Test

Only one person can claim a qualifying child, even if the child qualifies for more than one person. If more than one taxpayer *attempts* to claim the same child under the normal dependency rules, the tiebreaker rules apply, meaning the child is treated as a qualifying child in the following sequence:

- By the child's parents, if they file a joint return
- By the parent, if only one of the taxpayers is the child's parent
- By the parent with whom the child lived the longest during the year
- By the parent with the highest AGI, if the child lived with each parent for the same length of time during the tax year
- By the taxpayer with the highest AGI, if neither of the child's parents can claim the child as a qualifying child
- By a taxpayer with a higher AGI than either of the child's parents who can also claim the child as a qualifying child, but does not

Example: Rosita and her sister, Evita, live together. Their seven-year-old nephew, Martin, lived with his aunts all year while Martin's mother was incarcerated in a maximum-security prison. Rosita's AGI is $18,600. Evita's AGI is $29,000. Martin is a qualifying child of both Rosita and Evita because he meets the relationship, age, residency, and support tests for both of his aunts. However, Evita has the primary right to claim Martin as her qualifying child because her AGI is higher than Rosita's.

Note: Remember, the tiebreaker test only applies when two people <u>attempt</u> to claim the same child. In cases where the parents are in agreement, there is no tiebreaker test.

Example: Isabel is single and has a three-year-old son named Jeffrey. They live with Isabel's father, Robert (the child's grandfather). Isabel claims Jeffrey as her qualifying child, which means the child may not be the qualifying child of Robert, the grandfather.

Rules for a Qualifying Relative

A person who is not a qualifying child may still qualify as a dependent under the rules for qualifying relatives. Even an individual who is not a family member can be a qualifying relative. Unlike a qualifying child, a qualifying relative can be any age. The tests for qualifying relative are applied only when the tests for qualifying child are not met. To be claimed as a qualifying relative, the dependent must meet the following four tests:

- **Not a qualifying child test**
- **Member of household or relationship test**
- **Gross income test**
- **Support test**

Test #1: "Not a Qualifying Child" Test

If a child is already a qualifying child for any taxpayer, he cannot also be a qualifying relative of another taxpayer. A taxpayer cannot claim an individual who can be claimed as a dependent on another tax return.

Example: Theodore is 32 and single. Theodore has lived with his cousin, Melanie, the entire year. Melanie is 27 and has no taxable income and is not required to file a tax return. Theodore provided all the household support for Melanie. Therefore, Melanie passes the "not a qualifying child test" to be Theodore's dependent. If Theodore meets all other tests, Melanie may be claimed on Theodore's tax return as a qualifying relative.

Test #2: "Member of Household" or "Relationship" Test

A dependent that is not related to the taxpayer must have lived with the taxpayer the *entire tax year* in order to meet the member of household or relationship test. However, a family member who is related to the taxpayer in any of the following ways does not have to live with the taxpayer to meet this test:

- A child, stepchild, foster child, or descendant of any of them (for example, a grandchild)
- A sibling, stepsibling, or half-sibling
- A parent, grandparent, stepparent, or another direct ancestor (but not a foster parent)
- A niece or nephew, son-in-law, daughter-in-law, father-in-law, mother-in-law, brother-in-law, or sister-in-law

Example: Erick is 45 and single. Erick's 12-year-old nephew, David, lived with him for four months in 2018. For the remainder of the year, David lived with his mother, Clarissa, in another state. Clarissa is Erick's 32-year-old sister. Even though David and Clarissa lived in another state, Erick still provided all of their financial support. David is not Erick's qualifying child because he did not live with Erick for more than half the year and therefore does not meet the residency test. However, David does meet the requirements to be Erick's qualifying relative.

For the relationship test, "family members" do not include cousins, who are treated as unrelated persons for tax purposes. A cousin must live with the taxpayer for the entire year and also meet the gross income test to qualify as a dependent, and even then, a cousin cannot be a qualifying child—only a qualifying relative. Also, a taxpayer may not claim a housekeeper or other household employee as a dependent, even if the employee lives with the taxpayer all year.

> **Example:** Marianna is 20 years old and works as a live-in nanny for Henry. Marianna lives with Henry all year and takes care of his two toddlers. Henry cannot claim Marianna on his tax return as a dependent, because a qualifying relative cannot be a household employee.

Any relationship that is established by marriage does not end as a result of death or divorce. For example, if a taxpayer supports his mother-in-law, he can continue to claim her as a dependent even if he and his ex-spouse are divorced or if he becomes widowed.

> **Example**: Celeste and Giancarlo have always financially supported Celeste's elderly mother, Lucinda, and claimed her as their dependent on their jointly filed returns. In 2016, Celeste died and Giancarlo became a widower. Giancarlo remarries in 2018, but he continues to support his late wife's mother. Giancarlo can continue to claim his late wife's mother, Lucinda, as a qualifying relative, even though he has remarried.

> **Example:** Evangelista lived all year with her boyfriend, Oscar, and his two children in her home. Their cohabitation does not violate local laws. Oscar was unemployed for the entire tax year and has no taxable income. Oscar and his two children are not related to Evangelista as family members, but they may be qualifying relatives if they meet all the other tests. If Evangelista and Oscar were later to marry, then Evangelista would be able to claim Oscar's children as her stepchildren, and they would be qualifying children, instead of qualifying relatives.

Test #3: Gross Income Test

To meet the gross income test, the dependent's gross income for the tax year must be less than the threshold amount. In 2018, a qualifying relative cannot earn more than the "deemed exemption" amount, which is $4,150.

For the purposes of this test, "gross income" includes all income in the form of money, property, and services that is not exempt from tax.[45] Remember that there is no "gross income test" for a qualifying child—only for a qualifying relative.

> **Example:** Beatrice is 56 and earned $67,000 in wages for 2018. She financially supported her nephew, Jacob, who is 28 and a full-time college student. Jacob is not disabled. Jacob has a small part-time job, and he earns $4,950 in 2018. Although Beatrice financially supported Jacob, she cannot claim him as a dependent because Jacob does not meet the age test for a qualifying child. Jacob also does not meet the test for a qualifying relative, because his income exceeds the gross income test.

---

[45] For purposes of this test, the gross income of an individual who is permanently and totally disabled does not include income from a sheltered workshop.

Test #4: Support Test

In order to claim an individual as a qualifying relative, the taxpayer must provide *more than half* of the dependent's total support during the year. Support includes amounts from Social Security and welfare payments, even if that support is nontaxable. "Support" does not include amounts received from nontaxable scholarships. Support can include the fair market value of lodging. Note that this "support test" is very different from the one for a qualifying child.

> **Example:** Cherise supports her father, Albert, who lives with her. Albert received $3,700 from Social Security during the year, but he put $300 of it in a savings account and spent only $3,400 for his own support. Cherise spent $3,600 of her own income for Albert's support, so she has provided over half of his support for the year. Cherise can claim Albert as her qualifying relative.

Special Rules for Divorced and Separated Parents

Generally, to claim a child as a dependent, the child must live with the taxpayer for more than half the year. However, special rules apply if the dependent is supported by parents who are divorced, separated, or live apart.

In most cases, the child is the qualifying child of the custodial parent. However, a custodial parent may permit the noncustodial parent to claim the child. The noncustodial parent must attach Form 8332, *Release/Revocation of Release of Claim to Exemption for Child by Custodial Parent*, to his or her tax return. A child may be treated as the qualifying child of the noncustodial parent if *all* the following conditions apply:

- The parents are divorced or legally separated, or if they lived apart at all times during the last six months of the year.
- The child received over half of his support for the year from the parents
- The child is in the custody of one (or both) parents.
- The custodial parent signs a written declaration (Form 8332 or a similar statement) and the noncustodial parent attaches this declaration to his or her return.

This rule is an exception to the normal residency test for a qualifying child. It does not apply to the determination of head of household filing status or to eligibility for the Earned Income Tax Credit.

These benefits can be claimed only by the custodial parent, even if the noncustodial parent claims the child. If a divorce decree does not specify which parent is the custodial parent or which parent is allowed the claim the child, the dependent should be claimed by to the parent who has physical custody for the majority of the year.

> **Example:** Anders and Wilma are divorced and have one child. Wilma is the custodial parent, but she allows Anders to claim the child by signing Form 8332. Anders files as single and claims his son as his dependent. Wilma may still file as head of household, even though she does not claim her son as a dependent, because she maintained the home where the child lived for most of the year.

> **Example**: Johan and Penelope are legally divorced and live in separate homes. They share custody of their 8-year-old son, named Ludwig. In 2018, Ludwig stayed with Johan for 195 nights and with Penelope for 170 nights. Therefore, for federal tax purposes, Johan is considered the custodial parent and has the right to claim Ludwig as his qualifying child.

If the child lived with each parent for an equal number of nights during the year, the custodial parent is deemed to be the parent with the higher adjusted gross income.

The custodial parent can also revoke the release by using Form 8332. A copy of the revocation must be attached to the tax return for each year the child is claimed after the revocation.

Multiple Support Agreements

A *multiple support agreement* is when two or more people jointly provide for a person's support. This happens commonly when adult children are taking care of their parents. Under a multiple support agreement, family members together must pay *more* than half of the person's total support, but no one member individually may pay more than half.

In addition, the taxpayer who claims the dependent must provide more than 10% of the person's support. Only one family member can claim a dependent in a single year, but different qualifying family members can agree to claim the dependent in other years.

> **Example:** Sebastian, Valentin, and Yesenia are siblings who support their disabled mother, Victoria. Victoria is 83 years old and lives with Sebastian. In 2018, Victoria receives 20% of her financial support from Social Security, 40% from Valentin, 30% from Sebastian, and only 10% from Yesenia. Under the IRS rules for multiple support agreements, either Valentin or Sebastian can claim their mother as a dependent if the other signs a statement agreeing not to do so. Yesenia cannot claim her mother as a dependent, because she does not provide more than 10% of the support for Victoria during the year.

> **Example:** Yvette and Elinor are sisters who help financially support their 66-year-old father, Josef. Each pays approximately 20% of his care in a residential facility for elderly people. The remaining 60% is paid for by a wealthy friend who is not related to Josef. Because more than half of Josef's support is provided by someone unrelated to him, no one can claim Josef as a dependent.

(Test yourself first; then check the correct answers at the end of this quiz.)

1. Ingrid and Owen file for divorce. Ingrid has one son from a prior marriage named Gregory, age 17. After the divorce is final, Ingrid develops a drug problem and disappears. In 2018, Gregory lives for nine months with his former stepfather, Owen, who provides all of Gregory's support. Which of the following statements is correct?

A. Owen can claim Gregory as his qualifying child.
B. Owen can claim Gregory as his dependent but not as a qualifying child because the divorce dissolved any legal relationship between them.
C. Owen cannot claim Gregory as his dependent because they are not related persons.
D. Only Ingrid can claim Gregory as her dependent.

2. A taxpayer cannot claim a qualifying child as a dependent if that child provides more than how much of their own support?

A. 25%
B. 33%
C. 50%
D. 75%

3. All of the following statements are correct about the rules of dependents except:

A. One spouse is never considered the dependent of the other spouse.
B. A taxpayer may not claim a stillborn child as a dependent.
C. A taxpayer may claim a nanny as a dependent, as long as the nanny lives with the taxpayer all year.
D. A child is considered to have lived with the taxpayer during periods of time when either the child is temporarily absent.

4. Greta has three children: Luther, Silas, and Juliet. Each child contributes financially towards her support. Luther and Silas each provide 45%, and Juliet provides 10%. Which taxpayer would be eligible to claim Greta as a dependent under a multiple support agreement?

A. Luther or Silas
B. Juliet or Silas
C. Luther, Silas, or Juliet
D. No one is eligible to claim Greta.

5. Kingston provides the sole support for his mother. To claim her as a dependent on his Form 1040, Kingston's mother must be a resident or citizen of which of the following countries?

A. The United States
B. Mexico
C. Canada
D. Any of the above

6. Amber lives with Chad, her 17-year-old son. She provided $5,100 toward her son's support for the year. Chad also has a part-time job and provided $12,900 toward his own support. Can Amber claim her son as a dependent?

A. Yes; she can claim her son as a qualifying child because he is a minor.
B. Yes; she can claim Chad as a qualifying relative.
C. No; Chad provided more than half of his own support for the year. Therefore, he is neither Amber's qualifying child nor her qualifying relative.
D. None of the above

7. Dani and Xavier divorced years ago. They have six-year-old twins who live with Dani. Her AGI is $41,000, and Xavier's AGI is $48,000. Although Dani is the custodial parent, their divorce decree states that Xavier can claim the children on his tax return. However, Dani refuses to sign Form 8332. Which of the following statements is correct?

A. Xavier can claim one child as a dependent.
B. Xavier and Dani can each claim the children as dependents on their respective tax returns.
C. Since Dani is the custodial parent and refuses to sign Form 8332, Xavier cannot claim either child.
D. Neither Dani nor Xavier can claim the children as dependents.

8. Joseph, 52, is a single father who lives with his son Wyatt, who has Down syndrome. Wyatt is 32 years old and permanently disabled. Wyatt had $800 of interest income and $5,000 of wages from a part-time job. Joseph provided $25,000 toward Wyatt's support. Which of the following statements is correct?

A. Joseph can file as head of household, with Wyatt as his qualifying child.
B. Joseph does not qualify for head of household, but he could still claim Wyatt as his qualifying relative because Wyatt does not meet the age test for a qualifying child.
C. Joseph can file as head of household, with Wyatt as his qualifying relative.
D. Joseph must file as single, and he cannot claim Wyatt because of the amount of Wyatt's income.

9. Cheryl is 46 and unmarried. Her nephew, Bradley, lived with her all year and turned 18 years old on December 28, 2018. Bradley did not provide more than half of his own support. He had $4,200 of income from wages and $1,000 of investment income. Which of the following statements is correct?

A. Bradley is Cheryl's qualifying child.
B. Bradley is not a qualifying child; however, Cheryl can claim him as a qualifying relative.
C. Bradley is not a qualifying child or qualifying relative.
D. Cheryl can claim Bradley only if he is a full-time student since he is no longer a minor child.

10. Rebekah is 22 and a full-time college student. During the year, she lived at home with her parents for four months and lived in the college dorms for the remainder of the year. She worked part-time and earned $6,000, but that income did not amount to half of her total support. Can Rebekah's parents still claim her as a dependent?

A. No; because Rebekah earned more than the "deemed exemption" amount.
B. No; Rebekah did not live with her parents for more than half the year, and she does not meet the age test.
C. Yes; her parents can claim her as a qualifying child.
D. Yes; her parents can claim her as a dependent, but only as a qualifying relative.

11. Ursula and her son live together. Charlie is 34 years old, not disabled, and has a part-time job. Ursula provides more than half of Charlie's support. Ursula can claim Charlie as a qualifying relative, as long as he does not earn _____ or more in 2018.

A. $1,050
B. $3,500
C. $4,050
D. $4,150

Unit 3: Quiz Answers

1. The answer is A. A qualifying child must be related to the taxpayer by blood, marriage, or legal adoption. A "step" relationship formed by a legal marriage is not dissolved by divorce or death. Since Gregory did not live with his mother, but *did* live with his stepfather, Owen, for more than half the year, Owen is considered the custodial parent for tax purposes, and he can claim his stepson as a qualifying child.

2. The answer is C. A taxpayer cannot claim another person as a dependent if that person provided more than half of their own support.

3. The answer is C. A taxpayer may not claim a housekeeper or other household employee as a dependent, regardless of whether or not the employee lived with the taxpayer.

4. The answer is A. Only Luther or Silas is eligible to claim Greta under a multiple support agreement. Juliet is not eligible because she does not provide more than 10% of her mother's support.

5. The answer is D. A dependent must be a citizen or resident alien of the United States, Canada, or Mexico.

6. The answer is C. Chad provided more than half of his own support for the year, so he is not Amber's qualifying child or her qualifying relative. To meet the support test, the child cannot have provided more than half of his own support for the year.

7. The answer is C. Since Dani is the custodial parent and refuses to sign Form 8332, Xavier cannot claim either child. Without Form 8332, *Release/Revocation of Release of Claim to Exemption for Child by Custodial Parent,* signed and attached to the return, Xavier does not have the primary right to claim the children, since he is not the custodial parent.

8. The answer is A. Even though Wyatt is over the normal age threshold for a qualifying child, he is considered a qualifying child. This is because Wyatt is permanently disabled, and Joseph provides the majority of his financial support and care. The normal age thresholds for "qualifying children" do not apply in the case of permanently disabled individuals.

9. The answer is A. Bradley is Cheryl's qualifying child because he meets the age test, support test, and relationship test. Also, because Bradley is single, he is a qualifying person for Cheryl to claim head of household filing status. Bradley is not required to be a full-time student because any child under the age of 19 at the end of the tax year will be treated as a qualifying child if all the other tests are met. Bradley is only 18 years old and therefore passes the age test.

10. The answer is C. Rebekah meets all the qualifying child tests: the relationship test, the age test (because she is under 24 and a full-time student), the residency test (because the time spent at college is a legitimate temporary absence), and the support test (because she did not provide over half of her own support). Therefore, her parents can claim Rebekah as a dependent.

11. The answer is D. Charlie cannot be a qualifying child for Ursula because he does not meet the age test, but he can be claimed as a qualifying relative. The 2018 limit for gross income for qualifying relatives is $4,150. Therefore, if Charlie earns less than $4,150 during the year, his mother can claim him as a dependent on her tax return.

Unit 4: Taxable and Nontaxable Income

For additional information read:
Publication 525, *Taxable and Nontaxable Income*
Publication 15-B, *Employer's Tax Guide to Fringe Benefits*
Publication 3, *Armed Forces' Tax Guide*

The Internal Revenue Code (IRC) describes types of income that are taxable and nontaxable. Over the course of the next few units, we will cover the most common types of both. In this unit, we focus on various forms of employee compensation, but we start with a look at broader concepts regarding the taxability of income.

Federal tax law sets forth that all income is taxable unless it is specifically excluded. An *exclusion* is not the same as a *deduction*, and it is important to understand the distinction because some deductions and credits are phased out as a taxpayer's gross income increases. Excluded income, on the other hand, retains its character without regard to the amount of the taxpayer's gross income.

Most types of excluded income do not have to be reported on a tax return.

> **Example:** Lance is a popular recording artist who made more than $1,900,000 of taxable income last year. Because of his high income, some deductions and credits are phased out for Lance. However, in 2018, Lance is involved in an auto accident and sustains major injuries. Lance sues the other driver and receives an insurance settlement of $95,000 related to his injuries resulting from the accident. The settlement is excluded from his gross income because compensation for physical injuries is not taxable to the recipient, regardless of his taxable income level. Lance does not even have to report the injury settlement on his tax return.

Calculating Taxable Income

For a taxpayer to figure out how much tax he owes, he first needs to determine his **gross income. Gross income** is all income a taxpayer receives in the form of money, goods, property, and services that are not exempt from tax. In addition to wages, salaries, commissions, tips, and self-employment income, gross income includes other forms of compensation, such as interest, dividends, capital gains, taxable fringe benefits, and stock options.

Next, the taxpayer calculates his **adjusted gross income (AGI)** by subtracting from gross income certain specific deductions or adjustments. These deductions include IRA contributions, certain expenses for self-employed individuals, alimony payments,[46] and moving expenses.[47] The amount of a taxpayer's AGI is important because it helps determine eligibility for certain deductions and credits. Finally, the taxpayer calculates his **taxable income** by subtracting additional deductions (standard or itemized) from AGI.

---

[46] Before the TCJA was enacted, payments of alimony could always be deducted by the payor for federal tax purposes. For divorce decrees executed after December 31, 2018, the TCJA eliminates the deduction for alimony payments, however, prior divorce decrees are considered "grandfathered," and the old rules for deducting alimony payments still apply.
[47] Due to the TCJA, moving expenses are no longer deductible for most taxpayers. However, an exception exists for members of the armed forces on active duty who move pursuant to a military order and incident to a permanent change of station.

The table below is a simplified example of how to calculate income tax.

How to Calculate Taxable Income and Tax Liability
Start with gross income
Subtract adjustments to income ("above the line" deductions)
= Adjusted gross income (AGI)
Subtract greater of itemized deductions or standard deduction
= Taxable income
× Tax rate
= Gross tax liability
Subtract credits
= Net tax liability or refund receivable (based on the amount of prepaid tax, if any)

Earned Income vs. Unearned Income

Earned income such as wages, salaries, tips, professional fees, or self-employment income is received for services performed. *Unearned income* includes interest, dividends, retirement income, alimony, and disability benefits. Earned income is generally subject to Social Security and Medicare taxes (also called FICA taxes).

Investment income and other unearned income are generally not subject to FICA taxes. The amount of taxable income is used to determine the taxpayer's gross income tax liability before applicable credits.

Constructive Receipt of Income

The doctrine of constructive receipt requires that cash-basis taxpayers be taxed on income when it becomes available and is not subject to substantial limitations or restrictions, regardless of whether it is actually in their physical possession. Income received by an agent for a taxpayer is constructively received in the year the agent receives it.

Example: Logan is a landlord who owns several rental properties. On December 30, 2018, a customer delivers a $500 rent check to Logan's payment lockbox. Logan does not collect the rental deposits in the lockbox on December 30 and instead leaves town later that day to celebrate New Year's Eve. Logan does not take physical possession of the check until January 5, 2019, the same day he deposits the check in his bank account. He is considered to have constructive receipt in 2018 and must include the $500 of gross income on his 2018 tax return because the check was available to Logan at that time without any substantial limitations or restrictions.

Note: Most individuals are cash-basis taxpayers who report income when it is actually or constructively received during the tax year. This concept of constructive receipt would not apply to accrual-basis taxpayers who recognize income when it is earned rather than when it is received. We will cover accrual-basis taxpayers in Book 2.

Funds must be available without substantial limitations under the constructive receipt rules. If there are significant restrictions on the income, or if the income is not accessible to the taxpayer, it is not considered to have been constructively received. Income is also not considered to have been "constructively received" if a taxpayer declines it, as in the case of a prize or an award.

> **Example:** Lucia won front-row concert tickets valued at $1,200 from a local radio station. Lucia would be required to pay taxes based on the fair market value of the tickets. However, on the day of the concert, the radio station does not receive the tickets in time from the promoter, and Lucia is not able to attend the concert. Since she never received the tickets, the prize is not taxable to her because she never had constructive receipt of it.

> **Definition:** The IRS defines **fair market value** (FMV) in this way: The price at which a property would change hands between a buyer and a seller when both have reasonable knowledge of all the necessary facts and neither is being forced to buy or sell. If parties with adverse interests place a value on property in an arms-length transaction, that is strong evidence of FMV. If there is a stated price for services, this price is treated as the FMV unless there is evidence to the contrary.

The "Claim of Right" Doctrine

Under the "claim of right" doctrine, income received without restriction (over which the taxpayer has complete control) must be reported in the year received, even if there is a possibility it may have to be repaid in a later year.

If there is a dispute and income is later repaid, the repayment is deductible in the year repaid. As a result, the taxpayer is not required to amend his reported gross income for the earlier year.

> **Example:** In 2018, Marilyn sells a painting in her art gallery for $25,000. She properly includes $25,000 in her gross income and pays taxes on the income for the 2018 tax year. On March 2, 2019, the customer discovers the painting is a forgery and returns it for a full refund of $25,000. Since Marilyn pays back the $25,000 in 2019, she is entitled to deduct the amount from her gross income in 2019. She does not have to amend her 2018 tax return.

Worker Classification

For federal tax purposes, the IRS classifies workers in two broad categories: employees or independent contractors. These workers are taxed in different ways, and it is critical for businesses to identify the correct classification for each individual to whom it makes payments for services. In general, a business must withhold and remit income taxes, Social Security and Medicare taxes, and pay unemployment tax on salaries and wages paid to an employee. A business generally does not have to withhold or pay taxes on payments to independent contractors.

Self-Employed Taxpayers

Self-employment income is earned by taxpayers who work for themselves. A taxpayer who has self-employment income of $400 or more in a year must file a tax return and report the earnings to the IRS.

Taxpayers who are independent contractors usually receive Forms 1099-MISC from their business clients showing the income they were paid. The amounts from the Forms 1099-MISC, along with any other business income payments, are reported by most self-employed individuals on Schedule C, *Profit or Loss from Business*, of Form 1040.

Self-employed farmers or fishermen report their earnings on Schedule F, *Profit or Loss from Farming*, of Form 1040. Self-employment income also includes:

- Income of ministers, priests, and rabbis for the performance of services such as baptisms and marriages

- The distributive share of trade or business income allocated by a partnership to its general partners or by a limited liability company to its members. The income is reported on IRS Schedule K-1 (Form 1065).

A taxpayer does not have to conduct regular full-time business activities to be considered self-employed. A taxpayer may have a side business in addition to a regular job, and this is also considered self-employment.

Example: Nelson earned $45,000 as a full-time employee for Royal Roofing. He also advertises general handyman services online. During the year, Nelson did several handyman side-jobs on the weekends for clients. Nelson received payments of $9,000 from several different individuals for his handyman work. He did not receive Forms 1099-MISC for the $9,000 (because they were individuals who are not required to issue Forms 1099-MISC), but he must report the payments as self-employment income on Schedule C.

Example: Mia operates a popular taco truck with her brother, Orlando. They both split profits and losses equally, and they work together as a partnership. They correctly file Form 1065, *U.S. Return of Partnership Income*, to report the gross income from the taco stand. Mia and Orlando both receive a Schedule K-1 from the partnership every year. Mia and Orlando must each report their distributive share of income from the taco stand on their respective Forms 1040, Schedule E (Part 2). The income is considered self-employment income and is subject to self-employment tax.

FICA Tax (Payroll Taxes)

The Federal Insurance Contributions Act (FICA) tax includes two separate taxes: one is Social Security tax and the other is Medicare tax. The current rate for Social Security is 6.2% for the employer and 6.2% for the employee, or 12.4% total. The current rate for Medicare is 1.45% for the employer and 1.45% for the employee, or 2.9% total.

The combined FICA tax rate for 2018 is 15.3% and applies up to $128,400 of a taxpayer's combined earned income, including wages, tips, and net earnings from self-employment. If the taxpayer's combined earned income exceeds $128,400, a rate of 2.9%, representing only the

Medicare portion, applies to any excess earnings over $128,400. There is no cap on earnings subject to the 2.9% Medicare tax. An additional Medicare surtax of 0.9% is applied to wages and self-employment income above certain thresholds.[48]

> **Note:** The 7.65% tax rate is the combined rate for Social Security and Medicare. The Social Security portion (also called "OASDI") is 6.2% on earnings up to the applicable taxable maximum amount ($128,400 in 2018). *Remember:* the Medicare portion is 1.45% on *all* earned income. There is no yearly maximum for Medicare tax.

Self-Employment Tax

Self-employment tax (SE tax) is imposed on self-employed individuals in a manner similar to the Social Security and Medicare taxes that apply to wage earners. Self-employed individuals are responsible for paying the entire amount of Social Security and Medicare taxes applicable to their net earnings from self-employment. Self-employment tax is calculated on IRS Schedule SE, Self-Employment Tax. If a taxpayer has wages in addition to self-employment earnings, the Social Security tax on the wages is paid first. There are two adjustments related to the self-employment tax that reduce overall taxes for a taxpayer with self-employment income.

- First, the taxpayer's net earnings from self-employment are reduced by 7.65%. Just as the employer's share of Social Security tax is not considered wages to the employee, this reduction removes a corresponding amount from the net earnings before the SE tax is calculated.

- Second, the taxpayer can deduct the employer-equivalent portion of his self-employment tax in determining his adjusted gross income.

More Than One Business: If a taxpayer owns more than one business, he must net the profit or loss from each business to determine the total earnings subject to SE tax. However, married taxpayers cannot combine their income or loss from self-employment to determine their individual earnings subject to SE tax.

> **Example:** Brian is a sole proprietor who owns a barbershop. He has $49,000 of net income in 2018. His wife, Ellen, has a candle-making business, which has overall losses of ($12,000) in 2018. Brian must pay self-employment tax on $49,000, regardless of how he and Ellen choose to file. That is because married couples cannot offset each other's income from self-employment, even if they file jointly, for self-employment tax purposes. The income of each business is allocated to each individual.

> **Example:** Rocco is a married taxpayer who is a sole proprietor of two small businesses, a computer repair shop, and a car wash business that he runs only during the summer months. Rocco's wife is a homemaker and does not work in either business. Rocco's computer business has net income of $50,000 in 2018, while the car wash has a net loss of ($23,000) in 2018. Rocco only has to pay self-employment tax on $27,000 ($50,000 - $23,000) of income because he may net the income and losses from both his businesses.

---

[48] The Additional Medicare Tax applies to wages, railroad retirement (RRTA) compensation, and self-employment income over certain thresholds. This tax will be covered in more detail later.

Employee Compensation

Wages, salaries, bonuses, tips, and commissions are compensation received by employees for services performed. This compensation is taxable income to the employee and a deductible expense for the employer. Employers are required by January 31 to issue Forms W-2, which show the amounts of wages paid to employees for the previous year.

Employers are required by law to withhold Social Security and Medicare taxes from an employee's wages. If the employer fails to withhold these taxes, the employee is required to file Form 8919, *Uncollected Social Security and Medicare Tax on Wages.*

Example: Terrence works for a company as a delivery driver. He believes that he is an employee. At the end of the year, Terrence's employer issues him a Form 1099-Misc instead of a Form W-2. Terrence believes he was misclassified as an independent contractor. He files Form 8919, *Uncollected Social Security and Medicare Tax on Wages* with his tax return. Terrence lists the name of the employer, provides the employer's Federal Employer Identification Number, the reason he is filing, and his total wages with unreported Social Security and Medicare taxes.

Note: If a taxpayer has more than one employer and his total compensation is over the $128,400 Social Security base limit for 2018, too much Social Security tax may have been withheld. In this case, a taxpayer can claim the excess as a credit against his income tax.

Advance Wages: If an employee receives advance wages, commissions, or other earnings, he must recognize the income in the year it is constructively received, regardless of whether he has earned the income. If the employee is later required to pay back a portion of the earnings, the amount would be deducted from his taxable wages at that time.

Example: Jerry requests a modest salary advance of $1,200 on December 18, 2018, so he can take a two-week vacation. His employer gives him the check on December 20, 2018. Jerry must recognize the income on his 2018 tax return, even though he will not actually "earn" the money until 2019 when he returns from his vacation.

Supplemental Wages

Supplemental wages are compensation paid to an employee in addition to his regular pay. These amounts are listed on the employee's Form W-2 and are taxable just like regular wages, even if the pay is not actually for work performed. Vacation pay and sick pay are examples of supplemental wages that are taxable just like any other wage income, even though the employee has not technically "worked" for the income. Supplemental wages may also include:

- Bonuses, commissions, prizes
- Severance pay, back pay, and holiday pay
- Payment for nondeductible moving expenses

Garnished Wages

An employee may have his wages garnished for various reasons, such as when he owes child support, back taxes due, or other debts. Regardless of the amounts garnished from the employee's paycheck, the full amount of his gross wages must be included in his taxable wages at year end.

> **Example:** Joseph's employer garnishes part of his salary for back child support. Since the amount would have normally been included in Joseph's paycheck, he must recognize the income as if he had received it himself.

Property or Services in Lieu of Wages

Wages paid in any form other than cash are measured by their fair market value. An employee who receives property for services performed must generally recognize the fair market value of the property when it is received as taxable income. However, if an employee receives stock or other property that is restricted, the property is not included in income until it is available to the employee without restriction.

> **Example:** Leonard's company gives him 500 shares of stock, valued at $5,000. He cannot sell or otherwise use the shares for five years. If Leonard quits his job, he forfeits the shares. He does not have to recognize the stock as income in the year he receives it because the stock is subject to substantial restrictions. Leonard will report it as taxable income when the restrictions lapse and he gains complete control over the stock.

Another common arrangement is when colleges offer tuition reduction and/or free on-campus housing in lieu of wages to student teachers. Any portion of a grant or scholarship that is compensation for services is taxable as wages.

> **Example:** Adelaide is a doctoral student attending University in California. Adelaide received a grant of $32,500 to pay her tuition and on-campus housing. As a condition for receiving the scholarship, Adelaide must serve as a part-time teaching assistant. Of the $32,500 scholarship, $11,000 represents payment for teaching. The University gives Adelaide a Form W-2 showing $11,000 as wages. All the money was used to offset her tuition and course-related expenses. Assuming that all other conditions are met, $21,500 of her grant is tax-free. However, the $11,000 Adelaide received for teaching is taxable as wages.

Tip Income

Tips received by food servers, baggage handlers, hairdressers, and others for performing services are taxable income. An individual who receives $20 or more per month in tips must report the tip income to his employer. An employee who receives less than $20 per month in tips while working one job does not have to report the tip income to his employer. Tips of less than $20 per month are exempt from Social Security and Medicare taxes, but are still subject to federal income tax.

> **Example:** Christy works two jobs: as an administrative assistant during the week and as a bartender on the weekends. She reports her tip income from the bartending job of $3,000 to her employer. Her Forms W-2 show wage income of $21,000 (admin) and $8,250 (bartender). Christy must report $29,250, the total amount earned at both jobs, on her Form 1040. Since she reported the tip income to her employer, her bartending tips are already included on her Form W-2 for that job.

An employee who does not report all of his tips to his employer generally must report the tips and related Social Security and Medicare taxes on his Form 1040. Form 4137, *Social Security and Medicare Tax on Unreported Tip Income,* is used to compute the additional tax. Noncash tips (for example, concert tickets, or other items) do not have to be reported to the employer, but they must be reported and included in the taxpayer's income at their fair market value. Taxpayers who are self-employed and receive tips must include their tip income in gross receipts on Schedule C.

> **Example:** Matthew is a licensed barber who works for a popular salon franchise, Super-Duper Cuts. He is an employee of the franchise, and receives minimum wage as well as tips. He must report these tips to his employer. Matthew also cuts hair in the evenings in his garage, offering his barbering services to friends and family. All the income he earns cutting hair at home (including tips) is self-employment income, and must be reported on Schedule C.

Taxable Fringe Benefits for Employees

Employers often offer fringe benefits to employees; common fringe benefits include health insurance, retirement plans, and parking passes. Although most employee fringe benefits are nontaxable, some benefits must be reported on the employee's Form W-2 and included in his taxable income. Examples of taxable fringe benefits include:

- Off-site athletic facilities and health club memberships,
- Concert and athletic event tickets,
- The value of employer-provided life insurance over $50,000,
- Any cash benefit or benefits in the form of a credit card or gift card (an exception applies for occasional meal money or transportation fare to allow an employee to work beyond normal hours),
- Transportation benefits, if the value of a benefit for any month is more than a specified nontaxable limit,[49]
- Employer-provided vehicles, if they are used for personal purposes.

Starting in 2018, most entertainment expenses are no longer deductible. Therefore, the cost of entertainment provided to an employee is no longer a non-taxable fringe benefit.[50] This means that an employer can no longer provide occasional sporting event tickets as a nontaxable benefit to employees.

> **Example:** Great National Bank pays for country club memberships for all its top executives. Membership costs $8,000 a year per person. Bank executives use the club to entertain prospective clients and investors. Even though the club membership is used for business purposes, this type of fringe benefit is taxable compensation to the employees. Great National Bank must include the full amount of the club membership ($8,000) in the employee's wages.

---

[49] The nontaxable benefit for both mass transit and parking for 2018 is $260 per month, although the amounts are no longer deductible by the employer, they are still non-taxable to the employee if the employer continues to provide the benefit. Any expense over that amount is included in the employee's taxable income as wages. An employee can receive both parking and transit benefits in the same month.

[50] There is a narrow exception for entertainment expenses that are directly for the benefit of employees, other than highly compensated employees, (i.e., office parties or company picnics that include lower-paid staff).

> **Example:** Mayan Travel, Inc. is a travel agency that owns a timeshare on the Mayan Riviera that its employees may use free of charge. Lester, an employee of Mayan Travel, visits the resort with his family for 5 days in 2018. The fair market value of the stay is $5,000. Even though Lester paid nothing for the trip, the $5,000 FMV of the vacation must be included in his taxable wages.

Nontaxable Fringe Benefits for Employees

Most fringe benefits are not taxable and may be excluded from an employee's income. For example, the value of accident or health plan coverage provided by an employer is not included in an employee's income.

The following sections cover the rules for some common types of nontaxable employee fringe benefits.

Retirement Plans

Employer contributions on behalf of their employees' qualified retirement plans are not taxable to the employees when they are made. However, when an employee receives distributions from a retirement plan, the amounts received are taxable income. Retirement plans may also allow employees to contribute part of their pretax compensation to the plan. This type of contribution is called an elective deferral and is excluded from taxable compensation for income tax purposes but subject to Social Security and Medicare taxes.[51]

Cafeteria Plans

A cafeteria plan provides employees an opportunity to receive certain benefits on a pretax basis. Participants in a cafeteria plan must be permitted to choose from at least one taxable benefit (such as cash) and one qualified (nontaxable) benefit. Qualified benefits include:

- Accident, dental, vision, and medical benefits (but not Archer medical savings accounts or long-term care insurance)
- Health-care Flexible Spending Accounts (health FSA),[52]
- Adoption assistance and dependent care assistance

Employee contributions are usually deducted based upon salary reduction agreements (i.e., the money is withheld directly from the employee's paycheck and deposited into an account). Salary reduction contributions are not considered actually or constructively received by the employee and therefore are not treated as taxable wages.

Thus, they are generally not subject to income tax withholding, FICA (Social Security and Medicare taxes), or FUTA (unemployment tax). An employer may choose to make benefits available to employees, their spouses, and dependents.

---

[51] The tax provisions of retirement plans are covered in detail later.
[52] An FSA is *not the same* thing as an HSA. A health savings account is an account that a taxpayer may establish and fund on his own. An employee who is covered by an FSA generally cannot make contributions to an HSA.

Flexible Spending Arrangements (FSAs)

An FSA is a form of cafeteria plan benefit that reimburses employees for expenses incurred for certain qualified benefits, such as health care and daycare expenses. The benefits are subject to annual maximum limits and are typically subject to an annual "use-it-or-lose-it" rule, with a short (two-and-a-half-months) grace period after year end to use any remaining balance. In 2018, employee salary reduction contributions to a health-care FSA are capped at $2,650. The Dependent Care FSA (also known as Dependent Care Assistance Plan) limit remains at $5,000 in 2018.

Note: Both employer and employee may contribute to an employee's health-care FSA, but contributions from all sources combined must not exceed the annual maximum.

If a taxpayer *overcontributes* to their health-care FSA, the taxpayer must pay income tax, plus a 6% excise tax, on any excess contributions and related earnings for each tax year the excess contributions remain in the account. In order to avoid the excise tax on excess contributions, the taxpayer must remove the year's excess contributions and related investment earnings before the last day to file federal income taxes for the pertinent tax year, generally April 15.

Example: Max has a health care FSA at his current job. In 2018, he contributes the maximum of $2,650 to his account. In late November, he switches jobs and mistakenly contributes to the HSA that his new employer offers him. At the end of 2018, Max has contributed a total of $4,500 to both accounts. He has an excess contribution for the year. If Max does not withdraw the excess contribution by the filing deadline (April 15, 2019), he will be subject to a 6% excise tax, as well as income tax, on the excess contribution and any related investment earnings. These penalties will continue to accrue, year after year, until the excess contribution is corrected.

Up to $500 of unused FSA money per account may be carried over to the following year. An employer must choose between either the grace period or the carryover option.

Adoption Assistance in a "Cafeteria Plan": An employee can exclude amounts paid or reimbursed by an employer under a qualified adoption assistance program ($13,810 for 2018).

Dependent Care Assistance program: This is also sometimes called a Dependent Care FSA, or Dependent Care Flexible Spending Account (DCFSA). An employee can exclude up to $5,000 in 2018 ($2,500 if MFS) of benefits received under a qualified dependent care assistance program each year. The amounts can be used to pay for eligible daycare services, before or after school programs, including child or adult daycare. Amounts paid directly to the taxpayer or to a daycare provider qualify for exclusion.

Example: Jennifer has a six-year-old son. Jennifer participates in her employer's dependent care FSA. She fills out a form which directs the payroll department to set aside $400 each month from her paycheck. This amount is deposited into her dependent care FSA. At the end of each month, her daycare provider gives Jennifer a receipt, which she submits to her employer for reimbursement. Jennifer's employer then reimburses the funds directly from her FSA account. The money she contributes to her Dependent Care FSA is not subject to payroll tax or income tax, so she will end up paying less in taxes when she files her annual tax return.

Highly Compensated Employees (HCEs) and Key Employees

A cafeteria plan cannot have rules that favor eligibility for highly compensated employees to participate, contribute, or benefit from a cafeteria plan. If a benefit plan favors HCEs, the value of their benefits may become taxable. This is to discourage companies from offering excellent tax-free benefits to their top executives while ignoring the needs of lower-paid employees.

For purposes of a cafeteria plan, an HCE is any of the following:

- An owner of *more than* 5% of the interest in the business at any time during the year or the preceding year, regardless of how much compensation that person received,[53] or

- An employee with gross compensation in excess of $120,000 in the current or previous year[54]

- An officer of the company

- A family member of one of these employees.

The IRS uses a process called "family attribution" in order to make the determination of who qualifies as an HCE, which means that an employee can be determined to be an HCE merely by familial relationship.

An employee whose a spouse, child, grandparent or parent of someone who is a 5% (or greater) owner of the business, is also automatically considered an owner under the family attribution rules.[55] HCEs hired in the middle of the year will not receive HCE status until the start of the *following* year when they are eligible to collect the entirety of their salary. For example, an HCE hired in April 2018 does not qualify as an HCE until January 1, 2019, regardless of their salary level.[56]

> **Example:** Nolan is an employee-shareholder with 3% stock ownership in USA Rentals, Inc. His wife, Maddison, also works for USA Rentals, and owns 4% of the stock ownership in the company. Nolan and Maddison are both considered HCEs under the family attribution rules, because their combined stock ownership exceeds 5% (their total interest is 7%).

"Highly Compensated" Employees and "Key Employees" have similar-sounding names, but the rules for defining Key Employees are slightly different. Employer-provided benefits also cannot favor "key employees."

IRS guidelines define "Key Employees" as any of the following:

- A company officer of the employer with annual compensation greater than $175,000 in 2018, or

---

[53] The 5% ownership threshold is based on voting power or the value of company shares.

[54] For the 2019 plan year, an employee who earns more than $120,000 in 2018 is considered an HCE. For the 2020 plan year, an employee who earns more than $125,000 in 2019 is an HCE.

[55] In this case, family members include the spouse, parents, children, and grandparents. Family members for this purpose do not include grandchildren, siblings, aunts, uncles, or in-laws.

[56] Corporate executives often receive extraordinary fringe benefits that are not provided to other corporate employees. Any property or service that an executive receives in lieu of or in addition to regular taxable wages is a fringe benefit that may be subject to taxation. This is such an important issue to the IRS that they have developed an Audit Technique Guide about the subject (Executive Compensation-Fringe Benefits Audit Techniques Guide).

- A 5% owner of the company, or

- A 1% owner of the company with annual compensation of more than $150,000.

Although the compensation threshold is *lower* for HCEs than Key Employees, ($120,000 versus $175,000), an employee can be classified as a "key employee" without having any ownership in the company at all.

> **Example:** Colton is the vice-president of Grainger, Inc. a manufacturing firm. Colton is not an owner of the company. His salary is $200,000 in 2018, and was $195,000 in the previous year. Colton is classified as a "key employee," despite the fact that he does not have an ownership stake in the company.

A plan is considered to have improperly "favored" HCEs and key employees if more than 25% of all the benefits are given to those employees.

If a cafeteria plan or a retirement plan fails to pass IRS non-discrimination testing, highly compensated employees and key employees may lose the tax benefits of participating in the plan. If this happens, then the plans can lose their tax-favored status, and the HCEs or key employees must include the value of these benefits as taxable compensation. These types of "corrections" often take the form of taxable distributions to plan participants.

> **Example:** Dixie Motorsports is a small corporation with forty-five employees. The sole shareholder of the company, Randall, sets up a cafeteria plan as well as a 401(k) retirement plan. However, he only allows his spouse and his two sons to participate in the plans. The rest of the employees are not offered any type of benefits, and in fact, are never told about the plans. Later, Dixie Motorsports goes through a plan audit and the company fails discrimination testing. Randall is forced to recognize the value his pretax benefits as taxable income. Randall's spouse and his two sons are also considered HCEs because they are Randall's family members, so they are also forced to recognize their benefits as taxable income, as well.

> **Example:** Alloy Energy, Inc. is a C corporation with 300 employees, twenty-five of whom are considered highly compensated employees. Alloy Energy's cafeteria plan and its benefits are available to all full-time employees, and the benefits offered are the same for everyone, regardless of the employee's level of pay. Therefore, the discrimination rules do not apply, and the employees' benefits are not taxable.

Other Types of Employee Fringe Benefits

Educational Assistance: An employer can offer employees educational assistance for the cost of tuition, fees, books, supplies, and equipment. The payments may be for either undergraduate or graduate-level courses, and do not have to be work-related.

In 2018, $5,250 in educational assistance may be excluded per year per employee. If an employer pays more than $5,250, the excess is generally taxed as wages to the employee.[57] The cost of courses involving sports, games, or hobbies is not covered unless they are related to the

---

[57] There is an exception for job-related education. If the education is directly job related, amounts in excess of the $5,250 limit may qualify for exclusion as a working condition fringe benefit.

business or are required as part of a degree program. The cost of lodging, meals, and transportation is also not included.

Tuition Reduction Benefits: An educational organization can exclude the value of a qualified undergraduate tuition reduction to an employee, his spouse, or a dependent child. A tuition reduction is "qualified" only if the taxpayer receives it from, and uses it at, an eligible educational institution.

Graduate education only qualifies if it is for the education of a graduate student who performs teaching or research activities for the educational organization.

> **Example:** Mayra is a graduate teaching assistant at Northern California University. As part of her employment agreement with the college, Mayra is offered a 50% tuition waiver, reducing the cost of her own graduate tuition at the school. The normal graduate tuition cost is $14,000 per year. Because of the tuition waiver, Mayra only pays $7,000. The tuition reduction is not taxable to Mayra, but any wages that she receives as compensation for student teaching would be taxable.

Employer-Provided Meals and Lodging

An employer may exclude the value of meals and lodging provided to employees if they are provided:

- On the employer's business premises, and
- For the employer's convenience.

For lodging, there is an additional rule: it must be required as a condition of employment. Lodging can be provided for the taxpayer, the taxpayer's spouse, and the taxpayer's dependents and still not be taxable to the employee.

> **Example:** Patrick is a project supervisor for Birchwood Construction. He is provided free lodging at remote job sites in an RV, where he is required to stay on-site for months while timber is cleared and the grounds are prepared for construction projects. The value of the lodging and his meals is excluded from his income because it is primarily for the employer's security and convenience.

The exclusion from taxation does not apply if the employee can choose to receive additional pay instead of lodging. Meals may be provided to employees for the convenience of the employer on the employer's business premises for a number of reasons, such as when:

- Police officers and firefighters need to be on call for emergencies during the meal period
- The nature of the business requires short meal periods
- Eating facilities are not available in areas near the workplace
- Meals are furnished immediately after working hours because the employee's duties prevented him from obtaining a meal during working hours

Meals furnished to restaurant employees before, during, or after work hours are also considered furnished for the employer's convenience and are not taxable to the employee.

> **Example:** Paramedic Transport, Inc. regularly provides meals to employees during working hours so that paramedics are available for emergency calls during the meal. The employees are not permitted to take regular lunches or eat off-site because of the nature of their employment. The value of the free meals is therefore excludable from the employees' wages, and the employer is allowed to deduct the cost of the meals as a business expense, subject to the 50% limit.

Transportation Fringe Benefits

Employers may provide transportation benefits to their employees up to certain amounts without having to include the benefits in the employees' taxable income. Qualified transportation benefits include transit passes, paid parking, and a ride in a commuter highway vehicle between the employee's home and workplace. The nontaxable benefit for both mass transit and parking for 2018 is $260 per month.

Due to the TCJA, the amounts are no longer deductible by the employer, but transportation benefits are still non-taxable to the employee if the employer continues to provide the benefit (with the notable exception of bicycle commuting benefits, which became taxable to the employee in 2018 under the TCJA).

Any expense over that amount is included in the employee's taxable income as wages. An employee can receive both parking and transit benefits in the same month. The use of a company car for commuting purposes or other personal use is generally a taxable benefit. Therefore, the value of the vehicle's use for either of these purposes is considered taxable wages to the employee.

There is an exception in IRS regulations that exempts the personal-use of certain types of vehicles. Qualified nonpersonal use vehicles, such as police or fire vehicles, school buses, and ambulances are exempt from fringe benefit reporting, even if the vehicles are used for commuting purposes, as long as the employer is requiring their use in order for the employees to do their jobs.

> **Example:** Sienna was offered a lucrative new job in New York City as a computer programmer. As part of her employment contract, she negotiates a parking space for her car. Her new employer agrees to pay the cost of the space at the garage across the street from her work. Monthly parking is quite expensive in New York City, and the monthly parking fee at the garage is $550. Since this amount exceeds the allowable limit for parking fringe benefits, a portion of the parking costs will be taxable to Sienna as wages. In 2018, the allowable transportation benefit for parking is $260. Therefore, an additional $290 ($550-$260) would be taxable to Sienna each month.

> **Example:** Dominic is employed by a lumber company. He drives an employer-provided pickup truck, hauling equipment on job sites and delivering lumber to customers. He also gets to take the truck home in the evenings. In 2018, Dominic drives the truck 20,000 miles, of which 4,000, or 20%, are personal miles (4,000/20,000 = 20%). The truck has an annual lease value of $4,100. Personal use is therefore valued at $820 and is included in Dominic's taxable wages.

Cell Phones: The value of the business use of an employer-provided cell phone may be excluded from an employee's income to the extent that, if the employee paid for its use, the payment would be deductible. There must be substantial "noncompensatory" reasons for the use of a phone that relate to the employer's business.

Legitimate reasons include the employer's need to contact the employee in the event of work-related emergencies and the employee's need to be available to speak with clients when away from the office. If a cell phone is provided simply to promote goodwill, to boost an employee's morale, or to attract a prospective employee, the value of the cell phone must be added to the employee's wages.

Group-Term Life Insurance Coverage: Up to $50,000 of life insurance coverage may be provided as a nontaxable benefit to an employee. The cost of insurance coverage on policies that exceed $50,000 is a taxable benefit. If an employer provides more than $50,000 of coverage, the amount included in the taxpayer's income is reported as part of their taxable wages on their Form W-2. Also, the taxable amount is shown separately in box 12 of their Form W-2 with code C.

Work-Related Moving Expense Reimbursements: Starting in 2018, moving expenses are no longer deductible for most taxpayers, except for members of the armed forces. Therefore, moving expenses that are reimbursed or paid by an employer must be included in the employee's taxable income as wages. This is true even if the moving expenses are paid under an accountable plan.

Definition: An "accountable" plan is an employee reimbursement allowance arrangement or a method for reimbursing employees for business expenses that complies with IRS regulations.

There is an exception for qualified moving expenses that were incurred in 2017, but only reimbursed by the employer in 2018.[58] These moving expenses reimbursements may be excluded from the employee's wages and are not subject to federal income or employment taxes.

Example: Kamryn was offered a new job in another state on December 1, 2017. Her new employer offered to reimburse her qualified moving expenses as a condition of her employment. She accepted the position and moved on December 26, 2017. Kamryn submits the paperwork and her employer reimburses her moving expenses on January 15, 2018. Even though the reimbursement occurred in 2018, none of the amounts would be taxable to Kamryn, because her moving expenses were actually *incurred* in the previous year, when moving expenses were still deductible by most taxpayers. She does not have to include the amounts on her 2018 return, and the expenses are still fully deductible by the employer as a business expense.

No-Additional-Cost Services: Nontaxable fringe benefits also include services provided to employees that do not impose any substantial additional cost to the employer because the employer already offers those services in the ordinary course of doing business. Employees do not need to include these no-additional-cost services in their income. Typically, no-additional-

---

[58] IRS Notice 2018-75, *Guidance under Section 132(g) for the Exclusion from Income of Qualified Moving Expense Reimbursements.*

cost services are excess capacity services, such as unused airline seat tickets for airline employees or open hotel rooms for hotel employees.

> **Example:** Dalilah is a flight attendant with Starlight Airlines. She is allowed to fly for free on standby flights when there is an extra seat. This fringe benefit is allowed at no additional cost to the employer and is therefore nontaxable to Dalilah.

If an employee is provided with the free or low-cost use of a health club on the employer's premises, the value is not included in the employee's compensation. The gym must be used primarily by employees, their spouses, and their dependent children. However, if the employer pays for a fitness program or use of a facility at an *off-site* location, the value of the program is included in the employee's compensation.

Employee Achievement Awards: Employers may generally exclude from an employee's taxable wages the value of awards given for length of service or safety achievement. The tax-free amount is limited to the following:

- $400 for awards that are not qualified plan awards. A qualified plan award is one that does not discriminate in favor of highly compensated employees.

- $1,600 for all awards, whether or not they are qualified plan awards

The exclusion for employee awards does not apply to awards of cash, gift cards, or items such as vacations or tickets to sporting events.

De Minimis (Minimal) Benefits: This is a property or service an employer provides that has so little value that accounting for it would be impractical. Examples of de minimis benefits include the following:

- Occasional personal use of a company copying machine

- Holiday gifts with a low fair market value

- Beverages such as coffee or soft drinks for employees

Cash and gift cards are not excludable as de minimis benefits unless they are for occasional meal money or transportation fare. The benefit must be provided so that an employee can work an unusual, extended schedule.

> **Example:** Marcus works for Sunrise Dairy Farms as a farmhand. One day, there was an emergency on the farm where several dairy cows accidentally ingested tainted feed. The cows began to have seizures, and all the employees were forced to work overtime in order to stabilize the livestock and administer medicine. Sunrise Dairy Farms gives Marcus $20 in cash in order to purchase a meal during this unusual overtime shift. The cash can be excluded as a *de minimis* benefit because it is for the benefit of his employer that Marcus is working overtime, and it is an unusual and infrequent situation.

Employee Discounts: Employers may exclude the value of employee discounts from wages up to the following limits:

- For services, a 20% discount of the price charged to nonemployee customers

- For merchandise, the company's gross profit percentage multiplied by the price nonemployee customers pay

Reimbursement of Employee-Business Expenses

When a business *reimburses* its employees for certain business expenses, such as meals and travel, reimbursements are not taxable income if employees meet all of the following requirements of an accountable plan:

- Have incurred the expenses while performing services as employees
- Adequately account for travel, meals, and lodging
- Provide evidence of their employee business expenses, such as receipts or other records
- Return any excess reimbursement within a reasonable period of time

Under an accountable plan, a business may advance money to employees. The cash advance must be reasonably calculated to equal the anticipated expenses, and it must be advanced within a reasonable period of time. If any expenses reimbursed under this arrangement are not substantiated, they are considered taxable income for the employee.

Example: Miriam runs a tax preparation business as a sole-proprietor. She advances $250 to her employee, Nasser, so that he can become a notary. Nasser spends $90 on an online notary course and then another $100 to take the notary exam. Nasser returns the unused funds ($60), as well as copies of his receipts to Miriam. The expenses are qualified expenses under an accountable plan, so the amounts paid are not taxable income for Nasser, and still deductible as business expenses by Miriam.

Qualifying expenses for travel are excludable from an employee's income if they are incurred for temporary travel on business away from the area of the employee's tax home. Travel expenses paid in connection with an indefinite work assignment cannot be excluded from income. Any work assignment in excess of one year is considered "indefinite." Travel expense reimbursements include:

- Costs of travel to and from the business destination (such as flights and mileage reimbursements)
- Transportation costs while at the business destination (such as taxi fares and shuttles)
- Lodging, meals, and incidental expenses
- Cleaning, laundry, and other miscellaneous expenses

Example: Craig works for a travel agency in Seattle. He flies to Detroit to conduct business for an entire week. His employer pays the cost of the flight to and from Detroit, as well as lodging and meals while there. The reimbursements for substantiated travel expenses are excluded from Craig's income.

Taxation of Clergy Members

There are special rules regarding the taxation of clergy members, defined as individuals who are ordained, commissioned, or licensed by a religious body or church denomination. A clergy member's salary is reported on Form W-2 and is taxable. Offerings and fees received for performing marriages, baptisms, and funerals must also be reported as self-employment income on Schedule C.

Housing Allowance for Clergy: A clergy member who receives a housing allowance may exclude the allowance from gross income to the extent it is used to pay the expenses of providing a home. The exclusion for housing is limited to the lesser of:

- Fair market rental value (including utilities), or

- The actual cost to provide the home.

The housing allowance cannot exceed reasonable pay and must be used for housing in the year it is received. Salary, other fees, and housing allowances must be included in income for purposes of determining self-employment tax.

Even if a minister is considered an employee, churches cannot withhold Social Security and Medicare taxes from his wages. They are treated as self-employed for purposes of these taxes.

Example: Emanuel is an ordained minister who receives $32,000 in salary from his church. He receives an additional $4,000 for performing marriages and baptisms. His housing allowance is $500 per month, for a total of $6,000 per year, and is excluded from his gross income. Emanuel must report the $32,000 as salary and the $4,000 as self-employment income. The $6,000 housing allowance is subject to self-employment tax, but not to income tax.

Example: Dolores is a full-time ordained minister. Her church allows her to use a cottage that has a rental value of $8,000. She is paid a salary of $22,000, and her church does not withhold Social Security or Medicare taxes. Her income for self-employment tax purposes is $30,000 ($22,000 + $8,000).

A clergy member may apply for an exemption from self-employment tax if he is conscientiously opposed to public insurance because of religious principles. In order for a clergy member or a minister to claim an exemption from SE tax, the minister must file IRS Form 4029, *Application for Exemption From Social Security and Medicare Taxes and Waiver of Benefits.* The sect or religious order must also complete part of the form. The exemption does not apply to federal income tax, only to self-employment tax. If the exemption is granted, the clergy member will not pay Social Security or Medicare taxes on his earnings, and he will not receive credit toward those benefits in retirement.

If a clergy member is a member of a religious order that has taken a vow of poverty, he is exempt from paying SE tax on his earnings for qualified services. The earnings are tax-free because they are considered the income of the religious order, rather than of the individual clergy member.

Combat Pay and Veterans' Benefits

Wages earned by military personnel are generally taxable. However, there are a number of special rules for military personnel regarding taxable income. Combat zone wages (combat pay) are not taxable income.

Hazardous duty pay is also excludable for certain military personnel. Enlisted personnel who serve in a combat zone for any part of a month may exclude their pay from tax. For officers, pay is excluded up to a certain amount, depending on the branch of service.

Example: Ignatius is an Air Force pilot who served in a combat zone from January 1, 2018, to November 3, 2018. He is only required to report his income for December, because all of the other income is excluded from taxation as combat zone pay. Even though Ignatius only served three days in November in a combat zone, his income for the entire month of November is excluded.

Similarly, veterans' benefits paid by the Department of Veterans Affairs to a veteran or his family are not taxable if they are for education (the GI Bill), training, disability compensation, work therapy, dependent care assistance, or other benefits or pension payments given to the veteran because of disability.

Disability Payments

There are several types of disability payments, and the taxability of the income depends on several factors. There are also some types of disability-related payments that are given to workers that are not taxable at all. Worker's compensation is one such example. Worker's compensation should not be confused with disability insurance, sick pay, or unemployment compensation; it is a type of benefit that only pays workers who are injured on the job. Worker's compensation is paid to a taxpayer under a worker's compensation act or another state statute. The amounts are always exempt from tax.

Example: Hudson is a construction worker. In 2018, he is struck by falling concrete on a construction site. The concrete crushes his pelvis, causing catastrophic injuries and a long hospital stay. Worker's compensation covers Hudson's medical costs as well as a portion of his lost wages while he is recovering from the injury. The amounts are not taxable to Hudson and do not need to be reported on his tax return.

Workers' compensation is a type of mandatory insurance, meaning most large and mid-sized employers are required to have coverage for their employees.

Disability Insurance Benefits

A taxpayer may also receive long-term disability payments as a result of an insurance policy. As a general rule, long-term disability payments from an insurance policy are excluded from income if the *taxpayer* pays the premiums for the policy. If an *employer* pays the insurance premiums, the employee must report the payments as taxable income. If both an employee and his employer have paid premiums for a disability policy, only the employer's portion of the disability payments would be reported as taxable income.

Example: Margarete became disabled in 2018 and began to receive a long-term disability benefit of $4,200 a month. The original insurance policy was paid for by both her employer and herself. Before Margarete became disabled, her employer paid 80% of the disability insurance premiums. Margarete paid the remaining premium amount (20%) with post-tax dollars. In this case, because the employer paid 80% of the policy premiums, 80% of the benefits received would be taxable to Margarete. This means that $3,360 ($4,200 x 80%) would be taxable. The remaining benefits $840 (20% x $4,200) would not be taxable since Margarete paid that portion of the insurance premium with her own post-tax dollars.

Disability Insurance Premiums	Taxability of Benefits
The employer pays 100%	100% taxable
The employer pays a portion and employee pays the balance with post-tax dollars	Partially taxable; the taxable percentage is based on the premiums paid by the employer
The employer pays a portion and employee pays the balance with pretax dollars	100% taxable
The employee pays 100% with post-tax dollars	Not taxable
The employee pays 100% with pretax dollars	100% taxable

Disability Retirement Benefits

Disability *retirement* benefits are taxable as wages if a taxpayer retired on disability before reaching the minimum retirement age. The benefit is usually based on the employee's final average earnings and their years of actual service. Once the taxpayer reaches retirement age, the payments are no longer taxable as wages. They are taxable as pension income.

This type of disability retirement benefit is offered to most Federal government workers and U.S. Postal Service employees.[59] In order to apply for this benefit, the employee's disability generally must have caused them to discontinue working.

Example: Sloan is a U.S. Postal Service employee. She is age 50 and has worked for the postal service for over sixteen years, but she is still many years away from official retirement age. On January 10, 2018, Sloan sustains a life-altering spinal injury and becomes permanently disabled. She immediately applies for disability retirement under the Federal Employees Retirement System, or FERS, and is awarded disability retirement benefits. Her disability retirement benefits will be taxable as wages until she reaches retirement age (usually 62 years of age). After she reaches retirement age, the benefits will be taxable as pension income instead of wages.

Note: Do not confuse sick pay with disability pay. Sick pay, or sick leave, is always taxable as wages, just like vacation pay and holiday pay.

Veteran's Disability Benefits

Veteran's *disability* benefits (also called *VA Disability Compensation*) are a type of disability benefit paid specifically to a veteran for disabilities that are service-connected, which means the injury or disease linked to their military service. Generally, payments are designed to compensate for considerable loss of working time from illnesses. Veteran's disability benefits are exempt from taxation if the veteran was terminated through separation or discharged under honorable conditions. The VA typically does not issue Form W-2, Form 1099-R, or any other tax-related document for veterans' disability benefits.

---

[59] Social Security Disability Insurance (SSDI) benefits is a separate benefit from disability retirement benefits that are offered to federal and postal service employees.

> **Example:** Erica is an Army veteran who was discharged after she sustained a serious injury in Iraq. She lost vision in one eye and the use of one hand due to an explosion. Since Erica's discharge from the Armed Forces, she has received $1,950 per month in Veteran's disability benefits. She now has a civilian job working in a factory, where she earns regular wages as an employee. Her wages are taxable, but the disability compensation remains non-taxable to Erica. Her disability benefits do not need to be reported on her tax return.

Life Insurance Payments

Life insurance payouts generally are not taxable to a beneficiary if the payment was the result of the death of the insured. This is true even if the proceeds were paid under an accident or health insurance policy. However, interest income received as a result of life insurance proceeds is usually taxable. Further, if a taxpayer surrenders a life insurance policy for cash, he must generally include in income any proceeds that are more than the cost of the policy.[60]

Sometimes, a taxpayer will choose to receive life insurance proceeds in installments rather than as a lump sum. In this case, part of the installment generally includes interest income.

If a taxpayer receives life insurance proceeds in installments (also called a life insurance annuity), he can exclude part of each installment from his income. To determine the excluded part, the amount held by the insurance company (generally the total lump sum payable at the death of the insured person) is divided by the number of installments to be paid. The taxpayer would include any amount over this excluded portion as taxable interest income.

> **Example:** Molly's brother died in 2018, and she is the sole beneficiary of his life insurance. The face amount of the policy is $75,000. Rather than take a lump sum payment, Molly chooses to receive 120 monthly installments of $1,000 each. The excluded part of each installment is $625 ($75,000 ÷ 120), or $7,500 for an entire year. The rest of each payment, $375 a month (or $4,500 for an entire year), is taxable interest income to Molly.

---

[60] There are limited exceptions when the policy holder is deemed to be terminally or chronically ill.

Unit 4: Study Questions

(Test yourself first; then check the correct answers at the end of this quiz.)

1. Paxton is a flight attendant who earned wages of $61,000 in 2018. The airline provided free transportation on standby from his home in Little Rock to the airline's hub in Charlotte. The fair market value of the commuting flights was $5,000. Paxton also received advances under an accountable plan of $10,000 for overnight travel, but only spent $6,000. He returned the excess ($4,000) to his employer. Paxton was injured on the job and received worker's compensation of $4,000. What amount must he include in gross income?

A. $61,000
B. $65,000
C. $66,000
D. $67,000

2. Income was constructively received in 2018 in each of the following situations *except*:

A. Wages were deposited in the taxpayer's bank account on December 26, 2018, but were not withdrawn by the taxpayer until January 8, 2019.
B. A taxpayer was informed his check for services rendered was available on December 15, 2018. The taxpayer did not pick up the check until January 30, 2019.
C. A taxpayer received a check on December 31, 2018, but did not deposit the check until January 5, 2018.
D. A taxpayer's vacation property was sold on December 28, 2018. The payment was not received by the taxpayer until January 2, 2019, when the escrow company released the funds.

3. Chandra received the following income and fringe benefits in 2018:

Wages	$30,000
End-of-the-year bonus	2,000
Parking pass per month	90
Employer contributions to her 401(k) plan	900
Occasional free use of a copier on the employer's premises	15

How much income must Chandra report on her tax return?

A. $30,000
B. $32,000
C. $32,500
D. $34,480

4. Which of the following tip income is exempt from federal income tax?

A. Tips of less than $20 per month
B. Noncash tips
C. Tips not reported to the employer
D. All tips are taxable

5. Bartholomew is a naval officer who was injured while serving in a combat zone. He was later awarded Veterans Affairs (VA) disability benefits. How are these payments reported on Bartholomew's tax return?

A. 100% of the disability benefits may be excluded from income.
B. Up to 50% of the disability benefits may be excluded from income.
C. 100% of the disability benefits may be excluded from income for enlisted personnel, but not for officers.
D. The disability benefits are taxable.

6. Which of the following fringe benefits is taxable (or partially taxable) to the employee?

A. Health insurance covered 100% by the employer
B. An employer-provided company car that is used for commuting
C. Group-term life insurance coverage of $50,000
D. Employer contributions to an employee's 401(k) plan

7. What is adjusted gross income?

A. The sum of all sources of taxable income that the taxpayer receives during the year
B. The amount of earned income a taxpayer receives during the year
C. Another term for taxable income
D. Gross income minus certain allowable deductions or adjustments, calculated before the standard deduction or itemized deductions are taken

8. Flavian owns a restaurant. He furnishes his daytime waitress, Alida, two meals during each workday. Flavian encourages (but does not require) Alida to have her breakfast on the business premises before starting work so she can help him answer phones. She is required to have her lunch on the premises. How should Flavian treat this fringe benefit to Alida?

A. None of Alida's meals at the restaurant are taxable.
B. All of Alida's meals at the restaurant are taxable.
C. Alida's lunch is not taxable, but her breakfast is.
D. Alida's meals are taxed at a flat rate of 15%.

9. Self-employment income does not include:

A. Income of ministers, priests, and rabbis for the performance of services such as baptisms and marriages
B. The share of partnership ordinary income allocated to general partners on Schedule K-1
C. Wages earned by a temporary employee
D. Payments to independent contractors

10. Orrin is an ordained minister in the Evangelical Church of Chicago. He owns his home, and his monthly house payment is $900. His monthly utilities total $150. The fair rental value in his neighborhood is $1,000. Orrin receives a housing allowance from his church in the amount of $950 per month. What amount of his housing allowance would he include in his gross income for income tax purposes?

A. $0
B. $100 per month
C. $150 per month
D. $950 per month

11. Which of the following types of fringe benefits are deductible by an employer but not taxable to the employee?

A. De minimis fringe benefit
B. Use of an employer's apartment, vacation home, or boat
C. Membership in a country club or athletic facility
D. A gift card

12. Salvador is an enlisted soldier in the U.S. Army who served in a combat zone from January 30, 2018, to September 2, 2018. He returned to the United States and received his regular duty pay for the remainder of the year. How many months of his income are taxable in 2018?

A. Zero. All the income is tax-free.
B. Three months of wages are subject to tax.
C. Four months of wages are subject to tax.
D. Twelve months of wages are subject to tax.

13. Which of the following fringe benefits provided by the employer will result in taxable income to the employee?

A. A cell phone used by a salesperson to talk to clients while on the road
B. Reimbursements paid by the employers for qualified business travel expenses
C. Use of a company van for daily commuting
D. Occasional personal use of an office copy machine

14. Rasheed is employed as a staff accountant by a large CPA firm. When he travels for his audit work, he submits his travel receipts for reimbursement by his firm, which has an accountable plan for its employees. Which of the following statements is correct about accountable plans?

A. The reimbursed amounts are not taxable to Rasheed.
B. Rasheed may deduct his travel expenses on personal his tax return.
C. His employer cannot deduct the travel expenses, even though Rasheed was reimbursed in full.
D. Reimbursed expenses are taxable to the employee, and the employer can also deduct the expenses as they would any other current expense.

15. Of the following items, only _____ is not taxable income to an employee:

A. A holiday bonus
B. Overtime pay
C. Vacation pay
D. A mileage reimbursement under an accountable plan

16. Debby broke her leg in a car accident and was unable to work for three months. She received an accident settlement of $13,000 from her insurance company. During this time, she also received $7,500 of sick pay from her employer. In addition, she received $5,000 from an accident policy she had purchased herself. How much of this income is taxable to Debby?

A. $5,000
B. $7,500
C. $12,500
D. $18,000

17. Faye was the sole beneficiary on her mother's life insurance policy. Her mother died on December 12, 2018. Faye received the following payments on January 31, 2019:

- $160,000 death benefit from her mother's life insurance policy
- $175 of interest income on the life insurance proceeds

What is the proper treatment of these payments?

A. The life insurance and interest are both taxable in 2018, since that is the year that the policyholder died.
B. The insurance benefit and interest income are both taxable to Faye in 2019.
C. Only the $175 of interest income is taxable in 2019. The life insurance proceeds are not taxable.
D. None of these payments are taxable to Faye. Instead, they are taxable to her mother's estate.

18. Orval and Rainelle are married, and both are self-employed with their own businesses. Orval owns a business that has a $9,750 net profit during the year. His wife, Rainelle, has an overall business loss of ($11,100). They both file Schedules C to report their self-employment income. Which of the following statements is correct?

A. On their joint return, they will not have to pay self-employment tax, because the losses from Rainelle's business will offset Orval's income.
B. They can file MFS and offset each other's self-employment tax.
C. Orval must pay self-employment tax on $9,750, regardless of his wife's income or losses.
D. If they choose to file separate returns, they may split the profits and losses equally between their two businesses.

19. Elaine is a cash-basis taxpayer and sells cosmetics on commission (she is an employee). On December 25, 2018, Elaine receives $10,000 of income from commissions, plus an advance of $1,000 for future commissions. She also receives $200 of expense reimbursements from her employer after turning in her receipts as part of an accountable plan. How much taxable income should Elaine report on her 2018 tax return?

A. $0
B. $11,000
C. $11,200
D. $10,200

1. The answer is A. Paxton only has to include his wages on his tax return. The free flights offered on standby to airline personnel are considered no-additional-cost services and are not taxable to the employee. Reimbursements under an accountable plan and amounts paid for workers' compensation are nontaxable. Since Paxton returned the unspent amounts to his employer, the travel reimbursements qualify under an accountable plan, and the amounts spent are not taxable to him.

2. The answer is D. A taxpayer does not need physical possession of income to have constructive receipt. However, income is not considered constructively received if the taxpayer cannot access the funds because of restrictions. Since the taxpayer's control of the receipt of the funds in the escrow account was substantially limited until the transaction had closed, the taxpayer did not constructively receive the income until the following year.

3. The answer is B. Only the wages and the bonus are taxable ($30,000 + $2,000). The parking pass is a nontaxable transportation benefit, and the employer contributions are not taxable until Chandra withdraws the money from her retirement account. Chandra does not have to report the use of the copier, because it is considered a *de minimis* fringe benefit.

4. The answer is D. All tip income is subject to federal income tax, whether cash or noncash. An individual who receives less than $20 per month of tips while working one job does not have to report the tip income to his employer, but the income is still subject to federal income tax and must be reported on the taxpayer's Form 1040.

5. The answer is A. All of the disability benefits can be excluded from Bartholomew's taxable income. VA disability compensation is exempt from taxation if the veteran was terminated through separation or discharged under honorable conditions. The VA does not issue Form W-2, Form 1099-R, or any other tax-related document for veterans' disability benefits.

6. The answer is B. An employer-provided company car would be partially taxable if it was used for personal driving. The value of the personal use of the automobile must be added to the employee's wages. These valuation rules are covered in IRS Publication 15-B, *Employer's Tax Guide to Fringe Benefits.*

7. The answer is D. Adjusted gross income (AGI) is gross income (the sum of all income subject to taxation that the taxpayer receives during the year) minus certain allowable deductions or adjustments. AGI is calculated before the standard deduction or itemized deductions are taken.

8. The answer is A. Meals furnished to Alida are not taxable because they are for the convenience of the employer. Meals that employers furnish to a restaurant employee during, immediately before or after the employee's working hours are considered furnished for the employer's convenience. Since Alida is a waitress who works during the normal breakfast and lunch periods, Flavian can exclude from her wages the value of those meals. If Flavian allowed Alida to have meals without charge on her days off, the value of those meals would be included in her wages.

9. The answer is C. Wage income is never considered self-employment income. The other examples listed are all types of self-employment income and subject to self-employment tax on Form 1040.

10. The answer is A. Clergy members may exclude from gross income for income tax purposes, but not for self-employment tax purposes, the rental value of a home, or a rental allowance to the extent the allowance is used to provide a home, even if deductions are taken for home expenses paid with the allowance.

11. The answer is A. A *de minimis* fringe benefit is deductible by the employer but is not taxable to the employee. The IRS defines a de minimis benefit in this way: a benefit that, considering its value and the frequency with which it is provided, is so small as to make accounting for it unreasonable or impractical. For example, a de minimis fringe benefit might include occasional snacks, coffee, or doughnuts provided in a company's break room. The items in the other choices would be taxable to the employee.

12. The answer is B. If a taxpayer serves in a combat zone as an enlisted person for *any part* of a month, all of his pay received for military service that month is excluded from gross income. Since Salvador served for a few days in September, as well as January, all the income for those months is excluded as combat pay. Only October through December would be taxable.

13. The answer is C. Use of a company vehicle for commuting is not a qualified fringe benefit. Commuting expenses are not deductible. Use of a company van after normal working hours is personal use and not business use, so it would result in taxable income to the employee. The cell phone, reimbursements for business travel, and the occasional personal use of an office copy machine are noncash fringe benefits that are not taxable.

14. The answer is A. The reimbursed amounts are not taxable to Rasheed. Under an accountable plan, employee reimbursements are not included in the employee's income. In this scenario, the travel expenses incurred by the employee would be deductible by Rasheed's employer as an ordinary business expense.

15. The answer is D. Mileage reimbursements, if paid through an accountable plan, are not included in an employee's wages.

16. The answer is B. Only Debby's sick pay is taxable, because sick pay from an employer is always taxable as wages and is therefore included in Debby's gross income. Settlements for personal injuries from an accident are not taxable. If a taxpayer pays the full cost of an accident insurance plan, the benefits for personal injury or illness are not included in income. If the employer pays the cost of an accident insurance plan, the amounts are taxable to the employee.

17. The answer is C. Life insurance proceeds are not taxable to the recipient. Interest earned on life insurance proceeds is taxable. Faye must report the interest income in the year she receives it. Therefore, only the $175 of interest income is taxable in the year received.

18. The answer is C. Orval must pay self-employment tax on his earnings, regardless of how he and Rae choose to file. Taxpayers cannot combine both spouses' income or loss to determine their earnings subject to SE tax. However, if a taxpayer has more than one business, he must combine the net profit or loss from each to determine the total earnings subject to SE tax.

19. The answer is B. Elaine's commissions must be included in gross income, as well as advance payments in anticipation of future services ($10,000 + $1,000 = $11,000). The expense reimbursements from an accountable plan ($200) would not be included in her taxable income.

Unit 5: Investment Income and Expenses

> **For additional information read:**
> **Publication 550,** *Investment Income and Expenses*
> **Instructions for Schedule B**

The Tax Cuts and Jobs Act (TCJA) brought several important changes regarding the treatment of investment income and expenses. The TCJA did not change the rates on interest and dividends for most taxpayers, but it did change the treatment of investment income that is earned by minor children, (i.e., the "Kiddie Tax").

This unit covers interest and dividend income. Taxpayers who deposit cash or invest in securities such as stocks, bonds, and mutual funds may earn income from interest, dividends, and capital appreciation. Other types of income from investments, such as capital gains resulting from sales, are covered later.

Interest Income

Interest is a form of income that may be earned from deposits, such as in bank and money market accounts, notes receivable, and investments in instruments such as bonds. Some interest income is taxable, and some is not.

Certain distributions, commonly referred to as dividends, are actually reported as taxable interest income. These include "dividends" on deposits or share accounts in cooperative banks, credit unions, domestic savings and loan associations, and mutual savings banks. A taxpayer can also have taxable interest from certificates of deposits (CDs) and other deferred interest accounts.

Interest income is generally reported to the taxpayer on Form 1099-INT by the financial institution or another payor if the amount of interest is $10 or more for the year. Even if a taxpayer does not receive Form 1099-INT from a payor, all taxable interest income must be reported. If taxable interest income exceeds $1,500, the taxpayer must report the interest on Schedule B, *Interest and Ordinary Dividends*.

Gift for Opening a Bank Account: If a taxpayer receives noncash gifts or services for making deposits or for opening an account in a savings institution, the value of the gift may have to be reported as interest. For deposits of less than $5,000, gifts or services valued at more than $10 must be reported as interest. For deposits of $5,000 or more, gifts or services valued at more than $20 must be reported as interest. The value of the gift is determined by the financial institution.

A cash bonus for opening a new checking or credit card account is also taxable interest. Similarly, reward points or airline miles that a bank offers as a gift to customers who open new accounts are taxable. However, cash back and reward points earned on credit and debit card purchases are not taxable interest income.

Example: Trixie has three savings accounts in different banks. The total amount of interest earned from all her accounts is $1,950. Trixie will receive three Forms 1099-INT. She must list each payor and the amount of interest she receives from each bank on Schedule B and file it with her tax return.

Example: Renata has two savings accounts. In 2018, she earns $6 in interest from the first savings account and $8 in interest from the second account. Because the amounts are below the reporting threshold, she does not receive a Form 1099-INT from either bank. The interest is still taxable income and must be reported on her return, assuming that she has a filing requirement for the year.

Interest Earned on a Certificate of Deposit

Interest earned on a certificate of deposit (CD) is generally taxable when the taxpayer receives it or is entitled to receive it without paying a substantial penalty.

The interest a taxpayer pays on funds borrowed from a financial institution to meet the minimum deposit required for a CD, and the interest a taxpayer earns on the CD are two separate items. The taxpayer must include the total interest earned on the CD in income. If the taxpayer itemizes deductions, he can deduct the interest paid as investment interest, up to the amount of net investment income by using Form 4952, *Investment Interest Expense Deduction*.[61]

Example: Tiffany wanted to invest in a $10,000 six-month CD. She deposited $5,000 of her own money in a CD with a bank and borrowed an additional $5,000 from the same bank to make up the $10,000 minimum deposit required to buy the six-month CD. The certificate of deposit earned $575 at maturity in 2018, but Tiffany actually received a net amount of $265 for the year after taking into account the $310 of interest paid to the bank. This represented the $575 Tiffany earned on the CD, minus $310 interest charged on the $5,000 loan. The bank gives Tiffany a Form 1099-INT showing the $575 interest she earned. The bank also gives Tiffany a statement showing that she paid $310 in investment interest during the year. Tiffany must include the total interest amount that she earned, $575, in her gross income for the year. She can deduct the interest expense of $310 only if she itemizes deductions on Schedule A.

Tax-Exempt Interest

Interest earned on debt obligations of state and local governments (also commonly called *muni bonds* or *municipal bonds*) is generally exempt from federal income tax but may be subject to income taxes by state and local governments. However, interest on federally guaranteed state and local obligations is generally taxable.

In addition, even if interest on an obligation is nontaxable, the taxpayer may need to report a capital gain or loss when the investment is sold. The taxpayer's Form(s) 1099-INT may include both taxable and tax-exempt interest. Tax-exempt interest must be reported on Form 1040, even though it is not taxable.

---

[61] The TCJA suspended miscellaneous itemized deductions subject to 2%-of-AGI, which includes the deduction for investment expenses, starting in 2018. Other examples include: safe deposit fees, trustee fees, and investment advisor fees. However, the TCJA did *not* repeal the deduction for investment interest expense. Investment interest expense is any interest incurred on loans used to purchase taxable investments.

Interest on U.S. Treasury Bills, Notes, and Bonds

Interest on U.S. obligations, such as U.S. Treasury bills, notes, and bonds issued by any agency of the United States, is normally taxable for federal income tax purposes. The **Series EE bond** is the most common type of U.S. savings bond. These bonds are issued at a discount, and the difference between the purchase price and the amount received when the bonds are later redeemed (or "cashed in") is interest income.

Series I bonds are issued at face value with a maturity period of thirty years. The face value and accrued interest are payable at maturity. Individual taxpayers can generally report interest income from a Series EE or Series I savings bond either:

- When the bond matures or is redeemed (whichever occurs first), or

- Each year as the bond's redemption value increases.

However, a taxpayer must use the same reporting method for all the Series EE and Series I bonds he owns. When a taxpayer redeems savings bonds, he should receive a Form 1099-INT from the bank or another payor.

The Education Savings Bond Program

A taxpayer may be able to exclude interest from income all or part of the interest you receive on the redemption of qualified U.S. savings bonds during the year if you pay qualified higher education expenses during the same year. The expenses must be for the taxpayer, his spouse, or dependents. This exclusion is known as the Education Savings Bond Program.

The taxpayer must use both the principal and interest to pay for qualified education expenses. If the amount of savings bonds cashed during the year exceeds the amount of qualified educational expenses paid during the year, the amount of excludable interest is reduced.

To exclude interest earnings on Series EE and Series I bonds, a taxpayer must be at least twenty-four years old before the bond's issue date. For example, a bond bought by a parent and issued in the name of his or her child under age 24 does not qualify for the exclusion by the parent or the child. There are certain rules that must be followed for the educational exclusion to qualify:

- The bonds must be purchased by the owner. They cannot be a gift, although the bond proceeds can be used to pay the tuition expenses of a dependent child.

- Qualified higher education expenses must be reduced by certain tax-free benefits received and by expenses used to claim the American Opportunity and Lifetime Learning credits.

- The total interest received may be excluded only if the combined amounts of the principal and the interest received do not exceed the taxpayer's qualified higher education expenses.

> **Example:** Sonya is a full-time college student. She redeemed several education savings bonds in 2018 to pay for her college expenses. The total bond proceeds were $10,000 ($8,000 principal and $2,000 in interest). Sonya's qualified educational expenses were only $8,000. She used the remaining $2,000 to make a down payment on a new car. Therefore, since Sonya used only 80% of the bond proceeds for qualified expenses, she can only exclude 80% of the bond interest. The excludable portion would equal $1,600 (80% x $2,000 bond interest = $1,600). She would pay tax on the remaining $400 of bond interest.

Married taxpayers who file separately (MFS) do not qualify for the education savings bond interest exclusion. If a taxpayer cashes an education savings bond during the year, and then files MFS, all the interest would be taxable, regardless of whether or not the taxpayer had qualifying education expenses.

> **Example:** Izaiah is married, but files separately from his wife. In 2018, Izaiah cashed out qualified Series EE U.S. savings bonds with a total denomination of $10,000 that he bought fifteen years ago for $5,000. He received proceeds of $7,520, representing principal of $5,000 and interest income of $2,520. Izaiah paid $11,000 of college tuition for his graduate program using the bond proceeds. Normally, Izaiah would be able to exclude all the bond interest from his taxable income. However, since he is filing MFS, all the interest is taxable in the year received.

For the purposes of this exclusion, qualified educational expenses include:

- College tuition and fees (such as lab fees and other required course expenses), except for expenses for any course or other education program involving sports, games, or hobbies that are not part of a degree program

- Expenses paid for any course required as part of a degree or certificate program

> **Note:** The costs of room and board, as well as required textbooks, are *not* eligible expenses for the savings bond interest exclusion. However, the cost of required textbooks *is* a qualified educational expense for the purposes of the Lifetime Learning Credit and the American Opportunity Credit.

The amount of qualified expenses is reduced by the amount of any scholarships, fellowships, employer-provided educational assistance, and other forms of tuition reduction. The exclusion is calculated and reported on Form 8815, *Exclusion of Interest from Series EE and I U.S. Savings Bonds Issued After 1989.*

Dividend Income

A dividend is a distribution of cash, stock, or other property from a corporation or a mutual fund. The payor will generally use Form 1099-DIV to report dividend income to taxpayers. If a taxpayer does not receive Form 1099-DIV from a payor, the taxpayer must still report all taxable dividend income.

Generally, if a taxpayer's total dividend income is more than $1,500, it must be reported on Schedule B, *Interest and Ordinary Dividends*. Otherwise, it can be reported directly on Form 1040. Dividends are not subject to employment taxes. In 2018, the top rate on long-term capital gains[62] and qualified dividends of 20% remains in effect. This means that the maximum tax rate for dividends is 20%, regardless of the taxpayer's individual tax bracket.

> **Example:** Aiden earned $550,000 in wages in 2018. This puts him in the highest marginal tax bracket, at 37%. Aiden also earned $120,000 in dividend income from various investments. The dividends will be taxed at 20%, a much lower rate, and the dividends are also not subject to employment taxes. However, Aiden will be subject to the Net Investment Income Tax (NIIT) on a portion of his income, because his gross income is over the threshold amount (the NIIT is covered in detail later).

Ordinary Dividends: Ordinary dividends are corporate distributions in cash (as opposed to property or stock shares) that are paid to shareholders out of earnings and profits. Unless they are qualified dividends, they are taxed at ordinary income rates rather than at lower long-term capital gain rates. Ordinary dividends are reported in Box 1a of Form 1099-DIV.

Qualified Dividends: Qualified dividends are reported to the taxpayer on box 1b of Form 1099-DIV. These are ordinary dividends that are given preferred tax treatment as long-term capital gains if specific criteria are met. The top rates for qualified dividends and capitals gains in 2018 are as follows:

Qualified Dividend and Capital Gains Rate	Single/MFS Filers	MFJ/QW	HOH
0%	$0 - $38,600	$0 - $77,200	$0 - $51,700
15%	$38,601 - $425,800	$77,201 - $479,000	$51,701 - $452,400
20%	Greater than $425,800	Greater than $479,000	Greater than $452,400

In order for the dividends to qualify for these preferred tax rates, the following are the two most common requirements that must be met:

- The dividends must be paid by a U.S. corporation or a qualified foreign corporation,[63] and

- The taxpayer generally must have held the stock for *more than sixty days* during the 121-day period that begins sixty days before the ex-dividend date.

When figuring the holding period for qualified dividends, the taxpayer may count the number of days he held the stock, with the first day being the day after the stock was acquired (the date the taxpayer acquires the stock is not included in the holding period), and include the day he disposed of the stock.

---

[62] Note that *short-term* capital gains, which are generated by the sale of investments held for one year or less, are taxed at the individual taxpayer's ordinary income rate. This is why the holding period is so important. We will discuss holding period in more detail later.

[63] A "qualified foreign corporation" for the purposes of this rule is generally a foreign corporation whose stock is traded on a U.S. stock exchange or if a tax treaty between the U.S. and the foreign country of the corporation allows for qualified dividend status.

A longer holding period may apply for dividends paid on preferred stock. The "ex-dividend date" is the date a shareholder will no longer be entitled to receive the most recently declared dividend (typically the day following the record date).[64]

Nondividend Distributions: Distributions that are not paid out of earnings and profits are nondividend distributions. They are considered a recovery or return of capital and therefore are generally not taxable. However, these distributions reduce the taxpayer's basis in the stock of the corporation. Once the basis is reduced to zero, any additional distributions are capital gains and are taxed as such. Nondividend distributions are reported in Box 3 of Form 1099-DIV.

Money market funds: Money market funds pay dividends and are offered by nonbank financial institutions, such as mutual funds and stock brokerage houses. Generally, amounts received from money market funds should be reported as dividends, not as interest.

Stock Dividends and Stock Distributions

A stock dividend is a distribution of stock, rather than money, by a corporation to its own shareholders. A stock dividend is generally not a taxable event and does not affect the shareholder's income in the year of distribution, because he is not actually receiving any money and all shareholders increase their total number of shares pro rata.

When a stock dividend is granted, the total basis of the shareholder's stock is not affected, but the basis of individual shares is adjusted by the inclusion of the newly-issued shares.

> **Example:** Dragon Corporation declares a year-end stock dividend. Sharon is a shareholder in Dragon, and prior to the stock dividend, she owns 100 shares. Her basis in the shares is $5,000, or $50 per share. Sharon receives a stock dividend of 100 additional shares. After the dividend, Sharon owns 200 shares. Her overall basis in the shares does not change (it is still $5,000), but her new basis in each individual share is $25 per share ($5,000/200 = $25 per share). Sharon does not have any taxable income as a result of the stock dividend.

If a shareholder has the option to receive cash *instead* of stock, the stock dividend is taxable in the year it is distributed. The recipient of the stock must include the FMV of the newly issued stock in his gross income, and that same amount is the basis of the shares received.

> **Example:** The Pacific Corporation declares a year-end stock dividend and gives its shareholders the option of receiving cash instead of stock. Therefore, the stock dividend becomes a taxable event. Prior to the dividend, Gerry owns 1,000 shares in Pacific Corp., and his basis in the shares is $10,000, or $10 per share. Gerry decides to take the stock instead of cash and receives an additional 100 shares. The FMV of the stock at the time of the distribution is $15 per share. Gerry must recognize $1,500 of income ($15 FMV × 100 shares = $1,500), which also is his basis in the new shares.

---

[64] The "ex-dividend date" is the day on which a corporation's shares that are bought and sold no longer come attached with the right to receive the most recently declared dividend. This is important, because if a taxpayer purchases stock after its ex-dividend date, the taxpayer who bought the shares will not receive the next dividend payment. Instead, the seller of the stock receives the dividend.

Dividend Reinvestment Plans (DRIP)

A dividend reinvestment plan allows a taxpayer to use their dividends to purchase more shares of stock in a corporation instead of receiving dividends in cash. If the taxpayer uses his dividends to buy more stock at a price equal to its fair market value, he must still report the dividends as income.

Some plans also allow taxpayers to invest cash to buy shares of stock at a price less than fair market value. In this case, the taxpayer must report as dividend income the difference between the cash he invests and the FMV of the stock he purchases.

Example: Francesca owns 100 shares of Diamond Corporation, which is currently trading at $50 a share on the open market. Through Diamond's DRIP, Francesca buys 50 additional shares at a price of $40 per share. She must report $500 as dividend income ($10 per share difference between FMV and purchase price multiplied by 50 shares).

Mutual Fund Distributions

A mutual fund is an investment strategy that allows investors to pool their money for the purpose of investing in stocks, bonds, and other securities. The combined holdings of stocks, bonds, or other assets the fund owns are known as its "portfolio." Mutual funds are professionally managed by a portfolio manager. Mutual funds generally distribute all of their ordinary income to shareholders by the end of the year to obtain favorable tax treatment.

A taxpayer who receives mutual fund distributions during the year will also receive Form 1099-DIV identifying the types of distributions received. Mutual fund distributions are reported based upon the character of the income source and may include ordinary dividends, qualified dividends, capital gain distributions, exempt-interest dividends, and nondividend distributions. Ordinary dividends are the most common type of distribution from a mutual fund; these dividends are taxable as ordinary income.

Capital gain distributions from a mutual fund are always treated as long-term, regardless of the actual period the mutual fund investment is held. Distributions from a mutual fund investing in tax-exempt securities are tax-exempt interest and retain their tax-exempt character for the payee. Even so, the taxpayer must report them on his tax return.

If a mutual fund or Real Estate Investment Trust (REIT) declares a dividend payable to shareholders in October, November, or December, but actually pays the dividend during January of the following year, the shareholder is considered to have received the dividend on December 31 of the prior tax year and must report the dividend in the year it was declared.

Example: Andres has money invested in Great Shares Mutual Fund. The fund declared a $230 dividend on December 12, 2018. Andres did not receive the dividend until the following year, on January 6, 2019. Andres must report the dividend as taxable income in 2018. The dividend is taxable in the year *declared*, regardless of whether Andres withdraws the dividends or reinvests them.

Constructive Distributions

Certain transactions between a corporation and its shareholders may be regarded as constructive distributions. In general, constructive distributions are assessed under audit and they have very negative consequences for the company as well as the shareholder. They may be considered dividends or nondividend distributions and may be taxable to the shareholders. Examples of constructive distributions include:

- **Payment of personal expenses:** If a corporation pays personal expenses on behalf of an employee-shareholder, the amounts should be classified as a distribution, rather than expenses of the corporation.

- **Unreasonable compensation:** If a corporation pays an employee-shareholder an unreasonably high salary considering the services actually performed, the excessive part of the salary may be treated as a distribution.

- **Unreasonable rents:** If a corporation rents property from a shareholder and the rent is unreasonably higher than the shareholder would charge an unrelated party for the use of the property, the excessive part of the rent may be treated as a distribution. Conversely, if a corporation rents property_to a shareholder and the rent is unreasonably low, the discounted portion of the rent could be treated as a distribution as well.

- **Cancellation of a shareholder's debt:** If a corporation cancels a shareholder's debt without repayment by the shareholder, the amount canceled may be treated as a distribution.

- **Property transfers for less than FMV:** If a corporation transfers or sells property to a shareholder for less than its FMV, the excess may be treated as a distribution.

- **Below market or interest-free loans**: If a corporation gives a loan to a shareholder on an interest-free basis or at a rate below the applicable federal rate, the uncharged interest may be treated as a distribution.

> **Example**: Erika's father owns 95% of Spitfire Motorsports, Inc. and she and her siblings own the remaining 5%. Erika performs administrative assistant duties on a part-time basis for the corporation and is paid a salary of $700,000 a year. The corporation also pays for various personal expenses Erika incurs, such as monthly payments on the car she uses to commute to work. The IRS would likely consider Erika's salary as unreasonably high based on the nature of her duties, meaning that a portion of the salary and the personal expenses would be reclassified as constructive distributions. If that happens, then the constructive distribution becomes taxable to Erika as a taxable dividend, and the amounts are no longer deductible by the corporation as a business expense.

(Test yourself first; then check the correct answers at the end of this quiz.)

1. Giovanni opened a savings account at his local bank and deposited $28,900 as an initial deposit. He received a $25 calculator as a gift for opening the account, and he earned $20 of interest in 2018. Giovanni also received $100 of municipal bond interest in his mutual funds account. How much *taxable* interest income must Giovanni report on his Form 1040?

A. $25
B. $20
C. $45
D. $145

2. Which of the following dividends should be reported as interest income on a taxpayer's return?

A. Stock dividends
B. Preferred dividends
C. Dividends earned on deposits in credit unions
D. Qualified dividends

3. Six years ago, Derrick bought a U.S. Series EE savings bond and decided to report the interest earned each year until maturity. This year, he bought *another* Series EE savings bond. How should Derrick report the interest on this new bond?

A. He must wait until the second bond matures to report all the interest earned at that time.
B. He must report the interest earned each year until maturity.
C. He can use either method to report interest earned, as long as he makes the election on a timely filed return.
D. This type of interest is now exempt from federal income tax.

4. Alec received a Form 1099-DIV from his brokerage firm showing that he earned $1,200 of ordinary dividends in 2018. He received no other dividends during the year. How should this income be handled on Alec's tax return?

A. He must report the dividend income on Schedule B, but it is not taxable.
B. He must report the dividend income on Schedule B. It is taxable as ordinary income.
C. He can report the dividend income on page one of his Form 1040. It is taxable as ordinary income.
D. He does not have to report the dividend income until he sells the stock from the corporations that distributed the dividends.

5. Nondividend distributions are:

A. Considered a return of capital
B. Never taxable
C. Always taxable as ordinary income
D. Both A and B

6. A taxpayer must generally have held stock for _____ in order for his dividend income to be considered qualified dividends.

A. More than thirty days during the 121-day period that begins sixty days before the ex-dividend date
B. More than sixty days during the 121-day period that begins sixty days before the ex-dividend date
C. More than 120 days
D. More than one year

7. Robert is a 5% employee-shareholder of a family-owned corporation. Which of the following would the IRS likely classify as a constructive distribution?

A. Use of a company copy machine for making occasional personal copies
B. Payment of Robert's monthly gym membership by the corporation
C. Dental benefits paid by the corporation through a cafeteria plan
D. All of the above

8. Toni files as head of household and has modified AGI of $52,000 in 2018. She owns a Series EE savings bond, which she purchased as an investment to help pay for her daughter Holland's education. She redeems the bond in 2018 and immediately uses all the funds to pay college tuition expenses for Holland. Toni claims Holland as a dependent. The bond's interest is reported on:

A. Toni's tax return, and it is 100% taxable
B. Holland's tax return and it is 100% taxable
C. Toni's tax return, and it is exempt from taxes
D. Nowhere. It is not taxable and not required to be reported, as long as Toni uses all the funds to pay for qualified higher education costs.

9. All of the following statements about stock dividends are correct except:

A. When a stock dividend is granted, the basis of the stockholder's existing shares is adjusted to reflect the issuance of the new shares.
B. A stock dividend occurs when a corporation distributes stock to its own shareholders.
C. A taxpayer generally recognizes income only when he sells the stock received in a stock dividend distribution.
D. A stock dividend is never taxable, even if a taxpayer has the choice to receive cash instead of stock.

10. Araceli received $500 of interest from bonds issued by the state of New Jersey. How should she report this on her Form 1040?

A. It must be reported on her tax return, but it is not taxable income.
B. It must be reported as interest income, and it is 100% taxable.
C. She does not have to report the bond interest.
D. She must report the interest on her state tax return, but it does not have to be reported on her federal return.

11. Miguel deposited $4,000 of his own funds and also borrowed $12,000 from the bank to buy a six-month certificate of deposit for $16,000. The certificate earned $375 at maturity in 2018, and Miguel received $175, which represented the $375 he earned minus $200 of interest charged on the $12,000 loan. The bank gives Miguel a Form 1099-INT showing the $375 interest he earned. The bank also gives him a statement showing that he paid $200 of interest. How should Miguel report these amounts on his tax return?

A. He should report $175 of interest income.
B. He should report $375 of interest income. The $200 of interest he paid to the bank is not deductible.
C. He should report $375 of interest income and can deduct $200 on his Schedule A, subject to the net investment income limit.
D. He does not have to report any income from this transaction.

12. Leonardo invested in a mutual fund during the year. The fund declared a dividend, and Leonardo earned $19. He did not receive a Form 1099-DIV for the amount, and he did not withdraw the money from his mutual fund. Leonardo sold his investment in the mutual fund on January 2, 2019. Which of the following statements is correct?

A. The dividend is not reportable in 2018 because Leonardo did not withdraw the earnings.
B. The dividend is not reportable in 2018 because Leonardo did not receive a 1099-DIV.
C. The dividend is taxable and must be reported in 2018.
D. The dividend is taxable and must be reported in 2019.

13. Marcelo opened a savings account at his local bank and deposited $800. The account earned $20 interest during the year. On his credit card account, Marcelo received $100 worth of reward points for charging $10,000 of purchases, which he used to pay a portion of his credit card bill. How much interest income must Marcelo report on his Form 1040?

A. $20
B. $75
C. $120
D. $900

14. All of the following statements about dividends are correct *except*:

A. A taxpayer will pay a higher tax rate on an ordinary dividend than on a qualified dividend.
B. A taxpayer will pay a higher tax rate on a qualified dividend than on an ordinary dividend.
C. The ex-dividend date is the date a shareholder will no longer be entitled to receive the most recently declared dividend (normally right after the record date).
D. When figuring the holding period for qualified dividends, the taxpayer may count the number of days he held the stock (starting the day after the stock was acquired) and include the day he disposed of the stock.

15. Constance is using educational savings bonds to help pay her college expenses. Which of the following is a qualified expense for the educational savings bond exclusion?

A. College tuition
B. Room and board
C. Required textbooks
D. Student health fees

1. The answer is C. A gift for opening a bank account is normally taxed as interest income. The Form 1099-INT Giovanni receives will include the fair market value of the calculator and show a total of $45 of taxable interest for the year. The $100 of municipal bond interest is not taxable for federal tax purposes, but it must be reported on the return.

2. The answer is C. The dividends earned on deposits in credit unions are reported as interest income, rather than dividend income.

3. The answer is B. Derrick must report the interest earned each year until maturity. Savings bond owners must use the same interest-reporting method for all the Series EE and Series I bonds they own.

4. The answer is C. Ordinary dividends are taxable as ordinary income in the year they are earned. Only amounts over $1,500 must be reported on Schedule B, so Alec can report the $1,200 of dividend income directly on page one of his Form 1040.

5. The answer is A. Nondividend distributions are not paid out of a corporation's earnings and profits. They are considered a recovery or return of capital and therefore are generally not taxable. However, these distributions reduce the taxpayer's basis. Once basis is reduced to zero, any additional distributions are taxed as capital gains.

6. The answer is B. A taxpayer must generally have held stock for more than sixty days during the 121-day period that begins sixty days before the ex-dividend date. The ex-dividend date is the date a shareholder will no longer be entitled to receive the most recently declared dividend. When figuring the holding period for qualified dividends, the taxpayer may count the number of days he held the stock and include the day he disposed of the stock. The date the taxpayer acquires the stock is not included in the holding period. A longer holding period may apply for dividends paid on preferred stock.

7. The answer is B. The payment of personal expenses on behalf of an employee-shareholder is treated as a constructive distribution. In this case, the payment of his monthly gym membership is likely to be reclassified as a taxable dividend to Robert or a nondividend distribution, depending upon whether the corporation has earnings and profits. Choice C is incorrect because dental and medical benefits paid by an employer are an allowable employee benefit. Answer A is incorrect because the use of a company copier is an allowable de minimis fringe benefit. See Publication 5137, *Fringe Benefit Guide,* for more information.

8. The answer is C. As the buyer and owner of the bond, Toni reports the interest on her tax return, but excludes the interest from her taxable income because she used the funds to pay for qualified higher education expenses for her dependent daughter in the same year.

9. The answer is D. If a taxpayer is given a choice between receiving cash or stock, a stock dividend is taxable in the year it is distributed.

10. The answer is A. Interest earned on state and local bonds (municipal bonds or "muni" bonds) are generally tax-exempt at the federal level. Although the interest is not taxable, Araceli must still report the income on her federal return. Note that these bonds may be taxable at the state and local level, even if they are not taxable at the federal level.

11. The answer is C. Miguel must include the total amount of interest earned, $375, in his income. If he itemizes deductions on Schedule A, he can deduct $200 of interest expense, subject to the net investment income limit. He may not report the investment income and expenses on a net basis.

12. The answer is C. Leonardo earned the dividends in 2018, and whether or not he received a 1099-DIV is irrelevant. Mutual fund dividends are taxable in the year declared regardless of whether the taxpayer withdraws the dividends or reinvests them, so Leonardo must report the earnings in 2018.

13. The answer is A. If no other interest is credited to Marcelo during the year, the Form 1099-INT he receives will show $20 of interest for the year. The IRS does not count reward points or cash back from a credit card as taxable interest income, so Marcelo does not have to report the $100 in rewards points or pay any tax on it.

14. The answer is B. Ordinary dividends are taxed at higher ordinary income rates than qualified dividends. If certain conditions are met, qualified dividends are given preferred tax treatment. Qualified dividends must have been paid by a U.S. corporation or a qualified foreign corporation, and the taxpayer generally must have held the stock for more than sixty days during the 121-day period that begins sixty days before the ex-dividend date.

15. The answer is A. The savings bond education tax exclusion permits qualified taxpayers to exclude from their gross income all or part of the interest paid upon the redemption of eligible Series EE and I Bonds. Eligible educational expenses include tuition and required fees. The costs of room and board, as well as textbooks, are *not* eligible expenses.

Unit 6: Calculating the Basis of Assets

For additional information read:
Publication 551, *Basis of Assets*
Publication 544, *Sales and Other Dispositions of Assets*

Much of tax law deals with the taxation of assets. In order to calculate gains and losses from the sale or disposition of an asset, you need to be able to properly *classify* the asset first. There are two main types of assets: real property and personal property. "Real property" is real estate. Real property includes land, and anything permanently attached to it. Examples include: buildings, farmland, personal homes, commercial buildings, residential rentals, and subsurface mineral rights.

"Personal property" is *anything other* than real estate. Personal property includes: furniture, equipment, vehicles, household goods, collectibles, and even livestock. It also includes intangible assets, such as corporate stock, trademarks, cryptocurrency,[65] and copyrights. The tax treatment of an asset also varies based on whether the asset is personal-use, business property, or investment property.

Note: Do not get the term "personal property" confused with "personal-use property." The term "personal property" is an accounting and legal term which describes all movable assets, whether they are used in a business or not. "Personal-use" property refers to any property that is used *personally* by the taxpayer, and not used in a trade, business, or for investment.

When an asset is sold, the difference between the asset's basis and the selling price may be a taxable gain or loss. Sometimes, when an asset is disposed of or sold, no gain or loss is recognized until a later date. In order to correctly report a taxable gain or loss related to the disposition of an asset, a taxpayer needs to identify:

- Whether the asset is personal-use or used for business or investment;

- The asset's basis or adjusted basis:

    o As described above, the initial basis of an asset is usually its purchase cost, including certain ancillary charges.

    o Adjusted basis includes the original basis plus any increases or decreases resulting from events, transactions, or tax benefits that occur after the original purchase or acquisition by the taxpayer (such as subsequent improvements, depreciation deductions, casualty losses, rebates, and insurance reimbursements).

- The asset's holding period:

    o Short-term property is held for one year or less.

    o Long-term property is held for <u>more</u> than one year (at least a year, plus one day).

- The proceeds from the sale.

---

[65] The IRS views cryptocurrency, or virtual currency, as "property" and not as currency. The IRS deems cryptocurrency to be a capital asset, and gains or losses on the sale of cryptocurrency are capital in nature.

Basis in General

In order to correctly calculate gains and losses, you must also understand the concept of "basis". The initial basis of an asset is usually its cost. However, there are instances in which basis is determined based upon the fair market value of the asset when acquired by the taxpayer, rather than its cost, typically when property is acquired by inheritance and sometimes by gift. The basis of an asset may include:

- Sales taxes charged during the purchase

- Freight-in charges and shipping fees

- Installation costs and testing fees

- Delinquent real estate taxes that are paid by the buyer of a property

- The cost of any major improvements to the property

- Legal and accounting fees to transfer an asset

- Legal fees to obtain title to a property

All of these costs will *increase* an asset's basis. The result of these adjustments to the basis is the "adjusted" basis.

Example: Patrick paid $7,800 for an attorney's services in a title dispute for a parcel of farmland that he purchased. The farmland originally cost $45,000. The legal fees are added to the farmland's basis. Therefore, Patrick's adjusted basis in the farmland is $52,800 ($45,000 cost + $7,800 legal fees).

Example: Edwin purchases a new car for $15,000. The sales tax on the vehicle is $1,200. He also pays a delivery charge to have the car shipped from another dealership to his home. The freight charge is $210. Therefore, Edwin's basis in the vehicle is $16,410 ($15,000 + $1,200 + $210).

Example: Della is a self-employed writer. She purchases a new printer for her home office. The printer costs $540 with an additional $34 for sales tax. Therefore, Della's basis in the printer is $574 ($540 + $34).

Example: Bruce buys a house for $120,000. The following year, he paves the driveway, which costs $6,000. Bruce's adjusted basis in the home is now $126,000 ($120,000 original cost + $6,000 for major improvements).

Study Note: Understanding basis and how it is applied to various types of property is critical to your success in passing Part 1 *and* Part 2 of the EA exam. You may be expected to calculate basis in multiple scenarios.

Depreciation Deduction

Depreciation is an income tax deduction that allows a business to recover the cost or basis of property used in the business over time. Depreciation *decreases* the basis of an asset, usually over several years.

Depreciation is an annual allowance for the wear and tear, deterioration, or obsolescence of assets. The amount allowed as an annual depreciation deduction is intended to roughly approximate the reduction in the value of assets as they age. Property ceases to be depreciable when the business has fully recovered the property's tax basis, or when the taxpayer sells or retires it from service, whichever happens first.

Some types of property, such as land, cannot be depreciated. Most other types of tangible property, such as buildings, machinery, vehicles, furniture, and equipment, are depreciable.

Study Note: Depreciation is an important accounting concept, so it is tested most often on *Part 2: Businesses* of the EA exam. For Part 1 of the EA exam, test-takers must understand depreciation primarily in the context of residential rental property.

Basis of Real Property (Real Estate)

The basis of real estate usually includes a number of costs in addition to the purchase price. If a taxpayer purchases real property (such as land or a building), certain fees and other expenses are automatically included in the cost basis. The transaction might include real estate taxes the *seller* owed at the time of the purchase. If delinquent real estate taxes are paid by the buyer, those mounts must be added to the property's basis.

Example: Cora sells Anthony a home for $100,000. She had fallen behind on her property tax payments, so Anthony agrees to pay $3,500 of delinquent real estate taxes as a condition of the sale. Because a taxpayer is not allowed to deduct property taxes that are not his legal responsibility, Anthony must add the property taxes paid to his basis. His basis in the home is $103,500 ($100,000 + $3,500).

If a property is constructed rather than purchased, the basis of the property includes the expenses of construction. This includes the cost of payments to contractors, building materials, and inspection fees. Demolition costs and other costs related to the preparation of land prior to construction must be added to the basis of the land, rather than to any buildings constructed on it later.

Example: Dianne pays $50,000 for an empty lot where she plans to build her home. She also pays $2,800 for the removal of tree stumps and $6,700 to demolish an existing concrete foundation on the lot. These costs must be added to the basis of the land, not to the basis of the future house. Therefore, Dianne's basis in the land is $59,500 ($50,000 + $2,800 + $6,700).

Settlement Costs: Generally, a taxpayer must include settlement costs for the purchase of property in his basis. The following fees are some of the closing costs that can be included in a property's basis:

- Abstract fees
- Charges for installing utilities
- Legal fees (including title search and preparation of the deed)
- Recording fees and land surveys
- Transfer taxes
- Owner's title insurance

Also included in a property's basis are any other amounts the seller legally owes that the buyer agrees to pay, such as recording or mortgage fees, charges for improvements or repairs, and sales commissions. A taxpayer cannot include fees incidental to getting a loan in the basis of the property financed with proceeds from the loan.

Settlement costs do not include any amounts placed in escrow for the future payment of items such as taxes and insurance.

Basis of Securities

A taxpayer's basis in securities (such as stocks or bonds) is usually the purchase price plus any additional costs (e.g., brokers' commissions, settlement fees).

When a taxpayer sells securities, his investment broker should provide Form 1099-B, *Proceeds from Broker and Barter Exchange Transactions,* to him or her by February 15 following the end of the tax year, showing the proceeds of the sale. The IRS also receives a copy of Form 1099-B, which must be reported to the IRS by February 28 (March 31 if filed electronically).

If Form 1099-B does not identify a taxpayer's basis, the taxpayer must provide this information from his own records. If a taxpayer cannot provide evidence of his basis in an asset sold, the IRS may deem the basis to be zero.

A taxpayer may own more than one block of shares in a particular company's stock. Each block may differ from the others in its holding period (long-term or short-term), its basis, or both. When directing a broker to sell stock, a taxpayer may specify which block, or part of a block, to sell; this is called *specific identification*. The specific identification method requires good recordkeeping.

However, it simplifies the determination of the holding period and the basis of stock sold and gives the taxpayer better control over the recognition of taxable income and losses when selling part of an investment.

If the taxpayer cannot identify a specific block at the time of sale, shares sold are treated as coming from the earliest block purchased. This method is called First In, First Out (FIFO).

Example: Sharleen buys two blocks of 400 shares of stock (800 shares total). She buys 400 shares on May 1, 2013 for $11,200 and an additional 400 shares two months later for $11,600. On September 10, 2018, she sells 400 shares for $11,500 without specifying which block of shares she is selling. The sold shares are therefore treated as coming from the *earliest* block purchased (those purchased in May 2013). Since the basis and holding period defaults to the original block of shares, Sharleen realizes a long-term capital gain of $300 ($11,500 - $11,200).

Note: The IRS requires stockbrokers and mutual fund companies to report the basis for most stock purchased. The reporting is made to investors and to the IRS. You must understand how to calculate the basis of securities because this subject is frequently tested on Part 1 of the exam.

Events that occur after the purchase of stock can require adjustments (increases or decreases) to the basis per individual share.

For example, the original basis per share can be changed by events such as stock dividends and stock splits. Stock dividends and stock splits usually are not taxable events. However, a stock dividend may be taxable when shareholders have the option to receive cash or other property instead of stock.

- **Stock dividends** are additional shares a company grants to its shareholders in lieu of paying cash dividends. These additional shares increase the number of shares owned by an individual shareholder, so his original basis is spread over more shares, which decreases the basis per individual share. The total basis of all the shares remains the same.

- A **stock split** is similar to a stock dividend and occurs when a company issues additional shares of stock for every existing share an investor holds. Stock splits are a way for a company to lower the market price of its stock. The stock's market capitalization, however, remains the same. For example, in a 2-for-1 stock split, a corporation issues one share of stock for every share outstanding. This decreases a shareholder's basis per individual share by half. An original basis of $200 for 100 shares becomes $200 for 200 shares in a 2-for-1 stock split. However, the total basis in the stock remains the same even though the basis per share decreases.

Example: Leticia pays $1,050 for 100 shares of stock, plus a broker's commission of $50. Her basis in the 100 shares is $1,100 ($1,050 original cost + $50 broker's commission), or $11 per share ($1,100/100). Leticia later receives 10 additional shares of stock as a stock dividend. Her $1,100 basis must be spread over 110 shares (100 original shares plus the ten-share stock dividend). Her basis per share decreases to $10 ($1,100/110).

Example: Irwin buys 100 shares of Cortex, Inc. for $50 per share. His cost basis is $50 × 100 shares or $5,000. In 2018, Cortex declares a 2-for-1 stock split, and Irwin receives 100 additional shares of stock. Therefore, his new basis in each individual stock is $25 = ($5,000 ÷ [100 + 100]). His total basis in the shares remains $5,000.

Stock Options

A taxpayer may purchase *options* to buy or sell securities, (such as stocks or commodities), through an exchange or in the open market. He may realize a gain or loss from the sale or trade of an option itself, or he may exercise the option to buy or sell the underlying securities and realize a gain or loss from the disposition of those securities.

In addition, companies may grant options to their employees, as compensation for their service and as an incentive that allows them to purchase the company's stock at a later date.

If an employee receives stock options, he may have income when the options are granted, when he exercises them (to buy the company's stock), or when he sells or otherwise disposes of the options or the stock.

In general, there are two types of stock options:

- Options granted under an employee stock purchase plan (ESPP) or an incentive stock option (ISO) plan are **statutory stock options.**

- Stock options that are granted neither under an employee stock purchase plan nor an ISO plan are **nonstatutory stock options.**[66]

The nature, timing and amount of income that needs to be reported by the taxpayer depends on whether the options are considered to be *statutory* or *nonstatutory* options.

The tax advantage of a *statutory* stock option is that income is not reported when the option is granted or when it is exercised. Income is only reported once the stock is ultimately sold.

> **Note:** For Part 1 of the EA Exam, you must understand the concept of stock options from the perspective of the individual taxpayer *receiving* the options. For Part 2 of the EA Exam, you must understand stock options from the point of view of the corporation *issuing* the stock options.

Statutory Stock Options

If an employer grants an employee a statutory stock option, the employee generally does not include any amount in their gross income when they receive or exercise the option. However, a taxpayer may be subject to alternative minimum tax in the year they exercise an ISO. The employee will either have taxable income (or a deductible loss) when the employee eventually sells the stock they bought by exercising the option. The amount is treated as a capital gain or loss.

However, if the taxpayer does not meet special holding period requirements,[67] the taxpayer will have to treat income from the sale of the stock as ordinary income.

Incentive Stock Option (ISO)-After exercising an ISO, the taxpayer will receive from a Form 3921, *Exercise of an Incentive Stock Option*, from their employer. This form will report important dates and values needed to determine the correct amount of capital and ordinary income (if applicable) to be reported on the employee's individual tax return.

Employee Stock Purchase Plan (ESPP) - After the employee sells stock acquired by exercising an option granted under an employee stock purchase plan, the employee will receive Form 3922, *Transfer of Stock Acquired Through an Employee Stock Purchase Plan*, from their employer.

This form will report important dates and values needed to determine the correct amount of capital and ordinary income to be reported on the employee's individual tax return.

---

[66] Refer to Publication 525, Taxable and Nontaxable Income for more information on the treatment of statutory or nonstatutory stock options.

[67] If the taxpayer held the stock or option for less than one year, the sale will result in a short-term gain or loss, which will be taxed as ordinary income. Options sold after *a one year or longer* holding period are considered long-term capital gains or losses.

Example: Muscle Fitness, Inc. has an employee stock purchase plan (ESPP). The plan allows employees to purchase company stock at a discounted price. The option price is the lower of the stock price at the time the option is granted or at the time the option is exercised. Maria is an employee of Muscle Fitness, and she decides to take advantage of the ESPP that her employer provides. Muscle Fitness deducts $5 from Marla's pay every week for 48 weeks (total = $240 [$5 × 48]). The value of the stock when the option was granted was $25. When Maria exercises her options, the FMV of the stock is $20. Marla receives 12 shares of Muscle Fitness stock ($240 ÷ $20). Her holding period for all 12 shares begins the day *after* the option is exercised, even though the money used to purchase the shares was deducted from her pay on many different days. Marla's basis in each share is $20.

Basis Other Than Cost

The following are examples of situations in which an asset's basis is determined by something other than purchase cost.

Property in Exchange for Services: If a taxpayer receives property in payment for services, he must include the property's FMV in income, and this becomes his basis in the property. If two people agree on a cost for services beforehand, the agreed-upon cost may be used to establish the amount included as income and as the asset's basis.

Example: Jeremy is a CPA who prepares tax returns for a long-time client named Maryanne. Maryanne loses her job and cannot pay Jeremy's bill, which totals $400. Maryanne offers Jeremy an antique vase in lieu of paying her invoice. The fair market value of the vase is approximately $525. Jeremy agrees to accept the vase as full payment on Maryanne's delinquent invoice. Jeremy's basis in the vase is $400, the amount of the invoice that was agreed upon by both parties before the barter.

Basis After Casualty Loss: If a taxpayer has a casualty loss, he increases the basis in the property by the amount spent on repairs that restore the property to its pre-casualty condition. However, he must also decrease the basis of the property by any related insurance proceeds.

Example: Duke paid $5,000 for a car several years ago. His car was damaged in a flood, so he spends $3,000 to repair it. He does not have flood insurance on the car. Therefore, his new basis in the car is $8,000 ($5,000 + $3,000).

Basis After Mortgage Assumption: If a taxpayer buys property and assumes an existing mortgage on it, the taxpayer's basis includes the amount paid for the property plus the amount owed on the mortgage. The basis also includes the settlement fees and closing costs paid to buy the property. However, fees and costs for obtaining a loan on the property (points) are not included in a property's basis.

Example: Nadia buys a building for $22,000 cash and also assumes an existing mortgage of $80,000 on the property. Therefore, her basis in the building is $102,000 ($22,000 + $80,000 mortgage assumption).

Basis of Property Transfers Incident to Divorce

The basis of property transferred by a spouse (or former spouse if the transfer is due to divorce) is the same as the spouse's adjusted basis. Generally, there is no gain or loss recognized on the transfer of property between spouses (or between former spouses if the transfer is because of divorce).

For property transfers related to a divorce, the transfer generally must occur within one year after the date the marriage ends.

This nonrecognition rule applies even if the transfer was in exchange for cash, the release of marital rights, the assumption of liabilities, or other financial considerations.[68]

Example: Jeremiah and Adrienne finalized their divorce on January 23, 2018. Jeremiah owns a vacation home in Hawaii with a current adjusted basis of $225,000 and a fair market value of $450,000. Pursuant to their divorce agreement, Jeremiah agrees to transfer his ownership in the home to Adrienne. He transferred the property to Adrienne on December 1, 2018. Since the transfer was made within a year after their divorce was made final, there is no gain or loss recognized by either spouse; no tax reporting is required. Adrienne's basis in the property is the same as Jeremiah's basis before the transfer: $225,000.

Example: Adelynn and Graham jointly owned an antique collector Porsche that had a basis of $50,000 and an FMV of $150,000. When they divorced in 2018, Adelynn transferred her entire interest in the automobile to Graham as part of their property settlement. Graham's basis in the car is the same as their original joint basis of $50,000.

The Basis of Gifted Property

The basis of property received as a gift is determined differently than property that is purchased or inherited. The taxpayer must know the donor's adjusted basis in the property when it was gifted, its fair market value on the date of the gift, and the amount of gift tax the donor paid on it, (if any). The concept of "fair market value" is important when calculating any capital gains tax liability on a gift, so it's important to know how the basis and FMV is determined.

Generally, the basis of gifted property for the donee is equal to the donor's adjusted basis. This is called a "transferred basis." For example, if a taxpayer gives his son a car and the taxpayer's basis in the car is $2,000, the basis of the vehicle remains $2,000 for the son. The holding period of the gift would also transfer to the donee.

Example: Shira's father gives her 50 shares of stock that he purchased ten years ago. Her father has an adjusted basis in the stock of $500. Shira's basis in the stock, for purposes of determining gain on any future sale, is also $500 (this is a "transferred basis"). Shira is also considered to have "held" the stock for ten years, the same amount of time that her father held the stock.

---

[68] A divorce, for this purpose, includes the end of a marriage by annulment or due to violations of state laws, such as bigamy.

In situations where the fair market value of the property on the date of the gift is *less* than the transferred basis, the donee's basis for *gain* is the transferred basis. However, if the donee reports a *loss* on the sale of gifted property where the fair market value of the property on the date of the gift is less than the transferred basis, his basis is the FMV of gifted property on the date of the gift.

The sale of gifted property can also result in no gain or loss. This happens when the sale proceeds are greater than the gift's FMV but less than the transferred basis in situations where the fair market value of the property on the date of the gift is less than the transferred basis.

Example: Gabriel's aunt, Fatima, bought 100 shares of XYZ stock when it was at $92 per share. Fatima's basis for the 100 shares is $9,200. Fatima gives the stock to Gabriel when it is selling at $70 and has an FMV of $7,000 (it has lowered in value). In this case, Gabriel has a "dual basis" in the stock. He has one basis for purposes of determining a gain, and a different basis for determining a loss. Here are three separate scenarios that help illustrate how the gain or loss would be calculated when Gabriel sells the gifted stock:

Scenario #1: If Gabriel sells the stock for *more* than his aunt's basis, he will use her basis to determine his amount of gain. For example, if he sells the stock for $11,000, he will report a gain of $1,800 ($11,000 - $9,200).

Scenario #2: If Gabriel sells the stock for *less* than the FMV of the stock at the time of the gift ($7,000 in the example), he will use as his basis the FMV at the time of the gift to determine the amount of his loss. For example, if the stock continues to decline and Gabriel eventually sells it for $4,500, he can report a loss of $2,500 ($7,000 - $4,500).

Scenario #3: If Gabriel sells the stock for an amount in between the FMV and the donor's basis, no gain or loss will be recognized. For example, if Gabriel sells the stock for $8,000, there will be no gain or loss on the transaction (his basis will be deemed to be $8,000, the same as his sales price).

The Basis of Inherited Property

The basis of inherited property is treated very differently for tax purposes. In most cases, the basis is the FMV of the property on the date of the decedent's death, regardless of what the deceased person paid for the property or the adjusted basis of the property right before death. This means if the property is sold by the beneficiary, the gain will be calculated based on the change in value from the date of death. This usually results in a beneficial tax situation for anyone who inherits property because the taxpayer generally gets an increased or "stepped-up" basis.

Example: Rosanne's uncle bought 300 shares of stock many years ago for $500. Rosanne inherited the stock when her uncle died. On the date of his death, the stock was valued at $9,000, so Rosanne's basis is also $9,000. This is a "stepped up" basis. Roseanne later sells the stock for $11,000. She has a capital gain of $2,000 ($11,000 - $9,000).

However, there are cases in which this rule can work against taxpayers. Although the value of most property such as stocks, collectibles, and bonds generally increases over time, there are also instances in which a property's value drops. This creates a "stepped-down" basis.

> **Example:** Norbert purchased a home with cash in Connecticut for $240,000. His neighborhood becomes riddled with crime, and Norbert's home declines in value. In 2018, Norbert dies. On the date of his death, the home's FMV was only $185,000. Norbert's daughter Jayleen inherits the home. Her basis in the home is $185,000. This is a "stepped-down" basis.

> **Example:** Anson bought 100 shares of stock many years ago for $10,000. In 2018, Anson dies, and his daughter, Haley, inherits her father's stock. On the date of Anson's death, the value of the stock had plummeted to $5,000, meaning Haley's basis in the stock is "stepped down" for tax purposes to $5,000. The stock continues to decline, so six months later, she sells the stock for $4,000. Haley has a capital loss of $1,000 ($5,000 -$4,000), the difference between her inherited basis and the selling price.

Although the basis of an estate for estate tax purposes is usually determined on the date of death, a special rule allows the personal representative of the estate to elect a different valuation date of six months after the date of death. This is known as the alternate valuation date.

To elect the alternate valuation date, the estate's value and related estate tax must be less than they would have been on the date of the taxpayer's death. If the alternate valuation date has been elected for the estate, the basis for inherited assets is normally the fair market value of the assets six months after the date of death.

However, if any assets are received from the estate less than six months after the date of death, the basis in these inherited assets is the fair market value as of the date the asset was distributed to the heir.

If a federal estate tax return (Form 706) is not filed for the deceased taxpayer, the basis in the beneficiary's inherited property is the FMV value at the date of death, and the alternate valuation date does not apply.

Unit 6: Study Questions

(Test yourself first; then check the correct answers at the end of this quiz.)

1. Esteban installs artificial turf at a client's home and bills the client $1,500 for his services. After the installation, his client, Alice, receives a foreclosure notice and is unable to pay Esteban's bill. Alice has a Golden Retriever show dog that just had puppies. The FMV of each puppy is $1,800. Esteban loves animals and decides to take one of the puppies as full payment on Alice's delinquent bill. What is Esteban's basis in his new dog?

A. $0
B. $300
C. $1,500
D. $1,800

2. On January 1, 2018, Medi-Tech Corporation granted 1,000 Nonqualified Stock Options to Alexander (an employee of Medi-Tech). The exercise price on the shares was $33 per share. The market price of the shares on the date of the grant was $24 per share. Medi-Tech has a very profitable year, and as a consequence, the stock's market price increases significantly. On December 31, 2018, Alexander decides to exercise all of his options when the market price per share is $43. What is the basis of his stock, and what amount of income should be included on Alexander's Form W-2 as income from this transaction?

A. Basis $33,000; income $0
B. Basis $43,000; income $10,000
C. Basis $0; income $0
D. Basis $33,000; income $20,000

3. Flora gifted her grandson, Clifford, a residential rental property. She had purchased the property ten years ago for $120,000 and claimed $18,000 in depreciation. The fair market value of the rental house on the day of transfer was $144,000. Assuming no gift tax was paid, what is Clifford's basis in the property?

A. $102,000
B. $120,000
C. $126,000
D. $144,000

4. The basis of inherited property is generally:

A. The adjusted basis to the decedent
B. The fair market value of the property on the date of the decedent's death
C. The purchase price that the decedent paid
D. Determined nine months after the death of the decedent

5. On February 11, 2018, Henry bought 1,000 shares of stock for $4 per share and paid an additional $70 for his broker's commission. What is Henry's overall basis in the stock?

A. $1,000
B. $4,000
C. $4,070
D. None of the above

6. Mackenzie purchases an empty lot at auction for $50,000. She pays $15,000 in cash and finances the remaining $35,000 with a bank loan. The lot has a $4,000 tax lien against it for unpaid property taxes, which she also agrees to pay. Which of the following statements is correct?

A. Her basis in the property is $50,000. She can deduct the property taxes on Schedule A.
B. Her basis in the property is $19,000.
C. Her basis in the property is $54,000.
D. Her basis in the property is $46,000.

7. On January 3, 2018, Brigit purchased 1,000 shares of stock at the cost of $5,100, including the broker's commission. On August 14, 2018, she sold 500 shares for $3,300. What is the adjusted basis of the stock she sold?

A. $5,100
B. $2,550
C. $3,300
D. $3,255

8. Which statement is correct about the basis of assets?

A. The basis of an asset is always equal to its cost.
B. Depreciation increases the basis of an asset.
C. Inherited assets are treated as a gift to the beneficiary.
D. The cost basis of an asset generally includes sales tax and other expenses connected with the purchase.

9. Two years ago, Arnold paid $1,050 for 100 shares of Kirkner Corporation stock, plus a broker's commission of $50. During the year, Arnold received ten additional shares of Kirkner stock as a nontaxable stock dividend. What is the adjusted basis of Arnold's stock at the end of the year?

A. $9 per share
B. $10 per share
C. $11 per share
D. $25 per share

10. Julian owned one share of common stock that he bought for $45. The corporation distributed two new shares of common stock for each share held. Julian then had three shares of common stock. What is Julian's basis for each share?

A. $5
B. $45
C. $15
D. $135

11. If a taxpayer cannot determine his basis in a property and the property is sold, the IRS will deem the basis to be:

A. Zero
B. Fair market value
C. Actual cost
D. Average cost

12. During the year, Clementine bought 52 total shares of GRE Corporation for $624. That cost included a $40 broker commission. Later, in the year, GRE Corporation issued a 2-for-1 stock split. What is her basis per share after the split?

A. $12 per share
B. $6 per share
C. $24 per share
D. $26 per share

13. Which of the following must be added to the basis of a property, rather than deducted, as a current expense on a taxpayer's return?

A. Casualty loss
B. The cost of demolishing a building
C. Personal property tax based on the value of a car
D. Investment interest expense

14. David wishes to sell a home that he inherited from his mother last year. His mother paid $45,000 for the home ten years ago. She put a new roof on the property two years ago at a cost of $10,500. The fair market value of the home on the date of his mother's death was $120,000. An estate tax return was not required for his mother's estate, and the alternate valuation date was not elected. What is David's basis in the home?

A. $45,000
B. $55,500
C. $34,500
D. $120,000

15. Yoshiko owns two shares of common stock in Kirby Toys, Inc. She bought one share for $30 in 2015 and the other for $45 in 2016. In 2018, the corporation distributed two additional shares of common stock for each share held (a 3-for-1 stock split). Yoshiko had six shares after the stock split. How is Yoshiko's basis allocated between these six shares?

A. All six shares now have a basis of $12.50.
B. Three shares have a basis of $10 each and three have a basis of $15 each.
C. The shares are valued at $45 each.
D. None of the above.

16. Which of the following does not *decrease* the basis of an asset?

A. Depreciation
B. Manufacturers' rebates
C. Theft losses
D. Assessments for local improvements

17. Phoebe owns a piece of farmland that she purchased several years ago for $250,000. The land is now worth $750,000. During the year, she borrows $500,000 from the bank to improve the property. She uses $260,000 of the loan to demolish several existing buildings on the property and clear the land for construction of a stockyard and horse stable, which will begin next year. What is Phoebe's basis in the land after the demolition is completed?

A. $250,000
B. $460,000
C. $510,000
D. $750,000

18. Stephen purchases a truck for $15,000 to use in his carpentry business. He pays $5,000 in cash and finances the remaining $10,000 with a five-year loan. He also pays taxes and delivery costs of $1,300 and $250 to install a protective bedliner. What is Stephen's basis for depreciation of the truck?

A. $6,550
B. $10,000
C. $16,550
D. $16,300

19. Which of the following is not added to the basis of property?

A. Legal and accounting fees to transfer the title
B. Points on a loan
C. Sales tax
D. Freight-in charges

20. On June 1, 2018, Pharma Software Corporation granted 500 Incentive Stock Options to one of their executives, Wesley. The stock had an option price of $25. On December 31, 2018, Wesley exercised all of his options when the market price per share was $50. What is the basis of his stock and how much should be included on his Form W-2 as income for the year?

A. Basis $12,500; income $0
B. Basis $0; income $0
C. Basis $12,500; income $12,500
D. Basis $12,500; income $25,000

Unit 6: Quiz Answers

1. The answer is C. Esteban's basis in the animal is $1,500. If a taxpayer receives property as payment for services, he must include the property's FMV in income, and this becomes his basis. However, if the two parties agree on a cost beforehand, the IRS will usually accept the agreed-upon cost as the asset's basis.

2. The answer is B. The options were issued at an exercise price of $33, which means that $10,000 ($43 - $33 = $10 × 1,000), representing the difference between his exercise price and the stock's value at exercise, must be included in his W-2 for 2018. Alexander's basis of the stock would be the value on December 31, 2018, when he exercises his options ($43,000). His basis includes the amount he actually paid for the stock ($33,000) and the amount of taxable income recognized ($10,000). When the stock is later sold, the taxpayer would recognize gain or loss equal to the difference between his sales proceeds and his $43,000 basis in the stock. NQSO are normally issued with a strike price that exceeds its current FMV at the time of the grant. Note that the rules are different for Incentive Stock Options (ISOs) and Nonqualified Stock Options (NSOs). They are treated very differently for tax purposes.

3. The answer is A. The basis of gifted property for the donee is generally equal to the donor's adjusted basis, which is called a "transferred basis," when its FMV exceeds the donor's basis ($120,000 minus $18,000 depreciation = $102,000) at the time of the gift. While not the case here, if the fair market value of the property on the date of the gift is *less* than the transferred basis, the donee's basis for gain is the transferred basis. However, if the donee reports a loss on the sale of gifted property when the fair market value of the property on the date of the gift is less than the transferred basis, his basis is the lower of: the transferred basis *or* the FMV of the property on the date of the gift.

4. The answer is B. The basis of inherited property is generally the FMV of the property on the date of the decedent's death, regardless of what the deceased person paid for the property or the tax basis in the property in the hands of the decedent right before death.

5. The answer is C. Henry's basis in the stock is $4,070 ([1,000 × $4] = $4,000 + $70).

6. The answer is C. Mackenzie's basis is determined as follows: ($50,000 + $4,000 = $54,000). She cannot deduct the delinquent property taxes on her Schedule A. Any obligations of the seller assumed by the buyer increase the basis of the asset and are not currently deductible. Since Mackenzie did not owe the property taxes, but she still agreed to pay them, she must add the property tax to the basis of the property.

7. The answer is B. Brigit's original basis in the total stock was $5,100, which is $5.10 per share, so her basis in the 500 shares she sold is 500 × $5.10, or $2,550.

8. The answer is D. The cost basis of an asset includes sales tax and other expenses connected with the purchase. In most situations, the basis of an asset is its cost, including any sales tax, installation costs, or brokers' commissions paid. However, there are many other times when cost cannot be used to determine basis, such as when an asset is inherited or received as a gift. None of the other answers are correct.

9. The answer is B. Arnold's original basis per share was $11 ([$1,050 + $50 broker's commission = $1,100] ÷ 100). After the stock dividend, his $1,100 basis must be spread over 110 shares (100 original shares plus the additional 10 shares). Therefore, if Arnold's basis in the stock was $1,100 for 100 shares, the ten additional shares mean Arnold's basis per share decreased to $10 per share ($1,100 ÷ 110).

10. The answer is C. Julian's basis in each share is $15 ($45 ÷ 3). If a taxpayer receives a nontaxable stock dividend, he divides the adjusted basis of the stock by the total number of shares of stock (old and new). The result is the taxpayer's basis for each share of stock.

11. The answer is A. In order to compute gain or loss on a sale, a taxpayer must determine his basis in the property sold. If he cannot determine his basis in the property, the IRS will deem the basis to be zero.

12. The answer is B. The stock is $6 per share after the stock split. Figure the answer as follows:
Initial purchase: 52 shares = $624 ($40 broker commission already included in the price)
2-for-1 stock split doubles the shares to 104 total shares, so $624 (original basis) ÷ 104 shares
= $6 per share

13. The answer is B. Demolition costs are not deductible. They must be added to the basis of the land on which the building was located.

14. The answer is D. David's basis in the home is $120,000, the FMV on the date of his mother's death. Heirs can generally use a stepped-up basis for inherited property, regardless of what the deceased person actually paid for the asset. The basis of inherited property is generally the FMV of the property on the date of the decedent's death. When the property is ultimately sold, the beneficiary's gain or loss will be calculated based on the change in value from the date of death.

15. The answer is B. Yoshiko's shares are now valued as follows: three with a basis of $10 each ($30 ÷ 3), and three with a basis of $15 each ($45 ÷ 3). If a taxpayer receives a nontaxable stock dividend, she must divide the adjusted basis of the old stock by the number of shares of old and new stock. The result is the taxpayer's basis for each share of stock. The basis per share after the 3-for-1 stock split is calculated by dividing the original price by 3.

16. The answer is D. The basis of property must be increased for tax assessments the taxpayer is required to pay to finance local improvements, such as paving roads and building ditches. Basis is decreased for depreciation deductions and manufacturers' rebates received, and when the taxpayer incurs theft or other casualty losses.

17. The answer is C. Phoebe's basis in the land is calculated as follows: $250,000 (cost basis) + $260,000 (demolition costs) = $510,000. The loan amount is irrelevant because the act of borrowing alone does not increase basis; the amount spent on the improvement of the property increases its basis.

18. The answer is C. Stephen's basis in the truck includes the cost of acquiring the property (including any taxes associated with the purchase and delivery charges) and preparing it for use (in this case, installing the bedliner). Therefore, his basis is as follows: ($15,000 + $1,300 + $250) = $16,550. Any funds that are borrowed to pay for an asset are included in the basis.

19. The answer is B. Points related to a loan used to acquire property may be deductible in the year they are paid or amortizable over the term of the loan. Points are a type of mortgage interest. They are not added to the basis of the property.

20. The answer is A. For Incentive Stock Options (ISOs), the basis in the stock is the actual price per share paid upon exercise of the options. In this case, the executive's basis is 500 × $25 = $12,500. The bargain element attributable to the difference between the exercise price and the value at the date of exercise ([$50 - $25] × 500 shares = $12,500) is not recognized by the taxpayer until the stock is sold. However, the taxpayer may need to make an adjustment for alternative minimum tax (AMT) purposes for the bargain element. When the stock is sold, income will be recognized for the difference between his basis and the net proceeds of the sale. Note that the rules are different for Incentive Stock Options (ISOs) and Nonqualified Stock Options (NSOs). They are treated very differently for tax purposes.

Unit 7: Capital Gains and Losses

> **For additional information read:**
> Publication 550, *Investment Income and Expenses*
> Publication 523, *Selling Your Home*
> Publication 544, *Sales and Other Dispositions of Assets*

Capital Assets

In the previous chapter, we discussed assets in general. In this chapter, we will discuss capital gains and losses, which occur when a taxpayer sells or disposes of an asset.

Many of the items a taxpayer owns and uses for personal or investment purposes are classified as "capital assets" This means that the net gains that result from their sale or disposition may be subject to tax at favorable capital gains tax rates. Examples of capital assets include:

- A main home or vacation home

- Furniture, a car, or a boat

- Antiques and collectibles

- Stocks, bonds, and mutual funds (except when held for sale by a professional securities dealer)

- Cryptocurrency or virtual currency[69]

Note: Losses from the sale of personal-use property, such as a main home, a vacation home, personal-use furniture, or jewelry, are not deductible. However, *gains* from the sale of personal-use assets usually are taxable, subject to certain exclusions.

Example: Sanjay owns a station wagon that he uses to commute to work, run errands, and take on weekend ski trips. He purchased the car four years ago for $21,000. In 2018, he sells the car for $13,000. Sanjay cannot claim a loss from the sale of the car since it is his personal-use vehicle.

Example: Alexandros sold his personal computer to his friend for $750. Alexandros paid $5,000 for the computer five years ago. Alexandros used the computer to play games, surf the Internet, and pay bills online. He did not use the computer for business. Alexandros cannot deduct a loss on the sale of his personal computer.

Example: Judith collects antique coins as a hobby. She is not a professional coin dealer. Two years ago, Judith purchased an antique Roman coin at an estate sale for $50. In 2018, she is offered $1,000 for the coin, and she promptly sells it. Judith has a taxable capital gain that she must report on her tax return. Since she held the coin for more than one year, she will be eligible for favorable capital gains rates.

---

[69] IRS Notice 2014-21 states that, for federal tax purposes, virtual currency is treated as property.

The applicable capital gains tax rate depends on the holding period, the type of asset, and the taxpayer's ordinary income tax bracket.

Noncapital Assets

Assets held for business-use or created by a taxpayer for purposes of earning revenue (copyrights, inventory, etc.) are considered *noncapital* assets. Gains and losses from the sale of business property are reported on Form 4797, *Sales of Business Property*, and in the case of individual taxpayers, the amounts flow through to Form 1040, Schedule D, *Capital Gains and Losses.* The following assets are *noncapital* assets:

- Inventory or any similar property held for sale to customers

- Depreciable property used in a business, even if it is fully depreciated

- Real property used in a trade or business, such as a commercial building or a residential rental

- *Self-produced* copyrights, transcripts, manuscripts, drawings, photographs, or artistic compositions

- Accounts receivable or notes receivable acquired by a business

- Stocks and bonds held by professional securities dealers

- Business supplies

- Commodities and derivative financial instruments

Unlike capital assets, the costs of many noncapital assets may be deducted as business expenses when they are sold, and losses are generally deductible.

> **Example:** Olen is the sole proprietor of a health club. In 2018, he sells used fitness equipment to make room for new gym equipment. Since the used equipment was business property, Olen reports the sale on Form 4797. Also, during the year, Olen sells some stock at a substantial profit. He has a capital gain on the stock that he reports on Schedule D.[70]

> **Example:** Shawn is a self-employed fisherman who reports his income and expenses on Schedule F. In 2018, he sells some of his commercial fishing equipment. The fishing equipment is a noncapital asset, and the sale must be reported on Form 4797, *Sales of Business Property.* Also, during the year, Shawn sells his vacation home at a substantial loss. Unlike the fishing equipment, the vacation home is a capital asset, but since it is also personal-use property, he cannot deduct the loss.

Holding Period (Short-Term or Long-Term)

When a taxpayer disposes of investment property, his holding period affects the tax treatment of his capital gain or loss. This is important because long-term capital gains are taxed at lower rates than short-term gains. If a taxpayer holds investment property for more than one

---

[70] Certain capital asset sales must first be reported on Form 8949 before it flows onto Schedule D (to be discussed later).

year, any capital gain or loss is long-term capital gain or loss. If a taxpayer holds investment property for one year or less, any capital gain or loss is short-term capital gain or loss.

Long-term = <u>more</u> than one year (at least a year and a day)
Short-term = one year or less

To determine how long a taxpayer has held an investment property, he must begin counting on the date after the day he acquires the property. The day the taxpayer disposes of the property is part of the holding period.

Example: Nancy bought 50 shares of stock on February 5, 2018, for $10,000. She sells all the shares on February 5, 2019, for $20,500. Nancy's holding period is not more than one year, and so she has a short-term capital gain of $10,500. The short-term gain is taxed at ordinary income tax rates. If Nancy had waited just one more day, she would have received long-term capital gain treatment on her gain and been taxed at a lower rate.

Example: Karl bought 100 shares of stock on January 1, 2017, for $1,200. To determine his holding period, Karl must start counting his holding period on January 2, 2017 (the day *after* the purchase). He sells all the stock on January 2, 2018, for $2,850. Karl's holding period has been more than one year, and therefore, he will recognize a long-term capital gain of $1,650 in 2018 ($2,850 - $1,200).

Stock shares acquired as a result of a nontaxable stock dividend or stock-split have the same holding period as the original shares owned.

Example: Five years ago, Henry bought 500 shares of Stellar, Inc. stock for $1,500, including a broker's commission. On June 6, 2018, Stellar, Inc. distributes a 2% nontaxable stock dividend (10 additional shares). Three days later, Henry sells all his Stellar, Inc. stock for $2,030. Although Henry owned the 10 shares he received as a nontaxable stock dividend for only three days, a long-term holding period applies to all of his shares in the stock. Because he bought the stock for $1,500 and then sold it for $2,030 more than a year later, Henry has a long-term capital gain of $530 on the sale of the 510 shares.

The holding period for a gift is treated differently than the holding period for purchased property. If a taxpayer receives a gift of property, his holding period normally includes the donor's holding period. This concept is known as "tacking on" the holding period.

Example: Gena gives her nephew, Donnie, an acre of land. At the time of the gift, the land had an FMV of $23,000. Gena's adjusted basis in the land was $20,000. Gena only held the property for six months. Donnie holds the land for another seven months. Neither held the property for over a year. Regardless, Donnie may "tack on" his holding period to his aunt's holding period. Therefore, if Donnie were to sell the property, he would have a long-term capital gain or loss, because jointly they held the property for 13 months, or more than one year.

Inherited property is always considered long-term property. In other words, assets acquired from a decedent automatically receive long-term holding period treatment when sold by a beneficiary. This is true regardless of how long the beneficiary actually holds it.

Example: Nella inherited a vacation home from her father, who died on February 10, 2018. The FMV of the house is $210,000 on the date of her father's death. Nella immediately decides to sell the house. On March 20, 2018, the house is sold for $212,000. Nella has a long-term capital gain of $2,000 on the sale. The gain is treated as long-term, even though she held the property for only a few months.

Determining Capital Gain or Loss

A taxpayer determines gain or loss on a sale or trade of stock or property by comparing the amount realized with the adjusted basis of the property.

Example: Dustin receives Form 1099-B showing a net sales price of $1,200 on the sale of 600 shares of Centrex, Inc. He bought the stock six years ago and sold it on September 25, 2018. His basis in Centrex, Inc., including commissions paid, is $1,455. He will report a $255 loss on Schedule D.

A disposition of stock and the related income or loss must be reported in the year of sale, regardless of when the taxpayer receives the proceeds. Capital losses are netted against capital gains. A taxpayer can deduct up to $3,000 ($1,500 for MFS) of net capital losses against ordinary income in a tax year. Unused losses in excess of this limit are carried over to later years. The carryover losses are combined with gains and losses that occur in the next year.

Example: On April 1, 2018, Zayden sells Bitcoin for a total of $6,300. The Bitcoin was purchased on November 2, 2016, for $780. Zayden has a long-term capital gain of $5,520 on the sale. Also on April 1, 2018, Zayden sells Ethereum for $382. He had purchased Ethereum on February 2, 2018, for $966. Zayden therefore has a $584 short-term capital loss on the sale. His losses and gains are "netted" for the year. Zayden will report a long-term capital gain in 2018.

Virtual Currency	Basis	Sale Price	Gain or (Loss)
Bitcoin	$780	$6,300	Long-term gain $5,520
Ethereum	$966	$382	Short-term loss $584
Zayden's Net Capital Gain:			**$4,936**

Amounts carried over retain their character as either long-term or short-term and are reported on Schedule D. Thus, a long-term capital loss carried over to the next tax year will reduce that year's long-term capital gains before it reduces that year's short-term capital gains.

Note: Married taxpayers are actually at a disadvantage when deducting capital losses. On a joint return, the capital loss limit is $3,000, which is the same limit for single taxpayers. MFS filers only get half of that (a $1,500 capital loss limit).

Example: Kandi and Jerrod are married and file separate returns (MFS). In 2018, Kandi sells some stock and incurs a $5,000 capital loss. Jerrod also sells some stock and has a $12,500 capital gain. Kandi can only claim $1,500 of her loss on her tax return because she is filing MFS. Jerrod must pay tax on the entire gain on his separate tax return.

Example: Hubert purchased stock three years ago for $16,000. The stock declines in value, and he sells it in 2018 for $12,000. Hubert has a $4,000 long-term capital loss on the stock sale. He also has $60,000 of wages in 2018. He can claim $3,000 of his long-term capital loss against his ordinary income, thereby lowering his gross income to $57,000 ($60,000 - $3,000). The remainder of the long-term capital loss ($1,000) must be carried forward to the following tax year.

Example: Angelina is single. She purchased 50 shares of Formosa, Inc. stock five years ago for $19,000. Two years ago, she purchased 750 shares of Inertia, Inc. stock for $8,200. In 2018, Angelina sells all her stock. Her Formosa stock sells for $2,000, and her Inertia stock sells for $13,000. Angelina's gain and loss are both long-term because she held both stocks for more than one year. Her long-term loss and long-term gain are netted against each other, resulting in a net long-term capital loss, as follows:

Stock	Basis	Sale Price	Gain or (Loss)
Formosa Inc.	$19,000	$2,000	($17,000)
Inertia Inc.	$8,200	$13,000	$4,800

Angelina's net long-term capital loss in 2018: ($12,200)

Angelina also earned $55,000 in wages during the year. Angelina may deduct $3,000 of her capital losses against her wage income in the current year. The remaining capital losses must be "carried over" to a future tax year, starting with the next tax year.

A capital loss can be carried over indefinitely during the taxpayer's life. However, once a taxpayer dies, the capital losses not used on the final return cannot be carried over to a beneficiary or an heir. Capital losses always belong to the decedent. Any capital loss carryovers that are not used on the taxpayer's final return are essentially lost.

Example: Ethan has $15,000 of capital losses from the sale of cryptocurrency in 2018. On December 20, 2018, Ethan dies. His executor may claim the capital losses on his final individual tax return, up to the allowable limit. However, any unused capital losses cannot be carried over to a future year, because Ethan is dead. The losses do not transfer to Ethan's estate or to his heirs.

Worthless Securities

A taxpayer may choose to "abandon" a security that has lost its entire value in order to take advantage of the loss for tax purposes rather than retaining ownership. Stocks, stock rights, and bonds (other than those held for sale by a securities dealer) that became worthless during the tax year are treated as though they were sold for zero dollars on the last day of the tax year.

A loss from worthless securities receives special tax treatment. Unlike other losses, a taxpayer is allowed to amend a tax return for up to seven years in order to claim a loss from worthless securities. This is more than double the usual three-year statute of limitations for amending returns.

To abandon a worthless security, a taxpayer must permanently surrender all rights to it and receive no consideration in exchange. Taxpayers should report worthless securities on Form 8949, and indicate as a worthless security deduction by writing "WORTHLESS" in the applicable column of Form 8949.[71]

> **Example:** Leandro owned 500 shares of Crossroad Corporation stock. The company files for bankruptcy and the bankruptcy court extinguishes all rights of the former shareholders. Leandro learns of the bankruptcy court's decision in December 2018. Rather than wait for a formal notice from the court, he chooses to abandon all his Crossroad securities, knowing that his shares are essentially worthless. He takes a capital loss on his 2018 tax return, reflecting the value of his worthless shares as "zero."

Capital Gains from Mutual Funds

A mutual fund is a regulated investment company generally created by pooling funds of investors to allow them to take advantage of a diversity of investments and professional management. Two different types of transactions may result in taxable capital gains reporting by a taxpayer who invests in mutual funds.

First, profits resulting from investments made by the fund itself are reported to its own shareholders as capital gain distributions on Form 1099-DIV. The capital gain distributions are always taxed at long-term capital gains tax rates, without regard to how long a taxpayer has owned shares in the mutual fund.

In addition, if a taxpayer disposes of shares that represent all or a portion of his investment in the mutual fund itself, Form 1099-B will be issued. The taxable gain or loss that results from the sale or exchange of the taxpayer's shares in the mutual fund is reported on Form 1040, Schedule D. Brokers are now required to include the basis of mutual funds on Form 1099-B.

Wash Sales

A wash sale occurs when an investor sells a security to claim a capital loss, only to repurchase it again very soon thereafter. A taxpayer cannot deduct a loss on the sale of an investment if an identical investment was purchased within 30 days before or after the sale.

A wash sale is considered to have occurred when a taxpayer sells a security and, within 30 days:

- Buys the identical security,
- Acquires a substantially identical security in a taxable trade, or
- Acquires a contract or option to buy the identical security.

If a taxpayer's loss is disallowed because of the wash sale rules, he must add the disallowed loss to the basis of the new stock or securities. The result is an increase in the taxpayer's basis

---

[71] "Worthless securities" are stocks or bonds that have a market value of zero. A taxpayer may treat worthless securities as though they were sold or exchanged on the last day of the tax year.

in the new stock or securities. This adjustment postpones the loss deduction until the disposition of the new stock or securities.[72]

It is considered a wash sale if a taxpayer sells stock and his spouse then repurchases identical stock within 30 days, even if the spouses file separate tax returns.

> **Example:** Manuel sells 800 shares of Quanta Corporation stock on December 4, 2018, resulting in a loss of $3,200. He regrets selling the stock, so on January 2, 2019, he repurchases 800 shares of Quanta stock on the open market. Because of the IRS wash sale rules, all of the $3,200 loss is disallowed, and he must add the disallowed loss to the basis of the newly purchased shares. He cannot take the loss until he finally sells the repurchased shares at some later time.

For purposes of the wash sale rules, securities of one corporation are not considered identical to securities of another corporation. This means that a person can sell shares in one corporation and then purchase shares in a different corporation, and this will not trigger a wash sale. Similarly, preferred stock of a corporation is not considered identical to the common stock of the same corporation.

Home Sale Gain or Loss

The tax rules for the sale of a primary residence are advantageous for taxpayers. Most of the time, a home sale does not trigger a taxable gain. There are special rules regarding the sale of a taxpayer's primary residence. We will go over those rules later, in the chapter dedicated to nonrecognition property transactions (Unit 8). In this unit, we will only cover how to determine the basis of a home. The following are used to determine basis and figure the gain (or loss) on the sale of a home:

- Selling price
- Amount realized
- Basis
- Adjusted basis

Selling Price: The selling price is the total amount the taxpayer received for his main home. The "selling price" includes more than just cash. It includes all money, notes, mortgages, or other debts taken over by the buyer as part of the sale, and the fair market value of any other property or services that the seller received. Real estate sales proceeds are reported on Form 1099-S, *Proceeds from Real Estate Transactions*. If a taxpayer does not receive a Form 1099-S, he must rely upon sale documents and other records.

Amount Realized: The "amount realized" is the selling price minus selling expenses, which include commissions, advertising fees, legal fees, and loan charges paid by the seller, such as points.

Basis: The basis in a home is determined by how the taxpayer obtained the home. For example, if a taxpayer purchases a home, the basis is the cost of the home. If a taxpayer builds a

---

[72] Wash sale rules do not apply to trades of commodity futures contracts and foreign currencies. The rules also do not apply to professional securities dealers of stocks or securities.

home, the basis is the building cost plus the cost of land. If a taxpayer receives a home through inheritance or gift, the basis is either its FMV or the decedent's or donor's adjusted basis.

> **Example:** Misty is single. She sells her home for $350,000. She purchased the home 20 years ago for $50,000 and had lived in it continuously since then. She pays $4,000 in seller's fees to sell the home. Her amount realized in the sale is $346,000 ($350,000 - $4,000 = $346,000). Her basis is subtracted from her amount realized to figure her gain: ($346,000 - $50,000 basis) = $296,000.

If the taxpayer inherited the home, the basis is generally its FMV on the date of the decedent's death, or the later alternate valuation date chosen by the representative for the estate.

Adjusted Basis: The adjusted basis is the taxpayer's basis in the home increased or decreased by certain amounts. Increases include additions or improvements to the home that have a useful life of more than one year. Repairs that simply maintain a home in good condition are not considered improvements and should not be added to the basis of the property. Decreases to basis include deductible casualty losses, credits, and product rebates. Depreciation reduces basis for business assets, such as rental property, but is never taken on personal-use property.

> **The formula for figuring adjusted basis:**
>
> **Basis + Increases - Decreases = Adjusted Basis**

> **Example:** Raphael purchased his home ten years ago for $125,000. In 2018, he added another bathroom to the property at a cost of $25,000. Raphael's adjusted basis in the home is therefore $150,000 ($125,000 purchase price + $25,000 addition).

If the amount realized on the sale of a home is less than the adjusted basis, the difference is a loss. A loss on the sale of a primary residence can never be deducted.

If the amount realized is more than the adjusted basis of the property, the difference is a gain (but not always a *taxable* gain). As described in detail later, the taxpayer may be able to exclude all or part of the gain. If not excluded and the taxpayer owns a home for one year or less, the gain is reported as a short-term capital gain. If the taxpayer owns the home for more than one year, the gain is reported as a long-term capital gain.

Related Party Transaction Rules

Special rules apply to related party transactions, which are between two parties who are joined by a special relationship. If a taxpayer sells an asset to a close family member or to a business entity that the taxpayer controls, he may not receive all the benefits of the capital gains tax rates, and he may not be able to deduct his losses. The rules were made to prevent related persons and entities from shuffling assets back and forth and taking improper losses.

"50% Control" Rule: If a taxpayer controls *more than* 50% of a corporation or partnership, any property transactions between the taxpayer and the business are subject to related party transaction rules.

In general, a loss on the sale of property between related parties is not deductible. When the property is later sold to an unrelated party, a gain is recognized only to the extent it is more than the disallowed loss. If the property is later sold at a loss, the loss that was disallowed to the related party cannot be recognized. If a taxpayer sells or trades property at a loss (other than in the complete liquidation of a corporation), the loss is not deductible if the transaction is between the taxpayer and the following related parties:

- Members of an immediate family, including a spouse, siblings, half-siblings, direct ancestors (e.g., parents, grandparents) and lineal descendants of those persons (i.e., grandchildren.)

- A partnership or corporation that the taxpayer controls. A taxpayer "controls" an entity when he has more than 50% ownership in it. This also includes partial ownership by other family members.

- A tax-exempt or charitable organization controlled by the taxpayer or a member of his family

- Losses on sales between certain closely related trusts or business entities controlled by the same owners

Note: For purposes of this rule, the following are *not* considered related parties: uncles, aunts, nephews, nieces, cousins, step-children, step-parents, in-laws, and ex-spouses.

Example: Roxie purchases stock from her father for $8,600. Her father's basis in the stock is $11,000. Roxie later sells the stock on the open market for $6,900. Her recognized loss is $1,700 (her $8,600 basis minus $6,900). Roxie cannot deduct the loss that was disallowed to her father.

Example: Selma buys 300 shares of stock from her brother, Nolan, for $7,600. Nolan's cost basis in the stock is $10,000. Nolan cannot deduct the loss of $2,400 because of the related party transaction rules. Later, Selma sells the same stock on the open market for $10,500, realizing a gain of $2,900. Selma's reportable gain is $500 (the $2,900 gain minus the $2,400 loss that was not previously allowed to her brother).

Example: Irene sells 100 shares of stock to her stepbrother, Saul. She recognizes a $3,000 capital loss on the transaction. Since a stepbrother is not considered a related party for IRS purposes, she is allowed to take the loss on her tax return.

In the case of a related party transaction, if a taxpayer sells multiple pieces of property and some are at a gain while others are at a loss, the gains will generally be taxable while the losses cannot be used to offset the gains.

Installment Sales

An installment sale is a sale of property in which at least one payment is expected to be received after the tax year in which the sale occurs. If a taxpayer sells a property and receives payments over multiple years, he may use the installment method to defer tax by only reporting a portion of his gain as each installment is received. A taxpayer's gain, or gross profit, is the amount by which the selling price exceeds the adjusted basis in the property sold. A gross profit percentage is calculated by dividing the gross profit from the sale by the selling price.[73]

> **Study Note:** Test-takers may be required to determine gross profit percentage on an installment sale for either Part 1 or Part 2 of the EA exam.

Each payment received on an installment sale typically consists of the following three parts:

- Interest income

- Return of the adjusted basis in the property

- Gain on the sale (determined by applying the gross profit percentage to the amount of the payment received minus the interest portion)

In each year the taxpayer receives a payment, he must report the interest income and the portion that relates to his gain on the sale. The taxpayer does not include in income the part that is the return of his basis in the property.

> **Definition:** When a taxpayer disposes of certain types of property that have been depreciated, the property may be subject to **depreciation recapture**, which requires that the taxpayer report all or a portion of the prior depreciation deductions as ordinary income in the year of the sale.

> **Example:** In 2018, Sheri sells an empty lot with a basis of $40,000 for $100,000. Her gross profit is $60,000 ($100,000 - $40,000) for a gross profit percentage of 60%. She receives a $20,000 down payment and the buyer's note for $80,000. In 2018, Sheri must report $12,000 gain allocated from the down payment she received. The note provides for four annual payments of $20,000 each, plus 8% interest, beginning in 2019. Exclusive of the interest income, she must report $12,000 of her installment gain for each $20,000 payment received ($20,000 × .60 = $12,000).

The selling price includes the cash and any other property to be received from the buyer, any existing mortgage or debt the buyer pays or assumes, and any selling expenses the buyer pays.

However, if the buyer assumes or pays off a mortgage or other debt on the property sold, the calculation of gross profit percentage is affected. The mortgage assumption is considered a recovery of basis in the year of sale and is subtracted before calculating the gross profit percentage, except to the extent that it exceeds the adjusted basis of the property for installment sale purposes.

In contrast, if the property is sold to a buyer who holds a mortgage on it and the mortgage is canceled rather than assumed, the cancellation is treated as a payment received in the year of the sale and is not subtracted in calculating the gross profit percentage.

---

[73] For more information on installment sales and more extended examples, see Publication 537, *Installment Sales.*

Example: Sylvester sells property in an installment sale for $6,000. His gross profit is $1,500. The gross profit percentage on the sale is 25% ($1,500 ÷ $6,000). After subtracting interest, Sylvester reports 25% of each payment, including the down payment, as installment sale income in the year received. The remainder of each payment is the tax-free return of the property's basis.

If installment payments are made according to a schedule other than what was originally agreed, income is recognized according to the actual payments received. However, if the parties subsequently agree to adjust the selling price, the gross profit percentage must be recalculated, and income from future installments must be recognized based upon the adjusted gross profit.

If a taxpayer decides not to use the installment method, he must report all the gain in the year of the sale. Installment sale rules do not apply to property that is sold at a loss.

The installment method cannot be used for publicly traded securities, such as stocks and bonds. A taxpayer must report the gain on the sale of securities in the year of the sale, regardless of whether the proceeds are received in the following year.

Example: Wilmer owns 500 shares of stock, which he sells at a gain on December 29, 2018. Wilmer does not receive the proceeds until January 15, 2019. Wilmer is required to report the capital gain on the sale of the stock on his 2018 tax return. He cannot delay reporting the gain, and the sale is not considered an installment sale.

Installment sales to related persons are generally allowed. However, if a taxpayer sells a property to a related person who then sells or disposes of the property within two years of the original sale, the taxpayer will lose the benefit of installment sale reporting. Installment sales are reported on Form 6252, *Installment Sale Income,* which is attached to Form 1040. A taxpayer may also be required to complete Schedule D or Form 4797.

Example: Sam sells a plot of land to his daughter, Tamara. The sale price is $25,000, and Sam realizes a profit on the sale of $10,000. Tamara agrees to pay in five installments of $5,000. A year later, Tamara decides she no longer wants the property, and she sells the land to another person. Sam must report the entire profit of $10,000 on the sale, even though he may not have received all the installment payments. The installment sale method is disallowed on the related party sale because the property was disposed of during the two-year holding period.

Reporting Capital Asset Sales

An individual usually owns many assets, including investments, like stocks and bonds. The gain or loss on each asset is figured separately and the tax treatment depends on the type of asset that is sold. In the case of capital assets,[74] the gains and losses are typically reported on these two forms:

- Schedule D, *Capital Gains and Losses*, and

- Form 8949, *Sales and Other Dispositions of Capital Assets.*

---

[74] Capital assets include homes, rental properties, stocks, and even collectibles. In the case of individuals, a "capital asset" is typically anything the taxpayer owns for personal or investment purposes.

Schedule D is used to report gain or loss on the sale of investment property and most capital gain (or loss) transactions. However, before the taxpayer can calculate their net gain or loss on Schedule D, he may also have to complete Form 8949, *Sales and Other Dispositions of Capital Assets.* Form 8949 reports the details about each stock trade the taxpayer makes during the year. There are two parts to Form 8949. The first is for short-term assets, and the second part is for long-term assets.

Form 8949 is used to report the following:

- The sale or exchange of capital assets

- Gains from involuntary conversions (other than from casualty or theft)

- Nonbusiness bad debts and

- Worthless securities

Some transactions can be reported directly on Schedule D without needing to report them on Form 8949. A taxpayer can skip filing Form 8949 if both of the following are true:

- He received a Form 1099-B that shows basis was reported to the IRS and does not show a nondeductible wash sale loss in box 5, and

- He does not need to make any adjustments to the basis or type of gain or loss (short-term or long-term) reported on Form 1099-B, or to his gain or loss.

The information reported on Form 8949 describes all sales and exchanges of capital assets, including stocks, bonds, and mutual funds. This form must be filed along with Schedule D, which contains the summary of all capital gains and losses.

Example: Reese owns 2,000 shares of Boathouse Makers Inc. She purchased the stock five years ago for $7,500. In 2018, the company files for bankruptcy and Reese's stock becomes worthless. She chooses to abandon the securities to take a tax deduction in 2018. Then she reports the valueless stock on Form 8949 and treats the abandonment as a sale. For the sale date, she puts December 31, 2018, and she lists her proceeds as $0. She now has a long-term capital loss of ($7,500) that she can use to offset other taxable income.

Note: Once a corporation has been delisted from a stock exchange as a result of bankruptcy, the stockholder will often have to fill out a worthless securities processing request. Most brokerage firms will purchase worthless stock for a nominal amount (such as a penny), to provide closure and an official sale date to the customer on their brokerage statement.

Example: Argus receives a Form 1099-B reporting the sale of stock he had held for five years. It shows gross proceeds of $8,000 and cost basis of $3,000. Box 3 is checked, meaning that his basis was reported to the IRS. Argus does not need to make any adjustments to the amounts reported on Form 1099-B. He does not report the amounts on Form 8949. Instead, he enters the amounts directly onto his Schedule D.

(Test yourself first; then check the correct answers at the end of this quiz.)

1. Xavier owns 100% of the stock in XA Corporation. Gerald owns 100% of the stock in GA Corporation. In 2018, XA Corporation sold used machinery to GA Corporation at a $52,000 loss. Xavier and Gerald are stepbrothers. With regard to the related party transaction loss rules, how should this transaction between XA Corporation and GE Corporation be handled?

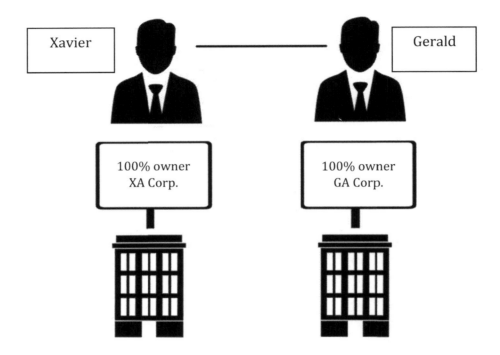

A. Any losses on the sale of property between the corporations would be disallowed.
B. The related party transaction rules do not apply to their corporations, but they would apply individually to Xavier and Gerald.
C. The related party transaction rules apply individually to Xavier and Gerald, but not to their corporations.
D. The related party transaction rules do not apply in this scenario.

2. When trying to determine the holding period for investment property, which of the following is important?

A. The cost of the property
B. In the case of gifted property, the amount of the gift
C. The date of acquisition
D. The amount realized in the transaction

3. Consuela purchased 1,000 shares of Hometown Mutual Fund on February 15, 2014, for $15 per share. On January 31, 2018, she sold all her shares for $3.75 per share. She also earned $45,000 of wages in 2018. She has no other transactions during the year. How should this transaction be reported on her tax return?

A. She has a capital loss of $11,250 that she can deduct against her wage income.
B. She must carry over the losses to a future tax year and offset future capital gains.
C. She can deduct a $3,000 capital loss on her tax return, and the remainder of the losses will carry forward to subsequent years.
D. She can deduct a $5,000 capital loss on her tax return, and the remainder of the losses will carry forward to subsequent years.

4. Noah bought two blocks (each of 400 shares) of Acme Corporation stock. He purchased the first block in April 2015 for $1,200 and the second block in March 2018 for $1,600. In June of 2018, he sold 400 shares for $1,500 but did not specify which block of stocks he sold. Noah's stock sale results in a:

A. Short-term loss of $100
B. Short-term gain of $300
C. Long-term loss of $100
D. Long-term gain of $300

5. Oliver operates an electronics repair business as a sole proprietorship. In 2018, Oliver sold equipment for $15,000 that was acquired for use in the business. The original purchase price of the property was $12,000, and Oliver had claimed depreciation of $3,000 related to the property. He accepted a down payment of $5,000 from the buyer, along with a note requiring additional payments of $2,500 plus interest in each of the next four years. Based on the information provided, what amount of taxable income will result in 2018 if Oliver uses the installment method to report the sale of this property?

A. Capital gain of $5,000 and ordinary income of $1,000
B. Capital gain of $1,000 and ordinary income of $3,000
C. Capital gain of $2,000
D. Capital gain of $1,000 and ordinary income of $1,000

6. Which of the following losses is deductible?

A. A loss on the sale of a primary residence
B. A loss on the sale of a vacation home
C. A loss on the sale of a personal-use mobile home
D. A loss on the sale of rental property

7. Nikhil's adjusted basis in 500 shares of Edico Corporation was $2,550. He owned the shares for three months. If he sold 500 shares for $3,300, what is the resulting gain or loss?

A. $750 short-term gain
B. $700 short-term gain
C. $750 long-term gain
D. $750 long-term loss

8. Ruben bought 100 shares of stock on October 1, 2017, when the share price was $26. He sold the stock for $20 a share on October 1, 2018. How should this trade be reported, and what is the nature of Ruben's gain or loss?

A. A short-term capital loss of $600
B. A long-term capital loss of $600
C. This is a wash sale, and there is no gain or loss
D. A short-term capital loss of $500

9. Five years ago, Marsha bought 100 shares of stock. Her sale date was March 10, 2018. Marsha's original cost for the stock was $10,110, plus an additional $35 of broker's fees. When she sold the stock, she received gross proceeds of $8,859. What is the net gain or loss from this transaction?

A. $1,286 long-term capital loss
B. $1,286 short-term capital loss
C. $1,251 long-term capital loss
D. $1,251 long-term capital gain

10. Emmanuel bought ten shares of Griffon Corporation stock on May 2, 2017. He sold them for a $7,000 loss on May 2, 2018. He has no other capital gains or losses. He also has $20,000 of wage income. How must Emmanuel treat this transaction on his tax return?

A. He can deduct the $7,000 as a long-term capital loss on his return.
B. He can deduct the $7,000 as a short-term capital loss on his return.
C. He can deduct $3,000 as a short-term capital loss to offset his wage income on his return. The remaining amount, $4,000, must be carried over to future tax years.
D. He cannot deduct any of the capital loss; it must be carried over to future tax years.

11. Norma sells an empty lot with an adjusted basis of $20,000. Her buyer assumes an existing mortgage on the property of $15,000 and agrees to pay Norma $10,000, with a cash down payment of $2,000 and then $2,000 every year (plus 12% interest) in each of the next four years. What is Norma's gross profit and gross profit percentage on the installment sale?

A. The gross profit is $5,000, and the gross profit percentage is 20%.
B. The gross profit is $10,000, and the gross profit percentage is 100%.
C. The gross profit is $15,000, and the gross profit percentage is 20%.
D. The gross profit is $5,000, and the gross profit percentage is 50%.

12. Mario purchased his main home five years ago for $150,000. He sold it at a loss for $115,000 in 2018. Which of the following statements is correct?

A. If he itemizes deductions, Mario can claim a loss of $35,000 on his 2018 tax return.
B. Mario can claim a loss of $3,000 in 2018 but must carry over the remainder to future years until the loss is completely deducted.
C. Mario can claim a loss of $35,000 because the home sale was an involuntary conversion.
D. Mario cannot claim a loss for the sale of his home.

13. Tahir purchased 100 shares in Foresthill Mutual Fund in April 2018 for $750. He received a capital gain distribution of $120 in 2018, but he did not sell his shares in the mutual fund during the year. The $120 was reported to him on Form 1099-DIV. How should this be reported on his tax return?

A. He must reduce his stock's basis by $120.
B. He must report the $120 as interest income.
C. He must report the $120 as a long-term capital gain.
D. He must report the $120 as a short-term capital gain.

14. Melissa purchased 1,000 shares of Sunshine Foods Inc. stock five years ago at $10 per share. She sold 900 shares on January 15, 2018, at $9 per share, resulting in a $900 loss. Melissa's husband, Alex, purchased 900 shares of Sunshine Foods Company stock on February 10, 2018. Alex and Melissa keep their finances separate and will file MFS. Which of the following statements is correct?

A. Melissa can deduct the $900 capital loss on her tax return.
B. Melissa has a wash sale, and her loss is not deductible.
C. Alex can deduct the loss on his separate tax return.
D. None of the above.

15. Phil and Sharon owned a vacation home for 14 months before selling it for $254,000. Their adjusted basis in the home was $232,000, and they incurred $12,500 of selling expenses. Prior to the sale, they did not rent the home. What is the nature and amount of their gain?

A. $22,000 long-term capital gain
B. $9,500 long-term capital gain
C. $9,500 short-term capital gain
D. $34,500 long-term capital gain

16. Colin purchased 100 shares of Entertainment Digital Media stock for $1,000 on January 1, 2018. He sold these shares for $750 on December 22, 2018. Colin has seller's remorse, and on January 19, 2019, he repurchases 100 shares of Entertainment Digital for $800. Which of the following statements is correct?

A. Colin can report a $250 capital loss in 2018.
B. Colin can report a taxable gain in 2019.
C. Colin cannot deduct his stock loss of $250 and must add the disallowed loss to his basis.
D. Colin can report a $250 capital loss in 2019.

17. What is the maximum number of years a taxpayer can carry over an unused capital loss?

A. One year
B. Two years
C. Five years
D. As many years as required to utilize the entire deduction

18. Francoise bought shares in the Vanest Mutual Fund four years ago for $8 a share. Since then, she received the following nondividend distributions:

- 2015: $2 per share
- 2016: $2 per share
- 2017: $3 per share
- 2018: $3 per share

What is Francoise's basis in the stock and what amount of gain (if any) must she report in 2018?

A. $0 basis; $6 gain
B. $14 basis; $0 gain
C. $0 basis; $2 gain
D. $8 basis; $3 gain

1. The answer is D. The related party transaction rules do not apply in this scenario. Related party transaction rules are designed to prevent improper deductions between two parties joined by a special relationship. However, the related party transaction rules do not apply to stepsiblings, so there are no related party issues between Xavier and Gerald or their corporations. Related party transaction rules do not apply to uncles, aunts, nieces, nephews, cousins, stepchildren, stepsiblings, stepparents, or in-laws.

2. The answer is C. To determine the holding period; a taxpayer must begin counting on the day *after* the acquisition date. If a taxpayer's holding period is not more than one year, the taxpayer will have a short-term gain or loss. The amount realized in the transaction has no bearing on the holding period.

3. The answer is C. Consuela cannot deduct all her stock losses in the current year. She can claim a $3,000 capital loss on her 2018 tax return, and the remainder of the losses will carry forward to subsequent years.

4. The answer is D. Noah realized a long-term gain of $300 because the basis and holding period would automatically default to the oldest block of shares. The "FIFO method" is used if the taxpayer cannot or does not specifically identify the shares sold.

5. The answer is B. The amount of depreciation deducted for the property ($3,000) is recaptured and reported in 2018 as ordinary income. This amount is added back to the adjusted basis of $9,000 to determine the adjusted basis for the installment sale ($12,000). This amount is subtracted from the total proceeds of the sale ($15,000) to determine the gross profit of $3,000, which derives a gross profit percentage of 20%. This percentage is applied to the portion of proceeds received in 2018 ($5,000) to determine Oliver's capital gain recognizable this year.

Original purchase price	$12,000
Minus depreciation deductions	(3,000)
Adjusted basis at date of sale	9,000
Depreciation recapture	3,000
Adjusted basis for installment sale	(12,000)
Proceeds of sale	15,000
Gross profit percentage	20%
Proceeds in 2018	5,000
Capital gain to be recognized	**$1,000**

6. The answer is D. Losses on the sale of personal-use property, including a loss on the sale of a primary residence or a vacation home, are not deductible. Only losses associated with business property and investment property (such as stocks and bonds or rental property) are deductible.

7. The answer is A. The sales price is $750 more than the adjusted basis of the shares. The gain is short-term since Nikhil did not own the shares for more than one year.

8. The answer is A. Ruben has a short-term capital loss of $600 = (100 shares × $26) - (100 shares × $20). Ruben's holding period was not more than one year, which means that the loss must be treated as short-term. To determine the holding period, you must begin counting on the day *after* the date the taxpayer acquires the property.

9. The answer is A. The answer is calculated as follows: The original basis is increased by the broker's commission. Therefore, Marsha's adjusted basis is $10,145 ($10,110 + $35). The gross proceeds from the sale are $8,859, which is subtracted from the basis, resulting in a long-term capital loss of $1,286 ($8,859 - $10,145) because she held the stock for more than one year.

10. The answer is C. Emmanuel has a short-term capital loss because he did not hold the stock for more than one year. He can deduct $3,000 of the loss in 2018, netting against his wage income. The remaining amount, $4,000, must be carried over to future tax years. A capital loss carryover retains its character as either long-term or short-term.

11. The answer is D. Norma's gross profit is $5,000, and the gross profit percentage is 50%. Her selling price is $25,000 ($2,000 down payment + $8,000 to be paid over four years + $15,000 for buyer's assumption of mortgage). Therefore, Norma's gross profit is $5,000 ($25,000 – $20,000 adjusted basis). If the entire selling price were payable in cash, her gross profit percentage would have been 20% ($5,000/$25,000). However, if a buyer assumes or pays off a mortgage or other debt on a property, the calculation of the installment sale gross profit percentage is affected. The mortgage assumption is subtracted before calculating the gross profit percentage, except to the extent that it exceeds the adjusted basis of the property for installment sale purposes, to derive what the IRS calls "contract price," rather than selling price. The mortgage assumption is considered a recovery of the seller's basis in the year of sale. Although the mortgage assumption is considered a payment, none of the gross profit is recognized in connection with the assumption. Instead, in this case, the contract price is considered to be $10,000 ($25,000 selling price - $15,000 mortgage assumption). Therefore, Norma's gross profit percentage is 50% ($5,000 ÷ $10,000). Norma must report half of each payment received as gain from the sale. She must also report all interest received as ordinary income.

12. The answer is D. Losses on the sale of personal-use property, including a personal residence, are never deductible. If the house had been a rental property, however, the loss would have been deductible and reported on Form 4797 and potentially Schedule D as well.

13. The answer is C. Tahir must report the $120 as a long-term capital gain. Mutual funds frequently distribute capital gains to shareholders. Capital gain distributions for mutual funds are always taxed as long-term capital gains, no matter how long a taxpayer has actually held the mutual fund shares.

14. The answer is B. The loss is disallowed. Melissa has a wash sale because her spouse repurchased identical securities within 30 days. It does not matter if they file separate returns. If a taxpayer sells stock and her spouse then repurchases identical stock within 30 days, the taxpayer has a wash sale. The fact that the taxpayers file MFS is irrelevant—the wash sale rules still apply, even if the taxpayers file separate returns.

15. The answer is B. The sale of a second home is a taxable event in the event of a gain. Since Phil and Sharon owned the property for longer than one year, their gain is long-term. The gain is calculated as follows:

Sale price	$254,000
Minus selling expenses	(12,500)
Net proceeds	241,500
Minus adjusted basis in the property	(232,000)
Taxable gain on the sale	**$9,500**

16. The answer is C. Because Colin bought shares in the same corporation within 30 days of its sale at a loss, this is considered a "wash sale" and he cannot deduct his loss of $250 on the sale. Instead, he must add the disallowed loss to the cost of the new stock to obtain his adjusted basis in the new stock. It would be treated as if he had never sold the shares in the first place.

17. The answer is D. Unused capital losses may be carried over indefinitely until they are utilized. There is no limit to how many years an individual taxpayer can claim the losses. However, capital losses do not transfer to an estate or surviving spouse after the taxpayer has died.

18. The answer is C. The first $8 of nondividend distributions per share reduces Francoise's basis to zero. In 2018, the final $2 of nondividend distribution must be reported as capital gain.

Unit 8: Nonrecognition Property Transactions

For additional information read:
Publication 544, *Sales and Other Dispositions of Assets*
Publication 523, *Selling Your Home*

For some transactions in which a taxpayer sells or exchanges property, gains may be nontaxable, partially taxable, or deferred. Three of the most common types of nonrecognition transactions involve:

- **Sale of a main home** (section 121, excluded gain)
- **Like-kind exchanges** (section 1031 nontaxable/deferred exchange)
- **Involuntary conversions** (section 1033 exchange)

Note: For Part 1 of the EA Exam, you will be tested primarily on the sale of a main home, involuntary conversions of personal-use property, and like-kind exchanges of residential rental property (Form 1040, Schedule E). For Part 2 of the EA exam, you will be tested on nonrecognition property transactions, but exclusively with business or rental property.

Sale of Main Home (Section 121 Exclusion)

In many cases, a taxpayer may exclude the gain from the sale of a main home. Up to $250,000 of gain may be excluded by single filers and up to $500,000 by joint filers. Generally, if the taxpayer can exclude all of the gain, it is not even necessary to report the sale. However, if part of the gain is taxable, the sale must be reported on Form 8949. Gain from the sale of a residence that is not the taxpayer's main home must be reported as taxable income.

The section 121 exclusion applies only to a "main home" and not to rental properties, vacation homes, or second homes. A taxpayer's main home is the residence where he lives most of the time. It does not have to be a traditional house. The main home can be a house, houseboat, mobile home, cooperative apartment, or condominium. To qualify as a home, it must have sleeping, kitchen, and bathroom facilities.

Example: Parker owns and lives in a house in Phoenix, Arizona. He also owns a lake cottage, which he uses only during the summer. The house in Phoenix is his main home; the lake cottage is not. Parker sells the lake cottage and has $100,000 of capital gain on the sale. The gain cannot be excluded because the cottage is not his main home. He must pay tax on the entire gain.

Example: Mickie lives in one-half of a duplex she owns and lets her best friend live in the other unit of the duplex rent-free. She purchased the duplex ten years ago for $200,000. In 2018, Mickie sells the duplex for $340,000, a gain of $140,000. Since only half of the duplex counts as her main home, Mickie may exclude only half of the gain ($70,000). She must report the other $70,000 as long-term capital gain.

If the home was used for business purposes or as rental property, the gain is reported on Form 4797, *Sales of Business Property.* If a taxpayer took depreciation deductions because he used his home as a rental or for other business purposes, he cannot exclude the part of the gain equal to any deductible depreciation. Section 121 applies only to the nonbusiness portion of a home.

Eligibility Requirements for Section 121

To be eligible for the section 121 exclusion, a taxpayer must:

- Have sold his main home
- Meet "ownership and use" tests
- Not have excluded gain in the two years prior to the current sale of a home

Ownership Test and Use Test

The IRS figures the ownership and use tests *separately*, and the time periods do not have to be continuous. During the five-year period ending on the date of the sale, the taxpayer must have:

- Owned the home for at least two years (the ownership test), and
- Lived in the home as his main home for at least two years (the use test).

Example: Lindsey is 25 years old and single. Since she was a born, Lindsay has lived with her parents in the home her parents owned. On January 6, 2018, she bought her childhood home from her parents. Her parents moved out of the home and purchased a home in another state. Lindsey continued to live in the home until December 14, 2018, when she sold it because she wanted a bigger house. Lindsay does not meet the requirements for exclusion. Although she *lived* in the property as her main home for more than two years, she did not *own* it for the required two years. Therefore, she does not meet both the ownership and use tests. She must report and pay tax on all her gain from the sale.

A taxpayer meets both tests if he *owned* and *lived* in the property as his main home for either 24 full months or 730 days (365 × 2) during the five-year period.

Note: The required two years of ownership and use do not have to be continuous. Further, ownership and use tests can be met during different two-year periods.

Example: Mabel bought a house in September 2013. After living there for ten months, she moved in with her boyfriend and kept her house vacant. They later broke up, and Mabel moved back into her own house in 2016. She lived there for an additional 16 months until she sold it in September 2018. Mabel meets the ownership and use tests because, during the five-year period ending on the date of sale, she owned the house for five years and lived in the house a total of 26 months.

Short, temporary absences, even if the property is rented during those absences, are still counted as periods of use. Short absences include vacations and other seasonal absences. Longer breaks, such as a one-year sabbatical, are not included.

Example: In 2010, Lionel began living in an apartment he rented from a landlord. The apartment was converted to a condominium, which he purchased on December 1, 2015. In 2017, Lionel became seriously ill, and on April 14, 2017, he moved into his daughter's home. After several months, he did not recover from his illness, so he decided to remain living in his daughter's home. He did not return to his condo, and on July 10, 2018, while still living in his daughter's home, Lionel sold his condo. He can exclude all the gain on the sale because he meets the ownership and use tests. His five-year "lookback" period is from July 11, 2013, to July 10, 2018 (five years before the date he actually sold the condo). He *owned* the condo from December 1, 2015, until July 10, 2018 (more than two years). He *lived* there from 2010 until April 14, 2017 (more than two years), so he would qualify to exclude all the gain, even though his ownership and use periods do not always overlap.

Example: Juanita bought her home on February 1, 2014. Each year, she left her home for a three-month vacation in Ecuador. Juanita sold the house on March 1, 2018. She may exclude up to $250,000 of gain. Her vacations are considered short temporary absences and are counted toward her periods of use.

Different Rules for Married Homeowners

The ownership and use tests are applied differently to married homeowners. Married homeowners can exclude gain of up to $500,000 if they meet all of the following conditions:

- They file a joint return.
- Either spouse meets the ownership test (only one is required to own the home).
- Both spouses meet the use test.
- Neither spouse has excluded gain in the two years before the current sale of the home.

If they do not satisfy these requirements, the couple cannot claim the maximum $500,000 exclusion for married couples. However, one spouse may figure his or her exclusion separately, if only one spouse qualifies.

Example: Irene owns her home and has lived in it continuously for the last seven years. She meets Harold and marries him in September 2018. They move in together, but Harold doesn't like Irene's house, and he convinces her to sell it a few months later. Irene sells the home on December 10, 2018, and has $350,000 of gain. Irene meets the ownership and use tests, but Harold does not meet the use test because he only lived in the house for a few months. Irene can exclude up to $250,000 of gain on her 2018 tax return, whether she files MFJ or MFS. The $500,000 exclusion for joint returns does not apply.

Example: Hubert owns a home that he has lived in continuously for a decade. On June 1, 2014, he marries Jasmine. She moves in, and they both live in the house together until December 1, 2018, when the house is sold. Hubert meets the ownership test and the use test. Jasmine does not own the home because Hubert is listed as the sole owner of the property. However, she meets the "use test" because she lived in the home for at least two years. Therefore, on a jointly filed return, they can claim the maximum $500,000 exclusion.

Note: This "special rule" for the holding period also applies to a home that is transferred by a spouse in a divorce. The receiving spouse is considered to have owned the home during any period of time that the transferor owned it.

Legally married same-sex spouses are eligible for the maximum $500,000 exclusion from gain on their jointly filed returns. If an unmarried couple owns and lives in a house together, and later gets married, the $500,000 exclusion applies if they file a joint return. If the couples file separate returns, each spouse would figure their exclusion separately on their own return.

Example: Royce and Felipe were legally married in California a year ago. In 2018, they sell the house they had co-owned and lived in together for ten years. They are both listed as co-owners on the deed, even though they were not married when they bought the home. The house sold for $575,000 more than they paid for it. Royce and Felipe may claim the maximum $500,000 exclusion for married couples when they file jointly in 2018. If they chose to file separate returns, each one would be eligible for a $250,000 exclusion on their own, separate returns. The remaining $75,000 of gain is taxable as long-term capital gain. Royce and Felipe would have to recognize the gain whether they file jointly or separately.

Unrelated Individuals: An unmarried couple or other taxpayers who own a home and live together may take the $250,000 exclusion individually on their separate returns if they meet the use and ownership tests.

Example: Salma and Carolyn are sisters. They are both widowed in 2018 and decided to purchase a home and live together. If they later sell the home, the ownership and use tests would apply to them individually. Each could claim an exclusion of up to $250,000 for her portion of the sale on her individual return.

Deceased Spouses: When a taxpayer's spouse dies, the taxpayer is considered to have owned and lived in a home during any period of time that the spouse owned and lived in it as a main home (provided that the taxpayer did not remarry before the date of sale). In effect, the holding period of the deceased spouse is "tacked on" for surviving spouses. As a result, the surviving spouse may exclude up to $500,000 of gain even if he sells the home within two years from the date of death of the deceased spouse.

Example: Harmony owned and lived in her home for seven years. She married Gerard in April 2018, and he moved into the home with her. Harmony died six months later, and Gerard inherited the property. He did not remarry. Gerard decides to sell the home on December 1, 2018. Even though he did not own or live in the house for two years, he meets the test requirements because his period of ownership and use includes the period that Harmony owned and used the property before her death. Gerard may exclude up to $500,000 of the gain under the special rule that applies to deceased spouses.

Military Personnel Exception: Members of the armed forces are often required to move and might have difficulty meeting the tests for ownership and use within the five-year period prior to the sale of a home. The five-year period can be suspended for up to ten years for U.S. military[75] and Foreign Service personnel, Peace Corps workers, and intelligence officers that

---

[75] This includes members of the U.S. Army, Navy, Air Force, Marine Corps, etc.

are on official extended duty. This provides the taxpayer a better opportunity to meet the two-year use test even if he and/or his spouse did not actually live in the home during the normal five-year period required of other taxpayers.

> **Example:** Ensign Smith is a naval officer. He is single and owns his own home. Ensign Smith bought and moved into his home on January 2, 2010. He lived in it as his main home for 2½ years. For the following 6 years, he didn't live in the home because he was on qualified official extended duty with the U.S. Navy. He did not return to the home. Ensign Smith sold his home for a $125,000 gain on December 26, 2018. To meet the use test, he may suspend the normal 5-year test period for the time he was on qualifying official extended duty. This means that Ensign Smith can disregard those 6 years when he is calculating his period of "ownership and use." He meets the "ownership and use" tests because he owned and lived in the home for at least 2½ years. Ensign Smith may exclude all the gain from the sale on his individual tax return.

Disability Exception: There is an exception to the use test if, during the five-year period before the sale of the home, a taxpayer becomes physically or mentally unable to care for himself, but he has owned and lived in the home for at least one year. The taxpayer is considered to have lived in the home during any time that he is forced to live in a licensed facility, including a nursing home. The taxpayer must still meet the two-year ownership test.

Reduced Exclusions

A taxpayer who owned and used a home for less than two years (and therefore does not meet the ownership and use tests), or who has used the home sale exclusion within the prior two-year period may be able to claim a reduced exclusion under certain conditions.

This may apply if a home sale has occurred primarily because of "unforeseen circumstances" during the taxpayer's period of use and ownership. Unforeseen circumstances include the following:

- Death, divorce, or legal separation
- Certain health reasons related to care for the taxpayer, a spouse, a child, or certain other related persons. The related person does not have to be a dependent for the reduced exclusion to apply.
- Unemployment or a job change. The job-change exclusion applies if a new job is at least 50 miles farther from the old home than was the former place of employment. If there was no former place of employment, the distance between the new place of employment and the old home must be at least 50 miles.
- Multiple births resulting from the same pregnancy
- Damage to the residence resulting from a disaster, an act of war, or terrorism
- Involuntary conversion of the property

The circumstances may involve the taxpayer, his spouse, a co-owner, or a member of the taxpayer's household. The IRS also has the discretion to deem other circumstances as "unforeseen."

Example: Farrell purchased his new home in Mississippi on January 10, 2018, but he lost his job shortly after he moved in. He found a new job in Alaska and sold his house in November 30, 2018, generating a small profit of $6,000 on the sale. Because the distance between Farrell's new place of employment and his former home is at least 50 miles, the sale satisfies the distance requirement. Farrell's sale of his home is due to a change in place of employment, and he is entitled to claim a reduced exclusion on his gain from the sale of his home.

The reduced exclusion amount equals the full $250,000 (or $500,000 for married couples filing jointly) multiplied by a fraction. The numerator is the *shorter* of:

- The period the taxpayer owned and used the home as a principal residence during the five-year period ending on the sale date, or

- The period between the last sale for which the taxpayer claimed the exclusion and the sale date for the home currently being sold.

The denominator is two years or the equivalent in months or days. Thus, the amount of the reduced exclusion is figured by multiplying the full exclusion amount by the number of days or months the taxpayer owned and used the property and dividing by either 730 days or 24 months.

Example: Elena, a single taxpayer, lived in her principal residence in San Francisco for one full year (365 days) before selling it. The sale generated a $260,000 gain. Even though she only lived in the house for a year, she qualifies for the reduced exclusion because she is pregnant with twins (multiple births exclusion). Elena can exclude $125,000 of gain ($250,000 × [365 ÷ 730]).

Land Sales: If a taxpayer sells the land on which his main home is located but not the house itself, he cannot exclude the gain. Similarly, the sale of a vacant plot of land with no house on it does not qualify for the section 121 exclusion.

Example: Bernarda purchased an empty lot three years ago for $90,000, planning to build her dream home. Construction was delayed and her house was never completed. In December 2018, Bernarda sells the land for $150,000. She owned the property for more than a year, so she has $60,000 of long-term capital gain. None of the gain can be excluded from income because there is no residence on the property. Section 121 only applies to homes, not to empty land.

If a taxpayer sells a vacant lot that is directly adjacent to his main home, he may be able to exclude the gain from the sale under some (rare) circumstances. Gain from the sale of vacant land that was used *in connection* with a principal residence may be excluded if the land sale occurs within two years before or after the sale of the home.

The land must have been adjacent to the land on which the home was located, and the taxpayer must have owned and used the land as part of their home and not for any business purpose. The sale of the land and the sale of the home are treated as one sale for purposes of the exclusion.

Like-Kind Exchanges (Section 1031 Exchange)

A section 1031 *like-kind exchange* occurs when a taxpayer exchanges business or investment property for similar property.

> **Note:** Starting in 2018, the TCJA changes the rules for like-kind exchanges. Going forward, like-kind exchanges will only apply to real property (real estate). They no longer apply to other property, such as machinery or livestock. Therefore any "exchange" of personal property will be treated as a non-cash sale and will not qualify for nonrecognition treatment.[76] This provision is permanent.

If the exchange qualifies under section 1031, the taxpayer does not recognize any resulting gain and cannot deduct any losses until he later disposes of the property received. To qualify for nonrecognition treatment, the exchange must meet all of the following conditions:

- The property must be held for investment or for productive use in a business. Property held for personal use, such as a personal residence, does not qualify.

- The property must NOT be "held primarily for sale" (such as inventory).

- There must be an actual exchange of two or more assets or properties (the exchange of *cash* for *property* is always treated as a sale, not as an exchange).

- For instances in which a property is transferred in exchange for like-kind property to be received later (known as a deferred exchange), the property to be received must be identified in writing (or actually received) within 45 days after the date of transfer of the property given up.

- A "qualified intermediary" must be procured to facilitate the exchange using escrow accounts. This type of qualified intermediary (sometimes also known as an exchange accommodator or facilitator) promises to return the proceeds of the exchange to the transferor of the property.

Further, the replacement property in a section 1031 exchange must be received by the earlier of:

- The 180th day after the date on which the property given up was transferred, or

- The due date, including extensions, of the tax return for the year in which the transfer of that property occurs. The IRS is very strict about these deadlines.

Taxpayers report like-kind exchanges on Form 8824, *Like-Kind Exchanges*. The most common type of section 1031 exchange is a simultaneous swap of one residential rental property for another. However, taxpayers may exchange different types of real property, including buildings, farmland, timberland, even undeveloped land.

In general, any exchange of any real property generally qualifies as like-kind, regardless of how each property is used or whether each property is improved or unimproved. For instance, the exchange of an office building for farmland would qualify, as would the exchange of an apartment complex for an office building.

---

[76] The prior law that allowed like-kind exchanges of personal property will still apply if one leg of the exchange was completed on or before December 31, 2017, as long as all the other requirements are met.

Nonqualifying Exchanges: Personal-use realty is not eligible for a like-kind exchange. So, the exchange of a personal residence for another personal residence does not qualify. The exchange of property within the United States for similar property *outside* the United States also would not be a qualifying exchange. Foreign realty is not eligible for nonrecognition treatment. And remember, inventory is never eligible for like-kind treatment.

Example: Lawrence is a professional real estate developer. Lawrence purchases large tracts of land and then markets and sells the subdivided lots for development. All of the lots he purchases are available for sale to customers. In this case, the land lots are not capital assets, because Lawrence is a professional real estate dealer: he is essentially selling inventory. Lawrence cannot use section 1031 to escape recognition of gain on the transfer or sale of his land lots.

Example: Madalynn is a full-time house-flipper. She buys distressed properties at auction, fixes them up, and then re-sells them. She does not rent them out or live in the properties while they are being rehabbed. In 2018, she has five houses that are in the process of being flipped. Once the restorations are complete, Madalynn intends to re-sell the homes to future buyers. The properties are treated as inventory, rather than capital assets. Therefore, none of the properties would be eligible for a section 1031 exchange.

Example: Rachel exchanges a residential rental in Hawaii with an adjusted basis of $100,000 with a vacation property in Cancun, Mexico. The Cancun property has a fair market value of $145,000. The exchange of foreign realty for real property in the United States does not qualify for section 1031 treatment. Instead, the transaction is treated as a sale. Since the exchange does not qualify for nonrecognition treatment, Rachel must recognize $45,000 of capital gain on the transaction. Her basis in the Cancun property is $145,000, which would be the same treatment if the property had been purchased with cash.

Taxable Exchanges: If a taxpayer receives property in exchange for other property that is not similar or related in use to the property exchanged, he may need to recognize gain if the fair market value of the property received is greater than the adjusted basis of the property exchanged. His basis in the property received is generally its FMV at the time of the exchange.

Cash Boot and Mortgage Boot

Although the Internal Revenue Code itself does not use the term "boot," it is frequently used to describe cash or other property added to an exchange to compensate for a difference in the values of properties traded. A taxpayer must generally not receive "boot" in an exchange in order for the exchange to be completely tax-free.

This doesn't mean that the exchange is not valid, but the taxpayer who receives boot may have to recognize taxable gain to the extent of the cash and the FMV of unlike property received, but the recognized gain when boot is received is still limited to the realized gain on the like-kind property. The amount considered boot would also be reduced by any qualified costs paid in connection with the transaction.

Example #1: Glenn exchanges a residential rental property in a 1031 exchange. The relinquished rental property has an FMV of $60,000 and an adjusted basis of $30,000. The replacement (like-kind) property Glenn receives has an FMV of $50,000, and he also receives $10,000 of cash as part of the exchange. Glenn, therefore, has a realized gain of $30,000 on the exchange (combined value of $60,000 received minus his basis of $30,000 in the property exchanged). He is required to pay tax and recognize gain on only $10,000, the cash (boot) received in the exchange. The rest of his gain is deferred until he disposes of the property at a later date.

Example #2: Noriko exchanges her rental property in a 1031 exchange. The relinquished rental property has an FMV of $90,000 and an adjusted basis of $86,000. The replacement like-kind property Noriko receives has an FMV of $70,000, and she also receives $20,000 of cash as part of the exchange. Noriko, therefore, has a *realized* gain of $4,000 on the exchange (combined value of $90,000 received minus her tax basis of $86,000 in the property exchanged). Even though she received $20,000 of boot (the cash) in the exchange, she is only required to pay tax on $4,000, (the amount of gain realized in the exchange).

When an exchange involves property that is subject to a liability (such as an existing mortgage), the assumption of the liability is treated as if it was a transfer of cash and thus considered boot by the party who is relieved of the liability. Sometimes this is called "mortgage boot" or "debt reduction boot." If each property in an exchange is transferred subject to a liability, a taxpayer is treated as having received boot only if he is relieved of a greater liability than the liability he assumes. When there is mortgage boot and cash boot in the same transaction, the mortgage boot paid does not offset any "cash boot" received. Net cash boot received is *always* taxable.

Example: Marjorie exchanges an apartment building with an existing mortgage of $100,000 for a commercial factory building with an existing mortgage of $150,000. Marjorie assumes the mortgage on the factory building, and also receives cash boot of $60,000 in the exchange. Marjorie may offset the mortgages, which means that she has paid $50,000 in mortgage boot in the transaction. She is not allowed to deduct the mortgage boot paid from the cash boot received, however. Therefore, her taxable boot in this transaction is $60,000, the amount of cash that she received.

The Basis of Property Received in a Like-Kind Exchange

The basis of property acquired in a Section 1031 exchange is the basis of the property given up with some adjustments. Gain is deferred, but not forgiven, in a like-kind exchange.

Example: Bernadette owns a residential rental property with an adjusted basis of $270,000. In 2018, she trades the rental property for a commercial parking lot with an FMV of $250,000. Bernadette's basis in the parking lot is $270,000, equal to the adjusted basis of the property she exchanged. The fair market value of the properties is irrelevant in this case.

If a taxpayer trades property and also pays money as part of the exchange, the basis of the property received is the basis of the property given up, increased by any additional money paid.

> **Example:** Gavin trades a parking lot with an adjusted basis of $30,000 for a parcel of farmland in another state with an FMV of $70,500. He pays an additional $4,000 of cash to complete the transaction. Gavin's basis in the new farmland is $34,000—his $30,000 basis in the old parking lot *plus* the additional $4,000 cash he paid.

If a taxpayer receives boot in connection with an exchange and recognizes gain, the basis of the property received is equal to the basis of the property given up plus the amount of gain recognized.

> **Example:** Ryan exchanges a residential rental with an adjusted basis of $500,000 for a tract of timberland with an FMV of $600,000. He receives cash of $100,000 in connection with the exchange and must recognize gain to the extent of the boot received. Ryan's basis in the timberland is $600,000 ($500,000 basis in the residential rental plus $100,000 recognized gain).

Related Party Transactions

Like-kind exchanges are permitted between related parties. However, if either party disposes of the property within two years after a 1031 exchange, the exchange is disqualified from nonrecognition treatment; any gain or loss that was deferred in the original transaction must be recognized in the year the disposition occurs. For purposes of this rule, a related person includes a close family member (such as a spouse, sibling, parent, or child). It also includes a corporation or partnership in which a taxpayer holds ownership or interests of more than 50%. The two-year holding period rule does not apply:

- If one of the parties involved in the exchange subsequently dies
- If the property is subsequently converted in an involuntary exchange (such as a fire)
- If it can be established to the satisfaction of the IRS that the exchange and subsequent disposition were not done mainly for tax avoidance purposes

The IRS gives close scrutiny to exchanges between related parties because they can be used by taxpayers to evade taxes on gains.

Involuntary Conversions (Section 1033 Exchange)

An involuntary conversion occurs when a taxpayer's property is lost, damaged, or destroyed, and the taxpayer receives an award, insurance money, or some other type of payment, as a result of:

- Casualty, disaster, or theft,
- The loss of a property due to an exercise of eminent domain, or
- Condemnation (or threat of condemnation).

Involuntary conversions are also called "involuntary exchanges." Involuntary conversions can occur with business property as well as personal-use property, but the rules differ for each.

185

Sometimes, a taxpayer will have a taxable gain from an involuntary conversion. This usually happens when a taxpayer's insurance reimbursement exceeds their basis in the property. Gain or loss from an involuntary conversion is usually recognized for tax purposes unless the property is a main home (covered later).

A taxpayer reports the gain or deducts the loss in the year the gain or loss is realized. This does not mean that an involuntary conversion is a taxable event, even when an insurance reimbursement exceeds the taxpayer's basis. Under section 1033, a taxpayer can elect to *defer* reporting the gain on an involuntary conversion if he receives proceeds from insurance or another source and reinvests in property that is similar to the converted property. In other words, the gain on an involuntary conversion can be deferred until (a later) taxable sale or exchange occurs. Unlike a section 1031 exchange, in general, replacement property cannot be purchased from a "related" party for an involuntary conversion to qualify for nonrecognition treatment.

Longer Replacement Period: While a section 1031 exchange only has a 180-day exchange period, a section 1033 exchange has a much longer time for completion. The replacement period for an involuntary conversion generally ends two years after the end of the first tax year in which any part of the gain is realized. There is no requirement under Section 1033 that a qualified intermediary be employed to hold the escrow funds or conversion proceeds.

Real property that is held for investment or used in a trade or business is allowed a three-year replacement period. The replacement period is four years for livestock that is involuntarily converted because of weather-related conditions.

Example: Stanford owns a drywall repair business. On September 1, 2018, a flood destroys his storage shed, which was filled with his tools and supplies. Stanford's insurance company reimburses him for the loss on October 26, 2018. He has until December 31, 2020 (two years) to replace the shed and supplies using the insurance proceeds. Stanford is not required to report the insurance proceeds on his 2018 tax return. If he reinvests all the proceeds in a replacement property, he will not have any taxable gain.

Example: Rossdale and Minerva are married and file jointly. They paid $100,000 for their home fifteen years ago, and it has gone up in value ever since. They receive an insurance payment of $700,000 after their home is destroyed in a mudslide, for a $600,000 gain on the conversion. They may exclude $500,000 of the gain under section 121, leaving $100,000 as taxable long-term capital gain. If they reinvest the insurance proceeds in a new home, under the rules for involuntary conversions, they may defer the remainder of the gain. If they choose not to reinvest the insurance proceeds, then they will be required to pay capital gains on $100,000.

If a taxpayer's main home is damaged or destroyed and is in a federally declared disaster area, the replacement period is extended to four years. A five-year replacement period has been applied to certain extreme disaster areas, but only if the replacement property is purchased in the same area.

Property Type	Replacement Period
Most property except those noted below. The two-year replacement period includes personal homes.	Two years
Real property (real estate) that is held for investment or business use, such as residential rentals and office buildings	Three years
Sale of livestock due to weather-related conditions	Four years
Main home in specific federally declared disaster area	Four to five years

If a taxpayer reinvests in replacement property similar to the converted property, the replacement property's basis is the same as the converted property's basis on the date of the conversion, subject to the following adjustments: The basis is **decreased** by the following:

- Any loss a taxpayer recognizes on the involuntary conversion
- Any money a taxpayer receives that he does not spend on similar property

The basis is **increased** by the following:

- Any gain a taxpayer recognizes on the involuntary conversion
- Any additional costs of acquiring the replacement property

Example: Miguel owns an apartment fourplex in Texas with a basis of $250,000. He receives an insurance settlement of $400,000 after the building is destroyed by a tornado. Two years later, Miguel purchases another apartment building in Wisconsin for $380,000. Miguel's realized gain on the involuntary conversion is $150,000 ($400,000 - $250,000 basis). He must recognize $20,000 of gain because he received an insurance payment of $400,000 but only spent $380,000 on the replacement property ($400,000 - $380,000). His basis in the new property is $250,000, which is calculated as the cost of the new property in Wisconsin minus the deferred gain ($380,000 - $130,000 = $250,000). If Miguel had used all the insurance proceeds and reinvested it in the new property, he would not have to report any taxable gain.

Example: A hurricane destroys Theresa's residential rental condo that had an adjusted basis of $49,000. The insurance company gives Theresa a check for $175,000, which is the FMV of the condo on the date that it was destroyed. Theresa buys a replacement rental property six months later for $175,000. Her gain on the involuntary conversion is $126,000 ($175,000 insurance settlement minus her $49,000 basis). However, Theresa does not have to recognize any taxable gain because she reinvested all the insurance proceeds in another, similar property under a qualified 1033 exchange. In this scenario, the basis of her replacement property is the same as the property that was destroyed: $49,000.

Condemnations and Eminent Domain

A "condemnation" is a specific type of involuntary conversion. If a building is dangerous to public health and safety, the property may also be legally condemned. Condemnation is also a legal process by which private property is taken from its owner for public use. Sometimes this process is called "eminent domain."

Eminent domain allows the government to take private property in exchange for compensation. A property may be condemned by a state or local government or by a private organization that has the legal power to seize it.

The owner generally receives a condemnation award (money or property) in exchange for the property that is taken. A condemnation is like a forced sale, with the owner being the seller and the government or other third party being the buyer.

Example: A local government informs Louis that his farmland is being condemned to create a public highway. Although Louis does not want to sell his land, the government forces the sale and issues a condemnation award to Louis, paying him the property's fair market value of $400,000. Louis's basis in the farmland was $80,000. Louis decides not to purchase replacement farmland. Therefore, he has a taxable event, and he must recognize $320,000 as income ($400,000 - $80,000 = $320,000). However, if Louis were to purchase replacement property with the condemnation award, he would have a nontaxable section 1033 exchange.

Example: Penny's timberland is destroyed by a massive mudslide. Her basis in the land is $60,000. The FMV of the land and timber was $110,000 just before it was destroyed. Her insurance company issues her a check for $110,000. Penny has a realized gain of $50,000 ($60,000 basis -$110,000 insurance proceeds). She decides to buy a smaller parcel and spends only $80,000 to purchase a new timber plot. She uses the remaining $30,000 of the insurance settlement to buy a car. Penny must recognize $30,000 as a taxable gain.

Amounts taken out of a condemnation award to pay debts on the property are considered paid to the taxpayer and are included in the amount of the award.

Example: The state condemned Kent's property to build a light rail system. The court award was set at $200,000. The state paid him only $148,000 because it paid $50,000 to his mortgage company and $2,000 in accrued real estate taxes. Kent is considered to have received the entire $200,000 as a condemnation award.

The time period for replacing condemned property is the same as other qualified section 1033 exchanges, two years after the end of the first tax year in which any part of the gain on the condemnation is realized.

For real property held for business use or investment, the replacement period is three years instead of two.

Example: Maia paid $118,000 for a rental property five years ago. After factoring in her depreciation deductions, her adjusted basis in the property is $75,000 at the beginning of 2018. The property is insured for $300,000 and is destroyed by a fire in June 2018. On December 15, 2018, Maia receives a $300,000 settlement from her insurance company. Maia reinvests all the insurance proceeds, plus $5,000 more of her own personal savings, into a new rental property. She qualifies to defer all of her gain. Her basis in the new property is $80,000 ($75,000 original basis + $5,000 of her additional cash investment).

Example: John owns a pool hall. In February 2018, the building is condemned by the city because asbestos is discovered in the ceiling. The building is torn down a few months later, and he receives his condemnation award from his insurance company in November 2018. He has until December 31, 2021, to replace the condemned pool hall with a similar building. This is because the pool hall is business-related real estate, so John has three full years to reinvest the proceeds in a similar property.

Condemnation or Destruction of a Main Home

If a taxpayer has a gain because his main home is condemned or destroyed, he can generally exclude the gain as if he had sold the home under the section 121 exclusion. Single filers can exclude up to $250,000 of the gain and joint filers up to $500,000.

Any excess gains above these amounts may be potentially excludable under section 1033 if the taxpayer reinvests the proceeds in another, similar property.

Example: Janice has owned and lived in her home continuously for seven years. In 2018, a local government informed Janice that it wished to acquire her home and surrounding land in order to create a public park. After the local government took action to condemn her property, Janice went to court to keep her home. The court decided in favor of the government. The governmental agency takes possession of Janice's home. This is a condemnation of private property for public use. Janice receives a $355,000 condemnation award from the government. Her basis in the home is $153,000. Even if she decides not to reinvest the proceeds of the condemnation award, Janice will not have a taxable gain, because the gain would have been excludable under section 121 if she had voluntarily sold the home ($355,000 award - $153,000 basis = $202,000 nontaxable capital gain).

Example: On February 8, 2018, a fire destroys Zyra's main home. She bought the home ten years ago for $80,000. Zyra's insurance company pays Zyra $400,000 for the house, which was the fair market value of the home when it was destroyed. Zyra realizes a gain of $320,000 ($400,000 insurance proceeds - $80,000 basis). On August 27, 2018, Zyra purchases a smaller condo at a cost of $100,000. Because the destruction of her old house is treated as a sale for purposes of section 121, Zyra may exclude $250,000 of the realized gain from her gross income. For purposes of section 1033, the amount "realized" is then treated as being $150,000 ($400,000 insurance proceeds - $250,000 section 121 exclusion) and the gain realized is $70,000 ($150,000 amount realized - $80,000 basis). Zyra elects under section 1033 to recognize only $50,000 of the gain ($150,000 amount realized - $100,000 cost of new house). The remaining $20,000 of gain is deferred and Zyra's basis in the new house is $80,000 ($100,000 cost - $20,000 gain not recognized).[77]

---

[77] Example modified from IRS Final Regulations, *Exclusion of Gain from Sale or Exchange of a Principal Residence,* [TD 9030]. RIN 1545-AX28.

(Test yourself first; then check the correct answers at the end of this quiz.)

1. A tornado destroyed Bryant's main home on July 15, 2018. He wants to replace the home using a section 1033 exchange for involuntary conversions. What is the latest date that Bryant can purchase replacement property to defer any gain from his insurance reimbursement that was paid to him on August 23, 2018?

A. December 31, 2020
B. July 15, 2019
C. August 23, 2020
D. July 15, 2021

2. Alistair and Gabrielle are married and file jointly. They moved after living in their home for 292 days because Gabrielle became pregnant with triplets and they needed a larger home. The gain on the sale of their home is $260,000. Since they lived there for less than two years but meet one of the exceptions, what is the actual amount of their reduced exclusion? (Two years = 730 days.)

A. $60,000
B. $200,000
C. $260,000
D. $500,000

3. Heather is single and bought her first home seven years ago for $350,000. She lived continuously in the house until she sold it in 2018 for $620,000. Which of the following statements is correct?

A. She may exclude $250,000 of gain and report the remaining amount as a long-term capital gain.
B. She may exclude the entire gain. There is no amount that needs to be reported.
C. She may not exclude the gain.
D. She may exclude $250,000 of gain. The remaining amount must be reported as a short-term capital gain.

4. Which of the following would not be an acceptable "unforeseen circumstance" for a taxpayer to take a reduced exclusion on the sale of his primary residence?

A. The home is condemned by the city.
B. A legal separation that will lead to a divorce
C. The birth of twin girls
D. Moving to another state to be closer to grown children

5. Chrystal exchanged a rental duplex with an adjusted basis of $160,000 for a warehouse. The fair market value of the warehouse she received was $200,000. She also received $10,000 of cash and paid $5,000 of exchange expenses. What is her recognized (taxable) gain on the transaction, if any?

A. $0
B. $5,000
C. $10,000
D. $45,000

6. Clayton trades a small building with an adjusted basis of $44,000 for a tractor with a fair market value of $77,000. What is the basis of the tractor and how much taxable gain, if any, must Clayton report?

A. $0 gain; $33,000 basis
B. $0 gain; $77,000 basis
C. $33,000 gain; $44,000 basis
D. This is not a qualifying like-kind exchange

7. Bailey exchanges his residential rental property with an adjusted basis of $50,000 and an FMV of $80,000 for a different rental property with an FMV of $70,000. What is Bailey's basis in the new property?

A. $50,000
B. $70,000
C. $80,000
D. $100,000

8. Aiden exchanges a residential rental property in Las Vegas with a basis of $100,000 for an investment property in Miami Beach valued at $220,000. Aiden also received $15,000 of cash boot in the exchange. What is Aiden's taxable gain on the exchange, if any, and what is his basis of the new property in Miami Beach?

A. Taxable gain: $15,000; basis: $115,000
B. Taxable gain: $0; basis: $235,000
C. Taxable gain: $15,000; basis: $135,000
D. Taxable gain: $15,000; basis: $220,000

9. Which of the following transactions cannot qualify for a section 1031 like-kind exchange?

A. An exchange of a building in Chicago for empty farmland in Nebraska
B. An exchange of an apartment building in Delaware for a factory building in Alaska
C. An exchange of a residential rental for an undeveloped lot of land
D. An exchange of land inventory for housing inventory

10. Geoff is a self-employed tax preparer. He sold his main home in 2018 at a $29,000 gain. He meets the "ownership and use" tests to exclude the gain from his income. However, he used one bedroom of the home for business for the last two years. His records show he claimed $3,000 of depreciation for a qualified home office, taking the deduction on his Schedule C. What is Geoff's taxable gain on the sale, if any?

A. $0
B. $1,000
C. $2,000
D. $3,000

11. Jonah exchanged an empty lot that he held for investment for a rental building. The original cost of the empty lot was $16,000, and he made $10,000 of improvements (such as permanent fencing) prior to the exchange. The fair market value of the rental building at the time of the exchange was $36,000. Jonah did not recognize any gain from the exchange. What is his basis in the new property?

A. $10,000
B. $16,000
C. $26,000
D. $36,000

12. Mitchell and Kaylie are married and file jointly. They owned and used their house as their main home for 15 months. Mitchell got a new job in another state, and they sold their home. What is the maximum amount they can exclude from income under the rules regarding a reduced exclusion?

A. $22,727
B. $250,000
C. $312,500
D. $500,000

13. Chayim is a farmer. He trades a plot of pastureland (adjusted basis $300,000), for agricultural land with an existing orchard (FMV $750,000) and in addition, he pays $60,000 of cash. What is his basis in the orchard?

A. $300,000
B. $360,000
C. $690,000
D. $750,000

14. Annalise sold her primary residence in Utah and moved to Iowa. She had purchased the house in 2010 for $200,000, and she sold it in 2018 for $550,000, net of selling expenses. During the time she lived in the house, she paid $25,000 for major improvements and $15,000 for general repairs. Assuming that Annalise utilizes the maximum available exclusion, what amount would she report as a taxable gain?

A. $0
B. $60,000
C. $75,000
D. $100,000

15. Eliseo bought a house for $189,000 in July 2015. He lived there continuously for 13 months and then moved in with his girlfriend. They later separated, and Eliseo moved back into his own house and lived there for an additional 12 months until he sold it in July 2018 for $220,000. What is the amount and nature of his gain?

A. Eliseo has no taxable gain because the sale qualifies for section 121 exclusion.
B. $31,000 long-term capital gain
C. $31,000 short-term capital gain
D. $30,000 long-term capital gain

16. Christian owned an office building with an adjusted basis of $400,000. The building was destroyed by a fire in 2018, and Christian received an insurance reimbursement of $600,000. He purchases a new office building for $450,000 and invests the rest of the insurance proceeds in cryptocurrency. Which of the following statements is correct?

A. He has $200,000 of taxable gain he must recognize on his tax return.
B. He has $150,000 of taxable gain he must recognize on his tax return.
C. He has $50,000 of taxable gain he must recognize on his tax return.
D. He does not have a taxable gain.

17. Isaiah has lived in and owned his home for 15 months when he decides to move in with his girlfriend, so he sells his home for $285,000. His adjusted basis in the home is $160,000. What is the amount and nature of his taxable gain on the sale?

A. $0
B. $35,000 long-term capital gain
C. $125,000 long-term capital gain
D. $125,000 short-term capital gain

18. Bobby and Grace were married on January 12, 2010. They purchased their first home together in March 2010 for $150,000. In February 2018, Bobby and Grace legally separated, and the court granted Grace ownership of the home as part of the divorce settlement. The divorce became final on June 10, 2018, and the fair market value of the home was $370,000 when ownership was transferred to Grace. She sells the house on December 23, 2018, for $480,000. What is Grace's taxable gain in the transaction?

A. $0
B. $80,000
C. $120,000
D. $210,000

Unit 8: Quiz Answers

1. The answer is A. Bryant must acquire qualifying replacement property by December 31, 2020 (*two* years from the *end* of the tax year during which any part of the gain is realized.) Since Bryant received the reimbursement check in 2018, he has two years from December 31, 2018, to acquire replacement property. Different types of property have different replacement periods. For example, if Bryant's main home had been located in a federally declared disaster area, he could have had four years to replace the property.

2. The answer is B. Alistair and Gabrielle are allowed to claim a *reduced* exclusion of $200,000 (292/730 multiplied by the $500,000 maximum exclusion available for married taxpayers). The remaining $60,000 would be considered taxable capital gain income and would be reported on Schedule D. This move qualifies for the reduced exclusion because multiple births from the same pregnancy are considered an unforeseen circumstance.

3. The answer is A. As a single taxpayer; Heather may exclude a maximum gain amount of $250,000 from the sale of her home. Her gain is $270,000 ($620,000 - $350,000). Her taxable gain is $20,000 ($270,000 gain - $250,000 exclusion), which must be reported as a long-term capital gain.

4. The answer is D. The move to be closer to grown children would not qualify. All of the following events would be qualifying events to claim a reduced exclusion from a premature sale:
- A divorce or legal separation
- A pregnancy resulting in multiple births or serious health issues
- The home is sold after being seized or condemned
- A move due to a new job or new employment

If any of these exceptions apply, the taxpayer may figure a reduced exclusion based on the number of days he owned and lived in the residence.

5. The answer is B. Although Chrystal's total gain on the transaction is $45,000, the recognized gain is only $5,000. The answer is calculated as follows:

FMV of like-kind property received (i.e., the warehouse)	$200,000
Cash boot received	10,000
Total received	210,000
Subtract: Exchange expenses paid	(5,000)
Amount realized	205,000
Subtract: Adjusted basis of property transferred	(160,000)
Realized Gain	$45,000
Cash received (boot)	$10,000
Subtract: Exchange expenses paid	(5,000)
Recognized (taxable) gain	**$5,000**

6. The answer is D. This is not an acceptable like-kind exchange, so the entire transaction is treated as a sale. This is a taxable exchange of property that is not similar, or "unlike" property.

7. The answer is A. Bailey's basis in the new property is the same as the basis of the property given up: $50,000.

8. The answer is A. Aiden's total gain on the exchange is $135,000 ($220,000 value of new property + $15,000 cash - $100,000 basis in the old property). However, only the cash boot received is taxable in this transaction. Aiden's basis in the new building is $115,000 (the original basis in the property he gave up plus the gain recognized as a result of the boot received).

9. The answer is D. Inventory never qualifies for like-kind exchange treatment, regardless of whether it is real property or not. The property in a section 1031 exchange must not be held "primarily for sale." Generally, real property exchanges will qualify for like-kind treatment, even though the properties themselves might be dissimilar, so all the other exchanges would be allowable.

10. The answer is D. Geoff can exclude $26,000 ($29,000 - $3,000) of his gain. He has a taxable gain of $3,000. He must report the depreciation recapture as ordinary income. If a taxpayer took depreciation deductions because he used his home for business purposes or as a rental property, he cannot exclude the part of the gain equal to any depreciation allowed as a deduction.

11. The answer is C. Jonah's basis in the new building is the same as his basis in the empty lot. The $10,000 spent on improvements is added to the $16,000 cost, so the adjusted basis of the relinquished empty lot was $26,000. Therefore, this is his basis in the new property, as well. The fair market value is irrelevant in this calculation.

12. The answer is C. A reduced exclusion is available, even though the taxpayers did not live in the home for two full years. They qualify for a reduced exclusion because they are moving for a change in Mitchell's employment. Their maximum reduced exclusion is $312,500 ($500,000 × [15 months/24 months]). The reduced exclusion applies when the premature sale is primarily due to a move for employment in a new location.

13. The answer is B. Chayim's basis is $360,000: the $300,000 basis of the relinquished pastureland plus the $60,000 cash paid. The fair market value of the property has no bearing on Chayim's basis in the new property.

14. The answer is C. Annalise's adjusted basis in the house would be the total of her original purchase price of $200,000 and the $25,000 cost of improvements. The cost of repairs would not be considered in determining her adjusted basis. Therefore, her gain on the sale would be $325,000, or the excess of her net proceeds over her adjusted basis. Since she met the requirements for ownership and use of the house as her primary residence, she qualifies for the maximum exclusion of $250,000 available to a single taxpayer, and the taxable portion of her gain would be $75,000.

The purchase price of house	$200,000
Cost of improvements	25,000
Adjusted basis	225,000
Net proceeds of the sale	**$550,000**
Gain on sale	325,000
Exclusion for a single taxpayer	(250,000)
Taxable gain	**$75,000**

15. The answer is A. This sale qualifies for section 121 treatment. Eliseo meets the "ownership and use" tests because, during the five-year period ending on the date of sale, he owned the house for three years and lived in it for a total of 25 months (over two years). The gain is not taxable and does not need to be reported.

16. The answer is B. Christian's realized gain is $200,000 ($600,000 - $400,000) and his taxable gain is $150,000. He purchased another building for $450,000 so he may defer $50,000 of the gain under section 1033 for involuntary conversions. The remainder of the gain, $150,000 ($600,000 - $450,000), must be recognized because he did not reinvest the remaining proceeds in like-kind property. If Christian had reinvested all the insurance proceeds in a new building, his entire gain would have been deferred.

17. The answer is C. Isaiah's gain is $125,000, the result of subtracting the adjusted basis in the home from the amount realized ($285,000 - $160,000 = $125,000). Since he does not meet the ownership or use tests or qualify for a reduced exclusion, he cannot exclude any of his gains under section 121, (because he hasn't lived in the house for two out of the last five years). He owned the property for more than a year, so the gain is taxed as a long-term capital gain.

18. The answer is B. Grace meets the ownership and use tests, and the basis in the property remains the same. Property transfers related to a divorce are generally nontaxable, and the FMV of the property at the time of the divorce has no bearing on the taxable outcome. Since she owned the property for longer than one year, the taxable portion of Grace's gain would be reported as a long-term capital gain. The gain is calculated as follows:

Original cost	$150,000
Sale price	480,000
Total realized gain	330,000
Section 121 exclusion	250,000
Taxable gain	$80,000

Unit 9: Rental and Royalty Income

For additional information read:
Publication 527, *Residential Rental Property (Including Rental of Vacation Homes)*
Publication 946, *How to Depreciate Property*
Publication 525, *Taxable and Nontaxable Income*

Rental income is any payment received for the use or occupation of property. Taxpayers must include amounts received as rent in their gross income. Royalty income is also a type of income received for the use of someone's property. Royalty income includes any payments received from a patent, a copyright, or some natural or mineral resource (such as forestland or a copper mine).

Example: Augustus owns a residential duplex. He has two tenants, one on each side of the duplex. He is not a real estate professional. He manages the rental property himself and does many of the repairs and general maintenance. The rental income he receives from his tenants is taxable and would be reported on Schedule E, *Supplemental Income and Loss.*

Example: Madeline owns 200 acres of forestland that she inherited from her grandfather. She leases the forestland to a lumber company that harvests and processes the timber. Madeline receives quarterly payments under a contract agreement with the timber company based on the value of the timber taken from the property during the year. At the end of the year, the timber company provides Madeline with a Form 1099-MISC reporting the payments as "Royalties" in Box 2. Madeline reports the royalty payments received as royalty income on Schedule E, *Supplemental Income and Loss.*

Rental Income Defined

Property owners can deduct the expenses of managing, conserving, and maintaining their rental properties. Common rental expenses include:

- Mortgage interest and property taxes
- Maintenance, repairs, and cleaning fees
- Advertising for new tenants
- Utilities, if paid by the homeowner
- Homeowner's insurance, liability insurance, and natural disaster insurance
- Depreciation

A taxpayer can deduct the expenses paid by a tenant if they are deductible rental expenses. The owner of the property would then include the fair market value of the property or services received in their rental income, and deduct that same amount as a rental expense.

Advance Rent: Taxpayers must report rental income when it is actively or constructively (i.e., available without restrictions) received. This includes advance rent, which is any amount received before the period that it covers. Thus, a taxpayer must include advance rent in income in the year he receives it, regardless of the period covered or the accounting method used.

> **Example:** Amos rents out a duplex. On December 20, 2018, his tenant Cynthia pays two months of rent in advance for January and February because she is leaving town on vacation. Amos cannot delay reporting the income. He must report all the advance rent as taxable income in 2018 (when he received it).

Lease Cancellation: If a tenant pays to cancel a lease, the amount received for the cancellation is rental income. The payment is included in the year received regardless of the taxpayer's accounting method.

Refundable Security Deposits: A security deposit is not considered income upon initial receipt if the deposit is refundable to the tenant at the end of the lease. However, if the taxpayer keeps the security deposit because the tenant did not live up to the terms of the lease or because he damaged property, the deposit amount is recognized as income in the year it is forfeited by the tenant.

Insurance Premiums Paid in Advance: If a cash-basis taxpayer pays an insurance premium for more than one year in advance, he can deduct only the part of the premium payment that applies to that year. He cannot deduct the total premium in the year he pays it.

Local Benefit Taxes: In most cases, a taxpayer cannot deduct charges for local taxes that increase the value of a rental property, such as assessments for streets, sidewalks, or water and sewer systems. These charges are non-depreciable capital expenditures that must be added to the basis of the property. Only taxes to maintain or repair such infrastructure, or to pay interest charges related to financing its construction, can be deducted.

Property or Services in Lieu of Rent: If a taxpayer receives property or services as payment for rent instead of cash, the fair market value must be recognized as rental income. If the tenant and landlord agree in advance to a price, the agreed-upon price is deemed the fair market value unless there is evidence to the contrary.

> **Example:** Loretta owns an apartment complex with five units. One of Loretta's tenants, Chaim, is a professional chimney sweep. Chaim offers to clean all of Loretta's chimneys in her apartment building instead of paying three months' rent in cash. Loretta accepts Chaim's offer. Loretta must recognize income for the amount Chaim would have paid for three months' rent. However, Loretta can deduct that same amount as a business expense for maintenance of the property.

If a tenant pays expenses on behalf of the landlord, the landlord must recognize the payments as rental income. However, the property owner can deduct the expenses as rental expenses.

> **Example:** Elizabeth owns an apartment building. While she is out of town on vacation, the furnace in the apartment building breaks down. Diego, Elizabeth's tenant, pays for the emergency repairs out-of-pocket and deducts the furnace repair bill from his rent payment. Elizabeth must recognize as rental income both the actual amount of rent received in cash from Diego and the amount he paid for the repairs. Elizabeth can deduct the cost of the furnace repair as a rental expense.

Vacant Property: Generally, a taxpayer cannot deduct any loss of rental income for the period a property is vacant. However, if the taxpayer is actively trying to rent the property, he can deduct ordinary and necessary expenses as soon as the property is "made available" for rent, even if the taxpayer doesn't find a tenant right away.

> **Example:** Finnegan purchased a rental property and made the property available for rent on March 1, 2018, by advertising it in the local newspaper. He found a tenant who moved in on June 1, 2018. Even though the rental was unoccupied from March through May, Finnegan can still deduct the mortgage interest and other expenses related to the property during that period, because the property was available and advertised to rent.

Depreciation of Rental Property

A taxpayer begins to claim deductions for depreciation of a rental property when he places it in service for the production of income. Rental property is considered "placed in service" when it is ready and available for rent. Depreciation ends when a taxpayer has either fully recovered his cost or other basis, or when the property is retired from service, whichever happens first. Three basic factors determine how much depreciation a taxpayer can deduct:

- Basis
- Recovery period for the property
- Depreciation method used, including certain conventions

The cost of land is never depreciated because land does not wear out, become obsolete, or get used up.

Most residential rental buildings are depreciated over 27.5 years. For example, a residential rental home with a cost basis of $137,500 would generate depreciation of $5,000 per year ($137,500/27.5 years) over most of the years of its depreciable life.

Nonresidential buildings are generally depreciated over 39 years, with a half-months' worth of depreciation allowed for the first and last month of the depreciable life of the property (i.e., the midmonth convention). An example of a nonresidential rental would be an office complex, where the offices are rented to business tenants, but nobody actually lives or sleeps in the building.

Converting a Home to Rental Use: Sometimes, taxpayers will convert their personal residence to a rental property. For a personal home that is later converted to rental property, the depreciable basis is the lower of:

- The taxpayer's adjusted basis in the property, or
- The fair market value of the property at the time of conversion.

If a taxpayer changes a main home or second home to rental use at any time other than the beginning of a tax year, he must divide his expenses between rental use and personal use. He can deduct as rental expenses only the portion that is for the part of the year the property was used or held for rental purposes.

For depreciation purposes, the property is treated as being placed in service on the conversion date. When a taxpayer converts property held for personal use to rental use, the basis for depreciation will be the lesser of fair market value or his adjusted basis on the date of conversion.

Example: In 2018, Bernice buys a rental property for $200,000. It has an assessed value of $160,000, of which $136,000 is for the house, and $24,000 is for the land. Bernice can allocate 85% ($136,000 ÷ $160,000) of the purchase price to the house and 15% ($24,000 ÷ $160,000) of the purchase price to the land. Therefore, her basis in the house is $170,000 (85% of $200,000) and her basis in the land is $30,000 (15% of $200,000). Bernice may use $170,000 as her basis for depreciation on the property.

Example: Mason purchased a residential rental building on January 1, 2018, for $395,000. The value of the house is $275,000. The assessed value of the land is $120,000. For tax purposes, a MACRS class life[78] of 27½ years is used. Using straight-line depreciation, the yearly depreciation amount is calculated as follows: $275,000/27.5 years = $10,000 depreciation expense per year.

Example: Five years ago, Albert purchased a home for $180,000. On the date of purchase, the assessed value of the land was $30,000. After living in the home for five years, Albert converted it to a rental property on April 1, 2018. Since land is not depreciable, Albert includes only the cost of the house when calculating his basis for depreciation. The allocated cost of the house is $150,000 ($180,000 - $30,000). In 2018, the county assessor's office assigned the home an FMV of $185,000, of which $40,000 was for land and $145,000 for the house. The basis for depreciation of the house is the FMV on the date of conversion ($145,000) because it is less than Albert's allocated cost ($150,000). Albert uses $145,000 to calculate depreciation, which is reported on Schedule E, *Supplemental Income and Loss.*

New Section 179 Rules for Certain Types of Rental Property

Starting in 2018, the TCJA increases the maximum Section 179 deduction to $1 million. In prior years, a taxpayer could not claim the section 179 deduction for any property that was used to produce rental income. The prohibition included any rental assets (such as furniture and appliances) as well as capital improvements, such as building additions and HVAC systems.

For the first time in 2018, the TCJA expands the section 179 deduction to certain types of tangible personal property that is used predominantly to furnish lodging. This new provision includes some types of lodging facilities, such dormitories and hostels or any other facility (or part of a facility) where sleeping accommodations are provided.

It also includes personal property used in apartment complexes and other residential properties that are rented out to tenants.

The TCJA also expands the definition of "eligible property" to include certain expenditures for nonresidential buildings: including roofs, heating, ventilating, and air conditioning (HVAC) equipment, fire protection and alarm systems, and security systems. Nonresidential

---

[78] Under MACRS, fixed assets are assigned to a specific asset class, which has a designated depreciation period associated with it. Residential rental property has a 27.5 year class life.

commercial property includes office buildings, medical centers, hotels, and malls. All these properties produce rental revenue for their owners, although the tax treatment of the revenue varies on a number of different factors. Under current IRS rules, if 80% or more of the annual gross rental income from the mixed-use building is generated from the residential rental apartments, the entire building and its structural components will qualify as a residential rental property.

> **Example:** Isaac owns a medical office building that he rents out exclusively to medical and dental professionals. In 2018, Isaac spends $7,525 on a new HVAC system for the building. He also installs a new alarm system, which cost $6,750. Isaac may deduct the entire cost of the equipment by taking the section 179 election on his tax return. He does not need to depreciate the HVAC system or the alarm system over their useful life.

Repairs vs. Improvements to Rental Property

A taxpayer can currently deduct the cost of repairs to rental property but cannot currently deduct the cost of improvements. Instead, the taxpayer must recover the cost of an improvement by taking depreciation deductions over its applicable recovery period. A repair generally keeps an asset or property in good working condition but does not add to the value of the asset or substantially prolong its life. Repainting, fixing leaks, and replacing broken windows are examples of repairs.

An improvement is anything that results in the betterment of a property, restoration of a property, or adaptation of a property to a new or different use. Examples of improvements include:

- Additions of an extra bedroom, bathroom, deck, or garage
- The installation of a new roof
- Installation of central air conditioning, new plumbing, wall-to-wall carpeting, or upgraded wiring
- Construction of a retaining wall, fence, or swimming pool

> **Note:** In September 2013, the IRS released its final tangible property regulations, a highly complex set of rules governing repairs and capitalization that affect all taxpayers who use tangible property in their businesses. The IRS is still issuing guidance on these regulations, even in the current year. These rules change the way businesses treat expenditures for tangible property. For the EA exam, most of the specific details of these regulations will likely not be tested. However, you should have a general understanding of the concept that a business may recover the costs of property either through current deductions or through periodic depreciation deductions for items required to be capitalized.

> **Example:** Odette owns a rental property. In 2018, she spent $18,000 to replace the roof, $6,540 to pave the driveway, and $175 to repair a couple of broken gutters. Only the gutter repair ($175) can be expensed on her 2018 tax return. The costs of the new roof and the new driveway must be capitalized and depreciated over time.

The capitalized cost of an improvement is depreciated separately from the original cost of the asset or property that is being improved.

> **Example #1:** Jeremiah owns a rental home. A baseball broke a window, so he replaced it with an upgraded model, an insulated double-pane window that helps control heating and cooling costs. Even though this window is a substantial upgrade from the previous one, it is still considered a repair, because the old window was broken and needed to be replaced. If Jeremiah were to replace all the windows in the house, the upgrade would be considered an improvement, and he would be required to capitalize the cost and claim depreciation deductions over a period of years.
>
> **Example #2:** Jeremiah also replaces the entire roof at the cost of $17,000. This is considered a substantial improvement, and the cost of the roof must be depreciated over time rather than deducted against current income.

Under a safe harbor rule of the tangible property regulations,[79] materials and supplies costing no more than $2,500[80] are generally deductible in the year they are used or consumed.

Deductible Rental Losses

The tax treatment of rental income, expenses, and losses depends on several factors: whether a taxpayer is a real estate professional or actively manages a property; whether there is any personal use of the rental property, and if so, whether the dwelling is considered a home; and whether the rental activity is for "carried on" for profit. We will briefly review the rules related to each of these situations next.

The deductibility of losses from passive activities is limited, and a taxpayer usually cannot deduct losses from passive activities to offset his nonpassive income (such as wages). In general, a trade or business activity is considered a passive activity if the taxpayer does not *materially participate* in it.

A taxpayer materially participates in an activity if he is involved in the operation of that activity on a regular, continuous, and substantial basis. Rental activities that require substantial services[81] along with the rental property may be classified as business activities, rather than passive rental activities.

An example of this would be a hotel owner, or the owner of a bed and breakfast. In this case, the rental income and expenses, including interest and taxes, would be reported on Schedule C. Generally, losses from passive activities that exceed income from passive activities in the same year are disallowed. The disallowed losses are carried forward to the next taxable year and can be used to offset future income from passive activities. There is a special exception to this rule, however, for rental real estate activities.

---

[79] The tangible property regulations are covered in more detail in Book 2, *Businesses*. For Part 1 of the exam, you may have to know how these new regulations apply to rental property.

[80] The Internal Revenue Service, in Notice 2015-82, increased the *de minimis* safe harbor threshold from $500 to $2,500 per invoice or item for taxpayers without applicable financial statements ($5,000 for taxpayers with applicable financial statements).

[81] For tax purposes, "substantial services" include such regular cleaning, changing linen, or daily maid service, such as a person might receive at a hotel.

Special $25,000 "Loss Allowance" for Real Estate Rental Activities

The passive activity loss rules for taxpayers involved in real estate rental activities are an exception, as most rental real estate activities are considered passive activities, even if the taxpayer does materially participate in them.

However, when a taxpayer *actively participates* in a rental real estate activity, he may be able to deduct up to $25,000 of losses against his nonpassive income. It should be noted that active participation is a different, and less stringent, standard than material participation.

Note: "Active participation" is not the same thing as "material participation." Material participation is a much stricter standard. For example, the owner of a rental property will generally be treated as actively participating if he makes management decisions such as approving new tenants, deciding rental contracts, approving repairs, and other similar management decisions.

In order to be considered "actively participating" in a rental activity, a taxpayer must own at least 10% of the rental property and must make management decisions in a significant and bona fide way, such as approving new tenants and establishing the rental terms. In this case, active participation can also include participation by the taxpayer's spouse.

Example: Clement owns a residential rental property in San Diego, California. He also lives in San Diego and has a regular job that he works full-time. Clement actively manages his rental by choosing his own tenants, hiring workers to do any required repairs, and collecting the rent. Clement is actively participating in this rental activity.

Note: If the IRS determines a taxpayer has not actively participated, rental losses are not currently deductible, and he is not eligible for the special $25,000 loss allowance.

Example: Corina owns a rental property in Hawaii. She lives in Nevada. Corina hired a management company to manage the property and screen new tenants. The management company handles all the repairs and collects the rent. The management company charges a fee for its services and then remits the net proceeds to Corina monthly. It has been several years since Corina has even visited the property. Corina is not actively participating in this rental activity. She is not eligible for the special $25,000 loss allowance.

Example: Joaquin owns two residential rental properties and provides basic services to his tenants. He manages the property and collects rents. He also has a full-time job as a restaurant manager. He is not a real estate professional. Joaquin should report his rental income and losses on Schedule E. His rental income is considered passive activity income, and it is not subject to self-employment tax. He is eligible for the $25,000 loss allowance.

The full $25,000 loss allowance is available for taxpayers, whether single or MFJ, whose modified adjusted gross income (MAGI) is $100,000 or less. If a taxpayer is married and files a separate return, but lived apart from his spouse for the entire tax year, the taxpayer's special allowance for rental losses cannot exceed $12,500; this full allowance would be available if his MAGI is $50,000 or less. However, if the taxpayer lived with his spouse at any time during the year and is filing MFS, the taxpayer cannot use any of his passive rental losses to offset nonpassive income.

Rental losses that cannot be deducted due to the limitations described above can be carried forward indefinitely and used in subsequent years, subject to the same limitations.

> **Example:** Delton and Emeline are married. They own a residential rental property that they manage themselves. In 2018, they have combined wages of $98,000 and a rental loss of $26,800. Because they meet both the active participation and the MAGI tests, they are allowed to deduct $25,000 of the rental loss as an offset to their nonpassive income (wages). The remaining amount over the $25,000 limit ($1,800) that cannot be deducted in the current year is carried forward and may potentially be used in the following year.

For every $2 by which a taxpayer's MAGI exceeds $100,000, the allowance is reduced by $1. If a taxpayer's MAGI is $150,000 or more (or $75,000 or more if married filing separately), the $25,000 allowance is fully phased out, and the losses must be carried forward.

> **Example:** Ernesto and Fabiola file jointly and have MAGI of $140,000. They have $25,000 of losses from the residential rental property that they actively manage. Because they actively manage the property, they potentially qualify to deduct up to $25,000 of losses against their nonpassive income. However, because their joint income is over $100,000, they are subject to the phaseout. Therefore, Ernesto and Fabiola's deduction for rental losses is reduced by $20,000 (0.5 × ($140,000 - $100,000). They can deduct $5,000 ($25,000 - $20,000) against their nonpassive income. The additional $20,000 of losses is carried forward to the following year.

> **Definition: MAGI** is a taxpayer's adjusted gross income with certain deductions added back in. These may include IRA contributions, rental losses, student loan interest, and qualified tuition expenses, among others. A taxpayer's MAGI is used as a basis for determining whether he qualifies for certain tax deductions.

> **Example:** Jerold owns a rental property in San Francisco. He actively participates in the rental activity. In the previous tax year, he incurred ($9,000) in losses on his rental. Jerold's modified adjusted gross income was $150,000 for the year. Because of his income threshold, Jerold's rental losses are suspended, and he is not allowed to deduct any rental losses. The following year, Jerold had $5,000 in losses from his rental activity. However, he also changed jobs in the middle of the year, and now his AGI is lower. In 2018, Jerold's AGI is $85,000, so his rental losses are now allowable. His suspended rental losses from the prior year ($9,000) and his current year losses ($5,000) will be allowed on his 2018 tax return, for a total deduction of ($14,000).

Renting Only Part of Property

A taxpayer who rents only part of a property must divide certain expenses between the part of the property used for rental purposes and the part used for personal purposes, as though there were actually two separate pieces of property. Expenses related to the part of the property used for rental purposes can be deducted as rental expenses on Schedule E. This includes a portion of expenses that normally are nondeductible personal expenses, such as painting the outside of a house. If an expense applies to both rental use and personal use, such as a heating bill for the entire house, the taxpayer must divide the expense between the two. The two most common methods for dividing such expenses are based on:

- The number of rooms in the house, and
- The square footage of the house.

> **Example:** Lucius rents out a single bedroom in his house. The room is 12 × 15 feet or 180 square feet. Lucius' entire house is 1,800 square feet. Lucius can deduct as a rental expense 10% of any expense that must be divided between rental use and personal use. Lucius' 2018 heating bills for the entire house totaled $600, and therefore $60 ($600 × .10) can be considered a deductible rental expense. The balance, $540, is a personal expense that Lucius cannot deduct.

A common situation involves a duplex in which the property owner lives in one side and rents out the other. Certain expenses, like mortgage interest and real estate taxes, apply to the entire property and must be split to determine rental and personal expenses.

> **Example:** Marisa owns a duplex with two units of the same size. She lives in one side and rents out the other. In 2018, Marisa paid $12,000 of mortgage interest and $4,000 of real estate taxes for the entire property. Marisa can deduct $6,000 of mortgage interest and $2,000 of real estate taxes on Schedule E. She can claim the other $6,000 of mortgage interest and $2,000 of real estate taxes attributable to her personal use on Schedule A as itemized deductions.

If a taxpayer owns a partial interest in rental property, he can deduct expenses paid according to the percentage of ownership.

Personal Use of Dwelling Unit

When a taxpayer has a residence (whether a main home or a second home) that is used personally at certain times and rented out at other times, he must divide his expenses between rental use and personal use. Rental expenses generally will be no more than a taxpayer's total expenses multiplied by the following fraction: the denominator is the total number of days the dwelling is used, and the numerator is the total number of days actually rented at a fair rental price. Any day the unit is rented at a fair rental price is a day of rental use. Any day the unit is available for rent but not actually rented is not a day of rental use.

> **Example:** Valerie owns a vacation home in Hawaii that she rented for 90 days in January, February, and March. She can deduct the rental expenses on Schedule E only for those 90 days. However, she can deduct expenses for mortgage interest and real estate taxes for the other 275 days of the year on her Schedule A.

Partial Rental Activity (with a Profit Motive)

If a taxpayer uses a property for both rental and personal purposes, the tax treatment of expenses depends on whether his personal use is considered to be usage as a "home." It is considered "usage as a home" if he uses the property for personal purposes during the year for more than the greater of <u>fourteen days</u>, or 10% of the total days it is rented at a fair rental price. Days of personal use are counted when:

- A member of the taxpayer's family uses the property without paying a fair rental price (this is treated as personal use of the property)

- Anyone uses the property at less than the fair rental price

- Use of the property is donated to a charitable organization

However, any day the taxpayer spends working on repairs and maintaining the property is not counted as personal use, even if his family is also staying there.

Renting a dwelling unit that is also used by the taxpayer for personal purposes during the year is not considered a passive activity. If a taxpayer's rental expenses are more than his rental income, he cannot use the excess expenses to offset income from other sources. However, excess deductions may be carried forward to the next year and treated as rental expenses for the same property, subject to the same limits.

> **Example:** Travis owns a condominium in the U.S. Virgin Islands. He uses it as a personal residence for five months out of the year and rents it out to tenants the rest of the year. He has a profit motive for the rental activity. Travis' rental income is $8,000 in 2018, and his rental expenses are $10,000. Travis cannot deduct the full $10,000 of rental expenses, because the condominium is not strictly a rental. It is also a personal home. Travis can carry over the remaining ($2,000) in unused losses and deduct that amount from future rental income on the condominium.

> **Example:** William owns a mountain cabin at Lake Tahoe that was used as follows in 2018: He rented it for 60 days during the ski season, spent a week at the cabin cleaning and making repairs before the rental period began, and donated a week of rental use to a local charity. In apportioning expenses:
>
> (1) Days used by the charity (7/67 days) would be treated as personal use; expenses such as mortgage interest and property taxes would be deductible in this ratio on Schedule A.
>
> (2) The remaining 60/67 days would be treated as rental use, and this fraction of total expenses incurred would be deductible on Schedule E.
>
> (3) The seven days cleaning and making repairs would not count as either personal or rental use for purposes of allocating expenses.
>
> William's cabin is not considered a "home" because his personal use was less than 14 days and less than 10% of the total days it was rented for fair market value. His losses are not limited.

Not-For-Profit Rentals and Below-Market Rentals

If a taxpayer does not rent the property with the intent to make a profit, the taxpayer cannot deduct any rental expenses that exceed the taxpayer's rental income. The presumption is made of whether a rental is for profit is when rental income exceeds rental expenses for three out of five years.

In the case of a "not-for-profit" rental, the rental income is not reported on Schedule E, and the taxpayer cannot deduct a loss. Any unused expenses on a "not-for-profit" rental cannot be carried forward to the next year.

When a taxpayer rents below fair market price, (such as rental to a close family member) the taxpayer would be considered to be renting "not for profit." Below-market rentals to a family member or another related party is the most common type of "not-for-profit" rental.

> **Example:** Sandra rents her second home to her grandson for less than market value, so there is no profit. Sandra's rental expenses exceed the income generated by the rental property. Since the rental activity does not have a profit motive, Sandra should report the rental income on Form 1040, as "other income." The rental expenses (such as mortgage interest and property taxes[82]) are deductible on Schedule A, just like they would be for any other second home. She would not use Schedule E to deduct the losses.

Not-for-profit rental income is reported on Form 1040 as "other income." If the taxpayer itemizes deductions, he can include mortgage interest and real estate taxes on the appropriate lines of Schedule A (Form 1040).

Minimal Rental Use (15-Day Rule)

If a taxpayer rents a main home or vacation home for fewer than 15 days, he does not have to recognize any of the income as taxable. He also cannot deduct any rental expenses. This is called the "15-day rule," or "minimal rental use."

> **Example:** Estelle owns a condo on the Gulf Coast which is her personal residence. While she was away on vacation, she rented her condo for 11 days, charging $100 per day for a total of $1,100. She also had $320 of rental expenses during that time. Estelle does not report any of the income or expenses based on the exception for minimal rental use.

Exception for Real Estate Professionals

If a taxpayer qualifies as a real estate professional, losses from rental real estate activities in which he materially participates are not considered passive activity losses and are fully deductible.[83] If the tests for material participation are not met, rental losses are considered passive and are normally deductible only up to $25,000, based upon the passive activity rules outlined previously.

In most instances, if a property owner provides only basic services to tenants, such as trash collection, he reports rental income and expenses on Schedule E, Form 1040. It is not subject to self-employment tax.

---

[82] Started in 2018 property taxes (along with other state and local taxes) for non-business and non-rental activities are generally subject to an overall deduction limit of $10,000 ($5,000 for those that file MFS). This will be covered in more detail in Unit 12.

[83] The determination of whether someone is a "real estate professional" is based on a number of factors. In general, a taxpayer qualifies as a real estate professional if (1) he performs more than 750 hours of services during the taxable year in real property trades or businesses in which he materially participates, and (2) more than one-half of the total personal services performed in trades or businesses by the taxpayer during the year are performed in real property trades or businesses in which the taxpayer materially participates.

In contrast, owners of property who provide significant services to the renter, such as maid cleaning and housekeeping services, are generally required to report revenue and expenses related to the property on Schedule C, *Profit of Loss from Business,* and any net profit is subject to self-employment tax. The most common examples of taxpayers who report their rental activities on Schedule C, instead of on Schedule E, are hotel owners and motel operators.

Hotels, Motels, and Bed and Breakfasts

Operators of hotels, boarding houses, and bed and breakfasts must report their income on Schedule C, not Schedule E. If the property is rented only for short periods and if the taxpayer provides "substantial services" to the tenant, such as daily maid service, laundry service, or regular breakfast service, the taxpayer should report the rental income and expenses on Schedule C (Form 1040), *Profit or Loss from Business,* rather than Schedule E.

In some cases, renting out all or part of a house can be classified for tax purposes as the equivalent of running a bed and breakfast. The facts and circumstances of each situation must be taken into account to determine if the taxpayer is providing "substantial services" to a tenant.

> **Example:** Moriah lives in a popular tourist area in Palm Springs, CA. She has a small granny cottage behind her home. Moriah listed her granny cottage on a popular website for vacation rentals, Airweb. She used Airweb to rent her cottage 140 days last year to several different tenants. She provided cleaning service, daily breakfast service, and fresh towels and linens, just like a hotel would. Even though she is not a real estate professional, Moriah would have to report the rental income on Schedule C, not Schedule E, because she is providing a short-term rental and "substantial services" to her tenants.

> **Example:** Stephanie owns a small motel in downtown Cincinnati. Stephanie does not offer long-term rentals. The hotel offers full maid service, cleaning, and breakfast daily. Since she provides "significant services" as a motel owner, the income would be treated as self-employment income, rather than rental income. Stephanie would report her income on Schedule C.

Royalty Income

Like rental income, royalty income is reported on Schedule E. Royalties from copyrights, patents, and oil, gas, and mineral properties are taxable as ordinary income.

> **Example:** Kirk owns 150 acres of farmland. In 2018, natural gas deposits were discovered on his property. Kirk negotiates a contract with an energy company who wishes to extract the natural gas from his land. The contract stipulates that Kirk will receive 12% of the revenue generated by the gas extracted from his property. In 2018, Kirk receives $98,000 in royalties from the energy company. The amounts were reported to Kirk on Form 1099-MISC, and he will report this income on his Schedule E, Form 1040.

In many cases, a taxpayer reports details of royalties on Schedule E, *Supplemental Income and Loss.* However, self-employed writers, musicians, and inventors report income on Schedule C, *Profit or Loss from Business,* and are subject to self-employment tax.

Example: In 2018, Orel's brother died. Orel inherited a copyright from his brother, who had written an instruction manual for woodworking. Orel then leased the copyrighted material to schools and colleges for their use. Since he had not created the copyright himself, Orel will report the royalty income on Schedule E. The income is subject to income tax, but not self-employment tax.

Royalties from copyrights on literary, musical, or artistic works, or from patents on inventions, are paid to a taxpayer for the right to use his work over a specified period of time. Royalties are often based on the number of units sold, such as the number of books, tickets to a performance, or machines sold.

Example: Nellie is the self-employed writer of a popular series of books for young children. She receives royalties from her publisher based on the number of books she has sold over a certain period of time. Nellie must report these royalties as taxable income on her Schedule C.

Royalty payments are always reported to the taxpayer on Form 1099-MISC. A taxpayer is required to issue Form 1099-MISC, *Miscellaneous Income,* to each person to whom he has paid at least $10 of royalties for the year.

Unit 9: Study Questions

(Test yourself first; then check the correct answers at the end of this quiz.)

1. Ian signs a three-year lease from a tenant who wishes to rent a building he owns. In December 2018, Ian receives $12,000 for the first year's rent and $12,000 as rent for the last year of the lease. He also receives a $1,500 security deposit that is refundable at the end of the lease. How much rental income must Ian include in his 2018 tax return?

A. $1,500
B. $12,000
C. $24,000
D. $25,500

2. In 2018, Jane is single and has $40,000 of wages, $2,000 of passive activity income from a limited partnership, and $3,500 of passive activity loss from a rental real estate activity in which she actively participated. Which of the following statements is correct?

A. The first $2,000 of Jane's $3,500 passive loss offsets her passive income. Jane can deduct the remaining $1,500 loss to reduce taxation of her wages.
B. Jane cannot deduct the passive loss to reduce taxation of her wages.
C. Jane cannot offset the rental loss against the passive income from the partnership because it is not the same type of passive activity.
D. Jane must carry over her loss to the subsequent tax year.

3. Rosemary's home is used exclusively as her residence all year, except for 13 days. During this time, Rosemary rents her home to alumni while the local college has its homecoming celebration. She made $3,000 of rental income and had $500 of rental expenses during this 13-day period. Which of the following statements is correct?

A. All of the rental income may be excluded.
B. Rosemary can exclude only $2,500 of the rental income.
C. Rosemary can deduct her expenses when she reports her rental income on Schedule E.
D. Rosemary must recognize all $3,000 of rental income, and deduct the $500 in rental expenses on Schedule E.

4. Pamela ordered an HVAC unit for her rental property on November 15, 2018. It was delivered on December 28, 2018, and was installed and ready for use on January 2, 2019. She paid for the unit using a credit card and paid off the card on February 3, 2019. On which date would the HVAC unit be considered "placed in service" for depreciation purposes?

A. November 15, 2018
B. December 28, 2018
C. January 2, 2019
D. February 3, 2019

5. Reba converted her primary residence to rental use during the year. Her original cost was $189,000, of which $13,200 was allocated to the land and $175,800 was to the house. On the date of the conversion, the property had a fair market value of $158,000, of which $11,000 was allocable to the land and $147,000 to the house. What is Reba's basis for depreciation on Schedule E?

A. $147,000
B. $189,000
C. $175,800
D. $158,000

6. Asher decides to convert his primary residence into a rental property. He moves out of his home in May 2018 and starts renting it on June 1, 2018. He has $12,000 of mortgage interest for the year. How should Asher report his mortgage interest expense?

A. Report the entire $12,000 on Schedule E.
B. Report the entire $12,000 on Schedule A.
C. Report $7,000 on Schedule E as interest expense and $5,000 on Schedule A as mortgage interest.
D. Report $8,000 on Schedule E as interest expense and $4,000 on Schedule A as mortgage interest.

7. Which of the following costs related to rental property should be classified as a capital improvement and depreciated rather than being expensed currently?

A. Replacing an entire deck
B. Repairing a broken toilet
C. Painting the family room
D. Patching a hole in the wall

8. Tina owns a residential rental house. Last year, she paid $968 to repair a broken window. The cost of the labor was $468, and the cost of the replacement window was $500. She replaced the broken window with a premium energy-saving window. What is the correct treatment of this expense?

A. She cannot deduct the cost since it was an improvement; she must add it to the basis of the property.
B. She can deduct $468 as a rental expense on Schedule E (the labor cost). The cost of the actual window ($500) must be capitalized and depreciated.
C. She can deduct the entire $968 as a rental expense on Schedule E.
D. She can deduct $968 on Schedule A as an itemized deduction.

9. Which of the following describes depreciation?

A. A business expense that applies only to rental properties
B. An improvement to an asset that must be capitalized
C. A common type of accounting method used by most partnerships
D. An annual tax deduction that accounts for the reduction in the value of an asset as it ages

10. In 2018, Travis and Brittany moved to Florida. They decided to rent their old house in California instead of selling it. They had purchased the home five years ago for $500,000 and had paid $80,000 for various improvements over the years. The purchase price of $500,000 was attributable to fair market values of $100,000 for the land and $400,000 for the house. Their new tenant paid a refundable security deposit of $6,000 and moved in on July 1, 2018. The FMV of the property on July 1 was $525,000, comprised of $105,000 for the land and $420,000 for the house. The tenant then paid rent of $3,000 each month from July through December of 2018. Travis and Brittany incurred the following expenses in 2018 related to the house:
- **Mortgage interest:** $10,000
- **Property taxes:** $10,000
- **Casualty insurance:** $1,000

In addition, they paid $500 for repairs during December. Exclusive of depreciation expense, what was Travis and Brittany's taxable rental income?

A. $1,500
B. $7,000
C. $7,250
D. $13,000

11. Based on the information in the previous question, what is the amount of basis on which depreciation should be calculated for the rental period?

A. $400,000
B. $480,000
C. $580,000
D. $420,000

12. Matthew and Diane are legally separated and have lived in separate residences for three years. They file separate tax returns (MFS). They own a rental property jointly; actively participate in the rental activity, and share income and losses equally. The rental property had $30,000 of losses during the year. Matthew has wage income of $48,000 in 2018. He has no other items of income or loss. What is the maximum amount of rental losses that Matthew can claim on his separate return?

A. $0
B. $12,500
C. $15,000
D. $25,000

1. The answer is C. Ian must include $24,000 in his income in the first year. He must recognize all the advance rent as income in the year of receipt. The security deposit does not have to be recognized as income because it is refundable to the tenant.

2. The answer is A. Jane can use $2,000 of her rental loss to offset the passive activity income from the limited partnership. The remaining $1,500 loss can be offset against her $40,000 of wages. A taxpayer can deduct up to $25,000 per year of losses for rental real estate activities in which she actively participates, as long as their modified AGI does not exceed a certain amount. This special allowance is an exception to the general rule disallowing losses in excess of income from passive activities against nonpassive income.

3. The answer is A. All the rental income may be excluded under the "15-day rule." Rosemary's home is primarily for personal use, and a rental period of fewer than 15 days is disregarded, which means the IRS does not consider it a rental. The rental income is not taxable, but the rental expenses (such as utilities or maintenance costs) are not deductible.

4. The answer is C. Depreciation begins on the placed-in-service date when an asset becomes ready and available for first use. Typically, the placed-in-service date and the purchase date are the same, but that is not always the case. Since Pamela did not have the HVAC unit installed and ready for use until January 2, 2019, she must wait until 2019 to begin depreciating the unit. The fact that the unit was paid for with a credit card is irrelevant (it is treated the same as if it was paid by check or cash).

5. The answer is A. Reba's basis for depreciation on the house is its fair market value on the date of the conversion ($147,000) because the FMV on the date of conversion is less than the amount of her original cost that was allocable to the house ($175,800). When a taxpayer converts property held for personal use to rental use (for example, the rental of a former home), the basis for depreciation will be the lesser of fair market value or adjusted basis on the date of conversion.

6. The answer is C. Asher must allocate his expenses between personal use and rental use. He can deduct as rental expenses seven-twelfths (7/12) of annual expenses, such as taxes and insurance. Starting in June, he can deduct as rental expenses the amounts he paid for items generally billed monthly, such as utilities. When figuring his allowable depreciation, he should treat the property as placed in service on June 1.

7. The answer is A. The replacement of the deck would be considered a depreciable improvement. The other choices are repairs and may be deducted as current expenses.

8. The answer is C. Tina can deduct the entire $968 as a rental expense on Schedule E. Generally, the expenses of renting a property, such as maintenance, insurance, taxes, and interest, can be deducted from rental income. This cost is a repair, not an improvement because the window was already broken. If *all* the windows had been replaced with energy-efficient windows, the cost would have been considered an improvement and added to the property's basis.

9. The answer is D. Depreciation is an income tax deduction that allows a business to recover the cost or basis of property it uses over time. It is an annual allowance for the wear and tear, deterioration, or obsolescence of assets.

10. The answer is B. Travis and Brittany must report six months of rental income at $3,000 per month, or $18,000, but the security deposit of $6,000 is refundable and therefore not recognized as income in 2018.

They can deduct 6/12 of the amounts incurred for mortgage interest, property taxes, and casualty insurance, or $10,500, plus the $500 cost of repairs while the house was rented. Thus, their reportable net rental income before considering depreciation would be $7,000. The calculations are as follows:

Taxable rental income:	
Six months of rent (at $3,000 per month)	$18,000
Minus deductible expenses:	
Mortgage interest (for six months)	5,000
Property taxes (for six months)	5,000
Casualty insurance (for six months)	500
Repair cost	500
Expenses before depreciation	(11,000)
Rental income before depreciation	**$7,000**

11. The answer is D. The basis for depreciation is the lesser of fair market value or the taxpayer's adjusted basis on the date the property was converted to rental use. The adjusted basis of the house on July 1, 2018, was $480,000 (original cost of $400,000 plus improvements of $80,000), but the FMV of $420,000 on the same date was lower. The basis of the land is not subject to depreciation and not included in the calculation.

Adjusted basis of house:	
Cost	$400,000
Improvements	80,000
Total adjusted basis	480,000
FMV of the house on July 1, 2018:	**$420,000**

12. The answer is B. Matthew is allowed to claim a maximum of $12,500 of losses on his separately filed return. If a taxpayer actively participated in a passive rental real estate activity that produced a loss, he can deduct the loss to offset his nonpassive income, up to $25,000. However, married persons filing separate returns who lived apart during the year are each allowed a maximum of $12,500 for losses from passive real estate activities. Married persons who file separate returns but lived together during the year are not allowed to take losses on rental real estate activity. Instead, the losses are suspended and must be carried over until the property produces income, or the property is disposed of.

Unit 10: Other Taxable Income

For additional information read:
Publication 525, *Taxable and Nontaxable Income*
Publication 4681, *Canceled Debts, Foreclosures, Repossessions, and Abandonments*
Publication 504, *Divorced or Separated Individuals*

In this unit, we discuss a number of other types of taxable income that must be reported on Form 1040. In 2018, the TCJA makes a number of significant changes to the treatment of hobby income, gambling income and losses, and the tax treatment of some types of court awards.

Taxable Recoveries

A "recovery" is a return of an amount a taxpayer deducted or took a credit for in an earlier year. The most common recoveries are refunds, reimbursements, and rebates of deductions itemized on Schedule A. A taxpayer must include a recovery in income in the year he receives it, to the extent the deduction or credit reduced his tax in the earlier year.

State and local income tax refunds are reported as taxable income in the year received only if the taxpayer itemized deductions in the prior year in which those taxes were overpaid. The payer should send Form 1099-G, *Certain Government Payments*, to the taxpayer by January 31, and also send a copy to the IRS.

Example: Kadam claimed the standard deduction on his prior year federal tax return. In 2018, he received a refund of $600 for state income taxes he paid during the prior year. The state tax refund is not taxable in 2018, as Kadam received no federal tax benefit from his state tax payments because he did not itemize deductions in the previous year.

Refunds of federal income taxes are not included in a taxpayer's income because they are never allowed as a deduction.

Alimony Received

Alimony is taxable income to the recipient and deductible by the payor.[84] In contrast, child support is not taxable income to the receiver and not deductible by the payer because it is viewed as a payment a parent makes simply to support his or her own child.

Alimony *received* is taxable income to the payee. Alimony *paid* is an adjustment to income for the payor. The payor does not have to itemize to deduct alimony payments made.

Example: Austin and Freya divorced two years ago. Their divorce decree requires Austin to pay Freya $200 per month as child support and $150 per month as alimony. Austin makes all of his child support and alimony payments on time. Therefore, in 2018, he can deduct $1,800 ($150 × 12 months) as alimony paid, and Freya must report $1,800 as alimony received as taxable income. The amount paid as child support, $2,400 ($200 × 12) is not deductible by Austin and is not reported as income by Freya.

---

[84] The Tax Cuts and Jobs Act changes the treatment of alimony after 2018, making it nondeductible to the payor and nontaxable to the recipient. Divorce agreements entered into before 2019 will be "grandfathered" so there will continue to be an alimony deduction and alimony income for individuals with divorce agreements that were finalized in prior years. For the 2018 tax year, the old rules still apply.

If a divorce agreement specifies payments of both alimony and child support and only partial payments are made by the payer, the partial payments are considered child support until that obligation is fully paid. Any additional amounts paid are then treated as alimony.

> **Example:** Dayna and Clemente are divorced. Their divorce decree requires Clemente pay Dayna $2,000 a month ($24,000 [$2,000 × 12] a year) as child support and $1,500 a month ($18,000 [$1,500 × 12] a year) as alimony. Clemente falls behind on his payments and pays only $36,000 during the year. In this case, the first $24,000 paid is considered child support and only the remaining amount of $12,000 ($36,000 - $24,000) is considered alimony. Clemente can deduct $12,000 as alimony paid. Dayna must report $12,000 as alimony income received.

If an alimony payment is subject to reduction based on a contingency relating to a child (e.g., attaining a certain age, marrying, or going to college), the amount subject to reduction is treated as child support for tax purposes. This is regardless of whether or not the contingency is likely to occur.

If alimony payments continue after the receiving spouse dies, they will automatically be considered child support, not alimony. In order for a payment to qualify as alimony:

- The divorce agreement may not include a clause indicating that the payment is something else (such as child support or repayment of a loan).

- If the spouses are legally separated, they cannot live together when the alimony payments are made, or the IRS will not consider the payments to be alimony.

- The payor must have no liability to make any payment (in cash or property) after the death of the former spouse.

Not all payments that are made to an ex-spouse qualify as alimony. Alimony does not include:

- Payments that are a former spouse's share of income from community property
- Payments to keep up the payer's property
- Free use of the payer's property
- Noncash property settlements
- Any payment made other than in cash

> **Note:** Property settlements are simply a division of property and are not treated as alimony. In general, property transferred to an ex-spouse as part of a divorce proceeding is not a taxable event.

> **Example:** Brooklynn and Galvin divorce in 2018. As part of their divorce agreement, Brooklynn must transfer a portion of her IRA account to Galvin. The IRA transfer is properly outlined in their property settlement agreement. On October 1, 2018, their divorce becomes final. Two days later, the IRA transfer is completed, and $105,000 is transferred directly from Brooklynn's IRA to Galvin's IRA. The transfer is considered a division of marital assets and is not alimony. It is also not subject to an early withdrawal penalty.

Payments made to a third party can be considered alimony in some cases. For example, if, under the terms of a divorce agreement, a spouse pays the medical bills of his ex-wife, a cash payment to the hospital can count as alimony.

For a jointly owned home, half of the mortgage payments and real estate taxes may be deducted as alimony, assuming the divorce decree or separation agreement requires a taxpayer to pay these expenses for his ex-spouse. The ex-spouse must include the payments as alimony received.

Government Benefits

Most government welfare benefits, including food stamps, heating assistance programs, and nonfederal assistance benefits from states or local agencies are exempt from federal taxation. Worker's compensation, which provides wage replacement and medical benefits to injured workers, is not taxable income. In contrast, unemployment compensation is taxable.

> **Example:** Haima was laid off from her job in 2018. She received $300 a week of unemployment compensation for 26 weeks. When she was unable to find another job, she began receiving benefits from her state's WIC program, which provided vouchers for food for her and her toddler. The unemployment compensation would be taxable income, but the welfare (WIC) benefits would not be taxable.

Social Security Income

Social Security income is reported to the taxpayer on Form SSA-1099, *Social Security Benefit Statement,* and these benefits are taxable in certain cases, depending upon a taxpayer's income and the amount of benefits received for the year. To determine if any percentage of his Social Security benefits is taxable, a taxpayer must compare the base threshold amount for his filing status with the total of:

- One-half of his benefits, plus
- All of the taxpayer's other income, including tax-exempt interest.

If the sum is less than the base amount for his filing status, none of the Social Security is taxable. If the sum is more than the base amount for his filing status, a percentage of the Social Security is taxable.

Base Amounts for Calculating Taxability of Social Security
MFJ: $32,000
Single, HOH, QW, or MFS (and lived apart from his/her spouse all year): $25,000
MFS (if lived with spouse at any time during the year): $0

The taxpayer calculates the taxable portion on a worksheet in the *Instructions for Form 1040*, or Publication 915, *Social Security and Equivalent Railroad Retirement Benefits.* The taxable portion of Social Security benefits is never more than 85% and, in most cases, is less than 50%. Spouses who file jointly must combine their incomes and Social Security benefits when figuring the taxable portion of their benefits, even if one spouse did not receive any benefits.

Example: George and Mabel are both over 65. They file jointly, and both received Social Security benefits during 2018. At the end of the year, George received a Form SSA-1099 showing net benefits of $7,500. Mabel received a Form SSA-1099 showing net benefits of $3,500. George also received wages of $20,000 and taxable interest income of $500. He did not have any tax-exempt interest.

1. Total Social Security benefits	$11,000
2. Enter one-half of Social Security	$ 5,500
3. Enter taxable interest and wages	$20,500
4. Sum ($5,500 + $20,500)	$26,000

George and Mabel's benefits are not taxable for 2018 because the total above is not more than the base amount ($32,000) for married filing jointly.

Other Income

"Other income" includes items that do not have separately identified lines on Form 1040. Starting in 2018, other income is reported directly on line 21 of Schedule 1, Form 1040. This line is the catch-all for all other types of taxable income that is not reportable on another schedule or area of Form 1040. Examples, which we cover in detail next, include:

- Gambling winnings
- Cancellation of debt income
- Hobby income
- Certain types of court awards
- Prizes and awards
- Taxable distributions from a Coverdell education savings account or a qualified tuition program if they are more than the qualified higher education expenses for a designated beneficiary

Note: Remember, taxpayers are required to report all taxable income, whether or not the taxpayer receives a document from the payor reporting the amount paid.

Gambling Winnings

Gambling income may include winnings from lotteries, raffles, horse races, and casinos. Gambling winnings will be reported to a taxpayer on Form W-2G if he wins:

- $600 or more from regular gambling (i.e., horse racing, card tables, etc.)
- $1,200 or more from bingo or slot machines
- $1,500 or more from keno
- Any amounts subject to federal income tax withholding

A taxpayer must report and pay tax on all gambling winnings, regardless of whether he receives a Form W-2G. In 2018, gambling losses are still deductible on Schedule A as a miscellaneous itemized deduction, but the deduction is limited to the amount of gambling winnings.

> **Example:** Janette had $11,000 of gambling winnings and $23,000 of gambling losses in 2018. Her deduction for gambling losses cannot exceed $11,000, the amount of her gambling winnings. In order to claim the deduction for her losses, Janette must itemize and list her gambling losses on Schedule A, Form 1040. If Janette does not itemize, she will not be able to deduct any of her gambling losses.

> **Note:** Starting in 2018, the TCJA expands the definition of "gambling losses." In prior years, professional gamblers who filed on Schedule C were able to generate an NOL from their wagering activities. In 2018, the TCJA modifies the limit on gambling losses so that all the deductions for expenses incurred in carrying out gambling activities, not just direct gambling losses, are limited to the extent of gambling winnings. For example, an individual who is a professional gambler can include expenses traveling to and from a casino as gambling losses as an offset against any gambling winnings, but cannot use the expenses to generate a loss on Schedule C.[85]

The taxpayer must keep an accurate diary or similar record of gambling winnings and losses, along with tickets, receipts, canceled checks, and other documentation. He is not required to include these supporting records with his tax return, but they should be retained in case of an audit.

Cancellation of Debt Income

Generally, if a taxpayer's debt is canceled or forgiven, the taxpayer must include the debt forgiveness in his gross income. If a lender cancels a debt and issues Form 1099-C, the lender will indicate on the form if the borrower was personally liable for repayment of the debt. The tax impact depends on the type of debt and whether the loan is recourse or nonrecourse.

A recourse debt holds the borrower personally liable. All other debt is considered nonrecourse. Cancellation of debt may include any indebtedness for which a taxpayer is personally liable, or which attaches to the taxpayer's property, such as an auto loan, credit card debt, mortgage, or home equity loan.[86]

> **Note:** A nonrecourse loan does not allow the lender to pursue anything other than the collateral. For example, if a borrower defaults on a nonrecourse home loan, the bank can only foreclose on the home. The bank cannot take further legal action to collect the money owed on the debt. Whether a debt is recourse or nonrecourse may vary from state to state, depending on state law. If a lender forecloses on property subject to a recourse debt and cancels the portion of the debt in excess of the FMV of the property, the canceled portion is treated as ordinary income. This amount must be included in gross income unless it qualifies for an exception or exclusion.

---

[85] The TCJA modifies IRC Sect. 165(d) to provide that all deductions for expenses incurred in carrying out gambling and wagering activities are limited to the extent of gambling winnings.

[86] There is no taxable income from a canceled debt if it is intended as a gift (for example, if a taxpayer owes his parents money, but they choose to forgive the debt).

Many home mortgages are "nonrecourse loans." This means that if the borrower defaults, the lender can seize the home, but cannot seek out the borrower for any further compensation, even if the FMV of the home does not cover the remaining loan balance. If the taxpayer abandons property that secures debt for which the taxpayer is not personally liable (a nonrecourse loan), the abandonment is treated as a sale or exchange.

If a loan is nonrecourse and the borrower does not retain the asset, the borrower does not have to recognize cancellation of debt income. However, there is a deemed sales price based on the amount of the nonrecourse loan at the time of the abandonment, foreclosure or short sale.

A taxpayer may question the taxability of canceled debt because it can apply in a tax year in which cash is not received. In a situation where a property is surrendered or repossessed, such as a foreclosure, the taxpayer may feel that by giving up the property, he should be relieved from any further obligation.

Example: Linus lost his home to foreclosure because he lost his job and could no longer make his mortgage payments. At the time of the foreclosure, Linus owed a balance of $170,000 to his mortgage lender, and the fair market value of the home was $140,000. The mortgage is a nonrecourse loan. Linus abandons the property, and the bank forecloses on the home. Linus is not personally liable for the debt (since it is a nonrecourse loan). The abandonment is treated as a sale (for tax purposes) and the "selling price" would be $170,000, which is the balance of the loan.

Example: Lisa borrows $10,000 to take a vacation and defaults on the loan after paying back only $2,000. She has the ability to pay back the loan but chooses not to. The lender writes off the remaining balance of the loan instead of pursuing Lisa for the balance of the loan. Therefore, there is a cancellation of debt of $8,000, which is taxable income to Lisa.

If the original debt is a nonbusiness debt, the canceled debt amount is reported as "other income" on line 21 of a Schedule 1, Form 1040. The taxpayer must generally report two transactions:

1. The cancellation of debt income
2. Gain or loss on the sale or repossession, generally equal to the difference between the FMV of the property at the time of the foreclosure and the taxpayer's adjusted basis in the property

If a personal asset such as a vehicle is repossessed, the repossession is treated as a sale for tax purposes, and a gain or loss must be computed. A loss related to a personal asset would be nondeductible.

Example: Julian lost his sailboat to repossession because he could no longer afford to make his payments. At the time of the repossession, he owed a balance of $170,000 to the lender, and the FMV of the sailboat was $140,000. Julian is personally liable for the debt (recourse loan), so the repossession is treated as a sale. The "selling price" from the repossession is $140,000, and Julian must recognize $30,000 in debt forgiveness income ($170,000 outstanding debt - $140,000 FMV).

Example: Larissa bought a new car for $15,000. She made a $2,000 down payment and borrowed the remaining $13,000 from her bank. Larissa is personally liable for the car loan (recourse debt). The bank repossessed her car because she stopped making payments. The balance due on the car loan at the time of the repossession was $10,000. The FMV of the car when repossessed was only $9,000. Since repossession is treated as a sale for tax purposes, the gain or loss must be computed. Larissa compares the amount realized ($9,000) with her adjusted basis ($15,000) to determine that she has a $6,000 nondeductible loss. She also has ordinary income from cancellation of debt. That income is $1,000 ($10,000 canceled debt – $9,000 FMV). Larissa must report the canceled debt as income.

Definition: A **nonrecourse debt** is a type of loan that is secured by collateral in which the borrower does not have personal liability for the loan. The most common type of nonrecourse debt is a home mortgage.

Nontaxable Canceled Debt

There are several circumstances in which canceled debt is not taxable. The law provides several exceptions in which the cancelled debt is excludible from income or nontaxable due to the nature of the debt.

Insolvency: A taxpayer is insolvent when his total debts are more than the FMV of his total assets. If a taxpayer is insolvent when the debt is canceled, the canceled debt is not taxable, but only to the extent of the insolvency (i.e., by how much his debts exceed his assets). For this purpose, the taxpayer's assets include the value of everything he owns, including pensions and retirement accounts.

Example: In 2018, Marnie had $5,000 of credit card debt, which she did not pay. The bank decided to cancel the entire $5,000 credit card balance. She received a Form 1099-C from her credit card company showing canceled debt of $5,000. Immediately before the cancellation, Marnie's total liabilities were $15,000 and the FMV of her total assets was $7,000. Therefore, at the time the debt was canceled, Marnie was insolvent to the extent of $8,000 ($15,000 total liabilities minus $7,000 FMV of her total assets). Marnie can exclude the entire $5,000 canceled debt from income. Even if the amount is not taxable, Marnie must report the amount of debt forgiven on her return by completing Form 982, *Reduction of Tax Attributes Due to Discharge of Indebtedness.*

Bankruptcy: Debts discharged through bankruptcy court in a Title 11 bankruptcy case (generally Chapters 7 and 13) are not considered taxable income. The taxpayer must attach Form 982, *Reduction of Tax Attributes Due to Discharge of Indebtedness,* to his federal income tax return to report debt canceled in bankruptcy.

Qualified Farm Indebtedness: If a taxpayer incurred the canceled debt in a farming business, it is generally not considered taxable income.

Canceled Debt that is Otherwise Deductible: If a taxpayer uses the cash method of accounting, he should not recognize canceled debt income if payment of the debt would have otherwise been a deductible expense.

Home Mortgage Debt: Under the *Mortgage Forgiveness Debt Relief Act*, mortgage debt on a primary residence that was forgiven was excluded from taxable income. This provision expired in 2018. Debt reduced through mortgage restructuring, as well as mortgage debt forgiven in connection with a foreclosure may now be taxable to the borrower.

Despite the expiration of this provision, canceled mortgage debt does not have to be included in taxable income if the debt was canceled in a bankruptcy case or while the taxpayer was insolvent (up to the amount of the insolvency of the taxpayer right before the debt cancellation).

Example: Alejandro's main home is subject to a $320,000 recourse mortgage. He stops making payments on the loan. Alejandro's mortgage lender forecloses on the home in January 2018, when the fair market value of the home was $280,000. The residence is later auctioned off by the bank for $280,000. Alejandro has $40,000 of canceled debt from the discharge of indebtedness because the recourse mortgage was $40,000 than the property's fair market value at the time of the foreclosure. However, right before the foreclosure, Alejandro was insolvent at the time of the foreclosure – with the amount of all his debts (including this mortgage) equaling $400,000 and the value of all of his assets being $350,000 at that time – resulting in an insolvency amount of $50,000. Since the $40,000 canceled debt is less than the $50,000 extent of his insolvency, the forgiven debt is not taxable. Alejandro must report the amount of debt forgiven on his return by completing Form 982, *Reduction of Tax Attributes Due to Discharge of Indebtedness*, and marking the box to report his insolvency.

Cancellation of Student Loans

Certain student loans contain a provision that all or part of the debt incurred to attend a qualified educational institution will be canceled if the student later works for a specified period of time in certain professions. The canceled debt does not have to be recognized as income on a taxpayer's return.

Example: Paula is a medical student completing her residency. In return for forgiveness of her student loans, she agrees to work for four years as a pediatrician in a state program in Minnesota that serves rural and poor communities. The canceled debt does not have to be recognized as income.

Starting in 2018, discharges of student loans (including private student loans) will not be taxable when the discharge is on account of death or permanent disability. It also excludes forgiveness in the event of death even if there is a cosigner on the loan. This new provision covers eligible student loans discharged from January 1, 2018, to December 31, 2025.

Example: Aurelius takes out a student loan of $32,500 and uses it to pay his college tuition and textbooks. He is personally responsible for the loan. On November 1, 2018, Aurelius dies in a car accident. The student loan is forgiven by the lender. The forgiven debt is not taxable to Aurelius on his final tax return, and the liability does not transfer to his estate or his heirs.

Example: Raima is a self-employed interior designer. A CPA firm agrees to file her business tax return and bill her at a later date. Raima receives $2,200 of tax preparation and bookkeeping services for her business on credit. Later, Raima loses a major account and has trouble paying her debts, so her CPA forgives the amount she owes. Raima does not include the canceled debt in her gross income because payment of the debt would have been deductible as a business expense had it been paid.

Hobby Income

A hobby is an activity typically undertaken primarily for pleasure. Even though it may produce income, a hobby is not considered a business because it is not carried on to make a profit. Income from a hobby is taxable and reported on Form 1040, Schedule 1, line 21. Hobby income is generally not subject to self-employment tax.

The IRS presumes that an activity is "carried on for a profit" if it makes a profit during at least three of the last five tax years, including the current year. However, determination of whether an activity is a hobby or a business is determined by a number of factors, including an analysis of the following:

- Does the effort put into the activity indicate an intention to make a profit?
- Does the taxpayer depend on income from the activity?
- If there are losses, are they due to circumstances beyond the taxpayer's control, or did they occur in the start-up phase of the business?
- Has the taxpayer changed methods of operation to improve profitability?
- Does the taxpayer or his advisors have the knowledge needed to carry on the activity as a successful business?
- Has the taxpayer made a profit in similar activities in the past?
- Does the activity make a profit in some years?
- Can the taxpayer expect to make a profit in the future from the appreciation of assets used in the activity?

Note: The use of hobby expenses offset hobby-related income is no longer permitted. The Tax Cuts and Jobs Act repealed most miscellaneous itemized deductions, including the deduction for hobby-related expenses. A taxpayer with hobby income is still allowed to deduct cost of goods sold (COGS), if it applies, in order to arrive at taxable income.[87]

Example: Stefan buys and breeds aquarium fish as a hobby. Twice a year, he goes to an Exotic Fish convention and sells some of his fish. Although he makes money on occasion, he mainly does this activity for pleasure. Stefan plans to continue attending the conventions whether he makes money or not. Therefore, the income is hobby income. His expenses are not deductible, and his income is taxable. Stefan is allowed to deduct the cost of goods sold (i.e., the cost of the fish he sells to customers) in order to calculate his hobby-related income.

---

[87] IRS Regulation 1.183-1(e) states that a taxpayer may determine gross income from <u>any activity</u> by subtracting the cost of goods sold (COGS) from the gross receipts so long as he consistently does so and follows generally accepted methods of accounting in determining such gross income.

Court Awards and Damages

Court awards for compensation for lost wages or profits are generally taxable as ordinary income, as are punitive damages. Compensatory damages for personal physical injury or physical sickness are not taxable income, whether they are from a settlement or an actual court award.

> **Example:** Terrill was injured in a car accident in 2018. His legs were broken, and he suffered other serious physical injuries. He received an insurance settlement for his injuries totaling $950,000. This is nontaxable income because it is payment for a physical injury.

Damages received for emotional distress due to "physical injury or sickness" are treated the same way as damages for physical injury or sickness, so they are not included in income. However, if the plaintiff's emotional distress is *not* due to a physical injury (for example, an employment lawsuit in which a taxpayer suffers emotional distress for injury to reputation), the proceeds are taxable, except for any damages received for medical care due to that emotional distress. Emotional distress includes physical symptoms such as headaches, insomnia, and stomach disorders.

> **Example:** Sheila won a court award for emotional distress caused by unlawful discrimination. The emotional distress resulted in her hospitalization for a nervous breakdown. The court awarded Sheila damages of $100,000, including $20,000 to refund the cost of her medical care for the nervous breakdown. In this case, $80,000 ($100,000 - $20,000) would be considered a taxable court award. The $20,000 of damages for her medical care would not be taxable.

Civil damages, restitution or other monetary awards that the taxpayer received as compensation for wrongful incarceration are not taxable.

> **Example:** Ryan was wrongfully convicted of murder and later released after spending almost 15 years in prison. Ryan was awarded $50,000 per year of wrongful imprisonment. None of the award is taxable income to Ryan.

Under the TCJA, effective for amounts paid or incurred after December 22, 2017, no deduction is allowed for any settlement, payout, or attorney fees related to sexual harassment or sexual abuse if the payments are subject to a nondisclosure agreement.

> **Example:** Santiago is a self-employed therapist who files on Schedule C. Santiago has several employees who work in his office. On January 4, 2018, Santiago's full-time secretary, Keira, sues him for sexual harassment. Rather than risk a public lawsuit that might damage his reputation, Santiago settles with Keira, coming to a confidential settlement with Keira and her attorney. The settlement was $25,000, and their settlement agreement was subject to a nondisclosure clause. Santiago also incurred $5,000 in legal fees for his own attorney to negotiate the settlement. Santiago cannot deduct the settlement or his legal fees as a business expense. However, Keira is required to report the full amount of the settlement as taxable income on her individual return.

Prizes and Awards

Prizes and awards are usually taxable and are reported on Form 1040, Schedule 1, line 21. If the prize or award is in the form of property rather than cash, the fair market value of the property is treated as the taxable amount.

The winner may avoid taxation of the award by rejecting the prize. The taxpayer may also avoid taxation by having the payer directly transfer the prize to a charity or other nonprofit organization.

> **Example:** A national education association chooses Paulo, a college instructor, as its teacher of the year. He is awarded $3,000, but he does not accept the prize. Instead, Paulo directs the association to transfer his winnings to a college scholarship fund. Paulo never receives a check or has control over the funds; therefore, the award is not taxable to him.

Employee awards for safety, length-of-service, or achievements are generally not taxable to the employee unless they exceed specified limits.[88]

Educational Assistance

Many types of educational assistance are tax-free if they meet certain requirements. Tax-free educational assistance includes scholarships, Pell Grants, and employer-provided educational assistance.

Scholarships and Fellowships: A scholarship is an amount paid to an undergraduate or graduate student to pursue a college degree. A fellowship is an amount paid to an individual to pursue research. A scholarship or fellowship is excluded from income only if:

- The taxpayer is a degree candidate at an eligible educational institution that has been nationally accredited.

- It does not exceed qualified educational expenses.

- It is not designated for other purposes, such as room and board.

- It does not represent payment for teaching, research, or other services.

Qualified educational expenses include: tuition, required fees, and course-related expenses such as books. An athletic scholarship is tax-free only if it meets the requirements described above.

> **Example:** Marybeth is a graduate student at a private university who received a scholarship of $30,000. Under its terms, she must serve as a part-time teaching assistant. From the $30,000 scholarship, she receives $12,500 for teaching, which is listed as income on her Form W-2. She had expenses of more than $18,000 for tuition and course-related books. Marybeth may exclude $17,500 of the scholarship funds from income, but the $12,500 she earned as a teaching assistant is taxable and must be included on her individual tax return.

---

[88] Employee awards are covered in greater detail in Book 2, *Businesses*, because they are a common employee fringe benefit. Fringe benefits are generally tested on Part 2 of the EA exam.

Pell Grants: A Pell Grant is a need-based grant that is treated as a scholarship for tax purposes. It is tax-free to the extent it is used for qualified educational expenses during the specified grant period.

Payment to Service Academy Cadets or Midshipmen: An appointment to a United States military academy is not a scholarship or fellowship. Cadets and midshipmen receive free tuition and room and board which is nontaxable. However, they also receive government pay while at the military academy; these amounts are taxable income.

Veterans' Educational Benefits: Veterans' benefits for education are tax-free if administered by the Department of Veterans Affairs.

> **Example:** Laurence served in Afghanistan and has since returned to college. He receives two education benefits under the GI bill: a $1,534 monthly basic housing allowance and $3,840 tuition paid directly to his college. Neither of these benefits is taxable to Laurence, and he is not required to report them on his tax return.

Qualified Tuition Programs

QTPs, also known as section 529 plans, are established and maintained by states or educational institutions. These plans allow a taxpayer to either prepay a student's qualified educational expenses at an eligible educational institution or contribute to an account that will be used to pay future expenses. A section 529 functions somewhat like a Roth IRA account: the amounts contributed to a section 529 plan are not deductible for federal tax purposes,[89] but the earnings grow tax-free.

Contributions to a section 529 are treated as gifts for tax purposes, which means that a donor can contribute up to $15,000 in 2018, per beneficiary, without incurring any gift tax. The amounts contributed to a 529 are removed from the calculation of a donor's gross estate (this is why 529 plans are commonly used for estate planning purposes).

Unlike a Coverdell ESA, a 529 plan does not impose age limits or income limits. Distributions from a 529 plan are reported to the taxpayer on Form 1099-Q. The part of a distribution representing the amount paid or contributed to the plan (the taxpayer's basis) is not included in income.

The beneficiary also generally does not have to include in taxable income any earnings distributed from a 529 plan if the total distribution is less than or equal to a student's qualified education expenses (after reduction of the latter by other tax-free education assistance received during the year). The definition of "qualified higher education expenses" for distributions from 529 accounts also includes the purchases of computer equipment and technology.

Eligible institutions include virtually all accredited colleges, universities, vocational schools, and postsecondary educational institutions.

---

[89] Although there is no federal tax deduction for contributions to a 529 plan, some states do allow a deduction for contributions. This can be a factor when taxpayers are deciding between different types of educational savings accounts.

Note: Starting in 2018, the TCJA modifies section 529 plans to allow distributions (not exceeding $10,000 per year) for tuition expenses incurred in connection with the enrollment or attendance at any public, private or religious elementary or secondary (K-12) school. This means that, for the first time, section 529 plans can be used for private elementary schools, middle schools, and high schools.

Qualified expenses include tuition, fees, books, computer equipment and software, and room and board for any time the beneficiary is enrolled in school. A beneficiary may be anyone the taxpayer designates: himself, a child, a grandchild, or an unrelated person.

If the total distribution is greater than a student's adjusted qualified expenses, an allocable portion of the earnings is taxable. In this type of taxable distribution, an additional excise tax of 10% generally applies to the amount included in income.

Example: Seven years ago, Kristina's parents opened a section 529 account for her maintained by the state of Virginia. Over the course of several years, they contributed $22,000 to the account. The total balance in the account was $33,000 on the date the first distribution was made. In September 2018, Kristina enrolled in college and had $10,000 of qualified education expenses for the rest of the year. She paid her college expenses from the following sources:

- QTP distribution: $7,500
- Partial tuition scholarship (tax-free): $4,000
- Gift from her parents: $1,000

Kristina must reduce her qualified educational expenses by the tax-free scholarship ($10,000 minus $4,000), so she has $6,000 of adjusted qualified educational expenses. Since that amount is less than the distribution, part of the earnings shown on Form 1099-Q is taxable and would be reported as "other income" on Line 21 of Schedule 1, Form 1040.

Any amount distributed from a 529 plan is not taxable if it is rolled over to another 529 plan for the use of the same beneficiary or for a member of the beneficiary's family. The amount must be rolled over to another educational account within 60 days after the date of distribution.

Example: Bernardo still had $3,000 left in his 529 plan after he graduated from college. He wanted to help his younger sister, who was still in high school. Within 60 days after distribution of the remaining portion of his 529 plan, he contributed the money to his sister's 529 plan, so the distribution was not taxable to him or his sister.

Coverdell Education Savings Accounts (ESA)

A Coverdell ESA[90] is a tax-advantaged investment account for higher education. A Coverdell is generally structured as a trust or custodial account set up to pay qualified elementary, secondary, or higher education expenses for a designated beneficiary. The funds in a Coverdell can be withdrawn tax-free when used for educational purposes. Coverdell ESAs have income and age limits, but under certain conditions they can offer more flexibility in investing.

---

[90] Formerly called "Education IRAs," these plans were renamed in 2002, after the late Senator Paul Coverdell, who was their primary backer.

Coverdell's are self-directed, which means that there are a variety of investment options available, whereas 529 plans are limited to the state's selected investment options.

In order to contribute fully to an ESA, the contributor's MAGI must be below $190,000-$220,000 (for joint filers) or $95,000-$110,000 (single). All contributions must be in cash (not property) and must be made by the due date of the contributor's tax return (not including extensions). So, for example, if a taxpayer wanted to set up a Coverdell account for his child in 2018, he would have until April 15, 2019, to set up the account and fund it.

Contributions to a Coverdell must be made before the beneficiary reaches age 18, and the use of account must be made by age 30 unless the beneficiary is special-needs. If there is a balance in the ESA when the beneficiary reaches age 30, it must be distributed within 30 days of turning 30 (or within 30 days after the death, if before age 30 of the beneficiary). The beneficiary can also choose to transfer the ESA to another beneficiary (such as a younger sibling or another family member) to avoid the tax.

> **Example:** Jeremiah earned a full scholarship to Stanford University. He enrolled when he was 19 and had a Coverdell ESA with a balance of $52,000. Since his tuition was already paid by his scholarship, Jeremiah only used the ESA for books and required lab fees. Jeremiah graduated from college four years later and had only used a total of $29,000 from his Coverdell. Rather than withdrawing the money and paying the 10% tax, Jeremiah transferred the Coverdell to his younger sister, who is 17 and still in high school. His sister can use the remaining amounts in the Coverdell for her own future college expenses.

If the beneficiary is special-needs, the Coverdell account can continue in existence (without transfer to another beneficiary) after the beneficiary turns 30. Contributions to a Coverdell ESA are not tax deductible, but amounts deposited in the account grow tax-free until they are later distributed.

There is no limit to the number of accounts that can be established for a beneficiary; however, the total contribution to all accounts on behalf of a beneficiary cannot exceed $2,000 per year, no matter how many accounts are established. However, if a taxpayer wants to do some year-end tax planning, they can set up a Coverdell as late as the filing deadline, and contribute $2,000 for 2018 and another $2,000 for 2019 up until April 15, 2019.

All contributions that exceed $2,000 for a single beneficiary in a taxable year will be treated as excess contributions. There will be a 6% excise tax if the excess contributions and earnings on them are not withdrawn from the child's accounts before June 1 of the following tax year. This tax will apply to each year that the excess remains in the account. Any earnings withdrawn as part of a corrective distribution are taxable in the year of the excess contribution, even if the corrective distribution occurs in the following year.

The penalty for excess contributions is imposed on the beneficiary of the account (usually a minor child), and not on the person who overcontributed to the account. The excise tax must be reported on the child's income tax return, using IRS Form 5329, Additional Taxes on Qualified Plans (Including IRAs) and Other Tax-Favored Accounts. This rule seems contrary to common sense, but the penalty is imposed on the child, not the child's parents, or the contributor of the excess funds.

Example: Three Coverdell ESAs were set up for Kendra when she was born: one by her parents, one by her grandparents, and one by her great-uncle. In 2018, her grandparents contribute $1,500 to Kendra's account. The most her parents and great uncle can contribute is a combined $500, because the maximum contribution per year for a single beneficiary is $2,000.

The beneficiary of a Coverdell account can receive distributions to pay qualified education expenses that are tax-free if the amount of the distributions does not exceed the beneficiary's adjusted qualified education expenses. If a distribution does exceed the beneficiary's qualified education expenses, a portion of the earnings is taxable and is reported as "other income" on line 21 of Form 1040.

An additional penalty tax of 10% applies to distributions that are not used for qualifying educational expenses.

There is no law that prevents a taxpayer from contributing to both a Coverdell and a 529 for the same beneficiary, so a taxpayer could potentially set up a Coverdell and a 529 for the same child, and the earnings would grow tax-free in both accounts. If a beneficiary receives distributions from both a 529 plan and a Coverdell ESA in the same year, and the total distributions exceed the beneficiary's adjusted qualified education expenses for that year, the expenses must be allocated between the distributions from each account.

The total expenses must also be reduced by any amounts used in claiming an American Opportunity or Lifetime Learning Credit for that year.

Miscellaneous Other Income

Other types of income that are taxable to the recipient and reported on line 21 of Schedule 1 include the following (this list is not exhaustive):

- Strike benefits
- Jury duty pay (when it is not turned over to the employee's employer and deducted as an adjustment to income)
- Fees paid by an estate to a personal representative/executor[91]
- Gifts or gratuities received by a host or hostess of a party or event where sales are made

Example: Shirley is retired and supports herself primarily with her Social Security income. In 2018, she receives a jury duty summons. She is chosen for the jury, and she is paid $40 a day for serving ten days on a jury trial. Shirley was also reimbursed by the court for reasonable transportation expenses and parking fees. The $400 she earned for jury duty is taxable and must be reported on her Form 1040 (Schedule 1). The reimbursement for transportation and parking fees is not taxable and does not have to be reported on her return.

---

[91] Executor fees are considered taxable income to the recipient. Executors of an estate will typically receive some type of compensation for their work on the estate. Some states follow the Uniform Probate Code, including the section on how to compensate the executor of a will. Most U.S. states have a specific flat percentage listed in their probate codes. We will cover estates more extensively in a later unit.

Example: Johanna hosts a cooking party for 15 friends, which includes a live demonstration by a Pampered Chef consultant. At the end of the evening, the women order $2,000 worth of Pampered Chef cookware and other merchandise from the consultant. Johanna receives a gift of $115 of products for hosting the party, which she must report as income at its fair market value.

Example: Samuel is the executor of his grandmother's estate. His grandmother died in 2018. Her estate includes several rental properties which must be managed after her death. Samuel is not an attorney or professional executor, but he did agree to manage his grandmother's estate. Samuel pays bills, files the estate's tax returns, manages his late grandmother's rental properties. His grandmother's final will stipulates that the executor should receive 4% of the income generated by the estate, as well as reimbursement for all estate-related business expenses. In 2018, Samuel receives $9,500 in executor fees, which he reports as other income on his Form 1040 (Schedule 1).

Table: Taxable vs. Nontaxable Income	
Taxable Income	**Nontaxable Income (or Variable)**
Wages, salaries, tips, bonuses, vacation pay, severance pay, commissions	Most employer-provided fringe benefits
Interest on bank and money market accounts; CDs; dividends; Treasury bonds	Interest on most state and local bonds
Gains from sales of property, stocks and bonds, stock options, etc.	Life insurance proceeds
Fees paid to an estate's executor	Gifts and inheritances
Alimony[92]	Child support
Social Security benefits (above the base amount and limited to 85% of benefits)	Welfare payments, food stamps, other forms of public assistance
Court awards for punitive damages, sexual harassment claims, and lost wages	Compensation or court awards for physical injury or illness, and awards for wrongful incarceration
Unemployment compensation; strike benefits	Worker's compensation
Barter and hobby income	Combat pay and certain veteran's benefits
Certain distributions from Coverdell savings accounts or qualified tuition programs	Scholarships, Pell grants, employer-provided educational assistance
Cancellation of debt income (unless excludable)	Canceled debt while in bankruptcy, or insolvency. Canceled student loans after death or permanent disability
Gambling winnings; most prizes and awards	Certain employee awards for safety, achievement, or service

---

[92] For alimony payments required under divorce decrees that are executed after December 31, 2018, the TCJA eliminates the deduction for alimony payments. Additionally, alimony payments are no longer taxable income by the recipient of the payments.

(Test yourself first; then check the correct answers at the end of this quiz.)

1. Penelope is under 18 and has two Coverdell accounts. One was set up by her grandparents, and the other was set up by her mother. Penelope received $3,200 in total contributions in her Coverdell accounts in 2018. Which of the following statements is true?

A. The contributions are deductible and can remain in the accounts until Penelope reaches 30 years of age.
B. Penelope has an excess contribution of $1,200. The excess contribution must be withdrawn, or it will be subject to an excise tax.
C. Penelope must invest the proceeds in a traditional IRA.
D. Penelope has an excess contribution of $200. She can transfer this excess contribution to another beneficiary.

2. Under Cary's divorce decree, he must pay his ex-wife, Eugenia, $30,000 of alimony per year. The decree also requires that Cary pays child support of $12,000 per year. The payments will stop after 15 years. However, if Eugenia dies before the end of the 15-year period, Cary must still pay Eugenia's estate the difference between $450,000 ($30,000 annually × 15 years) and the total amount paid up to that time. Eugenia dies at the end of the tenth year, and Cary must pay her estate an additional $150,000 ($450,000 – $300,000). How are the payments that occurred after Eugenia's death characterized for tax purposes?

A. Child support
B. Alimony
C. Other income
D. Taxable income

3. Alexander, age 64, is single and retired. He earned the following income in 2018. To determine if any of his Social Security is taxable, Alexander should compare how much of his income to the $25,000 base amount?

Part-time job	$8,000
Bank interest	5,000
Social Security	11,000
Taxable pension	6,000
Total	**$30,000**

A. $11,000
B. $24,500
C. $25,000
D. $30,000

4. In which of the following instances is canceled debt not excluded from income in 2018?

A. Mortgage debt of a rental property in foreclosure
B. Insolvency
C. Bankruptcy
D. Student loans discharged after death

5. Karly is trying to get her finances in order. During the year, she negotiated a settlement with her credit card company, to which she owed a delinquent debt. She owed $10,000 on her credit card. As part of the negotiation, the credit card company agreed to accept a $2,500 settlement as payment in full. Karly was not insolvent and not in bankruptcy when the debt was canceled. What amount should be reported as "other income" on Karly's Form 1040 (Schedule 1)?

A. $0
B. $10,000
C. $2,500
D. $7,500

6. Isabella had $9,000 of gambling winnings during the year. She also incurred $15,000 of gambling losses. How should these transactions be reported on her tax return?

A. The $9,000 of winnings are reported as income, and the $15,000 of losses are reported as an adjustment to income on Schedule 1.
B. The $9,000 of winnings are reported as income, and the $15,000 of losses are reported as an itemized deduction subject to the 2% limit on Schedule A.
C. The $9,000 of winnings are reported as income, and $9,000 of losses are reported as an itemized deduction not subject to the 2% limit on Schedule A.
D. The $9,000 of winnings are reported as income, but the gambling losses are not deductible.

7. Marcello received $32,000 of wages in 2018. He also won a prize from his homeowner's association for developing a new water conservation plan. The prize was free landscaping service for a year, valued at $600. Marcello also received $7,000 in child support and $2,000 in alimony from his ex-wife, whom he divorced five years ago. Marcello has full custody of his children. What is Marcello's taxable income (before deductions and adjustments) for 2018?

A. $32,000
B. $32,600
C. $34,600
D. $39,600

8. In 2018, Rosemary was discharged from her liability to repay $10,000 of credit card debt. The lender reported the discharged debt on Form 1099-C. Immediately prior to the debt cancellation, Rosemary had liabilities of $15,000 and the fair market value of her assets was $2,000. What portion of the canceled debt must Rosemary include in income?

A. $10,000
B. $3,000
C. $5,000
D. $0

9. Hank received Social Security in 2018 totaling $11,720. Hank also liquidated all of his stock and moved into senior housing during the year. He received $350,500 of taxable income from the stock sale. What is the maximum *taxable* amount of Hank's Social Security benefits?

A. $0
B. $5,860
C. $11,720
D. $9,962

10. Bethany and Clayton's divorce decree requires Clayton to pay Bethany $250 per month of child support and $1,500 per month of alimony. Their divorce was final on January 3, 2018. Clayton makes all of his child support and alimony payments on time during the year. How much of these payments is Bethany required to report as taxable income on her 2018 return?

A. $0
B. $1,500
C. $18,000
D. $21,000

11. Archer is a former National Football League cornerback. In 2018, he is awarded a sizable settlement in a class action lawsuit for concussion injuries for physical pain and suffering. The settlement will be paid in installments over a period of ten years. How should Archer report the damages he is awarded on his income tax return?

A. He must include the entire amount of his settlement in gross income for the year.
B. He must include in his gross income only the portion of the settlement paid to him each year when it is received.
C. He must report the settlement on his tax return, but it is not taxable income.
D. He may exclude the payments from his gross income.

12. Ginny had the following income and losses in 2018:

Source	Amounts
Wages	$14,000
Interest income	125
Gambling winnings	1,000
Gambling losses	2,000
Discrimination lawsuit settlement	10,000
Child support payments	9,000
Food stamp benefits	5,000

How much gross income must Ginny report on her tax return?

A. $14,125
B. $15,125
C. $25,125
D. $39,000

13. Which of the following is not taxable income to the recipient?

A. Long-term disability payments from a policy paid by the recipient's employer
B. Bartering income
C. Gains from the sale of stock
D. $25,000 of group-term life insurance coverage provided by an employer

14. Jean received the following income: wages, interest, child support, alimony, inheritance, worker's compensation, and lottery winnings. What amount of her income is taxable?

Source	Amounts
Wages	$13,000
Interest income	15
Child support	6,000
Alimony	2,000
Inheritance	10,000
Worker's compensation	1,000
Lottery winnings	5,000

A. $13,015
B. $16,015
C. $20,015
D. $30,015

15. Paulo, 72, experiences age-related discrimination on his job and sues his company. After he files the lawsuit, he is physically attacked by the company owner, who breaks Paulo's arm. The court awards Paulo the following amounts:

- $4,000 for emotional distress attributable to the age discrimination lawsuit
- $10,000 for loss of wages
- $35,000 for physical injury related to the assault
- $16,000 reimbursement for medical expenses

How much of this award is taxable to Paulo?

A. $4,000
B. $10,000
C. $14,000
D. $49,000

16. Anaya received payments of $20,000 for alimony and $15,000 for child support. Based upon the terms of her divorce settlement, her ex-spouse was also required to pay $14,000 of mortgage payments for the house they continue to own jointly. What portion of the amounts above must Anaya include in income?

A. $27,000
B. $34,000
C. $35,000
D. $49,000

17. Which of the following would be considered taxable income to the recipient?

A. Life insurance proceeds paid to a beneficiary
B. Adoption expense reimbursements
C. Unemployment compensation
D. Worker's compensation benefits

18. Sven and Samantha filed jointly and received the following income during the year. How much income should be reported on their joint return?

- W-2 income for Samantha for wages of $40,000
- 1099-MISC for Samantha for $2,000, the value of a prize trip she won to the Bahamas. She is planning to take the trip in the following year.
- Court settlement of $10,000 paid to Sven from a car accident for serious injuries he suffered
- $4,000 child support for Samantha's son from a previous marriage

A. $40,000
B. $42,000
C. $46,000
D. $52,000

19. Armando had a $15,000 loan from his credit union but stopped making payments. The credit union determined that the legal fees to collect might be higher than the amount Armando owed, so it canceled the remaining amount of $5,000 due on the loan. Armando did not file for bankruptcy, nor is he insolvent. How much income must he include from the debt cancellation?

A. $0
B. $5,000
C. $10,000
D. $15,000

1. The answer is B. Penelope has an excess contribution of $1,200. The excess contribution must be withdrawn by June 1 of the next tax year, or it will be subject to an excise tax of 6%, plus an additional 6% on any interest or profits derived from the excess contribution. This tax will apply to each year that the excess remains in the account. The maximum contribution to a Coverdell is $2,000 per year per beneficiary, regardless of how many accounts the beneficiary has. Any *earnings* withdrawn as part of a corrective distribution are taxable in the year of the excess contribution, even if the corrective distribution occurs in the following year.

2. The answer is A. For tax purposes; alimony cannot continue after the death of the receiving spouse. Since the payments are required even after Eugenia's death, none of the annual payments are considered alimony for tax purposes. The payments are considered "disguised child support" and cannot be deducted by Cary as alimony.

3. The answer is B. Alexander does not have to pay tax on his Social Security. In order to figure out the taxable portion of Social Security, the taxpayer's total income, including tax-exempt interest, must be compared to the base amount for his filing status, which is $25,000. The amount of income that should be compared to the $25,000 base amount is calculated as follows:

Part-time job	$8,000
Interest	5,000
½ of Social Security	5,500
Taxable pension	6,000
Total	**$24,500**

His income plus one-half of Social Security is less than the applicable base amount ($25,000). However, he is still required to file a tax return, because his overall income exceeds the minimum filing requirement.

4. The answer is A. Foreclosure of a rental property does not qualify for exclusion of canceled debt income. Canceled debt related to rental property, other business property, second homes, and vacation homes does not qualify, unless the taxpayer has filed bankruptcy or is insolvent.

5. The answer is D. Karly would report $7,500 in canceled debt income ($10,000 - $2,500) on her Form 1040 (Schedule 1).

6. The answer is C. Isabella must report $9,000 of her winnings as taxable income, and $9,000 of the losses are reported on Schedule A as an itemized deduction not subject to the 2% floor. The amount of losses deducted may not exceed gambling winnings.

7. The answer is C. The wages and the prize are both taxable income. Child support is not taxable to the receiver, nor deductible by the payer. The alimony is taxable to Marcello and deductible by his ex-wife. The answer is calculated as follows: ($32,000 + $600 + $2,000) = $34,600.

8. The answer is D. The amount of Rosemary's assets immediately prior to the debt cancellation exceeded the amount of debt that was discharged. Therefore, the entire amount of the debt cancellation can be excluded from income, due to her insolvency.

Liabilities	$15,000
The fair market value of assets	(2,000)
Amount of insolvency	13,000
Amount of debt cancellation	**$10,000**

9. The answer is D. The maximum amount that is ever taxable on net Social Security benefits is 85%, which in Hank's case is (11,720 x 85% = 9,962).

10. The answer is C. Alimony is taxable income to the *recipient* and deductible by the *payor*. Therefore, Clayton can deduct $18,000 ($1,500 × 12 months) as alimony paid, and Bethany must report $18,000 as alimony received. The amount paid as child support, $3,000 ($250 × 12), is not deductible by Clayton and is not reported as income by Bethany.

11. The answer is D. Gross income does not include the amount of damages received due to physical injuries or sickness, regardless of whether the damages are paid as lump sums or as periodic payments. Archer may exclude all the payments from gross income.

12. The answer is C. The wages, interest income, gambling income, and settlement from a discrimination lawsuit must all be reported ($14,000 + $125 + $1,000 + $10,000 = $25,125). The child support payments and the food stamp benefits are not taxable. The gambling losses do not affect the inclusion of the gambling income within gross income. However, if Ginny chooses to itemize deductions, her gambling losses may be deducted on Schedule A to the extent of her gambling income. If Ginny does not itemize, the gambling losses are not deductible.

13. The answer is D. An employer may provide up to $50,000 of life insurance coverage as a nontaxable benefit to an employee. The value of any insurance coverage that exceeds $50,000 is a taxable benefit. All of the other items are taxable.

14. The answer is C. Jean must report $20,015 in taxable income. The wages, interest, alimony, and lottery winnings are taxable income ($13,000 + $15 + $2,000 + $5,000 = $20,015). Child support, inheritances, and worker's compensation are non-taxable income.

Note: do *not* confuse worker's compensation with unemployment compensation. Worker's compensation is NOT taxable, while unemployment compensation is fully taxable.

15. The answer is C. Paulo must report $14,000 in taxable income. The amounts for loss of wages and emotional distress are taxable as ordinary income ($4,000 + $10,000 = $14,000). Damages for emotional distress that is not due to physical injury or sickness are usually taxable (as in this case where the distress was attributed to the job discrimination and lawsuit). The damages awarded for physical injury are not taxable.

16. The answer is A. Anaya must report the cash alimony payments and one-half of the mortgage payments as taxable alimony ($20,000 + $7,000). The child support payments are not taxable.

17. The answer is C. Unemployment compensation is taxable income. None of the other amounts would be taxable to the recipient.

18. The answer is B. The answer is $42,000 ($40,000 wages + $2,000 prize). Samantha must recognize the prize even though she has not taken the trip because she had constructive receipt of the winnings. The accident settlement and child support payments are not taxable.

19. The answer is B. Armando's inability to pay his debt is not a result of bankruptcy or insolvency, so he must include the full amount of the canceled debt ($5,000) in his gross income.

Unit 11: Adjustments to Gross Income

For additional information read:
Publication 504, *Divorced or Separated Individuals*
Publication 970, *Tax Benefits for Education*
Publication 590-A, *Contributions to Individual Retirement Arrangements*

An "adjustment to income" reduces taxable income and thus the amount of tax owed. The Tax Cuts and Jobs Act makes several significant changes to adjustments to gross income in 2018. They are reported on Form 1040, Schedule 1, *Additional Income and Adjustments to Income.* Adjustments are subtracted from gross income to derive adjusted gross income (AGI), whereas itemized deductions and the standard deduction are subtracted from AGI. Because adjustments are taken before AGI is calculated, they are designated as "above-the-line" deductions.

Adjustments are beneficial because they not only reduce taxable income, but a lower AGI may increase a taxpayer's eligibility for certain credits and deductions and the amounts that he can claim. Unlike "below-the-line" deductions, adjustments are not added back when calculating the alternative minimum tax.

Common Adjustments to Gross Income

There are many types of adjustments to gross income, and we will cover the most common ones in this unit. These are the adjustments listed in the order they are reported on Schedule 1, Form 1040:

- Qualified educator expenses (Line 23)
- Certain business expenses of reservists, performing artists, and fee-basis government officials.[93] (line 24)
- Deductible contributions to a health savings account (HSA) (Line 25)
- Moving expenses for members of the Armed Forces (Line 26)
- Deduction for ½ self-employment tax (Line 27)
- Contributions to self-employed SEP, SIMPLE, and qualified plans (Line 28)
- Self-employed health insurance deduction (Line 29)
- The penalty for early withdrawal of savings (line 30)
- Alimony paid (Line 31a)
- Deductible contributions to a traditional IRA (Line 32)
- Student loan interest deduction (Line 33)
- Miscellaneous write-in adjustments (Line 36)

---

[93] Although most employee-related business expenses are disallowed in 2018, business expenses for reservists, performing artists, and fee-basis government officials are still allowed. An employee with impairment-related work expenses is also still allowed to deduct those expenses. Form 2106 is used to calculate the Employee Business Expenses.

Line 23: Educator Expense Deduction

An eligible educator is allowed to deduct up to $250 of unreimbursed expenses for books, supplies, computer equipment (including related software and services), other equipment, and supplementary materials used in the classroom. Additionally, professional development expenses are also allowed.

Since this is an adjustment to income, teachers can deduct these expenses even if they do not itemize deductions. The PATH Act permanently extended the above-the-line deduction for eligible educators' classroom expenses. For courses in health and physical education, expenses are deductible only if they are related to athletics. Nonathletic supplies for physical education and expenses related to health courses do not qualify. Materials used for homeschooling cannot be deducted.

An eligible educator must work at least 900 hours a school year in a school that provides elementary or secondary education (K-12). College instructors do not qualify. For the purposes of this credit, an "educator" includes a:

- Teacher
- Counselor
- Principal
- Teacher's aide
- School coach

Example: Gayle is a third-grade teacher who worked 1,600 hours during the tax year. She spent $262 on supplies for her students. Of that amount, $212 was for educational software. The other $50 was for supplies for a unit she teaches on reproductive health. Only the $212 is a qualified expense that she can deduct.

Example: Donnie is a part-time math teacher at an elementary school. He spent $185 on qualified expenses for his students. During the tax year, he worked 550 hours at the school. Because Donnie does not have enough hours of documented employment as an educator during the tax year, he cannot deduct any of his unreimbursed educator expenses. The required minimum is 900 hours during the school year.

On a joint tax return, if both taxpayers are eligible, they each may take the deduction, up to a maximum of $500. In 2018, any educator expenses that exceed the $250 adjustment to income deduction may no longer be deducted as unreimbursed employee business expenses on Schedule A.

Line 24: Certain Business Expenses of Reservists, Performing Artists, and Fee-Basis Government Officials

Certain employees are allowed to claim specified work-related expenses as an adjustment to income. Although most employee-related business expenses are no longer deductible in 2018, business expenses for reservists, performing artists, and fee-basis government officials are still allowed.[94] However, no deduction is allowed for certain entertainment expenses, membership dues, and facilities used in connection with these activities for amounts paid or incurred in 2018.

Form 2106, *Employee Business Expenses*, is used to calculate the deduction. This adjustment applies only to reservists[95] (members of the reserve component of the Armed Forces of the United States, National Guard, or the Reserve Corps of the Public Health Service); qualified performing artists; and state or local government officials who are compensated on a fee basis.

Armed Forces Reservists are able to claim a deduction for amounts attributable to travel more than 100 miles away from their home, and return to their regular jobs once released. The travel must be reserve-related.

> **Example:** Anthony is an Army reservist. He also has a regular full-time job in addition to his job as a reservist. Anthony's drill location is 200 miles away from his home, where he normally reports for reserve drills and official meetings. He trains one weekend a month plus an additional two weeks per year. Anthony is allowed to deduct the mileage and other travel expenses related to his reservist duties on Form 2106. The amounts are then transferred to Schedule 1, Form 1040, and claimed as an adjustment to income.

Line 25: Health Savings Account Deduction (HSAs)

A high deductible plan (HDHP) can be combined with a health savings account (HSA), allowing the taxpayer to pay for medical expenses on a tax-preferred basis. The HSA contributions are deductible as an adjustment to income on Form 1040. Before a taxpayer can contribute to an HSA, the taxpayer must *first* be enrolled in a high-deductible health plan (HDHP). Once the HSA is set up, the taxpayer can take tax-free withdrawals from the HSA to pay for his qualifying medical expenses.

An HSA must be established *exclusively* to pay medical expenses for the taxpayer, his spouse, and his dependents. HSA accounts are usually set up with a bank, an insurance company, or through an employer. To qualify for an HSA, the taxpayer:

- Must not be enrolled in Medicare

- Cannot be claimed as a dependent on anyone else's tax return

- Must be covered under a high deductible health plan and have no other health coverage, other than for a specific disease or illness; a fixed amount for a certain time period of hospitalization; or liabilities incurred under worker's compensation laws or tort liabilities

An employee and his employer are both allowed to contribute to the employee's HSA in the same year. If an employer makes an HSA contribution on behalf of an employee, it is excluded from the employee's income and is not subject to income or payroll taxes. For 2018, taxpayers can contribute up to $3,450 for an individual and $6,900 for a family.

---

[94] An employee with impairment-related work expenses is also still allowed to deduct employee business expenses, if the expenses are directly related to his or her work and disability.

[95] These deductions for travel-related expenses are not available for active duty service members, only reservists.

HSA holders who are age 55 and older get to contribute an extra $1,000 as a catch-up contribution. Any excess contributions over these limits are subject to a 6% penalty.

2018 HSA contribution limits and HDHP guidelines	
HSA contribution limit	Self-only: $3,450
	Family coverage: $6,900
HSA catch-up contributions (55 and older)	$1,000
HDHP minimum deductibles	Self-only: $1,350
	Family coverage: $2,700
HDHP maximum out-of-pocket amounts	Self-only: $6,650
	Family: $13,300

Allowable medical expenses are those that would generally qualify for purposes of the deduction for medical and dental expenses and which are not paid or reimbursed by the taxpayer's high deductible health plan. Although an account holder can withdraw funds from an HSA at any time, withdrawals from an HSA for purposes other than payment of allowable medical expenses are subject to income tax. They may also be subject to a 20% penalty, except in the following instances:

- When a taxpayer turns age 65 or older

- When a taxpayer becomes disabled

- When a taxpayer dies

Example: Frederic is 67, single, and has an HSA through his employer. In 2018, his car breaks down, and he doesn't have the funds to repair it. Frederic withdraws $2,000 from his HSA to pay for the car repairs. Since he did not use the funds to pay for qualifying medical expenses, the entire withdrawal is subject to income tax. However, Frederic avoids the 20% additional penalty tax because he is over 65.

A taxpayer will receive Form 5498-SA from the HSA trustee showing the amount of contributions for the year. The deduction for an HSA is reported on Form 8889, *Health Savings Accounts*. To claim the HSA deduction for a particular year, the HSA contributions must be made on or before that year's tax filing date (without extensions). For 2018, HSA contributions must be made on or before the tax year filing deadline (before April 15, 2019).

Note: Do not confuse an HSA with a health-care FSA (Flexible Spending Arrangement). The two are not the same thing. Although both types of accounts are used to pay medical expenses on a pre-tax basis, there are significant differences between an HSA and a health-care FSA. An HSA is always paired with a high-deductible health plan. Self-employed individuals can set up and contribute to an HSA, (but not to an FSA). Unlike an FSA, funds in an HSA do not expire from year-to-year.

Line 26: Moving Expenses for Members of the Armed Forces

The Tax Cuts and Jobs act eliminated the moving expense deduction for most taxpayers in 2018, with the exception Armed Forces personnel moving pursuant to military orders or a permanent change of station. An employee of the armed forces is also allowed to deduct the costs of moving a spouse, dependents, and household goods or pets. A "permanent change of station" includes:

- A move from home to their first post of active duty,

- A move from one permanent post of duty to another, and

- A move from their last post of duty to a home or to a nearer point in the United States.

For 2018, the standard mileage rate for moving expenses is 18 cents a mile. A service member cannot deduct any amounts that were already reimbursed by the government. Form 3903, moving expenses, is used to calculate the qualifying moving expenses of Armed Forces personnel.

If a taxpayer is not a U.S. service member, and an employer reimburses their moving expenses in 2018, the reimbursement is taxable to the employee. Employers who reimburse employees for their moving expenses must now include the reimbursements on the employee's Form W-2, and the entire amount is taxable as wages.

The IRS issued guidance that an employer reimbursement for an employee move that actually occurred in the prior year (for example, a move that occurred in December 2017, but was not reimbursed until 2018) does not have to be included in the employee's wages.

Example: Cedro was offered a job at Xylocarp Engineering, Inc. on February 2, 2018. He agreed to accept the offer if Xylocarp paid all his moving expenses. The cost of his professional movers was $9,600, which the company paid. Xylocarp also reimbursed Cedro $7,500 for storage fees and other travel expenses. The total reimbursement was $17,100. Because moving expenses are no longer a deductible expense, the entire $17,100 is taxable as wages, and must be included on Cedro's Form W-2. The amount is deductible to Xylocarp, but it is categorized as a wage expense and therefore subject to payroll tax.

Example: Anaya is a cardiologist. She was offered a position with Banner University Medical Hospital on December 12, 2017. She moved on December 30, 2017, and submitted her receipts for reimbursement a few days later. The hospital did not reimburse Anaya's moving expenses until January 15, 2018. The moving expense reimbursement is not taxable to Anaya, even though she received the amounts in 2018, because the actual move occurred in the prior year.

Line 27: Deductible Part of Self-Employment Tax

A self-employed taxpayer can subtract from income 50% of self-employment tax, equal to the amount of Social Security and Medicare taxes that an employer normally pays for an employee, which is excluded from an employee's income. The deduction is figured on Schedule

SE. A self-employed taxpayer cannot deduct one-half of the Additional Medicare Tax on earned income.[96]

Line 28: Self-Employed Retirement Plans

When a taxpayer is self-employed, they have access to some of the same kinds of retirement plans that are utilized by larger employers. Self-employed individuals can deduct contributions to the following types of retirement plans:

- Simplified Employee Pension (SEP) plans

- Savings Incentive Match Plan for Employees (SIMPLE) plans

- Qualified plans

A taxpayer must have self-employment income to contribute to his own plan.[97] However, a self-employed taxpayer does not need to show a profit on Schedule C to contribute to an employee's retirement plan.

Example: Ricardo is a self-employed kickboxing instructor. He has a full-time receptionist named Benita that works in his training gym. In 2018, Ricardo makes a large fitness equipment purchase for his training gym. The fitness equipment qualifies for accelerated section 179 expensing. As a result, Ricardo reduces his taxable income to zero for the year. He cannot contribute to a retirement plan because he has no taxable income on his Schedule C. However, Ricardo is still allowed to contribute to Benita's retirement plan.

Line 29: Self-Employed Health Insurance Deduction

A self-employed taxpayer may be able to deduct up to 100% of his health insurance premiums as an adjustment to income. Premiums paid by the taxpayer for his spouse and dependents under age 27 at the end of the year are also deductible. However, the deduction is limited to the net profit or other earned income from the business under which the health coverage is arranged. The taxpayer must either:

- Be self-employed and have a net profit for the year

- Be a partner in a partnership with net earnings from self-employment, or

- Have received wages from an S corporation in which he was a more-than-2% shareholder.

Long-term care insurance is also considered health insurance for purposes of this deduction. The policy can be in the name of the business or in the name of the business owner.

A self-employed taxpayer may not take the deduction if either he or his spouse (if MFJ) is eligible to participate in an employer-sponsored and subsidized health insurance plan, even if they decline coverage.

---

[96] The Additional Medicare Tax and other provisions of the Affordable Care Act are covered later.
[97] SEP, SIMPLE, and qualified retirement plans are primarily tested on the businesses section of the EA exam (Part 2), so they are covered primarily in Book 2 of the PassKey EA Review.

> **Example:** Paige and Thomas are married. Thomas is self-employed and pays for his own individual insurance policy. Paige works for a grocery store as a cashier. Thomas was eligible to participate in a subsidized health plan through Paige's employer, but Thomas declined the coverage because he didn't want to switch doctors. Thomas cannot take an adjustment for the health insurance premiums that he paid because he declined to participate in his wife's employer-sponsored coverage.

Line 30: Penalty on Early Withdrawal of Savings

If a taxpayer withdraws money from a certificate of deposit (CD) or other time-deposit savings account prior to maturity, he usually incurs a penalty for early withdrawal. This penalty is charged by the bank or other financial institution and withheld from a taxpayer's proceeds.

Taxpayers can take an adjustment to income for early withdrawal penalties. The penalties are reported on a taxpayer's Form 1099-INT, *Interest Income*, or on Form 1099-OID, *Original Issue Discount*, which lists interest income as well as the penalty amount.

> **Example:** Early in 2018, Nikita invested in a $15,000 one-year certificate of deposit. In November, she had an unexpected medical expense and had to liquidate the CD. She paid a penalty of three months' interest, which totaled $150. Nikita can claim the penalty ($150) as an adjustment to income.

> **Note:** Don't be confused by this concept! It is frequently tested. Only the penalty for early withdrawal from a timed deposit (a certificate of deposit) is tax deductible. The penalty for early withdrawal from an IRA or a retirement plan is never deductible.

Line 31a: Alimony Paid

As described in the preceding unit, alimony received is taxable income. Alimony paid is generally treated as the mirror image and is a deductible expense that is claimed on Schedule 1 (Line 31a) of Form 1040.[98]

By definition, alimony is a payment to a former spouse under a divorce or separation instrument. The payments do not have to be made directly to the ex-spouse. For example, payments made on behalf of the ex-spouse for expenses such as medical bills, housing costs, and other expenses can also qualify as alimony. Voluntary payments not required by a divorce decree or separation instrument do not qualify as alimony.

> **Example:** Patrice's divorce settlement requires that she pay her ex-husband $16,000 a year. Per the divorce agreement, she also must pay his ongoing medical expenses. In 2018, her ex-husband had $9,500 of medical expenses. She can deduct the full amount ($25,500) as an adjustment to income because it is required by her divorce agreement.

---

[98] Due to the Tax Cuts and Jobs Act, alimony paid will no longer be deductible by the payor and alimony received will no longer be taxable to the receiver, effective for divorce agreements executed after December 31, 2018. Divorce agreements executed prior to that date will be "grandfathered" and the prior treatment of alimony will be allowable.

> **Example:** Under the terms of Anselmo's divorce decree, he must pay his ex-wife $12,600 in 2018 ($1,050 per month). As a personal favor, he also makes $2,400 in payments to cover part of her vehicle lease so she can keep steady employment. Anselmo can claim the $12,600 as an adjustment to income. He cannot count the lease payments because they were not required by the divorce agreement.

Line 32: Traditional IRA Deduction

An individual retirement arrangement (IRA) offers tax advantages for setting aside money for retirement. Some taxpayers can claim a deduction for the amounts contributed to a traditional IRA as an adjustment to gross income. Amounts that do not qualify for deduction include:

- Contributions to a Roth IRA

- Contributions to a traditional IRA that are nondeductible because the taxpayer and/or spouse is covered by an employer-sponsored retirement plan and modified adjusted gross income (MAGI) exceeds certain limits

- Contributions that apply to the previous tax year

- Rollover contributions

Deductions are allowed in full for contributions to a traditional IRA by a taxpayer (and spouse, if married) who is not covered by a retirement plan at work. If the taxpayer (and/or spouse) is covered by a retirement plan at work, deductions are phased out at certain income levels.[99]

Line 33: Student Loan Interest Deduction

Generally, personal interest (other than mortgage interest) is not deductible. However, interest on a qualified student loan is deductible. A qualified student loan is a loan used solely to pay qualified higher education expenses for the taxpayer, his spouse, or his dependents. A taxpayer can claim the deduction for 2018 if:

- He paid interest on a qualified student loan on which he was legally obligated.

- His filing status is not married filing separately.

- Neither he (nor his spouse, if filing jointly) can be claimed as a dependent on someone else's return.

In order for student loan interest to qualify, the student must have been enrolled in a higher education program leading to a degree, certificate, or other recognized educational credential. A student who used the loan to take classes for other purposes does not qualify. The maximum deduction for student loan interest in 2018 is $2,500. A phaseout applies for higher-income taxpayers. The deduction is phased out for taxpayers with modified adjusted gross income (MAGI) between $65,000-$80,000 and 135,000-$165,000 for MFJ in 2018. Taxpayers who file MFS are not allowed to take a deduction for student loan interest.

---

[99] The rules regarding IRA contributions, distributions (withdrawals), and rollovers are covered in detail later, in a dedicated unit for retirement plans.

Example: Socorro and her husband file jointly. Their modified adjusted gross income is $178,000. She completed her doctorate and paid $3,400 of student loan interest in 2018. Due to their high income, they cannot deduct any of their student loan interest as an adjustment to income.

Example: Rudy graduated from a technical college where he was enrolled full-time in a certificate program for automotive repair. Rudy is single and earned $40,000 in wages during the year. He had no other income. He may take the student loan interest deduction.

A student loan is not eligible if it is from certain related persons (such as family members or certain corporations, partnerships, or trusts). Loans from an employer plan also do not qualify. The student loan interest deduction limit is per return, not per student. For example, if a taxpayer has three children and pays $2,000 in student loan interest for each of them, the maximum deduction is still only $2,500. Qualified higher education expenses are the costs of attending an eligible educational institution, including graduate schools, such as:

- Tuition and fees

- Room and board

- Books, supplies, and equipment

- Other necessary school-related expenses, such as transportation

Qualified expenses must be reduced by the amounts of tax-free items used to pay them, such as the following:

- Employer-provided educational assistance benefits

- Tax-free withdrawals from a Coverdell Education Savings Account

- U.S. savings bond interest already excluded from income

- Tax-free scholarships and fellowships

- Veterans' educational assistance benefits

- Any other nontaxable payments (except gifts or inheritances) received for educational expenses

Example: Rhonda is an Army veteran receiving the GI Bill. Rhonda's college tuition expenses are $7,200. She also receives a gift of $1,000 from her aunt and $1,000 of her veterans' GI Bill. Therefore, Ronda's qualified higher education expenses are $6,200 because veterans' assistance benefits must be subtracted. The gift from her aunt does not have to be subtracted.

Lenders are required to send the taxpayer Form 1098-E, *Student Loan Interest*, when the amount of interest paid is at least $600 or more.

Line 36: Other Adjustments

Line 36 of Schedule 1, Form 1040 is reserved for more obscure deductions. This line on the form allows the taxpayer to manually indicate what type of adjustment is being taken. Some of the miscellaneous adjustments that may be entered on line 36 include deductions to an Archer MSA, jury duty pay remitted to an employer, and repayment of unemployment benefits.

Although these deductions are not frequently seen, they are still available under the Tax Cuts and Jobs Act. A taxpayer does not need to itemize in order to deduct these amounts. These "other adjustments" are listed in the instructions for Form 1040.

- Archer MSA deduction (see Form 8853).

- Jury duty pay remitted to an employer.

- Deductible expenses related to income reported on line 21 from the rental of personal property engaged in for profit (this would be income from the rental of personal property (such as equipment or vehicles), when the taxpayer was not "in the business" of renting personal property)

- Nontaxable amount of the value of Olympic and Paralympic medals and USOC prize money.

- Reforestation amortization and expenses

- Repayment of supplemental unemployment benefits (repayment exceeding $3,000)

- Contributions to section 501(c)(18)(D) pension plans

- Contributions by certain chaplains to section 403(b) plans

- Attorney fees and court costs for actions involving certain unlawful discrimination claims, but only to the extent of gross income from such actions.

- Attorney fees and court costs paid in connection with an award from the IRS for information provided that helped the IRS detect tax law violations, up to the amount of the award includible in the taxpayer's gross income. These awards are called "whistleblower awards."

(Test yourself first; then check the correct answers at the end of this quiz.)

1. Cleveland is 26 and has an HSA. He becomes permanently disabled in 2018 due to a serious auto accident. Which of the following statements is correct?

A. He may withdraw money from his HSA for nonmedical expenses, but the withdrawals will be subject to income tax and also an additional penalty of 20%.
B. He may withdraw money from his HSA for nonmedical expenses. The withdrawals will be subject to income tax but will not be subject to a penalty.
C. He may not take nonmedical distributions from his account.
D. He must be at least 65 to take nonmedical distributions from an HSA.

2. Deborah was a self-employed poultry farmer in 2018, and she files Schedule F. She had self-employment tax of $4,896 on her Schedule SE. Which of the following statements is correct?

A. She can deduct 100% of the self-employment tax she paid on Schedule C.
B. She can deduct 50% of the self-employment tax she paid on Schedule C.
C. She can deduct 50% of the self-employment tax she paid as an adjustment to income on Form 1040.
D. She cannot deduct self-employment tax.

3. Jermaine and Anna have MAGI of $85,000. They are married and file a joint return. Two years ago, they took out a loan so their daughter, Miranda, could earn her college degree. Miranda is 23 and their dependent. In 2018, they paid $3,000 of student loan interest. How much student loan interest can Jermaine and Anna deduct on their tax return?

A. $0
B. $1,000
C. $2,500
D. $3,000

4. Under his divorce decree, Rick must pay the medical expenses of his former spouse, Linda. In January 2018, Rick sends a check totaling $4,000 directly to General Medical Hospital to pay for Linda's emergency surgery. Which of the following statements is correct?

A. This payment qualifies as alimony, and Linda must include the $4,000 as taxable alimony on her individual tax return.
B. This payment does not qualify as alimony, but Rick can claim a deduction for the medical expenses on his return.
C. Linda must include the $4,000 as income on her return, but Rick cannot deduct the expense as alimony because it was paid to a third party.
D. None of the above

5. All of the following statements are correct about the educator expense deduction except:

A. A school counselor may qualify.
B. A part-time teacher may qualify.
C. A school principal may qualify.
D. A college instructor may qualify.

6. Chuck and Mallory are married and file jointly. Chuck is self-employed, and his net profit from his business was $50,000 in 2018. They pay $700 per month for health insurance coverage. Mallory was a homemaker until she started working for a construction company in early February. Mallory and Chuck became eligible to participate in her employer's health plan on March 1, 2018, but they did not want to switch insurance providers, so Mallory declined her employer's coverage. Which of the following statements is correct?

A. They can deduct $700 for both January and February, and $350 per month for each of the last ten months of the year, as self-employed health insurance premiums on Chuck's Schedule C.
B. They can deduct $1,400 in self-employed health insurance premiums, which is for January and February, the two months they were not eligible to participate in an employer plan.
C. They can deduct 100% of their health insurance premiums because they declined the employer coverage.
D. They can deduct 50% of their health insurance premiums on Chuck's Schedule C.

7. Carlie had an HSA account set up with her employer that had $3,000 in the account at the end of the year. She then quit her job in late December and withdrew all the funds from her HSA. She did not use the $3,000 for qualifying medical expenses. What is the consequence of this action?

A. Nothing; taxpayers are allowed to withdraw from their HSA accounts at any time.
B. Her withdrawal is prohibited and will result in a forfeiture of the funds.
C. Carlie must pay income tax and a 20% penalty on the withdrawal.
D. Carlie must pay income tax and a 6% penalty on the withdrawal.

8. Two full-time teachers who are married and file jointly can deduct a maximum of _____ in educator expenses:

A. $100
B. $250
C. $500
D. $750

9. Marshall lost his job last year and withdrew money from a number of accounts. He paid the following penalties:

The penalty for early withdrawal from a CD	$100
The penalty for early withdrawal from a traditional IRA	200
A late penalty for not paying his rent on time	50

What amount can Marshall deduct as an adjustment to income on his Form 1040?

A. $0
B. $100
C. $200
D. $250

10. Bruce makes an excess contribution to his HSA by accidentally contributing over the maximum allowable amount. What is the penalty on excess contributions if Bruce does not withdraw the overcontribution?

A. No penalty
B. 6% penalty
C. 10% penalty
D. 20% penalty

11. An adjustment to income is considered the most beneficial type of deduction because:

A. It favors taxpayers who choose to itemize their deductions.
B. It is simpler to figure out qualifying expenses for adjustments to income than it is other deductions.
C. It lowers a taxpayer's adjusted gross income and thus can affect the amounts of certain credits and deductions he may be able to claim.
D. There is no significant difference between an adjustment to income and other tax deductions.

12. Georgina was offered a position in another city on March 1, 2018. Her new employer reimburses her $4,000 for her moving expenses. Georgina had all the proper receipts. How should this reimbursement be treated?

A. The employer can reimburse Georgina on a pre-tax basis.
B. The expense is nontaxable as long as Georgina's employer gives her a gift card.
C. The reimbursement is tax-exempt because it is a qualified moving expense.
D. Because this is a reimbursement of a nondeductible expense, it is treated as taxable wages and must be included on Georgina's Form W-2.

13. Gael is a college instructor at California state university. In 2018, he paid $300 for materials that he used in the classroom. He also paid $210 in parking fees to park across the street from the university when the faculty lot was full. What amount of qualifying expenses does he have for purposes of the educator expense deduction?

A. $0
B. $250
C. $300
D. $510

14. Jasmine is a part-time art teacher at an elementary school. She spends $350 on qualified expenses for her art students and $75 on materials for a health course that she also teaches. She worked 440 hours as an educator during the tax year. How much can she deduct in educator expenses as an adjustment to income?

A. $0
B. $250
C. $350
D. $425

15. George paid $14,000 of alimony to his ex-wife during the year. Which of the following statements is correct?

A. He can deduct alimony paid as an adjustment to income.
B. The deduction for alimony is entered on Schedule B.
C. He can deduct alimony only if he itemizes deductions on his tax return.
D. He cannot deduct the alimony in 2018.

Unit 11: Quiz Answers

1. The answer is B. Withdrawals for nonmedical expenses from an HSA are allowed but are subject to income tax. Nonmedical distributions are also subject to an additional penalty tax of 20%, except when the taxpayer has turned 65, become disabled, or died. Cleveland has become permanently disabled, in which case his HSA withdrawals are not subject to penalty, but the withdrawals will still be subject to income tax.

2. The answer is C. Deborah can deduct 50% of the self-employment tax she paid as an adjustment to income on Schedule 1 of her Form 1040.

3. The answer is C. Jermaine and Anna's maximum deduction for student loan interest is $2,500. The deduction is limited to the lesser of $2,500 or the amount of interest actually paid. It doesn't matter how many qualifying student loans there are; the maximum is $2,500 per tax return (not per taxpayer).

4. The answer is A. This payment qualifies as alimony, and Linda must include the $4,000 as taxable alimony income on her return. The payment may be treated as alimony for tax purposes because the payments of Linda's medical expenses are a condition of the divorce agreement. Payments to a third party on behalf of an ex-spouse under the terms of a divorce instrument can be alimony, if they qualify. These include payments for a spouse's medical expenses, housing costs (rent and utilities), taxes, and tuition. The payments are treated by the ex-spouse as if they were received directly and included as income.

5. The answer is D. College instructors do not qualify. An eligible educator must work 900 hours a year in a school that provides elementary or secondary education (K-12). Part-time teachers qualify if they meet the yearly teachers' requirement for hours worked. The term educator includes instructors, counselors, principals, and aides.

6. The answer is B. Chuck and Mallory can deduct only $1,400 ($700 x two months) of self-employed health insurance for the months that they were ineligible to participate in an employer plan. No deduction is allowed for self-employed health insurance for any month that the taxpayer has the *option* to participate in an employer-sponsored and subsidized plan. This is true even if the taxpayer declines the coverage. A self-employed taxpayer can deduct 100% of health insurance premiums as an adjustment to income, but only if neither he nor his spouse was eligible to participate in an employer health plan.

7. The answer is C. Carlie must pay income tax and a 20% penalty on the withdrawal. Withdrawals from an HSA for non-eligible expenses are allowed, but the withdrawal is subject to a 20% penalty, in addition to regular income tax.

8. The answer is C. On a jointly filed tax return, if both taxpayers are teachers, they both may take the deduction, up to a maximum of $500 ($250 each).

9. The answer is B. Marshall can only deduct the $100 early withdrawal penalty from the CD. Early withdrawal penalties are deductible if made from a time deposit account, such as a certificate of deposit. The other types of penalties are not deductible.

10. The answer is B. Bruce will have to pay a 6% excise penalty if he does not correct the overcontribution. A 6% penalty applies to excess contributions to a health savings account.

11. The answer is C. Adjustments are deducted from gross income to derive adjusted gross income (AGI), and itemized and standard deductions are subtracted from AGI. The amount of a taxpayer's AGI is important, as it can affect his eligibility for certain deductions and the amounts that he can claim. For example, certain items are phased out at specified levels of AGI, and some itemized deductions must exceed specified percentages of AGI to be deductible. In addition, itemized deductions may be subject to the alternative minimum tax or may total less than the taxpayer's applicable standard deduction.

12. The answer is D. Starting in 2018, if an employer pays or reimburses moving expenses, the amounts are treated as taxable compensation and must be reported as wages on Georgina's Form W-2. The only exception to this rule is for moving expenses reimbursed by the government on behalf of U.S. Armed Forces personnel.

13. The answer is A. Gael cannot deduct any of his expenses. The educator expense deduction is only available for K-12 educators. College instructors do not qualify.

14. The answer is A. Because Jasmine worked only 440 hours as an educator during the tax year, she cannot deduct her educator expenses as an adjustment to income. An educator must have at least 900 hours of qualified employment during the school year to take this deduction as an adjustment to income.

15. The answer is A. George can deduct alimony paid as an adjustment to income. He does not need to itemize his deductions in order to take the deduction. He must file Form 1040 and enter the amount of alimony paid as an adjustment to income.

Unit 12: Standard Deduction & Itemized Deductions

For additional information read:
Publication 502, *Medical and Dental Expenses*
Publication 600, *State and Local General Sales Taxes*
Publication 936, *Home Mortgage Interest Deduction*
Publication 526, *Charitable Contributions*
Publication 561, *Determining the Value of Donated Property*

The Tax Cuts and Jobs Act made sweeping changes to the standard deduction and itemized deductions. The standard deduction has nearly doubled. As a result, fewer taxpayers will be forced to itemize.

Many itemized deductions have been eliminated or restricted in 2018 through 2025. The TCJA also removed the so-called "Pease limitation" on itemized deductions, which means that itemized deductions will no longer be phased out at higher income levels.

A taxpayer generally may choose either to claim a standard deduction amount or to itemize deductions. Depending on the option selected, either the applicable standard deduction amount or the taxpayer's total itemized deductions is subtracted from his adjusted gross income. The choice should be based on which option results in a lower tax liability.

The Standard Deduction

The standard deduction is a specific dollar amount that reduces the amount of income on which a taxpayer is taxed. The TCJA increased the standard deduction from $6,500 to $12,000 in 2018 for single filers, from $13,000 to $24,000 for joint filers and qualifying widow(ers), and from $9,550 to $18,000 for heads of household in 2018.

Using the standard deduction eliminates the need for a taxpayer to itemize his actual allowable deductions, such as medical expenses, charitable contributions, or state and local taxes. The standard deduction amounts are based on a taxpayer's filing status and are adjusted every year for inflation.

Filing Status	2018 Standard Deduction
Single	$12,000
Head of Household	$18,000
Married Filing Separately	$12,000
Married Filing Jointly	$24,000
Qualifying Widow(er)	$24,000
Dependent Standard Deduction[100]	$1,050

---

[100] Alternatively, if higher, the standard deduction for dependents is $350 plus their earned income for the year, up to $12,000 in 2018.

257

Additional Standard Deduction

An *additional* standard deduction is available to taxpayers who, at the end of the year, are:

- 65 or older, and/or
- Blind or partially blind.

The standard deduction is $1,300 higher for joint filers who are over 65 and/or blind, and $1,600 higher for unmarried taxpayers (Single and head of household). A taxpayer who is *both* blind and 65 or older may take the basic standard deduction, and additional standard deduction amounts for both age and blindness. For filing purposes, a taxpayer is considered to be age 65 in the tax year 2018 if they were 65 on December 31, 2018, or if they turned 65 on January 1, 2019.

Additional Standard Deduction Amounts–2018	
Taxpayers who are age 65 and/or blind	
Filing Status	Additional Amount Allowable
Single, HOH	$1,600
MFS, MFJ, QW	$1,300

The additional amount for blindness is allowed if the taxpayer is blind on the last day of the tax year, even if he was not blind the rest of the year. A taxpayer must obtain a statement from an eye doctor indicating that:

- The taxpayer cannot see better than **20/200**, even when corrected with eyeglasses, or
- The taxpayer's field of vision is not more than 20 degrees (the taxpayer has disabled peripheral vision).

Example: Wardell, 46, and Tamara, 33, file jointly. Neither is blind. They decide not to itemize their deductions. Their standard deduction is $24,000 in 2018.

Example: Samuel, age 52, and Priscilla, age 51, are married and do not itemize deductions. Because they file jointly, their base standard deduction is $24,000 in 2018. Priscilla is also blind, so she can claim an additional standard deduction amount of $1,300. Therefore, the total standard deduction of their joint return is $25,300 ($24,000 + $1,300) in 2018.

The standard deduction for a deceased taxpayer is the same as if the taxpayer had lived the entire year, with one exception: If the taxpayer died *before* his actual 65th birthday, the higher standard deduction for being 65 does not apply.

Example: Octavio is single and died on November 1, 2018. He would have been 65 if he had reached his birthday on December 18, 2018. He does not qualify for a higher standard deduction because he died before his 65th birthday, even though it would have happened during the 2018 tax year. His standard deduction is $12,000 on his final income tax return, which must be filed by his executor on or before April 15, 2019.

Standard Deduction for Certain Dependents

The standard deduction for a dependent which can be claimed on another person's return is limited to the greater of:

- $1,050, or

- The dependent's earned income (such as wages) plus $350, but not more than the regular standard deduction amount. For a single person, this is generally $12,000 in 2018. However, the standard deduction amount can be higher if the dependent is 65 or older and/or blind.

> **Example:** Clarence is 83 years old and single. Clarence is entitled to the regular standard deduction for single filers ($12,000) plus an additional standard deduction amount for being older than 65 ($1,600). He can take a standard deduction of $13,600 ($12,000 + $1,600).

> **Example:** Tessa is single, 22, and a full-time college student with a part-time job. Her parents provide the majority of her support, so they claim her as a dependent on their joint tax return. Tessa files a return and takes the standard deduction, which she is entitled to do, even though her parents are claiming her as a dependent. She has wages of $7,800 from her part-time job. Her standard deduction is $8,150 ($7,800 wages + $350).

Itemized Deductions

Itemized deductions may be taken in lieu of the standard deduction; they allow taxpayers to reduce their taxable income based on specific personal expenses. If a taxpayer's total itemized deductions are greater than his applicable standard deduction amount, they will normally result in lower taxable income and a lower tax liability. In most cases, a taxpayer may choose whether to claim itemized deductions or the standard deduction, depending on which is more beneficial. However, taxpayers are *required* to itemize in the following cases:

- If married and filing separately and one spouse itemizes, the other spouse also must itemize. In this case, the taxpayer's standard deduction is zero and they are both forced to itemize any deductions, even if the spouses do not have enough itemized deductions to exceed the standard deduction.[101]

- If the taxpayer is a nonresident alien or dual-status alien (who is not married to a U.S. citizen or U.S. resident)

- If the taxpayer files a tax return for a period of less than twelve months due to a change in accounting methods

If a taxpayer itemizes deductions, he must complete and file Schedule A along with his Form 1040. We will review the specific requirements for various itemized deductions in this and the next unit.

---

[101] This rule only applies when *both* spouses are filing MFS. If one spouse is MFS, but the other spouse qualifies for HOH filing status (Head of Household), then the spouses are not forced to itemize, and they may choose the standard deduction if they wish.

Medical and Dental Expenses

Medical and dental expenses (other than self-employed health insurance premiums) are deductible only if a taxpayer itemizes deductions. Qualifying medical expenses include the costs of diagnosis, cure, mitigation, treatment, or prevention of disease, and the costs of medical (but not cosmetic) treatments. The IRS defined qualifying costs as:

- Medically necessary equipment, supplies, and diagnostic devices

- Dental and vision care

- Transportation to obtain medical care

- Qualified health insurance and long-term care insurance

Deductible medical expenses include:

- Fees paid to doctors, dentists, surgeons, chiropractors, psychiatrists, psychologists, and nontraditional medical practitioners

- In-patient hospital care or nursing home services, including the cost of meals and lodging charged by the hospital or nursing home

- Acupuncture treatments

- Lactation supplies (breastfeeding supplies)

- Treatment at centers for alcohol or drug addiction, participation in smoking-cessation programs, and prescription drugs to alleviate nicotine withdrawal

- Weight-loss programs prescribed by a physician (but not diet food items)

- Insulin and prescription drugs (but prescription drugs brought in or shipped from a different country are generally not deductible)

- Admission and transportation to a medical conference relating to a chronic disease (but the costs of meals and lodging while attending the conference are not deductible)

- Veterinary care when it relates to the care of animals trained to assist persons who are visually impaired, hearing-impaired, or disabled.

Example: Carnell is a Gulf War Veteran. Carnell is recovering from severe Post-Traumatic Stress Disorder. He also has frequent seizures related to a head injury sustained during combat. Carnell's physician recommends that he obtain a service dog to help him with his recovery. The doctor gives Carnell a written physician's statement explaining the recommendation. With the help of a Veteran's support group, Carnell obtains a trained service dog in 2018. The dog's veterinary costs are deductible medical expenses on Carnell's individual tax return.

Note: Medical expenses must be primarily to alleviate or prevent a physical or mental defect or illness. Medical expenses do not include expenses that are merely beneficial to general health, such as vitamins, spa treatments, gym memberships, or vacations. In addition, the cost of over-the-counter medications cannot be deducted.

A taxpayer may only deduct medical expenses they paid during the year, regardless of when the services were provided.[102] Qualified medical expenses include expenses paid for:

- The taxpayer or the taxpayer's spouse
- Dependents (the individual must have been a dependent at the time the medical services were provided or at the time the expenses were paid). However, there is an exception to this rule for children of divorced or separated parents.

A taxpayer can deduct medical expenses paid on behalf of an adopted child, even before the adoption is final. A taxpayer can also deduct medical expenses paid for a dependent parent. All the standard rules for a dependency exemption apply, so the dependent parent does not have to live with the taxpayer to qualify.

Note: If a child of divorced or separated parents is claimed as a dependent on either parent's return, each parent can deduct medical expenses they individually paid for the child. This is true even if the other parent claims the child's dependency exemption. Basically, it doesn't matter which parent claims the child—the medical expenses are deductible for the parent that pays them.

Example: Bernard and Cindy are divorced. Their son, Micah, lives primarily with Cindy, who claims him as a dependent on her tax return. Cindy also deducts Micah's annual medical and dental bills, including orthodontia expenses for his braces. However, in April, Micah falls on the playground and fractures his arm. The out-of-pocket expenses for Micah's broken arm are $5,500. Micah's father, Bernard, pays for the emergency room visit and the expenses related to the injury. Therefore, Bernard can deduct the expenses on Schedule A, even though he does not claim his son as a dependent.

Taxpayers can deduct only the amount of unreimbursed medical expenses that exceed 7.5% of adjusted gross income in 2018.[103]

Example: Hattie, age 53, had unreimbursed medical expenses totaling $2,500 in 2018. Her AGI was $40,000. Hattie cannot deduct any of her medical expenses on Schedule A because they are not more than 7.5% of her AGI ($40,000 × 7.5% = $3,000).

Example: Garrison, age 46, paid $12,000 in out-of-pocket expenses for knee surgery in 2018. His AGI was $100,000. The amount of medical expenses in excess of $7,500 (AGI of $100,000 × 7.5% limitation), or $4,500, is allowed as an itemized deduction on Schedule A.

Example: Florinda had medical expenses of $8,000 in 2018. Her AGI was $70,000. She can deduct the amount in excess of the 7.5% AGI floor ($70,000 × 7.5% = $5,250). This means that she will have a deduction of $2,750 on Schedule A ($8,000 medical expenses - $5,250 AGI floor).

---

[102] An exception to this rule exists for deceased taxpayers (covered later).
[103] The Tax Cuts and Jobs Act restored the 7.5%-of-AGI base for medical expenses in 2018. The 10%-of-AGI base is effective again starting after December 31, 2018.

Example: Bianca pays all the medical expenses for her father, age 86, who is her dependent, but does not live with her. The medical expenses are deductible on Bianca's tax return as an itemized deduction to the extent they exceed the 7.5% threshold.

Medical Insurance: If a taxpayer receives insurance reimbursement for medical care expenses, those amounts are not deductible. Qualifying medical expenses include medical insurance and long-term care insurance premiums that the taxpayer paid with after-tax dollars.

Note: The cost of an employee's annual health care coverage is typically reported on Form W-2. The amount includes the portions paid by both the employer and the employee. Although this amount is reported on Form W-2, it does not mean the amount is taxable; it is for informational purposes only. This is a recent requirement of the Affordable Care Act.

Payments for medical expenses out of a health savings account (HSA) are not deductible, but contributions to HSAs may be deducted as an adjustment to gross income, and withdrawals from an HSA are tax-free as long as they are used to pay for qualifying medical costs.

Long-Term Care Premiums: A taxpayer may include limited amounts, paid for qualified long-term care services and insurance premiums in his medical expense deductions. Long-term care services include necessary diagnostic, preventive, therapeutic, rehabilitative, maintenance, and personal care services that are required by a chronically ill individual and provided under a plan of care by a licensed doctor.

The deductibility of costs of qualified long-term care premiums is limited by the age of the taxpayer. The expenses generally cannot include costs that would be reimbursed under Medicare. The limits on deductible long-term care premiums are per individual, not per tax return.

Deductibility of 2018 Long Term Care Premiums	
Age	Maximum deduction
Age 40 or under	$420
Over 40 but not more than 50	$780
Over 50 but not more than 60	$1,560
Over 60 but not more than 70	$4,160
Over 70 years of age	$5,200

Other Medical Expenses: If a taxpayer or a dependent is in a nursing home, and the primary reason for being there is medically related, the entire cost, including meals and lodging, is a medical expense.

A taxpayer can deduct legal fees necessary to authorize treatment for a mental illness. However, legal fees for the management of a guardianship estate or for conducting the affairs of a person being treated are not deductible as medical expenses.

Medical Expenses of Deceased Taxpayers: In addition to expenses paid before a taxpayer's death, a deceased taxpayer's executor (or personal representative) can elect to treat medical expenses paid by the estate within one year after his death as if the taxpayer had paid when the medical services were provided. In other words, an executor can elect to treat medical expenses as if they were paid at the time they were incurred, even if the expenses are paid the year *after* the taxpayer's death.

> **Example:** Nathan had heart surgery in November 2018 and incurred over $20,000 of medical bills. The surgery did not go well, and when he died on December 2, 2018, his 2018 medical bills had not yet been paid. The executor of Nathaniel's estate is his son, Damon. Damon pays his late father's outstanding medical bills on February 3, 2019. As the executor, Damon may elect to deduct Nathaniel's final medical expenses on his 2018 individual return (his final tax return), even though the medical expenses were not paid until 2019. This special election only applies to deceased taxpayers.

Cosmetic Surgery: Cosmetic surgery is only deductible if it is used to correct a defect or disease. A cosmetic procedure simply for the enhancement of someone's physical appearance is not a deductible medical expense.

> **Example:** Delia undergoes a mastectomy to remove her breasts as part of treatment for cancer. A cosmetic surgeon later reconstructs her breasts to correct the deformity that is directly related to cancer. The cost of her cosmetic surgery is deductible as a medical expense because the surgery corrects an earlier defect or disease.

Medically Related Transportation, Meals, and Lodging: Vehicle mileage may be deducted if transportation is for medical reasons, such as trips to and from doctors' appointments. If a taxpayer uses his own car for medical transportation, he can deduct actual out-of-pocket expenses for gas and other expenses, or he can deduct the standard mileage rate for medical expenses, which is 18 cents per mile in 2018. A taxpayer can also deduct the costs of taxis, buses, trains, planes, or ambulances, as well as tolls and parking fees.

A taxpayer can deduct the cost of meals and lodging at a hospital or similar institution if the principal reason for being there is to receive medical care. The care must be provided by a doctor, hospital, or medical care facility, and there must not be any significant element of personal pleasure or recreation.

Capital Improvements for Medical Reasons: Capital improvements such as home improvements are usually not deductible. However, a home improvement may qualify as a deductible expense if its main purpose is to provide medical care to the taxpayer (or to family members).

The deduction for capital improvements is limited to the excess, of the actual cost of the improvements, over the related increase in the fair market value of the home. Home improvements that qualify as deductible medical expenses may include:

- Wheelchair ramps
- Lowering of kitchen cabinets
- Railings and support bars
- Elevators
- Special lift equipment

Tenants can deduct the entire cost of disability-related improvements, even if they are not the owners of the property.

> **Example:** Elliott, age 61, has a heart condition. He cannot easily climb stairs or get into a bathtub. On his doctor's advice, he pays for the installation of a special sit-in bathtub and a stair lift in his rented house. The landlord did not pay any of the cost. Elliott can deduct the entire amount as a medical expense, subject to the 7.5% threshold.

State and Local Income Taxes

The Tax Cuts and Jobs Act instituted a cap on State and Local taxes (also called the "SALT cap") in 2018. The deduction for state and local income, sales or property taxes (on a combined basis) is now capped at $10,000 ($5,000 for MFS filers).

Taxpayers can deduct certain taxes if they itemize deductions. To be deductible, a tax must have been imposed on the taxpayer and paid by the taxpayer during the tax year. Deductible taxes include:

- State, local, and foreign income taxes[104]
- State and local sales taxes
- Real estate taxes (but not for foreign real estate)
- Personal property taxes

Any amount paid before January 1, 2018, for state or local income tax will be treated as paid on the last day of the tax year for which it was imposed.

State and Local Taxes: Taxpayers are allowed to deduct either *sales/use* taxes or state and local *income* taxes, depending on which provides the larger deduction, but not both. Income taxes paid include taxes withheld from salaries and wages, amounts paid for prior years, and estimated tax payments.

Real Estate Taxes: State and local real estate taxes, based on the assessed value of the taxpayer's real property (such as a house or land) are deductible. If the taxes are paid from a mortgage escrow account, the taxpayer can deduct only the amount actually paid out of the escrow account during the year to the taxing authority.

Some real estate taxes are not deductible, including taxes imposed to finance improvements of property, such as assessments for streets, sidewalks, and sewer lines. In addition, itemized charges for services and homeowner's association fees are not deductible.

> **Example:** Ernestine makes the following payments: state income tax, $2,000; real estate taxes, $900; local benefit tax for maintaining the sewer system, $75; and homeowner's association fees on her personal residence of $250. Her total deductible taxes are $2,900 ($2,000 + $900 = $2,900). The $75 local benefit tax and the $250 homeowner's association fee are not deductible.

---

[104] Foreign income taxes are not subject to the "SALT" cap. These taxes are still deductible in full.

If a property is sold, the real estate taxes are prorated between the buyer and the seller, according to the number of days that each owned the property, and adjustments are charged or credited on the settlement statement depending upon which party is responsible for paying the taxing authority.

Escrow accounts: If a portion of the taxpayer's monthly mortgage payment goes into an escrow account, and periodically the lender pays the real estate taxes out of the account to the local government, the taxpayer is only allowed to deduct the amount that was actually paid out of the escrow account during the year to the taxing authority.

Personal Property Taxes (DMV Fees): Personal property taxes are deductible if they are:

- Charged on personal property, including cars, boats, or items used in a business, such as equipment and furniture
- Based on the value of the property, and
- Charged on a yearly basis, even if collected more or less than once a year.

Example: Debbie receives an annual registration notice for her automobile from the California Department of Motor Vehicles. The bill is broken down as follows:

- Registration: $25
- Vehicle license fee: $58
- Weight fee: $32
- County fee: $13
- Owner responsibility fee: $15

The notice states that the vehicle license fee is based on the car's value. Only the vehicle license fee is tax deductible on Schedule A.

Example: Savannah lives and works in New York, which has a high cost of living. She earns $195,000 in wages per year. Savannah paid $14,000 in property taxes on her NY condo, and $11,900 in NY state income taxes. The state income tax was automatically withheld from her wages. She also owned a vacation home in Rio de Janeiro, Brazil. She paid $4,000 in foreign real estate taxes on her vacation home. In previous years, she would have been able to deduct all these taxes without limitation. In 2018, the foreign real estate taxes are not deductible at all, and the other taxes are limited because of the SALT cap. The maximum deduction that she can take for the taxes she paid on Schedule A is $10,000.

Note: Starting in 2018, the Tax Cuts and Jobs Act eliminates the deduction for foreign real estate taxes. These taxes are no longer deductible on Schedule A as an itemized deduction. Foreign *income* taxes are still deductible, however. Foreign income taxes are *not subject* to the SALT cap. State and local taxes are reported on lines 5a, 5b, and 5c of Schedule A. Foreign Income tax is listed on line 6, "Other taxes."

Foreign Income Taxes: Generally, a taxpayer can choose between claiming the Foreign Tax Credit or claiming an itemized deduction on Schedule A for income taxes paid to a foreign country, depending on which option results in the lowest tax. The rules regarding which foreign taxes qualify for either the credit or the deduction are covered later. Foreign income taxes are not subject to the "SALT cap."

Types of Deductible Interest

Taxpayers are allowed to deduct certain types of interest. Qualified interest payments are deductible as itemized deductions on Form 1040, Schedule A. Deductible interest includes:

- Home mortgage interest
- Points on a mortgage loan
- Investment interest expense

Home Mortgage Interest

Home mortgage interest is paid on a loan secured by a taxpayer's home. The loan may be a mortgage, a second mortgage, a home equity loan, or a line of credit. A taxpayer is allowed to deduct the interest related to a primary residence and a second home. Starting in 2018, the maximum amount of qualified acquisition Indebtedness secured by a qualified primary or secondary residence will be reduced to $750,000 ($375,000 for MFS). In 2018, home equity debt related to a main home and a second home is deductible only if the loan proceeds were used to acquire, build, or substantially improve the primary residence that secures the loan. Remember, the deductibility of mortgage interest on an equity loan depends primarily on what the loan is used for.

Example: Jared owns his own home. He decides to borrow a $45,000 home equity line to consolidate his credit card debt and buy a new car. None of the interest is deductible as mortgage interest in 2018.

Note: In 2018, mortgage insurance premiums (PMI) are no longer deductible as mortgage interest.

Regarding these changes in the law, December 15, 2017, is an important date going forward. The former $1,000,000 acquisition Indebtedness limit will continue to apply for future years for any mortgage loans incurred before December 15, 2017 (i.e., the prior acquisition limit is "grandfathered").

Example: Phillip has a $150,000 mortgage on his main home where he lives. He also has a $75,000 mortgage on a beach cottage in North Carolina and a $90,000 mortgage on a condo in Utah. Phillip can deduct the mortgage interest on his main home and on the condo, but he cannot deduct the mortgage interest on the cottage because the deduction is limited to two homes.

A second home can include any other residence a taxpayer owns and treats as a home, but the taxpayer does not have to actually use the second home during the year to deduct the mortgage interest paid on the related loan.

Note: Although a taxpayer can potentially deduct real estate taxes on more than two properties, he cannot deduct mortgage interest on more than two personal homes.

An empty lot does not qualify for the mortgage interest deduction. If a taxpayer builds a house that becomes a qualified home when ready for occupancy, he can deduct mortgage interest for a period of up to 24 months from when construction begins. A taxpayer can deduct late fees on a mortgage loan as mortgage interest.

> **Example:** Floyd owns his home and pays his mortgage on a monthly basis. In 2018, he falls behind on his mortgage payments and sends in his payment late on two occasions. The mortgage company charges Floyd a $35 fee for each late payment. The late fees are deductible as mortgage interest.

Mortgage Deduction Limits: Examples

A taxpayer can deduct the interest on home equity debt only if the home equity line is used to acquire, construct, or substantially improve the home, and the loan amounts do not add up to more than the $750,000 ($375,000 for MFS) mortgage limit. For example, if a taxpayer borrows $250,000 in a home equity line of credit, and all of the loan proceeds are used to substantially improve the home, then the entire amount would be considered a qualifying loan for the mortgage interest deduction.

> **Example:** Tessa has a mortgage of $800,000 against her primary residence, which she purchased on March 2, 2018, and another mortgage of $500,000 secured by a vacation home which she purchased on April 1, 2018. Both loans were used to acquire the homes, and not for any other purpose. The loan amounts add up to $1.3 million. Since the total loan amounts exceed $750,000 "acquisition limit" for home mortgage debt, Tessa's mortgage interest deduction is limited.

> **Example:** Keisha purchased her home ten years ago and paid cash. Its fair market value is now $80,000. She did not have a mortgage until last year, when she took out a $45,000 home equity loan, secured by her home, to pay for her daughter's college tuition. This loan is home equity debt. The mortgage interest is not deductible in 2018.

> **Example:** Jeannette is single and owns her home. She has an existing mortgage on the property totaling $475,000. In 2018, she decides to add an extra bedroom, a new bathroom, and she installs a new pool. The bedroom addition cost $66,000, the new bathroom cost $22,000, and the new pool cost $29,000, for a total cost of $117,000. Jeannette applies for a home equity line of credit to finance the improvements. Since the home equity loan was used entirely to improve the property, and her total acquisition debt does not exceed $750,000, all of the interest is deductible as mortgage interest.

Points and Prepaid Mortgage Interest

Points are interest charges a borrower pays up-front to obtain a loan. Points generally represent prepaid interest a borrower pays at closing to obtain a lower interest rate. Points may also be called loan origination fees, including VA and FHA fees, maximum loan charges, premium charges, loan discount points, or prepaid interest.

Loan fees paid for specific services, such as home appraisal fees, document preparation fees, VA funding fees, or notary fees are not interest and are not deductible. In order to deduct points, the following requirements must be met:

- The mortgage must be secured by the taxpayer's main home, and the mortgage must have been used to buy, build, or improve the home.

- The points must not be an excessive or unusual amount for the local area.

- The points paid must not be more than the amount of unborrowed funds.

- The points must be computed as a percentage of the loan principal, and they must be listed on the settlement statement.

If all these requirements are met, the taxpayer can deduct points in connection with the acquisition or construction of the home either in the year paid or over the life of the loan. Tax law treats "purchase" mortgage points differently from "refinance" mortgage points. Points paid to refinance a mortgage are generally not fully deductible in the year paid and must be deducted over the life of the loan unless the proceeds are used to improve a main home. A second home or vacation home would not qualify for this exception.

> **Example:** Tammy refinanced her home in January 2018 in order to get a lower interest rate. She paid $1,500 in points for a 15-year refinance of her existing home mortgage. She is entitled to deduct only $100 per year on her Schedule A ($1,500 ÷ 15 years, the life of the loan).

Investment Interest Expense

The TCJA suspended miscellaneous itemized deductions subject to 2%-of-AGI, which includes the deduction for investment expenses, (for example, safe deposit fees, trustee fee, or investment advisor fees). The TCJA did *not* repeal the deduction for investment *interest* expense. Investment *interest* expense is any interest incurred on loans used to purchase taxable investments.

A common type of investment interest expense is margin interest. One way investors borrow funds from brokerage houses is through margin accounts. The investor uses the loan to purchase stocks and bonds without having to invest the full amount in cash.

> **Example:** Anton likes to invest in stocks using his online brokerage account. He applies for a margin-approved brokerage account in order to buy more stock. At the beginning of the year, Anton has $100,000 in cash and stocks in his existing brokerage account. His brokerage firm approves him for a 20% margin loan. This means that Anton can purchase an additional $20,000 worth of marginable stock. The extra $20,000 is granted to him in the form of a margin loan, for which he will have to pay interest.

When a taxpayer borrows money to buy property held for investment, the interest he pays on that borrowed money is investment interest expense and may be deductible. The amount of investment interest expense a taxpayer can deduct each year is limited to the amount of net investment income earned. However, he can carry forward any disallowed investment interest expense to the next year.

Example: Maritza borrows money from a bank to buy $3,000 worth of short-term bonds. The bonds mature during the year, and Maritza makes $400 of investment interest income. She also has $210 in investment interest expense, which she paid on the loan originally taken out to buy the bonds. Maritza must report the full amount of $400 as investment interest income. She can deduct the $210 of investment interest expense on Schedule A.

Example: Randolph borrows money from a bank to buy $8,500 worth of U.S. gold coins. During the year, the coins lose value, and he has no investment income. Randolph paid $326 of investment interest expense on the loan he used to buy the coins. He may not take a deduction for the investment interest expense because he has no investment income, but he may carry over to the next tax year the investment interest expense he could not deduct.

The deductible amount of investment interest expense and any disallowed amount that may be carried over to the following year are calculated on Form 4952, *Investment Interest Expense Deduction.*

A taxpayer cannot deduct interest related to passive activities or incurred to produce tax-exempt income (such as state and local bonds that generate tax-exempt interest income) as investment interest expense.

Example: Melvin borrowed $15,000 to purchase muni bonds in 2018. The tax-free municipal bonds yield 5% in interest income, and Melvin paid 3% in investment interest expense on the loan. Since muni bond interest is exempt from federal tax, Melvin cannot deduct any of the interest he paid on the loan.

Nondeductible Interest and Investment Expenses: The following expenses cannot be deducted as investment interest:

- Interest on personal loans, such as car loans
- Fees for credit cards and finance charges for nonbusiness credit card purchases
- Loan fees for services needed to get a loan
- Interest on debt the taxpayer is not legally obligated to pay
- Service charges
- Interest to purchase or carry tax-exempt securities
- Late payment charges paid to a public utility
- Expenses relating to stockholders' meetings or investment-related seminars
- Interest expenses from single-premium life insurance and annuity contracts
- Interest incurred from borrowing against an insurance policy
- Short-sale expenses
- Fines and penalties paid to any government entity for violations of the law

> **Example:** Noah and Magdalena file a joint return. During the year, they paid:
>
> 1. $3,180 of home mortgage interest reported to them on Form 1098
> 2. $400 of credit card interest
> 3. $1,500 to for an appraisal fee on their personal residence
> 4. $2,000 of interest on a personal car loan
>
> Noah and Magdalena can deduct only their home mortgage interest ($3,180). None of the other charges are allowable as a tax deduction.

Charitable Contributions

The Tax Cuts and Jobs Act makes significant changes to the treatment of charitable contributions in 2018. Effective for 2018, the AGI limitation on most cash contributions is increased from 50% to 60% of AGI. The 30%-of-AGI limitation on contributions of appreciated assets still applies.[105]

Excess contributions that exceed the AGI limits may be deducted over a 5-year period. Carryovers are subject to the same percentage limits in the year to which they are carried. These same rules apply to the new 60% limit on cash charitable contributions made to qualified organizations.

Donors age 70 ½ or older may also donate up to $100,000 per tax year directly from a traditional IRA, in lieu of taking an annual required minimum distribution (RMD).

Taxpayers who itemize deductions can deduct certain charitable contributions to qualified organizations. Taxpayers may contribute cash, property (such as clothing and furniture), securities, or other assets. A taxpayer can only deduct a contribution in the year it is actually made. A donation charged to a credit card before the end of 2018 counts for 2018, even if the credit card bill is not paid until the following year. A donation made by check counts for 2018 if the donor mails it in 2018, even if the charity cashes the check in the following year.

In order to claim deductions for noncash donations, the donated items must be in good or better condition. In most cases, the taxpayer will be able to claim a deduction for the fair market value of the contribution (generally what someone would be willing to pay at a garage sale or thrift store). No deduction is allowed for items that are in poor or unusable condition. Deductible contributions may include:

- Unreimbursed expenses that relate directly to the services the taxpayer provided for the organization.
- The amount of a contribution in excess of the fair market value of items received, such as merchandise and tickets to a charity ball.
- Transportation expenses, including bus fare, parking fees, tolls, and either the actual cost of gas and oil or a standard mileage deduction of 14 cents per mile in 2018.

---

[105] In 2018, no deduction is allowed for any amount paid for the right to purchase tickets for seating at a college athletic event.

Volunteer Expenses: A taxpayer cannot deduct a monetary value for hours he spends volunteering. However, taxpayers are allowed to deduct out-of-pocket costs related to their volunteer work for qualifying organizations.

A taxpayer can deduct expenses incurred while traveling to perform services for a charitable organization only if there is no significant element of personal pleasure in the travel. However, a deduction will not be denied simply because the taxpayer enjoys providing the services. The taxpayer can take a charitable contribution deduction for the expenses if he is on duty in a genuine and substantial way throughout the trip.

> **Example:** Louisa is an attorney who donates time to her local church for its legal needs. In 2018, she spent ten hours drafting legal documents for the church, which is a qualified religious organization. She also had $200 of out-of-pocket expenses because she purchased a new printer for the church. The printer was delivered directly to the church rectory for its use. Louisa can take a charitable deduction for $200, the amount she spent on behalf of her church. She cannot deduct the value of her time.

> **Example:** Odessa regularly volunteers at her local animal shelter, a qualified animal rescue organization. She uses her own car to travel to and from the shelter. She is not reimbursed for mileage. Odessa also fosters kittens on behalf of the shelter. She pays for cat food for the foster kittens and other supplies out-of-pocket. She receives an annual statement from the animal shelter substantiating her donations. Odessa can deduct her mileage and her unreimbursed expenses as a charitable contribution but cannot deduct the value of her time.

Exchange Students: A taxpayer can deduct some expenses paid for a foreign or American student who is living with him. The student must be sponsored by a qualifying organization, not be related to the taxpayer, and be part of a program to provide educational opportunities.

> **Example:** The Taylor family hosts a high school student from Spain in their home for nine months during 2018. The exchange student is sponsored by AFS; Intercultural Programs USA, a qualifying organization. The Taylors can deduct up to $50 a month in expenses while the student lives with them.

Nonqualifying Organizations

Not all nonprofit organizations qualify as charitable organizations for purposes of donors being able to claim tax deductions. An organization may qualify for nonprofit status so that its own activities are not subject to income tax, but this designation does not automatically provide qualification for purposes of deductible contributions. The following are examples of items that do not qualify as deductible charitable contributions:

- Gifts to civic leagues, social and sports clubs, and Chambers of Commerce
- Gifts to groups run for personal profit
- Gifts to political groups, candidates, or political organizations
- Gifts to homeowner's associations
- Donations made directly to individuals

- The cost of raffle, bingo, or lottery tickets, even if the raffle is part of a qualified organization's fundraiser

- Dues paid to country clubs or similar groups

- Gifts and dues to labor unions

- Blood donated to a blood bank or to the Red Cross

- Any part of a contribution that benefits the taxpayer, such as the FMV of a meal eaten at a charity dinner

- Donors who purchase items at a charity auction may claim a charitable contribution deduction only for the excess of the purchase price paid for an item over its fair market value.

Example: Timothy goes to a church fundraiser that includes a bingo game. Timothy spends $200 on bingo cards but does not win anything. Even though the $200 went directly to the church, the cost of the bingo game is not considered a charitable gift (because it is a wagering activity) and is therefore not deductible.

Example: Tonya participates in a charity auction for her church. All the auction proceeds go to the church. She bids on a $100 gift certificate to a popular restaurant in town. She pays $135 for the gift certificate. The FMV for the gift certificate is $100, so her qualifying donation is $35 ($135 amount paid - $100 FMV).

Example: Scarlett paid the Chamber of Commerce a $30 entry fee to run in a 10K race it was sponsoring on behalf of a cancer-related charity. The Chamber is not a qualifying charitable organization, so none of Scarlett's entry fee is tax deductible as a charitable contribution. If the race had been organized by the charity itself, part of her entry fee might have been deductible.

Substantiation Requirements for Charitable Gifts

There are strict recordkeeping requirements for taxpayers who claim deductions for charitable contributions, depending upon the nature of the donation and the dollar amounts. The IRS imposes recordkeeping and substantiation rules on donors as well as disclosure requirements on the charities themselves. Here are the basic rules for ALL charitable gifts:

- At a minimum, the donor must have at least a bank record **or** a written receipt (or written acknowledgment) from a charity for **any** cash contribution before the donor can claim a charitable deduction.

- The *donor* is responsible for obtaining a written receipt from a charity for any single contribution of $250 or more before he can claim a charitable deduction.

- Charitable organizations are required to provide a written disclosure to a donor who receives goods or services in exchange for a single payment in excess of $75.[106]

---

[106] See Publication 1771, *Charitable Contributions Substantiation and Disclosure Requirements*

Rules for Cash Donations

Cash Donations of <u>LESS</u> than $250: Cash contributions include those paid by cash, check, debit card, credit card, or payroll deduction. If the value of an individual donation is *less* than $250, the taxpayer must keep a reliable written record, such as the following:

- A bank, credit union, or credit card statement that shows the name of the qualified organization, the date of the contribution, and the amount of the contribution

- A receipt (or a letter or other written communication) from the qualified organization showing its name, the date of the contribution, and the amount of the contribution

- For payroll deductions, a pay stub or Form W-2, plus a pledge card or other document showing the name of the qualified organization

- For text donations, a telephone bill, as long as it shows the name of the qualified organization, the date of the contribution, and the amount given

A donor should not attach the acknowledgment or receipt to his tax return but must retain it to substantiate the contribution.

> **Example:** Rodger donates $25 per month to the Humane Society. Rodger always pays by check, and he keeps the canceled check as a record of his contribution. This is a valid method of recordkeeping for donations under $250. He does not need to have an additional receipt from the organization to substantiate his deduction.

Cash Donations of $250 or <u>MORE</u>: For cash donations of $250 or more, the taxpayer must have a receipt or a written acknowledgment from the organization that includes:

- The amount of cash the taxpayer contributed

- The date of the contribution

- Whether the qualified organization gave any goods or services as a result of the contribution (other than certain token items and membership benefits). The absence of this simple statement by a charity has led to court cases in which major cash contributions have been challenged, and in some cases, disallowed.

- If applicable, a description and a good faith estimate of the value of goods or services provided by the organization as a result of the contribution

A single annual statement from the charitable organization may be used to substantiate multiple contributions of $250 or more.

> **Note:** The TCJA changes the substantiation requirements slightly in 2018. Prior law exempted donors from the "contemporaneous written acknowledgment" requirement if the *donee organization* receiving the donation instead filed a return reporting the same information that the donor would have received in a written acknowledgment. The TCJA eliminates this "donee reporting" exception. As a result, donors must always substantiate donations through contemporaneous written acknowledgments, without exception.

Rules for Noncash Donations (Gifts of Property)

Noncash Contributions of Less than $250: For each contribution of less than $250, the taxpayer must obtain a receipt from the receiving organization and keep a list of the items donated.

Example: Grant donated ten dress shirts to Goodwill during the year. He made a list of the items he donated and received a receipt from the organization when he dropped off his donation. In Grant's town, Goodwill sells dress shirts in their thrift shops for about $5 each. Based on the thrift store's valuation of his donation, Grant has made a charitable donation of $50 (10 shirts x $5 FMV each).

Noncash Donations between $250 and $500: For each contribution of at least $250, but not exceeding $500, the taxpayer must have the same documentation as described above, for noncash contributions less than $250. In addition, the organization's written acknowledgment must state whether the taxpayer received any goods or services in return and included a description and a good faith estimate of the fair market value of any such items.

Noncash Donations Over $500: If a taxpayer's total deduction for all noncash contributions for the year is more than $500, he must also file Form 8283, *Noncash Charitable Contributions.*

Noncash Donations Over $5,000: If any single donation or a group of similar items is valued at more than $5,000, a qualified appraiser is required to make a written appraisal of the donated property. The taxpayer must also complete Form 8283, Section B, and attach the form to his tax return.

The taxpayer generally does not have to attach the appraisal itself but must retain a copy for his records. For donations of artwork valued at more than $20,000, or property valued at more than $500,000, the appraisal itself must be included with the tax return.

Example: Michelle has AGI of $125,000 in 2018. She decides to donate a plot of land to her church, a qualified 501(c)(3) organization. The land is worth over $5,000, so Michelle hires a qualified appraiser to give her a written appraisal for the property before she donates it. The appraiser values the land at $18,000. She also requests a receipt for the donation from her church. When she files her tax return, she claims a charitable deduction of $18,000 on her Schedule A. She also attaches Form 8283 to her return. She is not required to attach the actual appraisal, but she must keep a copy of it for her records. Michelle has complied with all of the IRS' recordkeeping requirements for her property donation.

Special Rules for Donated Vehicles

Special rules apply to any donation of vehicles, including boats and airplanes. If the taxpayer claims a deduction of more than $500, he can only deduct the smaller of:

- The gross proceeds from the sale of the item by the charity, or

- The fair market value on the date of the contribution.

The charitable organization should provide Form 1098-C, *Contributions of Motor Vehicles, Boats, and Airplanes*, which shows the gross proceeds from the sale of the vehicle donated. If the taxpayer does not attach Form 1098-C, the maximum deduction that can be taken for the donation is $500. Vehicles not in working condition may have zero donation value.

> **Example:** Porter donates his used motorcycle to his church fundraiser. The FMV of the motorcycle is $2,500. The church sells the motorcycle 60 days later for $1,700 and sends Porter a Form 1098-C. He can deduct only $1,700 on his Schedule A (the smaller of the FMV or the gross proceeds from the sale) and must attach a copy of the Form 1098-C to his tax return.

Two exceptions apply to the rules regarding vehicle donations:

- If the charity keeps the vehicle for its own use, the taxpayer can generally deduct the vehicle's FMV.

- If the charity gives or sells the vehicle directly to a needy person, the taxpayer can generally deduct the vehicle's FMV.

Contribution Limits

In 2018, a taxpayer generally cannot deduct aggregate charitable contributions that exceed 60% of his adjusted gross income. For example, if a taxpayer had $100,000 of adjusted gross income in 2018, the maximum charitable contributions he could deduct would be $60,000 (60%-of-AGI).

The 60% of AGI limit applies to *cash contributions only*—not real estate, not stocks, not furniture or any other types of noncash donations.[107] The taxpayer's deduction may be further limited to 50%, 30%, or 20% of AGI, depending on the type of property donated and the type of organization the donor gives it to.

Contributions must be paid before the close of the tax year to be deductible. In 2018, there are four major AGI limits:

- **The 60% limit** (this applies to cash donations to most qualifying charities)[108]
- **The 50% limit** (this applies to noncash donations to most qualifying charities)
- **The 30% limit** (this applies to certain organizations and certain types of gifts of appreciated property, such as appreciated stock)
- **The 20% limit** (this applies specifically to gifts of appreciated property to certain types of nonprofits)

Any amounts disallowed as a result of this limit could be carried forward to future years. Be aware that the 50% limit still applies to most noncash charitable contributions, only cash donations are subject to the higher, 60%-of-AGI limit. This contribution limit applies to contributions made to:

- Churches, synagogues, and similar religious organizations
- Hospitals
- Most schools and colleges

---

[107] Cash contributions include those paid by cash, check, electronic funds transfer, debit card, credit card, payroll deduction, or a transfer of a gift card redeemable for cash.

[108] A higher limit applies to certain qualified conservation contributions and contributions made for disaster relief in certain presidentially-declared disaster zones.

- State or federal government entities

- Nonprofits organized solely for charitable, religious, educational, scientific, or literary purposes or for the prevention of cruelty to children or animals

- Certain organizations that foster national or international amateur sports competition also qualify (examples include the Olympics, Special Olympics, and the Paralympic Games).

A taxpayer's deductible contributions to certain other types of nonprofit organizations are limited to either 30% or 20% of his AGI.

The **30% limit** applies to organizations that include the following:

- Veterans organizations

- Fraternal benefit societies (such as the Knights of Columbus, the Freemasons, and the Shriners)

- Nonprofit cemeteries

In addition, a **separate 30% limit** applies in the following cases:

- Gifts for use by the charitable organization (such as the donation of a refrigerator the organization uses for itself)

- Gifts of appreciated property (also called capital gain property)

The **20% limit** applies to contributions of capital gain property to organizations subject to the 30% limit.

Example: Benita likes to volunteer and donate to her local animal shelter. In 2018, her AGI for the year was $30,000. She has money saved in her bank account, and she makes a large cash donation of $20,000 to the shelter. Her maximum charitable deduction for the year would be limited to $18,000 (60% of her $30,000 AGI). Her disallowed contribution, $2,000 ($18,000 allowable deduction -$20,000 donation), would be carried over to the following year and can be used on a future return.

Example: Daniel's adjusted gross income is $40,000. During the year, he gave appreciated land with an FMV of $11,000 to a local veteran's organization, which is a 30% limit organization. He has a qualified appraisal for the value of the property. The gift of land is appreciated property, so it is subject to an additional restriction—the 20%-of-AGI limit applies based on the nature of the organization. His allowable deduction is $8,000 (20% x $40,000 = $8,000). The remainder will have to be carried over to a future year ($11,000 FMV of the land - $8,000 allowable deduction= $3,000 carryover).

Charitable Contribution Carryovers

To the extent a taxpayer's deductions for contributions are limited; they may be carried over to subsequent years. However, the carryover period is generally limited to five years. Any carryover amounts that cannot be deducted within five years due to the AGI limits are lost. Any contributions made by the taxpayer and carried over to future years retain their original character. For example, contributions made to a 30% organization continue to be subject to the 30%-of-AGI limit in future years.

> **Example:** Amelia has an AGI of $100,000 in 2018. She makes a $60,000 cash donation to her synagogue during the year. She also donates $30,000 of appreciated stock. Amelia is allowed to deduct all her cash contributions, but her $30,000 gift of appreciated stock is disallowed in the current year, because she has already reached the 60%-of-AGI limit with her cash contributions. Her allowable deduction on Schedule A would be $60,000. She is required to carry forward the $30,000 contribution of appreciated stock to a future year. The carry forward will be subject to a 30%-of-AGI limitation in future years. She has up to five years to use the contribution carryforward.

Increased Contribution Limits for Disaster Areas

The Bipartisan Budget Act of 2018 was signed into law on February 9th, 2018. The act included several provisions aimed at helping victims of federal disasters. The Bipartisan Budget Act suspends AGI limits for any qualified contributions made for disaster relief efforts. This applies to disaster contributions made *between* October 7, 2017, and January 1, 2019.

Contributions to qualified charities may be earmarked for flood relief, hurricane relief or other disaster relief. However, a taxpayer cannot deduct any contributions earmarked for the relief of a particular individual or family.

The act also eliminated the 10% penalty for early withdrawal from eligible retirement plans for any individual whose principal residence is within the disaster area and sustained an economic loss by reason of the wildfires or hurricanes. This applies for up to $100,000 of IRA and 401(k) distributions. Taxpayers who made donations for qualified disaster relief organizations will not be subject to charitable contribution limitations if the contributions were made for this purpose.[109]

> **Example:** Eleonora has AGI of $130,000 in 2018. She decides to make a large cash donation of $100,000 to the California Disaster Charitable Fund, a qualified 501(c)(3) disaster relief organization. Normally, her charitable deduction would be limited to 60% of her taxable income, or $78,000 ($130,000 x 60% AGI). However, because the organization is a qualified disaster relief organization, Eleonora is allowed to deduct the full contribution of $100,000 on her Schedule A.

Special Rules for Conservation Easements

Many taxpayers choose to donate real estate to their favorite charities. Special rules apply to conservation easements. Conservation easements are gifts of real property (real estate) that are specifically for conservation purposes. In other words, conservation easements are used for land conservation purposes by restricting the use of the land. There are very unique rules that apply to charitable gifts of this type. The TCJA retains the deduction for conservation easements, but alters the filing requirements for claiming the deduction.[110]

---

[109] The new IRS Publication 3833, *Disaster Relief, Providing Assistance Through Charitable Organizations,* describes the rules for taxpayers and charitable organizations that provide assistance to victims of disasters or other emergency hardship situations.

[110] The IRS has issued recent guidance on syndicated conservation easements, listing these contributions as tax-avoidance strategies. As a result, syndicated conservation easements are now considered "listed transactions" that require disclosure statements to the IRS by both investors and material advisors. Notice 2017-10.

Unlike other capital gain property, if the real property has appreciated in value, the charitable deduction is not limited to 30% of adjusted gross income. In 2018, the charitable deduction allowed for conservation property is 50% of adjusted gross income, regardless of whether or not the property has appreciated. There is also a separate, higher AGI threshold that applies specifically to farmers and ranchers.[111]

The carryforward period for a donor to take tax deductions for a conservation agreement is fifteen years, rather than the usual five years for other types of charitable gifts.

> **Example:** In 2018, Jordan decides to make a donation of property to The Nature Conservancy. Jordan donates 500 acres of land with the intent to preserve the area for fishing and wildlife. Jordan purchased the land twenty years ago for $1,000,000. The land has appreciated in value. Jordan obtains a qualified appraisal of the property, stating that the land has a current fair market value of $1,400,000. In 2018, Jordan's AGI is $400,000. Because of the special threshold that applies to conservation easements, Jordan will be able to take a charitable deduction of up to 50% of his $400,000 AGI. Therefore, his $1,400,000 gift permits a deduction of $200,000 ($400,000 AGI x 50% = $200,000) in 2018 and charitable carryforward of $1,200,000 that he can use in future years to offset his taxable income. The carryforward is valid for fifteen years, rather than the usual five. If Jordan had been a qualified farmer or rancher, he would have been able to deduct up to 100% of his AGI for the year, for a full $400,000 deduction on Schedule A.

Personal Casualty and Theft Losses

For tax years 2018 through 2025, the TCJA suspended the itemized deduction for most personal (i.e., non-business, non-production of income) casualty and theft losses. Only losses derived from federally declared disaster areas are deductible.

Taxpayers in a federal disaster area who incur disaster-related casualty losses can deduct their unreimbursed losses on either their tax return in the year the disaster occurred, or if elected, in the year *prior* to the year of the disaster event.

This special rule about being able to potentially claim a casualty loss in the *prior* tax year allows taxpayers in a presidentially-declared disaster area to quickly obtain the tax benefits associated with the deduction without having to wait (up to) a year from the casualty event before their tax return for the year of the event can be filed.

The casualty loss deduction on a personal-use asset is the *lesser* of (1) the decrease in the fair market value of the property (before and after the casualty event) or (2) the taxpayer's adjusted basis in the property at the time of the casualty event. The loss casualty loss deduction is further limited to a $100 limit per casualty and 10% of the taxpayer's adjusted gross income (AGI). The $100 and 10%-of-AGI limitations only apply to personal casualty losses (losses of nonbusiness property). Casualty losses of business property and rental property are 100% deductible, but those losses are not reported on Schedule A. Business casualty losses are covered in more detail in Part 2, *Businesses.*

---

[111] The PATH Act made the enhanced conservation easement donation deduction permanent.

Example: On November 9, 2018, Kelsey's mobile home was completely destroyed in a California wildfire. The area was declared a federal disaster area by the president. Kelsey did not have insurance on her mobile home, so she did not receive any insurance reimbursement. The fair market value of the mobile home before the wildfire was $80,000. Since it was completely destroyed, its FMV was $0 afterward. Her basis in the home was $13,800 at the time of the fire. As such, her loss on the home was $13,800. Her AGI was $25,000 in 2018. Kelsey would figure her deductible casualty loss as follows:

Loss on the mobile home	$13,800
Subtract $100	($100)
Loss before AGI limitations	$13,700
Subtract 10% of her AGI ($25,000 X 10%)	($2,500)
Allowable casualty loss deduction on Schedule A	**$11,200**

Miscellaneous Itemized Deductions

The TCJA suspended most miscellaneous itemized deductions in 2018, including most unreimbursed employee travel and moving expenses.[112] This TCJA suspension applies to taxable years between 2018 and 2025. There are still some miscellaneous expenses that a taxpayer can deduct on Schedule A. These are less commonly seen, but some of them are still tested on the EA exam. Miscellaneous tax deductions that are still allowable in 2018 include:

- The amortizable premium on taxable bonds
- Casualty and theft losses from "income-producing" property
- Federal estate tax on income "in respect of a decedent" (IRD)
- Gambling losses to the extent of gambling winnings
- Impairment-related work expenses of persons with disabilities.
- Losses from Ponzi-type investment schemes.
- Repayments of more than $3,000 under a claim of right
- Unlawful discrimination claims.
- Unrecovered investment in an annuity

The amortizable premium on taxable bonds: If the amount a taxpayer pays for a bond is greater than its stated principal amount, the excess is called a bond premium. Annual amortization of the premium is treated as a miscellaneous itemized deduction.

Casualty or theft losses from "income-producing" property: A taxpayer can deduct a casualty or theft loss as a miscellaneous itemized deduction, if the damaged or stolen property was income-producing property (meaning property held for investment, such as gold coins,

---

[112] There is an exception in the law for military personnel.

silver coins, artwork, and vacant lots). The taxpayer must report the loss on Form 4684, *Casualties and Thefts,* Section B.

Gambling losses to the extent of gambling winnings: The full amount of a taxpayer's gambling winnings must be reported on Form 1040. Gambling *losses* are deducted on Schedule A, up to the total amount of gambling winnings. Taxpayers must have kept a written record of their losses. Gambling losses in excess of winnings are not deductible.

Example: Nathan likes to gamble at the blackjack tables at his local casino. In 2018, he wins $6,200 playing blackjack but has $9,500 in gambling losses. He is required to report the full amount of the winnings on Form 1040. His deduction for gambling losses is limited to $6,200 on Schedule A. He cannot write off the remaining $3,300 in losses. He also cannot carry the losses forward to future years. If Nathan chooses not to itemize his deductions, then none of his gambling losses would be deductible.

Work-related expenses for individuals with a disability: These are expenses that enable a disabled person to work, such as special equipment or attendant care services at his workplace. Impairment-related work expenses must be incurred in connection with the taxpayer's place of work, or necessary for the taxpayer to be able to work.

Example: Norma has a serious visual disability, macular degeneration. She requires a large screen magnifier to see well enough to perform her work. Norma purchased her screen magnifier for $550. Her employer did not reimburse the cost. She can deduct its cost as an itemized deduction. This means she is able to deduct the full cost of the magnifier on Schedule A without any income limitations.

Estate tax on income in respect of a decedent: Income in respect of a decedent (IRD) is income owed to a decedent at the time he died. If a decedent's estate has paid federal estate taxes on IRD assets, a beneficiary may be able to claim an IRD tax deduction. IRD is covered more extensively later, in the chapter that covers estate tax.

Repayments of more than $3,000 under a claim of right: On occasion, a taxpayer may have to repay income that was included on a previous year's tax return because at the time the taxpayer received it, they thought they had an unrestricted right to it. One example could be when a taxpayer has to repay the unemployment benefits that they received.

Example: Katie lost her job and promptly applied for unemployment. She received unemployment all year. Katie's former employer appealed to the state, and it was determined that Katie made false statements and held back important information on her unemployment claim. Katie is now required to repay the benefits she received earlier. Katie will be forced to repay $8,000 in unemployment benefits. She is allowed to take an itemized deduction for these repayments on her Schedule A, because the amount of the repayment exceeds $3,000.

Losses from Ponzi-type investment schemes: Victims of fraudulent investment schemes can claim a theft loss deduction if certain conditions apply. Under IRS rules, an investor who is a victim of a Ponzi scheme is entitled to deduct Ponzi losses as a *theft* loss, instead of a *capital* loss from an investment. Ponzi scheme losses are not limited to the $3,000 annual limit that applies to other capital losses.[113]

> **Example:** Alanna is a potential investor. She is looking for a financial advisor to help her invest. Bernie holds himself out to the public as an investment advisor and securities broker. In 2018, Alanna is persuaded to invest with Bernie. She opens an investment account with Bernie and contributed $100,000 to the account and provided Bernie with a power of attorney to use the funds to purchase and sell securities on her behalf. Unbeknownst to Alanna, Bernie only invests a small amount of her funds and embezzles the rest into his own personal accounts. Later, it is discovered that Bernie's purported investment advisory and brokerage activity was, in fact, a fraudulent investment arrangement known as a "Ponzi" scheme. Bernie is convicted of securities fraud and sentenced to prison. Alanna is only able to recover $5,000 of her original $100,000 investment. Therefore, Alanna has a $95,000 deductible theft loss. She would report the loss on Schedule A as an itemized deduction, and the losses are not limited.

Deductions for Nonresident Aliens

Specific limitations on deductions apply to nonresident aliens who are required to file Form 1040NR. They cannot claim the standard deduction. Further, except for certain allowable itemized deductions, they can claim deductions only to the extent they are connected with income related to their U.S. trade or business. The following itemized deductions are allowed:

- State and local income taxes
- Qualifying charitable contributions to U.S. nonprofit organizations (not foreign nonprofits)
- Casualty and theft losses in a presidentially declared disaster area
- Some miscellaneous itemized deductions

Itemized deductions related to mortgage interest are not allowed. There are special exceptions in the law for tax treaty partners, but the IRS will not test on any specific tax treaties with other nations.

Nondeductible Expenses

The IRS has a lengthy list of expenses that individual taxpayers cannot deduct.[114] These are just a sample of personal expenses the IRS lists as nondeductible:

- Lunch with coworkers or meals while working late
- Country club dues, athletic club fees, and gym memberships
- Home repairs, insurance, and rent
- Losses from the sale of a home, furniture, or a personal car
- Brokers' commissions
- Burial or funeral expenses, including the cost of cemetery lots

---

[113] A "Ponzi scheme" is a type of criminal fraud or embezzlement. For more guidance on the IRS' official position regarding Ponzi schemes, see IRS Revenue Ruling 2009–9 and Revenue Procedure 2009-20.
[114] A basic rule is that most personal, living, or family expenses are not deductible.

- Fees and licenses, such as car license or registration costs (except certain portions that may be considered deductible property taxes), marriage licenses, and dog tags
- Fines and penalties for breaking the law, such as parking tickets
- Life and disability insurance premiums
- Investment-related seminars
- Lost or misplaced cash or property
- Political contributions
- Expenses of attending stockholders' meetings
- Voluntary unemployment benefit fund contributions
- Adoption expenses (although a taxpayer may be able to claim an adoption credit)
- Travel expenses for another individual
- Interest on a personal credit card
- Expenses of earning or collecting tax-exempt income

Unit 12: Study Questions

(Please test yourself first; then check the correct answers at the end of this quiz.)

1. Connor is deaf. He purchased a special device to use at his workplace so he can identify when his phone rings. He paid for the device out-of-pocket, and his employer did not reimburse him. How should Connor report this on his tax return?

A. Connor can deduct the purchase as an itemized deduction on Schedule A.
B. Connor can deduct the purchase as an adjustment to income.
C. Connor cannot deduct the purchase because he is not totally disabled.
D. Connor cannot deduct the purchase because he is not self-employed.

2. Christopher and Ariel file a joint return. During the year, they paid:

Home mortgage interest on their primary residence	$5,000
Credit card interest	600
Auto loan interest	4,000
Loan interest on an empty lot that was purchased to build a second home	3,000

What amount can they report as deductible mortgage interest?

A. $0
B. $5,000
C. $8,000
D. $8,600

3. Which of the following taxes can taxpayers potentially deduct on Schedule A?

A. Federal income tax
B. Real estate taxes on a U.S. property
C. Taxes on alcohol and tobacco
D. Foreign real estate taxes

4. Which of the following taxpayers must either itemize deductions or claim zero as their deduction?

A. Mindy, who files a joint return with her husband.
B. Leslie, who is single, claims two dependents, and files Form 1040.
C. Pearl, whose itemized deductions are more than the standard deduction.
D. Gabriel, whose wife files a separate return and itemizes her deductions.

5. Clemens owns three homes and has an AGI of $128,000 in 2018. His primary residence is in Chicago. He also owns a mountain cabin in Lake Tahoe and a small condo in Las Vegas, which he uses several times a year. In 2018, Clemens did not use the mountain cabin, and it sat empty all year. He pays property tax and mortgage interest on all three properties.

Home Location	Mortgage Interest	Property Tax
Main home in Chicago	$18,500	$7,500
Cabin in Tahoe	$5,200	$2,800
Condo in Las Vegas	$4,500	$1,950

Based on the information above, which of the following statements is correct?

A. Clemens may claim a mortgage interest deduction of $18,500 and a property tax deduction of $7,500 on Schedule A.
B. Clemens may claim a mortgage interest deduction of $23,700 and a property tax deduction of $10,300 on Schedule E.
C. Clemens may claim a mortgage interest deduction of $28,200 and a property tax deduction of $12,250 on Schedule A.
D. Clemens may claim an allowable mortgage interest deduction of $23,700 and a property tax deduction of $10,000 on Schedule A.

6. Emelie donates $430 in cash to her church. Which of the following is required on the receipt to substantiate the donation correctly for IRS recordkeeping requirements?

A. The reason for the contribution
B. Emelie's home address
C. The amount of the donation
D. Emelie's method of payment

7. Julio spent the entire day attending his human rights organization's regional meeting as a delegate. He spent $250 on a plane ticket to the meeting and $25 on materials for the meeting. In the evening, Julio went to the theater with two other meeting attendees. He spent $50 on theater tickets. The charity did not reimburse Julio for any of his costs. How much can he deduct as a charitable expense?

A. $0
B. $250
C. $275
D. $125

8. Which of the following home improvements cannot be deducted as an itemized medical expense?

A. The cost of installing stairlifts for a disabled individual
B. The cost of lowering cabinets to accommodate a disability
C. The cost of making doorways wider to accommodate a wheelchair
D. An elevator that costs $14,000 and adds $15,000 to the FMV of the home

9. Which of the following taxes can taxpayers deduct on Schedule A?

A. Local sales taxes
B. Fines for speeding
C. Social Security taxes
D. Homeowner's association fees

10. Which of the following taxpayers is required to itemize deductions and cannot take the standard deduction?

A. Sophie, who has one dependent child.
B. Andrea, who wants to deduct the alimony she paid to her ex-husband.
C. Gabrielle, whose itemized deductions are more than the standard deduction.
D. Samir, who is a nonresident alien.

11. Justin had the following medical expenses in 2018:

- Contributions to health savings account (HSA): $6,000
- Treatment of a broken leg: $9,000 (of which $8,000 was reimbursed by his insurance)
- Doctor-prescribed back brace: $1,900
- Child care while in the hospital: $200

What is his medical expense deduction before limitation based on the 7.5%-of-AGI threshold?

A. $1,900
B. $2,900
C. $7,900
D. $8,900

12. For a tax to be deductible, all of the following must be correct except:

A. The tax must be imposed during the tax year
B. The taxpayer must be legally liable for the tax
C. The tax must be paid during the tax year
D. The tax must be paid by the taxpayer

13. Iris is single and has the following income and expenses:

Wages	$70,000
Net investment interest income	3,000
Mortgage interest paid on a primary residence	24,000
Investment interest expense	5,000
Personal credit card interest	3,400
Car loan interest on her personal vehicle	1,200
Late fees on her mortgage	50

What is Iris' total allowable deduction for interest expense on her Schedule A?

A. $24,000
B. $27,000
C. $27,050
D. $32,400

14. All of the following factors determine the amount of a taxpayer's standard deduction except:

A. The taxpayer's filing status
B. The taxpayer's adjusted gross income
C. Whether the taxpayer is 65 or older, or blind
D. Whether the taxpayer can be claimed as a dependent

15. Thomas donates to his church multiple times during the year. Which one of the donations listed below will require a qualified appraisal before the contribution can be deducted on his return?

A. A cash donation of $12,000
B. A donation of antique furniture valued at $6,500
C. A donation of appreciated stock with a fair market value of $12,500
D. A donation of an old motorcycle valued at $450

16. Herschel and Angeline will file separate tax returns in 2018. Herschel plans to itemize his medical expenses, therefore, what must Angeline do?

A. They will have to file jointly.
B. Angeline must take the standard deduction.
C. Angeline must either itemize her deductions or claim zero as their standard deduction.
D. Angeline may choose to itemize or take the standard deduction.

17. Kiara donates her used car to a qualified charity. She bought it three years ago for $15,000. A used car guide shows the FMV for this type of car is $5,000. Kiara's friend, Buck, offered her $4,500 for the car a week ago. Kiara receives Form 1098-C from the organization showing the car was sold for $1,900. How much is Kiara's charitable deduction?

A. $15,000
B. $5,000
C. $4,500
D. $1,900

18. Oscar donated a leather coat to a thrift store operated by his church. He paid $450 for the coat three years ago. Similar coats in the thrift store sell for $50. What is Oscar's charitable deduction?

A. $0
B. $50
C. $400
D. $450

19. Which of the following taxes is not deductible on Schedule A?

A. Property taxes paid on a vacation home located in Hawaii.
B. State income taxes
C. Property taxes based on a vehicle's value (DMV fees)
D. Property taxes paid on a home in Mexico

20. Bowen donated to all of the following nonprofit organizations in 2018. What is his allowable deduction for charitable gifts on Schedule A?

Organization	Amount
Methodist church	$100
County animal shelter	120
Salvation Army	75
American Red Cross	25
Democratic party	50
Chamber of Commerce	300
Total contributions	$670

A. $320
B. $370
C. $220
D. $670

21. Enrique and Crystal had adjusted gross income of $75,000 in 2018 and incurred the following expenses:

Homeowner's association dues	$1,000
Fine from homeowner's association for violation of bylaws	100
Applicable losses from Hurricane Maria, (a federal disaster area)	9,000
Political contributions to the Green Party	250

Based on the information provided, what is the amount of expenses they can deduct for 2018 on Schedule A?

A. $1,750
B. $10,250
C. $1,350
D. $1,400

22. All of the following miscellaneous itemized deductions are allowable in 2018 except:

A. Union dues
B. Impairment-related work expenses of persons with disabilities
C. Federal estate tax on income in respect of a decedent
D. Gambling losses to the extent of gambling winnings

23. Angie and Sheldon, both age 41, file a joint return and claim their two children as dependents. They have adjusted gross income of $125,000. In 2018, the family accumulated $12,120 of unreimbursed medical and dental expenses that included the following:

Prescription medications filled in the U.S.	$6,500
Prescription medications ordered and shipped from another country	1,320
Prescription contact lenses for Angie	500
Teeth whitening procedure by Angie's dentist and custom bleach trays	2,600
Prescribed smoking cessation program for Sheldon	1,200

What amount can they deduct for their medical expenses?

A. $6,500
B. $9,375
C. $8,200
D. $0

24. Isaac's main home was damaged by a Hurricane Maria, and his county was later deemed a federal disaster area. He incurred $90,000 worth of flood damage, but $80,000 was reimbursed by his homeowner's insurance company. His basis in the home was $200,000 at the time of the hurricane. Isaac's employer had a disaster relief fund for its employees. Isaac received $4,000 from the fund and spent the entire amount on repairs to his home. What is Isaac's casualty loss *before* applying the $100 limit per casualty and 10%-of-AGI limits?

A. $0
B. $4,000
C. $6,000
D. $10,000

25. Gonzalo is a visiting professor from Spain who is teaching at a U.S. university on a J-1 visa. He is classified as a nonresident alien for tax purposes and will file Form 1040NR. Which of the following is he allowed to claim as an itemized deduction on his income tax return?

A. Disability insurance premiums.
B. A charitable gift of $150 to the American Cancer Society.
C. Mortgage interest on his main home.
D. The standard deduction.

1. The answer is A. Connor can deduct the expenses for the special device as an impairment-related work expense. If a taxpayer has a physical or mental disability that limits employment, he can deduct the expense as a miscellaneous itemized deduction.

2. The answer is B. Only their home mortgage interest ($5,000) is potentially deductible as interest on Schedule A. The other types of interest are all personal interest, which is not deductible. Interest paid on a plot of land is not deductible as mortgage interest, even if the taxpayer later decides to build a home on the property. Only the interest secured by an actual home (not land) is deductible as mortgage interest.

3. The answer is B. Only the real estate taxes incurred on a U.S. property are deductible. Taxpayers can deduct real estate tax on Schedule A as an itemized deduction.

4. The answer is D. A married taxpayer who files separately and whose spouse itemizes deductions must either itemize his deductions or claim zero as his deduction. Gabriel is not permitted to utilize the standard deduction.

5. The answer is D. The mortgage interest and property tax on both his main home in Chicago and the mountain cabin are deductible (assuming the ceiling on qualifying mortgage debt is not an issue). The mortgage interest on the third home is not deductible. The property tax on all the homes is *potentially* deductible, but the deduction is limited to $10,000 by the SALT cap in 2018. The mortgage interest on a second home is deductible, even if the taxpayer did not use the home during the year. A taxpayer may deduct mortgage interest on up to two homes. The answer is calculated as follows:

Home Location	Mortgage Interest	Property Tax
Main home in Chicago	$18,500	$7,500
Cabin in Tahoe	5,200	2,800
Condo in Las Vegas	3rd home Not Deductible	1,950
Totals before limitations	**$23,000**	**$12,250**
Allowable deduction	**$23,700**	**$10,000 SALT limit**

6. The answer is C. Emelie can claim a deduction for a contribution of $250 or more only if she has a receipt or acknowledgment from a qualified organization. The receipt must include:
- The amount of cash contributed
- Whether the qualified organization gave the taxpayer any goods or services in return
- If applicable, a description and good faith estimate of the value of any goods or services provided in return by the organization

A receipt must also show the date of the donation and the name of the organization that was paid.

7. The answer is C. Julio's charitable contribution is $275 ($250 plane ticket + $25 materials = $275). He can claim his travel and meeting expenses as charitable contributions because they are directly related to his charitable activities. However, he cannot claim the cost of the evening at the theater, as that is a personal entertainment expense.

8. The answer is D. The deduction for capital improvements is limited to the excess of the actual cost of the improvements over the increase in the fair market value of the home. Since the increase in the fair market value of the home exceeds the cost of the elevator, none of the cost can be deducted as a medical expense.

9. The answer is A. A taxpayer has the option of claiming sales taxes as an itemized deduction on Schedule A instead of claiming state and local income taxes. A taxpayer cannot claim both. The other expenses listed are not deductible on Schedule A.

10. The answer is D. A nonresident or dual-status alien (who is not married to a U.S. citizen or resident) must itemize deductions. Samir cannot use the standard deduction. The other taxpayers listed are not required to itemize their deductions but may elect to do so if they wish.

11. The answer is B. Justin's medical expense deduction (before any AGI limitations) is $2,900 ($1,900 + $1,000). The childcare cost is not deductible, even though it was incurred while Justin was obtaining medical care. The amount reimbursed by insurance is not deductible. Contributions to an HSA may be claimed as an adjustment to gross income, but not as a medical expense deduction. Payments for medical expenses out of an HSA are not deductible.

12. The answer is A. Taxpayers can deduct taxes imposed during a *prior* year, as long as the taxes were *paid* during the current tax year.

13. The answer is C. The answer is calculated as follows: $24,000 + $3,000 + $50 = $27,050. The deduction for investment interest expense is limited to net investment income of $3,000. The excess amount of interest expense of $2,000 ($5,000 - $3,000) must be carried over to the next tax year and may be used to offset net investment income in future tax years. Late fees paid on a qualifying mortgage are deductible as interest. The credit card interest and car loan interest are not deductible.

14. The answer is B. The standard deduction amount is based on the taxpayer's filing and dependent status, and whether the taxpayer is blind or at least 65 years old. It is not based on a taxpayer's income.

15. The answer is B. The antique furniture donation would require an appraisal. Thomas must also complete Form 8283 and attach it to his tax return. The IRS requires a taxpayer to obtain a written appraisal by a qualified appraiser for any *noncash* contribution of more than $5,000. The antique furniture would require a qualified written appraisal before the taxpayer could deduct the donation on his tax return. Thomas must retain a copy of the appraisal for his own records, but in most cases, does not have to attach the appraisal to his tax return. Answer A is incorrect because a cash donation does not require an appraisal. Answer C is incorrect because the donation of stock or other securities does not require an appraisal. A donation of a vehicle valued at less than $500 does not require an appraisal or any other type of documentation beyond a written acknowledgment from the organization.

16. The answer is C. Since they are both filing MFS, Angeline is forced to either itemize her deductions or claim a zero as their standard deduction. A taxpayer whose spouse itemizes deductions must either itemize deductions or claim zero as the standard deduction. This only applies in situations when both taxpayers are filing MFS. If one spouse qualifies for Head of Household filing status, then neither spouse would be forced to itemize.

17. The answer is D. Kiara can deduct $1,900 for her donation. She is allowed to take the lesser of the car's FMV or the amount for which the charity was able to sell the car. Since the charity sold the car for only $1,900, that is the amount of her allowable deduction, regardless of any other estimates of its value.

18. The answer is B. Oscar's donation is limited to $50. Generally, the FMV of used clothing and household goods is far less than the original cost. For used clothing, a taxpayer should claim as the value the price that a buyer typically would pay in a thrift shop or at a garage sale.

19. The answer is D. Property taxes paid on a home in Mexico are not deductible. The deduction for foreign real property taxes is no longer allowed in 2018.

20. The answer is A. The contributions to the political organization and the Chamber of Commerce are not deductible on Schedule A. Bowen's allowable deduction is calculated as follows: $100 + $120 + $75 + $25 = $320.

21. The answer is D. Only the casualty loss is deductible. Neither the homeowner's association dues, nor the fine or political contribution are deductible. The applicable amount of the hurricane loss[115] in a federal disaster area, minus $100, that exceeds 10% of adjusted gross income is deductible as a casualty loss. Enrique and Crystal's deductible casualty loss on Schedule A is $1,400, figured as follows:

Applicable loss from hurricane	$9,000
Minus $100 threshold	(100)
Loss after $100 limit	8,900
Adjusted gross income	75,000
Multiply by 10% AGI limit	7,500
Casualty loss deduction ($8,900 - $7,500)	**$1,400**

22. The answer is A. The union dues are not deductible as a miscellaneous itemized deduction in 2018. All of the other expenses would be deductible on Schedule A.

23. The answer is D. Angie and Sheldon cannot deduct any of their medical expenses. In 2018, only the medical expenses that exceed 7.5% of the taxpayer's AGI are deductible. The total of Angie and Sheldon's *qualifying* medical expenses, $8,200, is less than $9,375 ($125,000 × 7.5%). Of the items listed, only the smoking cessation program, the contact lenses, and the prescription medications filled in the United States are qualified medical expenses. Prescription medications shipped from other countries are ineligible. The teeth whitening procedure would be considered a cosmetic enhancement and would not be a qualified medical expense, whether performed by a dentist or not.

24. The answer is C. Isaac's casualty loss before applying the deduction limits is $6,000. Isaac must reduce his loss ($90,000) by the $80,000 insurance proceeds and the $4,000 he received from his employer.

---

[115] The *lesser* of (1) the decrease in the fair market value of the property (before and after the casualty event) or (2) the taxpayer's adjusted basis in the property at the time of the casualty event.

25. The answer is B. Gonzalo is allowed to deduct the charitable gift to a U.S. charity on his Form 1040NR. Nonresident aliens are limited as to the types of itemized deductions they can claim. Among other restrictions, they are not allowed to claim the deduction for mortgage interest. Answer "D" is incorrect because nonresident aliens cannot claim the standard deduction.

Unit 13: Individual Tax Credits

For additional information read:
Publication 972, *Child Tax Credit*
Publication 503, *Child and Dependent Care Expenses*
Publication 596, *Earned Income Credit*
Publication 970, *Tax Benefits for Education*

A tax credit directly reduces a taxpayer's liability on a dollar-for-dollar basis, which means it is usually more valuable than a tax deduction of the same dollar amount that only reduces the amount of taxable income. Various types of tax credits are either refundable or nonrefundable.

Nonrefundable Tax Credits

A nonrefundable tax credit reduces a taxpayer's liability for the year to zero but not beyond that, so any remaining credit is not refunded to the taxpayer. Among the most common nonrefundable tax credits are:

- Foreign Tax Credit (covered later)
- Child and Dependent Care Credit
- Child Tax Credit (CTC)
- Adoption Credit
- American Opportunity Tax Credit (also has a refundable component)
- Lifetime Learning Credit
- Retirement Savings Contributions Credit
- The new "Credit for Other Dependents" (ODC)

Refundable Tax Credits

A refundable tax credit can reduce a taxpayer's liability to zero and also generate a refund to the taxpayer for the amount by which the credit exceeds the amount of tax he would otherwise owe. Refundable tax credits include the following:

- Additional Child Tax Credit (ACTC)
- Earned Income Tax Credit (EITC)
- Premium Tax Credit (related to the Affordable Care Act, covered later)
- American Opportunity Tax Credit (AOTC, partially refundable)
- Credit for excess Social Security and RRTA tax withheld

Note: A provision in the *Protecting Americans from Tax Hikes Act* prevents retroactive claims of the Earned Income Tax Credit, the Child Tax Credit, and the American Opportunity Credit for any individual that did not have a valid tax identification number for the taxable year. In the past, a taxpayer was allowed to amend their return to claim these credits retroactively after a valid taxpayer identification number was issued.

Note: New due diligence requirements apply to Tax Preparers who prepare returns claiming the Earned Income Tax Credit (EITC), the Child Tax Credit (CTC), and the American Opportunity Tax Credit (AOTC). Starting in 2018, the new due diligence requirements also apply to the determination of Head of Household filing status. Tax preparers must complete Form 8867, *Paid Preparer's Due Diligence Checklist*, for each EITC, CTC/ACTC or AOTC claim they prepare. This new requirement is covered in more detail in Book 3, *Representation*.

Child and Dependent Care Credit

The Child and Dependent Care Credit allows a taxpayer a credit for a percentage of child care expenses for children under age 13 and for disabled dependents of any age. This is a nonrefundable credit for child care expenses that allow taxpayers to work or to seek work. The credit offsets regular tax and the alternative minimum tax. The credit ranges from 20% to 35% of qualifying expenses, depending on a taxpayer's income.

For 2018, the limit on qualifying expenses is $3,000 for one child and $6,000 for two or more children. If a taxpayer receives a reimbursement under a flexible spending account, the amount is treated as being pretax, and the taxpayer must deduct the reimbursed amount from his qualified expenses to determine the credit. A taxpayer must pass five eligibility tests to qualify for the Credit for Child and Dependent Care Expenses:

- **Qualifying person test**
- **Earned income test**
- **Work-related expense test**
- **Joint return test**
- **Provider identification test**

Test #1: Qualifying Person Test

For purposes of the Child and Dependent Care Credit, a "qualifying person" is:

- A dependent child under the age of 13 (at the time the care was provided)
- A spouse who is physically or mentally unable to care for himself
- Any other disabled person who is unable to care for himself and that the taxpayer either claims as a dependent or could claim if not for certain specified circumstances

Example: Conrad paid someone to care for his disabled wife, Dacia, so he could work. Dacia requires a full-time in-home care aide. Conrad also paid to have someone prepare meals and babysit his 12-year-old daughter, Tammy. Both Dacia and Tammy are qualifying persons for the Child and Dependent Care Credit.

Test #2: Earned Income Test

Both the taxpayer and his spouse, if married, must have "earned income" during the year to qualify for this credit. This generally means both spouses must work (if filing a joint return). The credit is not available to MFS filers. In the event one spouse does not have earned income, for purposes of this test the taxpayer's spouse is treated as having earned income for any month he is:

- A full-time student, or

- Disabled.

For any month that a spouse has no actual earned income, but has "deemed earned income" because they were a full-time student or disabled, the amount of deemed earned income by that nonworking spouse is $250 per month if the couple has a prequalifying individual for this credit, or $500 per month if the taxpayer has two or more dependents.

> **Example:** Stephanie and Ralph are married. Ralph worked as a custodian in 2018. Stephanie attended college full-time from January 1 to June 30. She was unemployed during the summer and did not attend school for the rest of the year. Stephanie is treated as having earned income for the six months she attended school full-time.

The amount of work-related expenses to figure the credit cannot be more than:

- The taxpayer's earned income for the year, if he is single at the end of the year, or

- The smaller of his or his spouse's earned income for the year if he is married at the end of the year.

Test #3: Work-Related Expense Test

Child and dependent care expenses must be "work-related" to qualify for this credit, meaning a taxpayer must be working (or actively searching for work). Expenses incurred so that a spouse may do volunteer work or take care of personal business, or so that a married couple can go on a "date night" do not qualify.

> **Example:** Nikita is a stay-at-home mom who volunteers several hours a week for a local suicide hotline. Her husband works full-time as a maintenance worker. They pay a babysitter to stay with their daughter during the hours Nikita volunteers. The couple does not qualify for the credit because the babysitting expense is not work-related. Since Nikita does not have a job, is not disabled, and is not a full-time student, the child care expenses are ineligible.

> **Example:** Maureen's four-year-old son attends a daycare center while she works three days a week. The daycare charges $150 for three days a week and $250 for five days a week. Sometimes Maureen's pays the extra money so she can run errands on her days off. This extra charge is not a qualifying expense. Maureen's deductible expenses are limited to $150 a week, the amount of her work-related daycare expense.

The following kinds of expenses qualify for the credit:

- Education: Preschool or other programs *below* the level of kindergarten; before or after-school care for a child in kindergarten or above

- Childcare for a child under 13 or adult daycare for a disabled dependent or spouse (of any age)

- Transportation costs for a care provider to take a qualifying person to or from a place where care is provided

- Fees and deposits paid to an agency or preschool to acquire child care

- Household services, (such as the services of a full-time nanny) if they are at least partly for the well-being and protection of a qualifying person

Example: Randy's 10-year-old child attends a private school. In addition to paying for tuition, Randy pays an extra fee for before and after-school care so he can be at work during his scheduled hours. Randy can count the cost of the before and after-school program when figuring the credit but cannot count the cost of private school tuition.

Example: Marina is single and her elderly mother, Lula, is her dependent. Lula is completely disabled and must be in an adult daycare. Marina pays $8,000 per year for Lula to be in the adult daycare. Marina may take the credit because Lula is disabled and incapable of self-care.

Examples of child care expenses that do *not* qualify for the credit include:

- Tuition costs for children in kindergarten and above

- Summer school or tutoring programs

- The cost of sending a child to an overnight camp (but day camps generally do qualify)

- The cost of transportation not provided by a daycare provider

- A forfeited deposit to a daycare center (since it is not for care and therefore not a work-related expense)

Example: Laurie is divorced and has custody of her 12-year-old daughter, Janessa, who takes care of herself after school. In August, Laurie spends $2,000 to send Janessa to an overnight camp for two weeks. She also sends Janessa to a Girl Scout day camp for a week in July while Laurie is working. The cost of the Girl Scout camp is $75. Laurie may only count the $75 toward the credit because the cost of sending a child to an overnight camp is not considered a qualifying expense. Next summer, when Janessa turns 13, she will no longer be a qualifying child under the rules for this credit.

Care expenses do not include amounts paid for food, clothing, education, or entertainment. Small amounts paid for these items, however, can be included if they are incidental and cannot be separated from the cost of care.

Example: Irma takes her three-year-old child to a nursery school that provides lunch and activities as part of its program. The meals are included in the overall cost of care, and they are not itemized on her bill. Irma can count the total cost when she figures the credit.

Payments for child care will not qualify for the credit if made to a family member who is either:

- The taxpayer's own child under age 19

- Any other dependent listed on the taxpayer's tax return

Taxpayers may combine costs for multiple dependents. For example, if a taxpayer pays daycare expenses for three qualifying children, the $6,000 limit on qualifying expenses does not need to be divided equally among them.

Example: Hank has three children. His qualifying daycare expenses are $2,300 for his first child; $2,800 for his second child; and $900 for his third child. Hank can use the total amount, $6,000, when figuring his credit.

Example: Gilles and Francine both work and have three children. They have $2,000 of daycare expenses for their first child, $3,000 for their second child, and $4,000 for their third child. Although their total child care expenses are $9,000, they may use only the first $6,000 as their basis for the credit.

Example: Elyse is a single mother with a five-year-old son. She takes him to daycare five days per week so she can work. Elyse makes $46,000 of wages and spends $5,200 per year on daycare. The maximum amount of qualifying expenses she can claim for the credit is $3,000 since she only has one qualifying child, even though her actual expenses exceed that amount.

Test #4: Joint Return Test

The joint return test specifies that married couples who wish to take the credit must file jointly. However, a married taxpayer can be "considered unmarried" for tax purposes if he qualifies for head of household filing status. With divorced or separated taxpayers, only the custodial parent is allowed to claim the credit.

Test #5: Provider Identification Test

This test requires that taxpayers provide the name, address, and taxpayer identification number of the person or organization who provided the care for the child or dependent. If a daycare provider refuses to supply its taxpayer identification information, the taxpayer may still claim the credit. If the provider refuses to provide a tax ID, the taxpayer must report whatever information he has (such as the provider's name and address) and attach a statement to Form 2441, *Child and Dependent Care Expenses,* explaining the provider's refusal to supply the information.

There is also an exception for foreign providers, who are not required to have a U.S. tax ID.

Example: Ephraim is a U.S. contractor working temporarily overseas in Israel. Ephraim has sole custody of his 11-year old daughter, Leah. Ephraim pays a nanny to watch his daughter while he is working. Since the care was provided in a foreign country, the nanny is not required to have a U.S. tax ID, and Ephraim is still allowed to claim the full amount of the credit.

The Child Tax Credit and Additional Child Tax Credit

The TCJA made the following changes to the Child Tax Credit (CTC) and the Additional Child Tax Credit (ACTC) for tax years 2018 through 2025:

- The nonrefundable Child Tax Credit increased to $2,000 per qualifying child

- The Additional Child Tax Credit was increased to a maximum of $1,400 per qualifying child.

- The AGI phaseout for the Child Tax Credit also increased in 2018 to $200,000 ($400,000 for joint filers).

- Starting in 2018, the child must have a valid SSN to qualify for the $2,000 Child Tax Credit.

Taxpayers with income below certain threshold amounts can claim the Child Tax Credit for each qualifying child under the age of 17. A taxpayer whose tax liability is zero cannot take the Child Tax Credit because there is no tax to reduce. In addition, the Child Tax Credit is limited to the amounts of regular income tax and any alternative minimum tax owed.

However, a taxpayer with zero tax liability may be able to take the Additional Child Tax Credit, which is a refundable credit. In order to qualify for the Additional Child Tax Credit, the taxpayer must have "earned income," such as wages or income from self-employment.

Example: Eduardo files as head of household and has two children, ages 5 and 7. Both children qualify for the Child Tax Credit. His MAGI is $54,000, and his tax liability is $4,680. Eduardo is eligible to take the full credit of $2,000 per child ($2,000 X 2 children = $4,000) because his MAGI is less than $200,000 and his tax liability is greater than $4,000.

Example: Mendel and Jada file jointly and have two children who qualify for the Child Tax Credit. Their MAGI is $36,000, and their tax liability is $954. They can offset the $954 in tax using the Child Tax Credit, reducing their tax to zero. Since their tax liability is zero, Mendel and Jada cannot claim the maximum Child Tax Credit of $2,000 per child, but they may be eligible for the Additional Child Tax Credit, which is a refundable credit.

Example: Joshua and Anika are married and file jointly. They have one 13-year old child. Joshua has wage income of $195,000. Anika has rental income of $50,000 and dividend income of $250,000. Their joint AGI is $495,000. They are not eligible to take the Child Tax Credit, because their joint AGI is above the phase-out threshold for joint filers ($400,000 is the phaseout)

Note: Unlike the Earned Income Tax Credit, disability has no effect on the eligibility for this credit. The child's age is the primary determining factor.

Definition of a Qualifying Child for the Child Tax Credit: To be eligible to claim the Child Tax Credit, the taxpayer must have at least one qualifying child. To qualify, the child must meet the following tests:

- **Age Test:** The child must have been younger than 17 on December 31, 2018.

- **Relationship Test:** The child must be the taxpayer's son, daughter, stepchild, foster child, brother, sister, stepbrother, stepsister, half-brother, half-sister or a descendant of any of them. For example, a qualifying child could include grandchildren, nieces, and nephews. Adopted children always qualify as the taxpayer's own child.

- **Support Test:** The child must not provide more than half of their own support for the year.

- **Dependency Test:** The child must be a dependent the taxpayer claims on their federal tax return. A noncustodial parent may claim the child tax credit for his or her child if he or she is allowed to claim the child as a dependent and otherwise qualifies to claim the child tax credit.

- **Joint Return Test:** The child cannot file a joint return for the year unless the only reason they are filing is to claim a refund, and otherwise the child would not have a tax liability.

- **Citizenship Test:** The child must be a U.S. citizen, U.S. national or U.S. resident alien with a valid Social Security Number. An ITIN or ATIN is no longer acceptable. Citizens or residents of Mexico and Canada no longer qualify for this credit.

- **Residency Test:** In most cases, the child must have lived with the taxpayer for more than half of the year (over six months). Exceptions exist for temporary absences[116] and children who are born or die within the year.[117]

Example: Lissette's adopted son, Louie, is 14. His adoption was finalized on November 1, 2018, but before that date, he lived with Lisette all year as her foster child. Louie is a U.S. citizen. Lissette provided all of her son's support. Louie is a qualifying child for the Child Tax Credit because he was under age 17 at the end of the tax year; he meets the relationship requirement; he lived with Lissette for more than six months of the year, and Lissette provided his support.

Example: Jose and Yolanda file jointly and have four dependent children under the age of 17. Jose and Yolanda both have valid SSNs. Their children have Individual Taxpayer Identification Numbers (ITINs). They cannot claim the Child Tax Credit.

Example: Isaiah's son, Ken, turned 17 on December 31, 2018. He is a U.S. citizen and has a valid Social Security number. According to the Child Tax Credit rules, he is not a qualifying child for this credit because he was not *under* age 17 at the end of the year.

Example: Jennifer gave birth to a son on December 30, 2018. The baby stayed at the hospital for several days after his birth, receiving treatment for jaundice. Jennifer was finally able to take her son home on January 10, 2019. Even though the baby did not technically live with Jennifer for a single day in 2018, the child meets the residency requirement, because hospitalization is considered a temporary absence. The baby is a qualifying child for the purposes of the Child Tax Credit and the Additional Child Tax Credit.

---

[116] Temporary absences include: school, vacation, medical care, military service, or incarceration in a juvenile facility. These absences count as time lived at home. The same is true if the child lived with the taxpayer more than half the year except for any required hospital stay following birth.

[117] There are special rules for children of divorced or separated parents, as well as children of parents who never married. In some cases, the noncustodial parent may be entitled to claim the child as a dependent and thus the Child Tax Credit and Additional Child Tax Credit. In addition, there is an exception for an infant who is born during the tax year and has not lived long enough to meet the six-month requirement.

Additional Child Tax Credit (ACTC)

The Additional Child Tax Credit is available for certain individuals who do not qualify for the full amount of the nonrefundable Child Tax Credit. In order to claim the Additional Child Tax Credit, a taxpayer must be able to claim the Child Tax Credit, even if he does not qualify for the full amount.

Since the Additional Child Tax Credit is refundable, it can produce a refund even if the taxpayer does not owe any tax. The additional child tax credit allows eligible taxpayers to claim up to $1,400 for each qualifying child. The credit is based on the *lesser* of:

- 15% of the taxpayer's taxable earned income that is over $2,500 or

- The amount of unused child tax credit (caused when tax liability is less than the allowed Child Tax Credit)

Note: In 2018, the "earned income" threshold for claiming the ACTC has decreased from $3,000 to $2,500, which means that the taxpayer only has to have a minimum of $2,500 in earned income in order to qualify for the refundable portion of the credit.

Schedule 8812, *Child Tax Credit*, is used to report both the Child Tax Credit and the refundable Additional Child Tax Credit. A taxpayer cannot claim the refundable Additional Child Tax Credit if he files Form 2555, *Foreign Earned Income Exclusion*.

New Credit for Other Dependents (ODC)

The new $500 Credit for Other Dependents applies to dependents who do not qualify for the $2,000 Child Tax Credit, such as children who are age 17 and above or dependents who meet the relationship test (such as elderly parents). Taxpayers cannot claim the credit for themselves or a spouse; in other words, the credit is only available for dependents who are listed on the return.

The dependent must be a U.S citizen, U.S. national, or U.S. resident.[118] The AGI phaseout for the Credit for Other Dependents is the same as the phaseout for the Child Tax Credit (to $200,000 for unmarried taxpayers in 2018 and $400,000 for joint filers).

Example: Robert and Susan file a joint return and they both have valid SSNs. Their tax liability is $2,000. They have three qualifying dependents. Amber is their 19-year-old daughter, has an SSN, and meets the qualifying child test. Paulo is their 17-year-old adopted child, has an ATIN, and meets the qualifying child test. Robert's mother, Esther, is 75 years old, has a valid SSN, and meets the qualifying relative test. They are all U.S. residents for tax purposes. Amber, Paulo, and Esther are not qualifying dependents for the Child Tax Credit, but they are *all* qualifying dependents for the Credit for Other Dependents.

To claim the Credit for Other Dependents, the dependent must have a valid identification number (ATIN, ITIN, or SSN) by the due date of the return (including extensions).

---

[118] Dependents who are residents of Canada or Mexico do not qualify for either the Child Tax Credit or the Credit for Other Dependents in 2018.

Adoption Credit

In 2018, a nonrefundable credit of up to $13,810 per child can be taken for qualified expenses paid to adopt a child. An eligible child is:

- Under 18 years old, or

- Physically or mentally disabled, regardless of age.

For a special needs child, the maximum credit amount is allowed even if the taxpayer does not have any adoption expenses.

If an employee receives employer-provided adoption benefits that are excluded from income, the employee may still be able to take the Adoption Credit. However, the exclusion and the credit cannot be claimed for the same expenses, and any allowable exclusion must be claimed before any allowable credit. The exclusion is limited to the same dollar amount as the credit. The phaseout ranges are the same for all taxpayers, regardless of filing status. Married taxpayers generally must file jointly to claim either the credit or the exclusion.

Although the Adoption Credit is nonrefundable, any unused credit may be carried forward for up to five years. Qualified adoption expenses are directly related to the adoption of a child. These include:

- Adoption fees and court costs

- Attorney fees

- Travel expenses related to the adoption, including meals and lodging

- Re-adoption expenses to adopt a foreign child

Qualified adoption expenses do not include; any illegal adoption expenses, any surrogate parenting arrangement, or the adoption of a spouse's child.[119]

Special-Needs Adoptions

A taxpayer can claim the full credit for a special-needs child regardless of actual expenses paid or incurred. For the purposes of this rule, a special-needs child must be a United States citizen or U.S. resident when the adoption begins.[120] Further, one of the following must apply:

- The state has determined the child cannot (or should not) be returned to the parents' home, or

- The state has determined the child will not be adopted unless assistance is provided to the adoptive parents.

In making the determination about special needs, a state may take into account the following factors: a child's ethnic background and age; whether he is a member of a minority or

---

[119] Although a taxpayer cannot deduct adoption expenses to adopt a spouses' child, qualified adoption expenses *does* include expenses paid by a registered domestic partner to adopt his or her partner's child, as long as those expenses otherwise qualify for the credit.

[120] Foreign children, if not a U.S. citizen or U.S. resident, are not considered to have special needs for purposes of the adoption credit.

sibling group; and whether he has a physical, mental, or emotional handicap. The child does not have to be disabled in order for the child to qualify as "special needs."

> **Example:** Sandra adopts two special-needs children in 2018. She incurs only $2,100 in adoption expenses; however, because both children are special-needs, she is allowed an adoption credit of $27,620 ($13,810 x 2). This credit may be used to offset income tax on her return.

> **Example:** Roman and Marylou adopt a special needs child, and the adoption is finalized in 2018. Their actual adoption expenses are $7,500. They are allowed to claim the full $13,810 credit because they adopted a special needs child. Their income tax liability is $8,000 so the adoption credit will reduce their tax liability in 2018 to zero. They can carry forward any unused adoption credit for up to five years.

Unsuccessful Adoptions: A taxpayer who has attempted to adopt a child in the U.S. and been unsuccessful is still eligible for the credit. Eligible expenses may include those related to unsuccessful attempts to adopt as well as an adoption attempt that is ultimately successful. However, if the eligible child is from a foreign country, the taxpayer cannot take the credit or exclusion unless the adoption becomes final. A foreign child is defined as a child who was not a citizen or resident of the United States at the time the adoption effort began.

The Timing of Payment: For a domestic adoption, qualified expenses paid before the year in which the adoption becomes final may be claimed in the year after the expenses were paid. Once the adoption becomes final (or if it is unsuccessful), the taxpayer can claim the expenses in the year paid. For a foreign adoption, expenses paid before or during the year of finality are allowable in that year.

Education Credits

Two education credits are available based on qualified expenses a taxpayer pays for postsecondary education:

- **American Opportunity Tax Credit (also called the AOC or AOTC)**
- **Lifetime Learning Credit**

Certain general rules apply to both of these credits, in addition to specific rules for each. A taxpayer may take education credits for himself, his spouse, and his dependents who attended an eligible educational institution during the tax year. Eligible educational institutions include colleges, universities, vocational schools, and community colleges. Taxpayers can claim payments that are prepaid for an academic period that begins in the first three months of the next calendar year.

> **Example:** James is 29 years old and single. He pre-paid $1,500 in December 2018 for college tuition for the spring semester that begins in January 2019. James can claim $1,500 of education credits on his 2018 return, even though he will not start college until 2019.

A taxpayer cannot claim education credits if he:

- Can be claimed as a dependent on someone else's tax return

- Files MFS

- Has adjusted gross income above the phase-out limit for his filing status

- Has a spouse who was a nonresident alien for any part of the tax year[121]

To claim the credit for a dependent's education expenses, the taxpayer must claim the dependent on his return, but he does not necessarily have to pay for all of the dependent's qualified education expenses. If a taxpayer does not claim the eligible student as a dependent, the student may be able to claim an education credit on his own return.

> **Example:** Natalia, age 52, has a 20-year-old son named Raul who is a full-time college student. Natalia and Raul do not have enough money to pay for Raul's college tuition. As a gift, Raul's grandmother pays his tuition directly to the college. For purposes of claiming an education credit, either Natalia or Raul is treated as receiving the money as a gift and paying for the qualified tuition and related expenses. If Natalia claims Raul as a dependent, she can claim an education credit. Alternatively, if Raul's mother does not claim him as a dependent, he can claim the credit.

If a taxpayer incurs education expenses for more than one student, he may be eligible to take the American Opportunity Credit for one student and the Lifetime Learning Credit for another student on the same tax return.

> **Example:** Moshe is 49 and pays college expenses for himself and his dependent daughter, Sarah, age 18. Moshe is attending graduate school to earn a doctorate degree. Moshe qualifies for the Lifetime Learning Credit. Sarah is an undergraduate and qualifies for the American Opportunity Credit. Moshe can take both credits on his tax return for each eligible student— Sarah and himself.

Form 8863, *Education Credits,* is used to figure and claim both education credits. Qualified education expenses are tuition and related expenses, such as books and other course materials required as a condition of enrollment. Any course involving sports, games, or hobbies is not a qualifying expense *unless* the course is part of the student's degree program (or if taken to improve job skills, in the case of the Lifetime Learning Credit). Qualified education expenses must be reduced by the amount of any tax-free educational assistance received, such as Pell grants, tax-free portions of scholarships, and employer-provided educational assistance. Education expenses that do not qualify include:

- Room and board, (even if the housing is on-campus and a condition of enrollment)

- Any medical expenses, including student health fees, even if charged by the college

- Other insurance costs

- Transportation costs

---

[121] This rule does not apply if the nonresident spouse elects to be treated as a resident alien for tax purposes.

- Personal, living, or family expenses

Tuition expenses are reported to the student on Form 1098-T, *Tuition Statement*, issued by the school.

> **Example:** Lillian received Form 1098-T from the college she attends. It shows that her tuition was $9,500 and that she received a $1,500 tax-free scholarship. Her maximum qualifying expenses for the education credit are $8,000 ($9,500 - $1,500 scholarship).

> **Example:** Arlene paid $3,000 for tuition and $5,000 for room and board at her university. She was also awarded a $2,000 tax-free scholarship and a $4,000 student loan. To qualify for an education credit, she must first subtract the tax-free scholarship from her tuition, her only qualified expense. A student loan is not considered tax-free educational assistance because it must be paid back. To calculate her education credit, Arlene has $1,000 of qualified expenses ($3,000 tuition - $2,000 scholarship).

American Opportunity Tax Credit (AOTC)

The American Opportunity Tax Credit (also referred to as the AOTC or AOC) allows taxpayers to claim a maximum credit of up to $2,500 for each eligible student. The credit covers 100% of the first $2,000 and 25% of the second $2,000 of eligible expenses per student. Qualified expenses include tuition and required fees, books, supplies, equipment, and other *required* course materials (but not room and board).

> **Example:** Bradford is a college senior studying to be a dentist. This year, in addition to tuition, he pays a fee to the university for the rental of the dental equipment he is required to use in the program. Bradford's equipment rental fee is a qualified education expense.

Unlike other education credits and deductions, the American Opportunity Credit is partially refundable. Up to 40% of the credit is refundable, which means the taxpayer can receive up to $1,000 even if no taxes are owed. The credit is not refundable if the student is subject to the "kiddie tax" rules. Requirements for the AOC are as follows:

- **Degree requirement:** The student must be enrolled in a program that leads to a degree, certificate, or other recognized educational credential.

- **Workload:** For at least one academic period of the year, the student must carry at least half of the normal full-time workload for his course of study.

- **No felony drug conviction:** The student must be free of any felony conviction for possessing or distributing a controlled substance.

- **Four years of postsecondary education:** The credit can be claimed only for expenses related to a student's postsecondary education and only for the first four years.

> **Example:** Miriyam started college in 2014. She has not yet completed her first bachelor's degree, but she expects to graduate in 2018. Miriyam was eligible for the American Opportunity Tax Credit for 2014, 2015, 2016, and 2017. Since the credit has been claimed for four years, the credit can't be claimed on any additional returns, including her 2018 return.

For 2018, the AOTC phases out for joint filers with modified adjusted gross income between $160,000-$180,000, and between $80,000-$90,000 for taxpayers filing as single, head of household, or qualifying widow(er). The credit is not available to taxpayers with MAGIs over $90,000 or $180,000 (if filing jointly).

> **Example:** Bella age 24, and Jonathan, age 33, are married and file jointly. Bella is a full-time student working towards her first bachelor's degree. Bella incurs $15,000 in qualifying tuition expenses during the year. Jonathan works full time and has $220,000 of taxable income. Their joint AGI is over $180,000, so they cannot claim the American Opportunity Credit. They are phased-out because of their income level.

If a student does not meet all of the conditions for the American Opportunity Credit, he may still be able to take the Lifetime Learning Credit.

Lifetime Learning Credit

The Lifetime Learning Credit is a nonrefundable tax credit of 20% of qualified tuition, fees and any amounts paid directly to the educational institution for required books, supplies and equipment, up to $10,000, paid during the tax year. The maximum credit is $2,000 per tax return, not per student. A family's maximum credit is the same regardless of the number of qualified students. The requirements for the Lifetime Learning Credit differ from those for the AOTC as follows:

- **No workload requirement:** A student is eligible no matter how few courses he takes.
- **Nondegree courses eligible:** A student qualifies if he is simply taking a course to acquire or improve job skills. There is no degree requirement.
- **All levels of postsecondary education:** A student may be an undergraduate, graduate, or professional degree candidate. The courses can also be just for professional development.
- **An unlimited number of years:** There is no limit on the number of years for which the credit can be claimed for each student.
- **Felony drug convictions permissible:** A student can be convicted for a felony drug conviction and still qualify.

> **Example:** Brent attends Creek Community College after spending twelve months in prison for a felony cocaine conviction. He paid $4,400 for the course of study, which included tuition, equipment, and books required for the course. The school requires that students pay for books and equipment when registering for courses. The entire $4,400 is an eligible educational expense under the Lifetime Learning Credit. Although he meets all the other requirements for the American Opportunity Credit, Brent does not qualify for the AOC because he has a felony drug conviction. He may claim the Lifetime Learning Credit instead.

> **Example:** Carey works full-time and takes one course a month at night school. Some of the courses are not for credit, but she is taking them to advance her career. She is not pursuing a degree. The education expenses qualify for the Lifetime Learning Credit, but not for the American Opportunity Credit.

For 2018, the Lifetime Learning Credit is phased out for unmarried filers with modified adjusted gross income between $57,000 – 67,000. For joint filers, the phaseout is between 114,000 – 134,000 of MAGI. If a taxpayer's MAGI is over $67,000 (for unmarried taxpayers) or $134,000 (for joint filers), the taxpayer cannot claim the Lifetime Learning Credit.

Earned Income Tax Credit (EITC)

The Earned Income Tax Credit (EITC), also commonly known as the Earned Income Credit (EIC), is a fully refundable federal income tax credit for lower-income people who work and have earned income and adjusted gross income under certain thresholds. This credit is claimed on Schedule EIC, *Earned Income Credit.* There are strict rules[122] and income guidelines for the EITC. To claim the EITC, a taxpayer must meet all of the following tests:

- Have a Social Security number that is valid for employment. Any dependent must also have a valid SSN.

- Have earned income from wages, combat pay, or self-employment

- Not have investment income that exceeds $3,500 in 2018

- Not file as MFS

- Not be claimed as a dependent by another taxpayer

- Be a U.S. citizen or legal resident all year (a nonresident alien married to a U.S. citizen or resident alien filing jointly can still qualify)

Qualifying Income for the EITC: Only earned income, such as: wages, tips, combat pay, union strike benefits, and net earnings from self-employment, qualifies for the EITC. For EITC purposes, "earned income" does not include the following income:

- Social Security benefits or welfare payments

- Alimony or child support

- Pensions or annuities[123]

- Unemployment benefits

- Inmate wages, including amounts paid while in work release programs

- Income from investments, rental activities, or other passive sources.

Income that is excluded from tax is generally not considered earned income for the EITC. Nontaxable combat pay is an exception. A taxpayer can choose to include their nontaxable combat pay in their earned income if it gives them a better tax result.

Low-income taxpayers *without children* may qualify for the EITC in certain cases, but the rules are stricter, and the amount of the credit is lower. A taxpayer with a qualifying child can

---

[122] Among the EITC rules is a requirement that practitioners make reasonable inquiries to determine that the information the taxpayer is giving is correct. We cover the due diligence for the EITC, CTC, and other credits in Book 3, *Representation.*
[123] Although uncommon, some disability retirement benefits qualify as earned income to claim the Earned Income Tax Credit.

claim the EITC without any age limitations, but a taxpayer *without* a child can only claim the EITC if all of the following tests are met:

- Must be at least age 25 but under 65 at the end of the year (if married, either spouse can meet the age test)

- Must live in the United States for more than half the year

- Must not qualify as a dependent of another person

- Cannot file Form 2555 (related to foreign earned income exclusion[124])

Example: Chelsea is single and age 26. She has no children. She earns $10,100 in wages during 2018. Her wages would normally qualify her for the Earned Income Tax Credit, but she also has $4,000 of investment income during the year, from a certificate of deposit that she inherited from her grandmother. A taxpayer with $3,500 or more of investment income in 2018 does not qualify for the EITC, regardless of her earnings, so Chelsea would not qualify for the EITC due to her investment income.

Qualifying Children for EITC Purposes

The definition of a "qualifying child" for purposes of the EITC is stricter than it is for being able to claim someone as a dependent. The taxpayer's qualifying child must meet <u>all</u> the following tests:

- **Relationship test**

- **Age test**

- **Joint return test**

- **Residency test**

Relationship Test: The child must be related to the taxpayer in one of the following ways:

- Son, daughter, stepchild, eligible foster child, adopted child, or descendant of any of them (for example, a grandchild), or

- Brother, sister, half-brother, half-sister, stepbrother, stepsister, or descendant of any of them (for example, a niece or nephew)

Example: Curtis is 27 and supports his younger sister, Betty, who is 16. He has taken care of Betty since their parents died five years ago. Betty is Curtis' qualifying child for purposes of the Earned Income Tax Credit.

An adopted child is generally treated as the taxpayer's own child. However, special rules apply for foreign adoptions. Any qualifying child listed on Schedule EIC also must have a valid SSN. Since an ATIN is not sufficient, then a taxpayer with an ATIN is not a qualifying child for EITC purposes.

---

[124] The mere act of *earning* foreign income would not automatically disqualify a taxpayer from claiming EITC. A taxpayer who elects not to exclude foreign income from his gross income may still be eligible for the EITC.

A foster child can also be an eligible child, but they must be placed in the taxpayer's home by an authorized placement agency or by the courts in order to be eligible.

Age Test: To qualify for the EITC, the child must be:

- Age 18 or younger,
- A full-time student age 23 or younger, or
- Any age, if permanently disabled.

In addition, the qualifying child must be younger than the taxpayer claiming him, unless the child (dependent) is permanently disabled.

> **Example:** Caleb, age 45, supports his older brother, Brian, age 56. Brian, who is mentally challenged and permanently disabled, lives with Caleb. Caleb financially supports his disabled brother and also pays for his adult daycare program. In this case, Brian meets the criteria to be Caleb's qualifying child for purposes of the EITC, even though Brian is older than the taxpayer claiming him.

Joint Return Test: The qualifying child (dependent) cannot file a joint return with a spouse, except to claim a refund.

> **Example:** Daniela's 18-year-old son and his 18-year-old wife had $1,010 of interest income and no other income. Neither is required to file a tax return. Taxes were taken out of their interest income due to backup withholding, so they file a joint return to get a refund of the taxes withheld. The exception to the joint return test applies, so Daniela's son may still be her qualifying child if all the other tests are met.

Residency Test: The child must have <u>lived with</u> the taxpayer in the United States for more than half the year. For purposes of the EITC, U.S. military personnel stationed outside the United States on extended active duty are considered to live in the U.S. during that duty period, so their children meet the residency test. This means that only a custodial parent can claim the EITC. A child who was born or died during the year would meet the residency test for the entire year if the child lived with the taxpayer the entire time he was alive in 2018.

> **Example:** Catherine gave birth to a baby girl in March. The infant died one month later. The child is still a qualifying child for purposes of the EITC because she meets the other tests for age and relationship.

Earned Income and AGI Limits

Both the taxpayer's earned income and his AGI must be less than the following limits:

Filing Status	2018 Income limits for Qualifying Children Claimed			
	Zero Children	One Child	Two Children	Three or more
Single, HOH, or QW	$15,270	$40,320	$45,802	$49,194
MFJ*	$20,950	$46,010	$51,492	$54,884

*MFS filers do not qualify to take the EITC, so they are not listed in this table.

Example: Barton is single and his AGI is $45,950 in 2018. He has one qualifying child. Barton cannot claim the EITC because his AGI exceeds the income threshold for unmarried filers with one child.

EITC Fraud and Penalties: If the IRS audits a taxpayer's return and disallows all or part of the EITC, the taxpayer:

- Must pay back the amount in error with interest,
- May need to file Form 8862, *Information to Claim Earned Income Credit after Disallowance*,
- Cannot claim the EITC for the next two years if the IRS determines the error is because of reckless or intentional disregard of the rules, or
- Cannot claim the EITC for the next ten years if the IRS determines the error is because of fraud.

Retirement Savings Contributions Credit (Saver's Credit)

The amount of the credit is 50%, 20% or 10% of a taxpayer's retirement plan or IRA contributions up to $2,000 ($4,000 if married filing jointly), depending on their adjusted gross income. Eligible contributions must be made to an IRA or an employer-sponsored retirement plan.[125] The amount of the credit is the eligible contribution multiplied by the applicable credit rate, which is based on filing status and AGI.

Note: On past exams, the IRS has sometimes referred to this credit as the "Saver's Credit." Either term may be used on the EA exam, since both terms are currently used on the IRS website as well as IRS publications.

The credit percentages for the credit (based on AGI) for 2018 are as follows:

Filing Status	2018 AGI Limits	Applicable Credit Amount
Single/MFS/Qualifying Widow(er)	$0-$19,000	50% credit
	$19,001-$20,500	20% credit
	$20,501-$31,500	10% credit
	more than $31,500	No credit allowable
Married Filing Joint	$0-$38,000	50% credit
	$38,001 - $41,000	20% credit
	$41,001 - $63,000	10% credit
	more than $63,000	No credit allowable
Head of Household	$0-$28,500	50% credit
	$28,501 - $30,750	20% credit
	$30,751 - $47,250	10% credit
	more than $47,250	No credit allowable

---

[125] Eligible contributions include those to both traditional IRAs and Roth IRAs, elective deferrals to 401(k) or other qualified employer-sponsored retirement plans, and voluntary employee contributions to other qualified retirement plans.

To be eligible for this credit, the taxpayer must fulfill all the following requirements:

1. Be at least age 18 or older;

2. Not a full-time student; and

3. Not claimed as a dependent on another person's return.

Most workers who contribute to traditional IRAs already deduct all or part of their contributions. The Saver's Credit is in addition to these deductions. In essence, a taxpayer could potentially deduct their traditional IRA, and then also receive the Saver's Credit in the same year. When figuring the credit, a taxpayer generally must subtract the amount of distributions received from his retirement plans, in the two years before the year the credit is claimed; the year the credit is claimed; and the period after the end of the credit year but before the due date, including extensions, for filing the return for the credit year.

Also, note that foreign income cannot be included in the taxpayer's adjusted gross income for the purposes of calculating this credit. Beginning in 2018, the Saver's Credit can be taken for contributions to an ABLE account if the taxpayer is the designated beneficiary of the ABLE account.[126]

> **Example:** Alonzo is 24 and earns $35,000 during the year. He is single and contributes $3,000 to his 401(k) plan at work. Alonzo is not eligible for the credit because his income exceeds the threshold limit for single filers.

> **Example:** Karen works at a bank. She is married and earned $37,000 in 2018. Karen's husband is disabled and didn't have any earnings for the year. Karen contributed $1,000 to her traditional IRA in 2018. After deducting her IRA contribution, the adjusted gross income shown on her joint return is $36,000. Karen may claim a 50% credit, or $500, for her $1,000 IRA contribution.

This credit is claimed on Form 8880, *Credit for Qualified Retirement Savings Contributions*.

Credit for Excess Social Security and RRTA Tax Withheld

This credit is for workers who overpay their tax for Social Security, which usually happens when an employee is working two jobs and both employers withhold Social Security tax. Each year, a limit is set as to how much Social Security tax an individual should have withheld from his earnings. If the taxpayer's withholding for Social Security tax exceeds the annual maximum,[127] he can request a refund of the excess amount. This also applies to overpaid Railroad Retirement taxes. Beginning 2018 tax year, this credit amount will be calculated on Schedule 5, *Other Payments and Refundable Credits*, of the 1040. This credit is fully refundable.

If a single employer overwithheld too much social security (or RRTA tax), this is an error and the employer should adjust the excess for the taxpayer. If a single employer refuses to

---

[126] Rollover contributions (money that moved from another ABLE account or from a Qualified Tuition Plan (QTP) account do not qualify for the credit.

[127] In 2018, the Social Security contribution and benefit base is $128,400, which means the maximum Social Security tax a taxpayer will be required to pay in Social Security for the year is $7,960.80. Any amount over this threshold will be credited to the taxpayer when their file their annual return.

refund the over-collection, the taxpayer can file a claim for refund using Form 843, *Claim for Refund and Request for Abatement.*

> **Example:** Zachary is a medical doctor. In 2018, he works for two different hospitals as an employee. His first employer pays him $108,400 in wages during the year. The second hospital pays him $40,000. His total wages exceed the 2018 Social Security contribution limit of $128,400, because each of his employers is required by law to withhold Social Security tax from the entire amount. When Zachary files his 2018 tax return, his overpayment of Social Security tax is calculated by adding up the combined Social Security tax withheld from all his wages. He will receive a credit for the overwithheld amounts.

(Test yourself first; then check the correct answers at the end of this quiz.)

1. Orlando is a university senior studying to be an optometrist. Which of the following expenses is a qualifying expense for the American Opportunity Tax Credit?

A. The rental of the equipment he is required to use to enroll in this program
B. Student health fees
C. Room and board
D. A physical education course not related to his degree program

2. Beatrice has three dependent children, ages 10, 12, and 18, who live with her. Assuming she meets the other criteria, what is the maximum Child Tax Credit she can claim on her 2018 tax return?

A. $1,400
B. $2,000
C. $4,000
D. $6,000

3. Abigail's earned income from wages is $13,900 in 2018. She has interest income of $3,550. She deposits $1,000 into her traditional IRA in 2018. She is single and has a valid Social Security number. She does not have any dependents and no other income for the year. Which of the following credits may she qualify for in 2018?

A. Earned Income Tax Credit
B. Child Tax Credit
C. Credit for Other Dependents
D. Retirement Savings Contribution Credit

4. Which of the following individuals could be a qualifying child for the Child Tax Credit?

A. An 18-year-old dependent who is a full-time student
B. A six-year-old nephew who lived with the taxpayer for seven months.
C. A child actor who is 15 years old and provides over half of his own support
D. A foster child who has lived with the taxpayer for four months

5. Which of the following expenses is not a qualified expense for purposes of the Adoption Credit?

A. Court costs
B. Re-adoption expenses to adopt a foreign child
C. Attorney fees for a surrogate arrangement
D. Travel expenses

6. Danika and Ralph got divorced eight years ago. They have one child together, Amelie, age 16, who lives with Danika. Amelie is a full-time student at a private high school. All are U.S. citizens and have SSNs. Together, Danika and Ralph provide more than half of Amelie's support, including $10,000 in tuition expenses for Amelie's private high school. Danika's AGI is $31,000, and Ralph's AGI is $39,000. Ralph is the noncustodial parent, but Danika signs Form 8332, giving Ralph the right to claim Amelie on his tax return. Based on this information, which credit might Ralph qualify for if he claims his daughter as a dependent?

A. The Earned Income Tax Credit
B. The Adoption Credit
C. The Child Tax Credit
D. The American Opportunity Credit.

7. In 2018, John and Hannah adopt a special-needs child. The child is a U.S. citizen. Their adoption expenses are $7,000, and their travel expenses related to the adoption are $1,200. What is their maximum Adoption Credit?

A. $7,000
B. $8,200
C. $13,810
D. $0

8. Scott is 43 and unmarried. Scott's half-brother, Alexander, turned 16 on December 30, 2018. Alexander lived with Scott all year, and he is a U.S. citizen. Scott claimed Alexander as a dependent on his return. Which of the following statements is correct?

A. Alexander is a qualifying child for the Child Tax Credit.
B. Alexander is not a qualifying child for the Child Tax Credit because he is too old to be eligible.
C. Alexander is not a qualifying child for the Child Tax Credit because siblings do not qualify.
D. Alexander only qualifies for the Child Tax Credit if he is a full-time student.

9. All of the listed expenses are deductible for the Lifetime Learning Credit except:

A. Required books
B. On-campus childcare in order to attend class
C. Tuition
D. Required fees

10. The American Opportunity Credit has a maximum credit of up to _____.

A. $2,500 credit per eligible student
B. $2,000 credit per eligible student
C. $2,500 credit per tax return
D. $4,000 credit per eligible student

11. Rocco has three kids in college. They are all his dependents:

- Cosima, age 21, a college sophomore working on her first bachelor's degree
- Marico, age 19, a college freshman working on his first bachelor's degree
- Kasha, age 23, a graduate student, working on her first master's degree. Kasha had a four-year bachelor's degree from the same college

Based on the above scenario, what is the maximum amount of American Opportunity Credits (AOC) Rocco can claim on his tax return?

A. $2,500
B. $6,000
C. $5,000
D. $7,500

12. Samira and Rishi are married and file jointly. Their daughter, Chetana, was enrolled full-time in college during the year. Samira and Rishi obtained a student loan in 2018 and used the entire loan proceeds to pay for Chetana's tuition and related fees for 2018. They repaid the loan in 2019. When will they be entitled to claim an education credit?

A. They cannot claim an education credit, because they used a loan to pay the tuition, rather than cash.
B. 2018
C. 2019
D. Either 2018 or 2019

13. Edwin is a professional bookkeeper. He takes an accounting course at the local community college to improve his work-related skills. Edwin is not a degree candidate. Which educational credit does he qualify for?

A. The American Opportunity Credit
B. The College Saver's Credit
C. The Lifetime Learning Credit
D. The General Education Credit

14. To qualify for the Earned Income Tax Credit, which of the following statements is correct?

A. The taxpayer must have a dependent child.
B. The taxpayer must be a U.S. citizen or legal U.S. resident all year.
C. The taxpayer's filing status can be MFS or MFJ.
D. The taxpayer's only income can be from Social Security benefits.

15. Nina pays for daycare costs for the following individuals so she can work. Each is a qualifying individual for purposes of the Child and Dependent Care Credit except:

A. Nina's husband, who is disabled
B. Nina's son, Cameron, age 13, who is Nina's dependent
C. Nina's nephew, Andy, age 12, who is also Nina's dependent
D. Nina's daughter, Polly, who is 22, and is disabled

16. Vincent has two children in graduate school. His wife, Olivia, also attends a doctorate program at a local university. Vincent and his wife file jointly. What is the maximum amount of the Lifetime Learning Credit that Vincent and Olivia can claim on their joint return?

A. $2,000 per student (up to a maximum of $6,000 per tax return)
B. $2,500 per student
C. $4,000 maximum ($2,000 per qualifying student)
D. $2,000 per tax return

17. Zoe attends college full-time, pursuing an undergraduate degree in architecture. Because she changed majors in her junior year, she is now in her fifth year of college. She received a $4,000 Pell grant for 2018, and her parents have claimed the American Opportunity Credit for Zoe the past four years. What amount can they claim for the AOC in 2018 based upon the following expenses for Zoe?

Tuition	$15,000
Room and board	12,000
Required Student Health Fees	1,000

A. $0
B. $2,500
C. $2,000
D. $11,000

18. For purposes of the EITC, the following type of income is considered earned income:

A. Alimony
B. Interest and dividends
C. Capital gains
D. Household employee income reported on Form W-2

19. Generally, which is most beneficial to taxpayers when it comes to reducing income tax liability: a nonrefundable credit, a refundable credit, or a deduction?

A. A nonrefundable credit
B. A refundable credit
C. A deduction
D. All are equally beneficial in reducing income tax liability

20. Which of the following education tax benefits listed below is refundable?

A. The educator expense deduction
B. The American Opportunity Credit
C. The Lifetime Learning Credit
D. Student Loan Interest Deduction

21. Which of the following individuals is eligible for the American Opportunity Credit?

A. Garrett, who is enrolled full-time as a postgraduate student pursuing a master's degree in biology after having completed a four-year undergraduate degree.
B. Lucy, who is taking a ceramics class at a community college for fun.
C. Douglas, who is a full-time undergraduate student and was convicted of a felony for distribution of cocaine.
D. Bethany, who is pursuing a degree in computer science degree and who attended classes the entire school year.

22. Which of the following filing conditions would prevent an individual from qualifying for the Earned Income Tax Credit?

A. MFS filing status
B. A taxpayer with nontaxable combat pay
C. Investment income of $3,000
D. A taxpayer who is 68 years old with one qualifying child

23. All of the following are qualified expenses for purposes of the Child and Dependent Care Credit except:

A. A $500 payment to a grandparent for child care while the taxpayer is employed
B. A $300 payment to a daycare center while the taxpayer is looking for employment
C. A $500 child care expense while the taxpayer obtains medical care
D. A $600 adult daycare expense for a disabled spouse while the taxpayer works

24. Orrin was audited in 2018, and the IRS determined that he claimed the Earned Income Tax Credit erroneously due to reckless disregard of the EITC rules. For how many years is Orrin prohibited from claiming the EITC?

A. None
B. Two years
C. Five years
D. Ten years

25. Which of the following credits are refundable in 2018?

A. Lifetime Learning Credit
B. Retirement Savings Contribution Credit
C. The Additional Child Tax Credit
D. The Child and Dependent Care Credit

Unit 13: Quiz Answers

1. The answer is A. Because Orlando's equipment rental fee must be paid to the university as a condition for enrollment, it is considered a qualified related expense. For AOTC purposes, "qualified education expenses" do not include insurance or medical expenses (such as student health fees), room and board, transportation, or similar personal, living, or family expenses, or any course of instruction or other education involving sports, games, or hobbies, unless the course is part of the student's degree program.

2. The answer is C. Beatrice can claim $4,000 as a maximum Child Tax Credit, or $2,000 for each qualifying child. For purposes of this credit, she only has two qualifying children, because one of her dependents is already over 17 and therefore no longer eligible for the credit.

3. The answer is D. She may qualify for the Retirement Savings Contribution Credit. Abigail does not qualify for the Earned Income Tax Credit because her investment income exceeds $3,500 in 2018. She does not qualify for the Child Tax Credit or Credit for Other Dependents because she does not have a qualifying child.

4. The answer is B. A nephew who lived with the taxpayer for seven months may qualify. In order to qualify for the Child Tax Credit, the taxpayer must have a qualifying child who lived with him for more than six months and who is under the age of 17. The child cannot have provided more than half of his own support.

5. The answer is C. Expenses related to a surrogate arrangement are not a qualified adoption expense. Qualified adoption expenses are expenses directly related to the legal adoption of an eligible child. These expenses include adoption fees, court costs, attorney fees, travel expenses (including amounts spent for meals and lodging) while away from home, and re-adoption expenses to adopt a foreign child.

6. The answer is C. Ralph, the noncustodial parent, can claim the Child Tax Credit if Danika signs Form 8332. He cannot claim the Earned Income Tax Credit because he is not the custodial parent. He cannot claim the Adoption Credit because the Adoption Credit is only for qualified adoption expenses. He cannot claim the American Opportunity Credit, because the credit only applies to expenses incurred for postsecondary education (i.e., college expenses, not private school tuition for K-12 students).

7. The answer is C. John and Hannah can take the full Adoption Credit of $13,810 in 2018 because they adopted a special needs child. Under a special rule for taxpayers who adopt special needs children, the maximum Adoption Credit is allowed, even if the taxpayer has a lesser amount of adoption expenses.

8. The answer is A. Alexander is a qualifying child for the Child Tax Credit because he was under age 17 at the end of 2018. Siblings can be qualifying children for purposes of this credit, and half-siblings are treated the same as full siblings for tax purposes.

9. The answer is B. Childcare is not a qualifying education expense, even if the childcare is offered on-campus. For purposes of the Lifetime Learning Credit, qualified education expenses are tuition and certain related expenses required for enrollment or attendance at an eligible educational institution.

10. The answer is A. The American Opportunity Tax Credit is worth up to $2,500 per eligible student. The maximum credit equals 100% of the first $2,000 and 25% of the next $2,000 of qualified expenses.

11. The answer is C. The American Opportunity Tax Credit is worth up to $2,500 per qualifying student. Rocco can potentially claim $5,000 in AOC credits on his tax return ($2,500 each for Cosima and Marico). Cosima and Marico would be qualifying students for AOC purposes because they are working on their first undergraduate degree. Kasha would not qualify, because she is working on a graduate degree after having completed a four-year undergraduate degree. The American Opportunity Credit is only available for four years of postsecondary school. Kasha's educational expenses may be eligible for the Lifetime Learning Credit, however.

12. The answer is B. Samira and Rishi are eligible to claim an education credit for 2018. The credit should be claimed for the year in which the taxpayer paid the qualifying expenses, not the year in which the loan is repaid.

13. The answer is C. Edwin qualifies for the Lifetime Learning Credit. He does not qualify for the American Opportunity Credit because he is not a degree candidate and because his course does not meet the requirements. The "College Saver's Credit" and the "General Education Credit" do not exist.

14. The answer is B. The taxpayer must be a U.S. citizen or legal U.S. resident all year. A taxpayer cannot claim the EITC if his filing status is MFS. Taxpayers do not need to have a dependent child to qualify for the Earned Income Tax Credit. However, the amount of the credit is greatly increased if the taxpayer has a qualifying child. A taxpayer must have earned income to qualify for the EITC; Social Security benefits do not qualify.

15. The answer is B. Nina's son, Cameron, does not qualify because he is over the age limit for the credit. To qualify for the Child and Dependent Care Credit, the dependent must be *under* the age of 13 or disabled.

16. The answer is D. Vincent and Olivia can claim a maximum credit of $2,000 on their joint tax return. The Lifetime Learning Credit is allowed for 20% of the first $10,000 of qualified tuition and fees paid during the year. The credit is per tax return, not per student, so only a maximum of $2,000 can be claimed each year, no matter how many qualifying students a taxpayer may have.

17. The answer is A. Zoe does not qualify for the AOC because she is in her fifth year of college and her parents have already claimed the credit the prior four years. If she had been eligible for the credit, she would have had $11,000 of qualifying expenses. Room and board and student health fees are not qualifying expenses for the AOC, and the qualifying tuition cost must be reduced by any tax-free scholarships, such as the Pell grant. The AOC is a maximum credit of $2,500 per student (100% of the first $2,000 of eligible expenses and 25% of the next $2,000). Zoe qualifies for the Lifetime Learning Credit.

18. The answer is D. Household employee income is considered earned income because it is a type of wage. Alimony, workfare payments, and interest and dividends are not considered earned income for purposes of the EITC.

19. The answer is B. A refundable credit, such as the Earned Income Tax Credit, is not limited by an individual's tax liability. The taxpayer can receive a refund even if he has zero tax liability.

20. The answer is B. Up to 40% of the American Opportunity Tax Credit is refundable, meaning that the taxpayer can receive a refund even if they have zero tax liability.

21. The answer is D. Bethany is eligible for the American Opportunity Credit because she is pursuing a degree and is enrolled at least half-time for at least one academic period during the year. Courses that do not lead to a degree, certificate or other recognized credential do not qualify for the AOC. Students with felony drug convictions are ineligible for this credit.

22. The answer is A. Taxpayers cannot claim the EITC if they file Married Filing Separately. All the other choices would not disqualify a taxpayer from claiming EITC. Combat pay is considered qualifying income for EITC purposes. The investment income threshold for EITC in 2018 is $3,500. A taxpayer who is 68 years old may be eligible for EITC if they have a qualifying child.

23. The answer is C. Childcare costs to obtain medical care are not a deductible expense. Deductible costs must be work-related and for a child under 13, a disabled dependent, or a disabled spouse of any age. Childcare costs incurred so that the taxpayer can volunteer, obtain medical care, run errands, or do other personal businesses do not qualify.

24. The answer is B. Orrin cannot claim the EITC for two tax years. There are restrictions on EITC claims by taxpayers for whom a previous claim was denied or reduced due to any reason other than a math or clerical error. If a taxpayer was determined to have claimed the EITC due to reckless or intentional disregard of the EITC rules, he cannot claim the EITC for two tax years. If the error was due to fraud, the taxpayer cannot claim the EITC for ten tax years.

25. The answer is C. The Additional Child Tax Credit is refundable, meaning it can result in a refund even if a taxpayer does not owe tax.

Unit 14: The Affordable Care Act for Individuals

For additional information read:
Publication 5187, *Health Care Law: What's New for Individuals & Families*
Publication 974, *Premium Tax Credit (PTC)*

The Affordable Care Act[128] (ACA) is a comprehensive health care reform law enacted in March 2010 (it is sometimes known as ACA or "Obamacare"). The Affordable Care Act tax provisions are administered by the IRS. In 2018, the law requires most U.S. citizens and U.S. residents to have qualifying health insurance or to pay a penalty for not doing so.

Note: In this unit, we provide an overview of the key ACA tax provisions you should understand for the EA exam. The ACA is extremely complex, and its provisions affect taxpayers in many different ways depending upon their individual situations. In this book, we will cover the ACA from the individual taxpayer's perspective. The ACA from the *employer's* perspective is covered in detail in Book 2, *Businesses*.

In recent years, a universal mandate, known as the *individual shared responsibility provision*, took effect. This is also known as the "ACA penalty" or "healthcare penalty."

Starting in tax year 2019, the Tax Cuts and Jobs Act eliminates the penalty under the Affordable Care Act's individual mandate (i.e., the penalty for failing to maintain minimum essential coverage).

The employer-shared responsibility provisions remain in place, which means that employers must still offer qualifying health coverage to their employees or face the prospect of an excise penalty.

In 2018, the penalty remains in effect, unless the taxpayer qualifies for an exemption. In 2018, the healthcare tax penalty is the greater of:

- $695 per individual (up to a maximum of $2,085) or

- 2.5% of household income, less the taxpayer's filing threshold amount.

The maximum penalty in 2018 is $2,085 per family, *regardless of the family's size.*

The Shared Responsibility Payment is capped at the national average premium for a bronze-level qualified health plan available through the Marketplace that would cover everyone in the tax household who does not have coverage or qualify for an exemption. In 2018, the monthly national average premium for a bronze level health plan available through the Marketplace is $283 per individual, up to a family maximum of $1,415 per month for families of five or more members.[129]

A taxpayer calculates the amount due for the shared responsibility payment by using the instructions to Form 8965, *Health Coverage Exemptions.*

---

[128]Although commonly known as Obamacare, the actual name of the health care law is the "Patient Protection and Affordable Care Act," often shortened to the Affordable Care Act or ACA.

[129] For more information, see Revenue Procedure 2018-43.

Important Forms for the ACA

In order to simplify reporting, the IRS has created a new group of forms to help handle some of the requirements of the ACA. If the taxpayer is covered by health insurance, he will most likely receive one of the forms listed below. The taxpayer must use the information from these statements when preparing his taxes. The forms are provided to different groups of people.

- **Form 1095-A**, *Health Insurance Marketplace Statement:* This form is for individuals who enroll in Marketplace[130] coverage. This form reports basic information about the insurance company that issued the taxpayer's policy, the exchange where he enrolled, and document coverage for each month.

- **Form 1095-B,** *Health Coverage:* This is for people whose insurance comes from a source other than the Marketplace.

- **Form 1095-C**, *Employer-Provided Health Insurance Offer and Coverage*: Individuals who work for applicable large employers will get this form (employees will also get this form if they enroll in self-insured coverage provided by an applicable large employer).

Some taxpayers will receive multiple forms in the same year. For example, if a taxpayer purchased health insurance through the Marketplace and then started a new job in the middle of the year that offered health coverage, he may receive both Forms 1095-B and 1095-C.

Minimum Essential Coverage (MEC)

Under the Affordable Care Act, each individual must have qualifying health care coverage, known as *minimum essential coverage*, or MEC, for each month of the year. This requirement applies to individuals of all ages. Coverage that qualifies includes:

- Employer-sponsored coverage, including self-insured plans, COBRA, and retiree coverage

- Coverage purchased in either federal or state health insurance Marketplaces (also known as exchanges)

- Medicare Part A and Medicare Advantage plans

- Most Medicaid coverage

- Certain types of veterans' health coverage and most types of TRICARE coverage

Coverage that provides only limited benefits generally does not qualify as minimum essential coverage. For example, this includes stand-alone dental and vision insurance plans, accident or disability income insurance plans, worker's compensation insurance, and Medicaid family planning services. An employer-sponsored plan provides minimum value if the plan covers at least 60% of the expected total allowed costs for medical services. The plan also must provide substantial coverage of in-patient hospitalization and physician services.

---

[130] The "Marketplace," also called the "Health Insurance Marketplace," is an online resource where taxpayers can learn about their health coverage options and sign up for health insurance.

Taxpayers are required to "self-report" their coverage by checking the box on Form 1040. Taxpayers are not required to send in proof of health care coverage to the IRS when filing their tax returns.

> **Example:** Consuela, age 58, had qualifying health insurance through her employer for every month of 2018. Her husband, Adolfo, age 67, is retired and had Medicare coverage for all of 2018. On their joint return, they check the box attesting that they had full-year insurance coverage. They have fulfilled their "shared responsibility" of the Affordable Care Act and will not owe a penalty to the IRS.

Health Coverage Exemptions

There are multiple coverage exemptions that will excuse an individual from the requirement to have minimum essential health insurance coverage. A taxpayer must apply to the Health Insurance Marketplace for certain types of exemptions. If an exemption is approved by the Health Insurance Marketplace, the taxpayer will receive an *exemption certificate number* (ECN), which must be entered into most software programs to e-file. Form 8965, *Health Coverage Exemptions*, is the form used for reporting ACA Exemptions. Below are all health coverage exemptions for the current tax year.

Note that there is no "hardship" exemption based only on employment status. So, if a taxpayer becomes unemployed during the year, that in itself is not considered a valid hardship. However, several exemptions apply to people with low income. Remember, taxpayers who otherwise do not have a filing requirement, do not need to file a tax return solely to report coverage or to claim an exemption from the coverage requirement.

Income-Related Exemptions

- **Affordability exemption:** Taxpayers who do not have access to coverage considered affordable based on their projected household income may be exempt from paying penalties. In this case, if the lowest-priced coverage available to the taxpayer, (either through a Marketplace or job-based plan), would exceed 8.05% of household income in 2018, the taxpayer is exempt from the penalty.

- **No filing requirement:** If the taxpayer does not have to file a tax return because his income is below the filing requirement, then he is exempt from the healthcare penalty.

Health Coverage-Related Exemptions

- **Short-Term Coverage Gap:** The taxpayer was uninsured for less than three consecutive months of the year. A taxpayer with a coverage gap of *three months or more* is not exempt for any of those months.

- **State Did Not Expand Medicaid:** The taxpayer lived in a state that didn't expand its Medicaid program, but the taxpayer would have qualified if it had. In order to qualify for this exemption, the taxpayer would need to provide a copy of his Medicaid denial of eligibility notice.

> **Example:** Douglas starts the year with qualifying health coverage through his employer. He was laid off from his job on March 1, 2018. His health benefits ceased on March 31, 2018. He searched for work and started a new job on April 15, 2018. His new employer-sponsored health coverage started on May 1, 2018. Douglas is eligible for the short coverage gap exemption because he was without coverage for less than three consecutive months. He will not owe a healthcare penalty in 2018.

Group Membership Exemptions

- **Recognized Tribe:** The taxpayer is a member of a federally recognized tribe or eligible for services through an Indian Health Services provider.

- **Health Sharing Ministries:** The taxpayer is a member of a recognized health care sharing ministry.

- **Religious Objections:** The taxpayer is a member of a recognized religious sect with religious objections to insurance, including Social Security and Medicare.

Other Allowable Exemptions

- **Incarceration:** Taxpayers who are in jail, prison, or another correctional facility.

- **Citizens Living Abroad/Some Noncitizens:**

  - U.S. citizens or residents who spent at least 330 days outside of the U.S. during a twelve-month period

  - U.S. citizens who are bona fide residents of a foreign country

  - Certain resident aliens who are citizens of a foreign country that has an income tax treaty with the U.S.

  - Taxpayers who are not legally present in the U.S. (undocumented aliens)

- **Acceptable Hardships:** If the taxpayer experienced one of these listed hardships an exemption may potentially be granted:

  - The taxpayer was homeless.

  - The taxpayer was evicted or was facing eviction or foreclosure.

  - The taxpayer received a shutoff notice from a utility company.

  - The taxpayer experienced domestic violence.

  - The taxpayer experienced the death of a close family member.

  - The taxpayer experienced a fire, flood, or other natural or human-caused disaster that caused substantial damage to his property.

  - The taxpayer filed for bankruptcy.

  - The taxpayer had medical expenses that resulted in substantial debt.

  - The taxpayer experienced unexpected increases in necessary expenses due to caring for an ill, disabled, or aging family member.

- The taxpayer expects to claim as a dependent a child who has been denied coverage for Medicaid, and another person is required by court order to give medical support to the child. In this case, the taxpayer doesn't have to pay the penalty for the child.

- As a result of an eligibility appeals decision, a taxpayer is eligible for enrollment in a qualified health plan (QHP) through the Marketplace, lower costs on his monthly premiums, or cost-sharing reductions for the time period when he was not enrolled in health insurance through the Marketplace.

- The taxpayer's individual insurance plan was canceled during the year, and the taxpayer believes that other Marketplace plans are unaffordable.

Example: Deena is single. Her gross income for 2018 was $9,800. She did not purchase health insurance, but she is exempt from the individual shared responsibility payment because her income is below the filing threshold for filing a return. She does not file a tax return, and she is not required to file Form 8965 since she is automatically exempt from the penalty.

Example: Elijah and his four children live in Wyoming, a state that did not expand Medicaid under ACA. Their household income is below 138% of the federal poverty line. They do not have qualified health coverage. When Elijah files his tax return, he attaches Form 8965 and claims an exemption to the individual shared responsibility provision. Elijah will not owe a penalty for failing to have minimum essential coverage.

The Shared Responsibility Payment (ACA Healthcare Penalty)

If a taxpayer (or any of his dependents) does not have minimum essential coverage for each month of the year and does not qualify for an exemption, he will face a penalty called the *shared responsibility payment* (SRP) when he files his tax return. This is also called the "ACA penalty" or the "healthcare penalty."

The IRS is specifically prohibited from using enforcement actions such as liens and levies to collect an SRP that a taxpayer does not pay. However, if a taxpayer is due a refund, the IRS may offset the liability by subtracting the SRP amount from his current or future refund.

When filing a return, the taxpayer is required by law to answer the health coverage question regarding the Affordable Care Act (ACA). A "silent return" is any Form 1040 return where the question on page one entitled "Full-year health care coverage or exempt" is not checked. The IRS will not accept electronically filed silent returns. At the time of this book's printing, all the current legislative provisions of the ACA law are still in force, and taxpayers remain required to follow the law and pay what they may owe.

Example: Evan and Galina are married and have two dependent children under age 18. For half of the year, no member of their family had minimum essential coverage, and no one qualified for an exemption. Evan and Galina must calculate the shared responsibility payment for the six months of the year they did not have qualified health coverage.

Premium Tax Credit

The Premium Tax Credit is a refundable federal tax credit to help eligible taxpayers pay for health insurance premiums. The credit is based on a taxpayer's income and is only available for taxpayers who purchased their insurance through a federal or state healthcare exchange.

The amount of the Premium Tax Credit is based on a sliding scale, so the higher the household income, the lower the amount of the credit. This credit is *only available* to taxpayers who purchase their insurance from the federal exchange (i.e., the "Marketplace")[131]; it is not available to taxpayers who obtain insurance through their employer. To be eligible for a Premium Tax Credit, a taxpayer must generally meet all of the following requirements:

- Purchase health insurance through the Marketplace

- Be a U.S. citizen or legal U.S. resident

- Be unable to get coverage from an employer or the government (i.e., cannot be enrolled in Medicare)

- Not be claimed as a dependent on anyone else's tax return

- If married, the couple must generally file a joint tax return.[132] In general, taxpayers who file separate returns will not qualify for the credit.

- The taxpayer must meet certain household income requirements. Household income must be at least 100%, but not more than 400%, of the federal poverty line for the family size. For purposes of the Premium Tax Credit, a taxpayer's household income is the total of the taxpayer's modified adjusted gross income (MAGI), the taxpayer's spouse's MAGI (if filing jointly) and the MAGI of all dependents required to file a federal income tax return.

> **Example:** Hendrik and Vidalia are married and file jointly. They have two dependent children. Vidalia works part-time and does not receive health insurance through her employer. Hendrik was unemployed for several months during 2018 before starting a new job in April. His employer-sponsored health insurance started May 1, 2018. From January through April, the family purchased health insurance through the federal exchange (the Marketplace). Assuming they meet the income guidelines, Hendrik and Vidalia can claim the Premium Tax Credit for the four months that they had Marketplace coverage.

Advance Premium Tax Credit Payments

When a taxpayer first applies for a Marketplace plan, the amount of the credit is estimated using information the taxpayer provides about family size and projected household income. Since it can be difficult to know exactly how much income a taxpayer will earn in a given year

---

[131] The Health Insurance Marketplace, also called simply the Marketplace, is the place where you will find information about private health insurance options, purchase health insurance, and obtain help with premiums and out-of-pocket costs if you are eligible. The Department of Health and Human Services (HHS) administers the requirements for the Marketplace and the health plans offered.

[132] In the case of married taxpayers who file separately (MFS), certain eligibility exceptions to the Premium Tax Credit apply, such as for domestic abuse or spousal abandonment.

and family circumstances can change during the year, the actual amount of the credit can vary from the estimated amount.

When enrolling in a plan, a taxpayer must choose whether to have some or all of the benefit of the expected credit paid in advance to his insurance company or wait to claim all of the benefits on his tax return.

A taxpayer who chose advance credit payments must file a tax return, regardless of whether he meets any other filing requirements, in order to reconcile the advance credit payments with the actual Premium Tax Credit earned. This reconciliation is calculated on Form 8962, *Premium Tax Credit*. If the credit allowed is *less* than the advance credit payments received, normally the difference will be subtracted from the taxpayer's refund or added to his balance due.

Example: Mariano is self-employed, and his income varies from year to year. When he enrolled in a health insurance plan through his state exchange, he estimated his 2018 earnings based on his prior year income. He learned he was eligible for the Premium Tax Credit, which he chose to take in full as advance credit payments. Mariano's business did well in 2018, and he made substantially more money than he expected, meaning his actual household income did not meet the guidelines for the Premium Tax Credit. He reconciles the advance credit payment amounts on Form 8962 and discovers he received a benefit of $4,000 in payments for which he is no longer eligible. Mariano is not owed a refund, so he must enter $4,000 on the excess advance premium tax credit repayment line 46 of Schedule 2 (Form 1040). That amount is added to his overall tax liability.

Example: Adela was enrolled in a qualified health plan through the Marketplace. She turned 65 on July 1, 2018 and became eligible for Medicare. Adela applied to Medicare in September and became eligible to receive Medicare benefits beginning on December 1. Adela can get the Premium Tax Credit for her coverage in the qualified health plan for January through November. Beginning in December, Adela cannot get the Premium Tax Credit for her coverage in the qualified health plan because she is eligible for Medicare.

Note: The Premium Tax Credit is refundable. If the amount of the credit is more than the amount of the tax liability of the return, a taxpayer may receive the difference as a refund. If no tax is owed, a taxpayer can receive the full amount of the credit as a refund.

Changes in family size due to marriage, death, divorce, birth, or adoption can affect the amount of the credit. A taxpayer is supposed to report changes in circumstances to the Marketplace so the amount of the advance credit payments can be recalculated during the year. A taxpayer should also report changes in eligibility for government-sponsored or employer-sponsored health coverage, a move to a new address, an increase or decrease in the number of dependents, and other factors that may affect eligibility for the Premium Tax Credit.

Although the IRS is restricted in its ability to collect the shared responsibility payment, the agency may use full collection actions, including levies and liens, against a taxpayer who does not repay excess advance premium tax credits.

Net Investment Income Tax (NIIT)

The Affordable Care Act imposes a net investment income tax on higher-income taxpayers. It applies to individuals, estates, and trusts. For individuals, a 3.8% tax is imposed on the lesser of:

- The individual's net investment income for the year, or

- Any excess of the individual's modified adjusted gross income for the tax year over the following thresholds:

Filing Status	Threshold Amount
MFJ or QW	$250,000
MFS	$125,000
Single or HOH	$200,000

These threshold amounts are not indexed for inflation. The NIIT is imposed only on U.S. citizens and resident aliens; nonresident aliens are not subject to the NIIT. Net investment income that is subject to the tax includes:

- Interest income, unless it is otherwise tax-exempt

- Dividends

- Capital gains

- Rental and royalty income

- Nonqualified annuities

- Income from businesses involved in trading of financial instruments or commodities

- Income from businesses that are passive activities for the taxpayer

Net investment income does not include: wages, self-employment income, Social Security benefits, veterans' benefits, unemployment compensation, alimony payments, or distributions from IRAs or certain qualified retirement plans.

To the extent that gains are not otherwise offset by capital losses, the following are common examples of items included in computing net investment income:

- Gains from the sale of stocks, bonds, and mutual funds

- Capital gain distributions from mutual funds

- Gains from the sale of investment real estate

- Gains from the sale of interests in partnerships and S corporations, to the extent the partner or shareholder was a passive owner

Example: Mike is single and earned a salary of $175,000 in 2018. He also had $15,000 of income from dividends and capital gains, for MAGI of $190,000. This amount is less than the $200,000 threshold for single filers, so Mike is not subject to the Net Investment Income Tax.

> **Example:** Rosalind is single and earned a salary of $175,000 in 2018. She also received $80,000 of dividend income, for a total MAGI of $255,000, which exceeds the threshold for single filers by $55,000. The Net Investment Income Tax is based on the lesser of $55,000 (the amount by which her MAGI exceeds the threshold for single filers) or $80,000 (her total "net investment income"). Rosalind owes NIIT of $2,090 ($55,000 × 3.8% = $2,090).

The NIIT does not apply to any gains or investment income that is excluded from gross income for regular income tax purposes.

For example, muni bond interest is exempt from federal tax, so it is not included in the calculation for the NIIT. Additionally, net investment income does not include any gain on the sale of a personal residence excluded from gross income (Section 121 exclusion).

> **Example:** Sebastian and Myrna are married and file jointly. They sell the main home that they have lived in for fifteen years for $1.8 million and realize a gain of $850,000 on the sale. They may exclude $500,000 under section 121, so their gain subject to regular income tax is $350,000. They also have $75,000 of net investment income from other sources, for a total of $425,000. Their MAGI is $525,000, which exceeds the MFJ threshold amount of $250,000 by $275,000. They are subject to the NIIT on the lesser of $425,000 (NII) or $275,000 (the amount of excess MAGI). Sebastian and Myrna owe NIIT of $10,450 ($275,000 × 3.8% = $10,450).

A gain from the sale of a second home that is not a primary residence would not be eligible for section 121 exclusion and therefore would be fully subject to the NIIT. Federal income tax credits generally may be used to offset net investment income.

Investment interest expense can also be deducted to determine gross investment income, which is used to arrive at net investment income.

The NIIT is subject to estimated tax provisions, so taxpayers may need to adjust their withholding or estimated payments to avoid underpayment penalties. Employers are not required to withhold the NIIT from an employee's wages. The tax is computed on Form 8960, *Net Investment Tax: Individuals, Estates, and Trusts.*

Additional Medicare Tax

The Additional Medicare Tax was legislated as part of the Affordable Care Act, and has been in effect since 2013. The tax only applies to a taxpayer's earned income. An employer is required to withhold the Additional Medicare Tax if an employee is paid more than $200,000, regardless of an employee's filing status or whether the employee has wages paid by another employer.

A taxpayer may be subject to the Additional Medicare Tax even if amounts are not withheld from his wages. A taxpayer's earned income (including wages, taxable fringe benefits, bonuses, tips, commissions, and self-employment income) that is subject to regular Medicare tax is also subject to the Additional Medicare Tax to the extent it exceeds the applicable threshold amount for his or her filing status.

There is no employer share of the Additional Medicare Tax. Self-employed taxpayers cannot deduct one-half of the 0.9% Additional Medicare Tax.

The Additional Medicare Tax is withheld at a rate of 0.9%, and computed on Form 8959, *Additional Medicare Tax.* The tax is assessed only on earned income in excess of the following thresholds:

Filing Status	Threshold Amount
MFJ	$250,000
MFS	$125,000
Single, HOH, or QW	$200,000

Filing status determines the threshold amount. For those who are married and file a joint return, they must combine the wages, compensation or self-employment income of their spouse with their own. These thresholds are not adjusted for inflation. The tax is reported on Form 8959, *Additional Medicare Tax.*

Example: Annabelle is unmarried and files head of household. She has $130,000 in self-employment income and $23,000 in wages during the year. Annabelle is not liable for the Additional Medicare Tax because her combined self-employment income and wages is less than the $200,000 threshold for HOH filers.

Example: Naomi is single. She earns $350,000 in wages during 2018. The additional 0.9% tax will be calculated on her earnings above $200,000. This means that $150,000 will be subject to Additional Medicare Tax ($350,000 wages - $200,000 threshold amount). She will pay $1,350 in Additional Medicare Tax on her tax return ($150,000 x 0.9% = $1,350). This additional tax is withheld from Naomi's wages automatically by her employer.

Extended Example #1: Regan is single and earned $145,000 of salary in 2018. Because his earnings are below the $200,000 threshold for single filers, his company did not withhold any amount for the Additional Medicare Tax. He also had $85,000 of self-employment income from selling custom watercolor paintings he created. Regan's total earned income is $230,000. He would be required to pay Additional Medicare Tax on the $30,000 of earned income that exceeds the $200,000 threshold. Regan would owe $270 in Additional Medicare Tax on his 2018 income tax return ($30,000 × 0.9% = $270). He must calculate the tax and attach Form 8959, *Additional Medicare Tax*, to his tax return.

Extended Example #2: Regan gets married on December 31, 2018, to Patty, who earned wages of $7,000 during the year. Because they are married as of the last day of the year and file jointly, their threshold for the Additional Medicare Tax is $250,000. Their combined earned income is now $237,000, below the $250,000 threshold for MFJ. Regan and Patty do not owe the Additional Medicare Tax.

If an employer withholds amounts for an employee who earns more than $200,000, but the employee and his spouse's combined earnings are less than the $250,000 MFJ threshold, they can apply the overpayment against any other type of tax that may be owed on their income tax return.

Example: Stanley and Ophelia are married and file jointly. Stanley earned $120,000 of salary in 2018, and Ophelia earned $190,000. Their employers do not withhold amounts for the Additional Medicare Tax because neither earned wages above $200,000. However, their combined earned income is $310,000, which exceeds the $250,000 threshold for joint filers by $60,000. Stanley and Ophelia will owe $540 of Additional Medicare Tax on their 2018 income tax return ($60,000 × 0.9% = $540). They must calculate the tax and attach Form 8959, *Additional Medicare Tax*, to their tax return.

(Test yourself first; then check the correct answers at the end of this quiz.)

1. Laverne had Minimum Essential Coverage (MEC) all year. On which form would she report her qualifying coverage?

A. Form 1040
B. Form 8965
C. Form 1095-A
D. Form 1095-B

2. Terry and Lulu are married but choose to file separately because of Terry's past-due child support. Their household income for 2018 is at 200% of the federal poverty line. They enroll in the federal Marketplace for health coverage. Which of the following statements is correct?

A. They are not eligible for the Premium Tax Credit because their household income is too high.
B. They are not eligible for the Premium Tax Credit because of their filing status.
C. They are not eligible for the Premium Tax Credit and will owe a shared responsibility payment.
D. They are eligible for the Premium Tax Credit.

3. Which of the following taxpayers would be subject to the Additional Medicare Tax in 2018?

A. Randy, who files as HOH and earned $180,000 of wages and $50,000 of interest income.
B. Kerrie, who is single and earned $196,000 of wages, taxable fringe benefits, and bonuses.
C. Lizzie, who files separately from her husband and earned $140,000 of wages.
D. Reginald; who is a qualifying widower and has $200,000 in wages.

4. Which of the following taxpayers would not be subject to the net investment income tax (NIIT)?

A. An estate
B. A nonresident alien
C. A trust
D. An individual with only rental income in 2018

5. In 2018, Suzanne had qualifying health insurance through her employer for every month of the year. She does not receive Form 1095-B from her employer. All of the following statements are correct *except*:

A. Suzanne must attach proof of health coverage when she files her income tax return.
B. Suzanne will not owe the individual shared responsibility payment.
C. Suzanne's employer is required to provide Form 1095-B.
D. Suzanne is not eligible for the Premium Tax Credit.

6. Which of the following individuals would be eligible for the Premium Tax Credit, assuming he met applicable income guidelines?

A. A taxpayer who had minimum essential coverage through his employer
B. A taxpayer who was enrolled for two months through the federal Marketplace
C. A taxpayer who received Medicaid coverage for twelve months of the year
D. A taxpayer who is a full-time U.S. military employee

7. The Additional Medicare Tax is:

A. 0.9% on a taxpayer's earned income above a certain threshold
B. 3.8% on a taxpayer's earned income above a certain threshold
C. 0.9% on a taxpayer's investment income above a certain threshold
D. 3.8% on a taxpayer's investment income above a certain threshold

8. Which of the following does not qualify as minimum essential coverage (MEC) under the Affordable Care Act?

A. COBRA
B. Coverage purchased through a state Marketplace
C. Medicare
D. Worker's compensation insurance

9. Milka is single. She has the following income in 2018:

- $73,000 interest income
- $200,000 gain from selling her home that she had lived in and owned for 7 years
- $245,000 MAGI

Calculate Milka's net investment income tax, if any, for 2018:

A. $0
B. $1,710
C. $2,774
D. $10,374

10. The Premium Tax Credit is:

A. Nonrefundable
B. Refundable
C. Available to all taxpayers with minimum essential coverage
D. Available to all taxpayers with minimum essential coverage who purchased insurance through the federal Marketplace (but not from a state exchange)

11. Which of the following is a correct statement about the net investment income tax?

A. The tax is 3.8% of the excess of MAGI over a threshold amount.
B. The tax is 3.8% of net investment income.
C. The tax is 3.8% of the greater of net investment income or the excess of MAGI over a threshold amount.
D. The tax is 3.8% of the lesser of net investment income or the excess of MAGI over a threshold amount.

12. The IRS may take the following actions to collect the shared responsibility payment from a taxpayer:

A. Offsetting his tax refund
B. Offsetting his tax refund and putting a lien on his property
C. Offsetting his tax refund, putting a lien on his property, and levying his property
D. None of the above is allowed.

13. Kyong enrolled in the federal Marketplace for 2018 to obtain health insurance. She estimated her household income for the year, qualified for the Premium Tax Credit, and chose to have half of the expected credit paid in advance to her insurance company. What must Kyong do when she files her income tax return?

A. She must repay half of the credit that she received in advance.
B. She will not owe any additional tax but may be eligible for a larger amount of the credit.
C. She must reconcile the advance premium tax credit payments with the actual Premium Tax Credit that she calculates on Form 8962. Any excess amount will be counted as household income and used to project her credit for the next year.
D. She must reconcile the advance premium tax credit payments with the actual Premium Tax Credit she calculates on Form 8962. She may receive a refund, or she may have to repay any excess advance premium tax credit payments, depending on her individual situation.

14. Adrienne and Otis are married and file jointly. Adrienne has $133,000 of self-employment income. Otis earned $184,000 in wages. Compute the amount of their Additional Medicare Tax, if any.

A. $2,853
B. $1,053
C. $603
D. They do not owe the Additional Medicare Tax.

1. The answer is A. Laverne would report her coverage on Form 1040. Taxpayers who have Minimum Essential Coverage all year will indicate this on Form 1040, page 1, by checking the box next to the "Spouse standard deduction" section. Answer B is incorrect because coverage exemptions are reported on Form 8965. Answers C and D are incorrect because these forms are used by the Healthcare Marketplace and employers, not individual taxpayers.

2. The answer is B. Terry and Lulu have minimum essential coverage because they purchased health insurance through the federal exchange. However, they are not eligible for the Premium Health Credit because they file separate returns. Unless one of a limited number of exceptions applies, a married couple cannot claim the Premium Tax Credit unless they file jointly.

3. The answer is C. The Additional Medicare Tax is applied to MFS taxpayers whose earned income exceeds $125,000 in 2018. Lizzie will owe an additional 0.9% tax on the $15,000 of earned income that exceeds the $125,000 threshold ($15,000 × .009 = $135 Additional Medicare Tax).

4. The answer is B. A nonresident alien would not be subject to the net investment income tax (NIIT). The net investment income tax applies to individuals, estates, and trusts. Only U.S. citizens and U.S. residents are subject to the tax.

5. The answer is A. Because Suzanne had employer-sponsored health coverage for all twelve months of 2018, she has fulfilled her obligations under the Affordable Care Act and does not owe the shared responsibility payment. She must check the box for "full-year health care coverage or exempt" on Form 1040, but she is *not* required to send in proof to the IRS when she files her return. She must retain documentation of her coverage, as she would any other records needed to substantiate items on her tax return.

6. The answer is B. To be eligible for the Premium Tax Credit, a taxpayer, his spouse, or his dependents must have been enrolled in either the federal Marketplace or a state exchange at some point during the year. A taxpayer enrolled in an employer-sponsored plan, including retiree coverage, is not eligible for the Premium Tax Credit, even if the plan is unaffordable. A taxpayer who received coverage through Medicaid or other government health plans outside of the Marketplace is not eligible for the PTC.

7. The answer is A. The Additional Medicare Tax applies to 0.9% of a taxpayer's earned income above a threshold based on his filing status. For single, head of household, and qualifying widow(er) filers, the threshold is $200,000. For married couples filing jointly, the amount is $250,000. For married couples filing separately, the amount is $125,000.

8. The answer is D. Worker's compensation insurance, and other plans that offer only limited benefits, do not fulfill the minimum essential coverage requirements. Employer-sponsored plans, including self-insured, COBRA, and retiree plans, generally offer qualifying coverage. All plans purchased through a federal or state exchange also qualify as minimum essential coverage, so Medicare, Medi-Cal, and Medicaid would all qualify.

9. The answer is B. The NIIT applies to the lesser of Milka's investment income ($73,000) or her MAGI above the threshold for her filing status, which is $200,000 for a single filer ($245,000 MAGI - $200,000 threshold = $45,000). Thus, her NIIT is calculated as follows: $45,000 × 3.8% = $1,710. The $200,000 gain from selling her home is excluded from taxation under section 121 and is therefore not part of the calculation for the NIIT.

10. The answer is B. The Premium Tax Credit is refundable, meaning that a taxpayer may be able to receive the full amount of credit as a refund, assuming he has no other tax liability. The PTC is available only to a taxpayer, his spouse, or his dependents that had health coverage through a federal or state exchange for all or part of the year.

11. The answer is D. For individuals; the net investment income tax (NIIT) is 3.8% of the lesser of net investment income, or the excess of modified adjusted gross income over a threshold amount. For example, the threshold for spouses filing joint returns is $250,000; the threshold is $200,000 for single filers.

12. The answer is A. The IRS is not allowed to take any enforced collection measures to collect a taxpayer's liability related to the shared responsibility payment. However, if a taxpayer is owed a tax refund, it can be used to offset the unpaid SRP. In contrast, the IRS is not restricted in the collection methods it may use against a taxpayer who does not repay excess advance premium tax credits. Both liens and levies are allowed to collect excess advance premium tax credit payments.

13. The answer is D. Kyong must do a monthly calculation to determine the actual amount of her PTC, which must then be reconciled with the advance premium tax credits paid to her insurer to lower her premium payments. Kyong must enter the amount of any excess advance premium tax credit payments made on her behalf on her return and normally repay the excess. Any taxpayer who claims the Premium Tax Credit (whether advance credit payments were made or not) must file a tax return and include Form 8962, *Premium Tax Credit* (PTC). If there were no excess advance premium tax credit payments and the amount of the PTC is more than the amount of her tax liability, she may receive the difference as a refund.

14. The answer is C. Adrienne and Otis are subject to the Additional Medicare Tax. Their combined compensation is $317,000, which is $67,000 above the applicable threshold of $250,000 for joint filers. Their Additional Medicare Tax is $603 ($67,000 × 0.9%).

Unit 15: Additional Taxes and Credits

More Reading:
Publication 54, *Tax Guide for U.S. Citizens and Resident Aliens Abroad*
Publication 926, *Household Employer's Tax Guide*
Publication 519, *U.S. Tax Guide for Aliens*
Publication 514, *Foreign Tax Credit for Individuals*
Tax Topic 556, *Alternative Minimum Tax*
Form 5405, *Repayment of the First-Time Homebuyer Credit (Instructions)*

In this unit, we cover a variety of other taxes and credits, including the taxation and reporting of foreign income, the "nanny tax," and the "kiddie tax." We start with a look at the Alternative Minimum Tax (AMT).

Note: Under the Tax Cuts and Jobs Act, starting in 2018, the *corporate* alternative minimum tax is repealed. The AMT repeal for corporations will be permanent. The TCJA does not repeal the AMT for individuals, but it does increase the AMT exemption amount for 2018 through 2025. The TCJA raises the AMT phaseout threshold for individuals to $500,000 for taxpayers who file and single, head of household and married filing separately, and $1 million for married couples who file jointly and qualifying widow(er).

Alternative Minimum Tax

The Alternative Minimum Tax (AMT) gives an alternative set of rules to calculate an individual's taxable income. For this reason, the AMT is sometimes called a "parallel tax" system. Congress adopted the AMT in 1969 in an attempt to ensure that individuals and corporations pay at least a minimum amount of tax.[133]

The TCJA made a number of significant changes to the AMT in 2018. First, the AMT exemption was increased substantially. The AMT exemption amounts are as follows:

- Single or HOH: $70,300

- MFJ or QW: $109,400

- MFS: $54,700

This means that taxpayers who make below this threshold will not be subject to AMT, regardless of how many tax deductions or credits they may have. These exemption amounts are indexed each year for inflation after 2018.

Individuals compute AMT on Form 6251, *Alternative Minimum Tax, Individuals, Estates, and Trusts.* As described in the preceding units, federal tax law provides special treatment for certain types of income and allows deductions and credits for certain types of expenses. These tax benefits can significantly reduce the regular income tax liabilities for some taxpayers.

---

[133] The AMT for corporations was completely repealed in 2018. The corporate AMT was permanent. This provision is covered more extensively in Book 2, *Businesses.*

AMT Preference Items

The AMT *limits* the extent to which deductions and credits can be used to reduce the total amount of income tax paid by higher-income taxpayers. These are called "tax preference" items. When calculating the AMT, many common items considered in the computation of the regular income tax liability are either adjusted downward or eliminated entirely.

In 2018, fewer adjustments are required. For taxpayers who itemize, only state and local taxes and foreign income taxes need to be adjusted when figuring alternative minimum taxable income. In addition, the benefits of the following tax preference items may also be eliminated when calculating the AMT:

- Depletion

- Excess intangible drilling costs

- Interest on private activity bonds

- Accelerated depreciation on property placed in service before 1987

- Exclusion of gain on qualified small business stock (QSBS)

The AMT is the excess of the tentative minimum tax over the regular income tax. Thus, the AMT is owed only if the tentative minimum tax is greater than the regular tax. In general, the tentative minimum tax is computed by:

1. Starting with AGI minus itemized deductions, if any, for regular tax purposes,

2. Eliminating or reducing certain adjustments and preferences (the exclusions, deductions, and credits that are allowed in computing the regular tax, such as those mentioned above), to derive alternative minimum taxable income (AMTI),

3. Subtracting the AMT exemption amount,

4. Multiplying the amount computed in (3) by the applicable AMT rate, and

5. Subtracting the AMT Foreign Tax Credit.

The AMT exemption in step 3 is an amount that is deducted from alternative minimum taxable income before calculating the tentative minimum tax. Most tax preparation software will automatically compute whether a taxpayer owes the AMT. If a taxpayer received or claimed any of the following items in the tax year, he is required to complete, but may not necessarily need to file, Form 6251, *Alternative Minimum Tax, Individuals, Estates, and Trusts*:

- Accelerated depreciation

- Stock received through incentive stock options that were not sold in the same year

- Tax-exempt interest from private activity bonds

- Intangible drilling, circulation, research, experimental, or mining costs

- Amortization of pollution-control facilities or depletion

- Income (or loss) from tax-shelter farm activities or passive activities

- Interest from long-term contracts not figured using the percentage-of-completion-method

- Mortgage interest that is not used to: buy, build, or substantially improve a home

- Investment interest expense reported on Form 4952

- Net operating loss deduction

- Alternative minimum tax adjustments from an estate, trust, electing large partnership, or cooperative

- Section 1202 exclusion (gains from qualifying small business stock)

- Any general business credit in Part 1 on Form 3800

- Empowerment zone and renewal community employment credit

- Qualified electric vehicle credit

- Alternative fuel vehicle refueling property credit

- Credit for prior year minimum tax

Credit for Prior Year Minimum Tax

A nonrefundable credit may be available to individuals, estates, and trusts for alternative minimum tax paid in prior years to the extent that a taxpayer's regular tax in the current year is greater than his tentative minimum tax. If applicable, the credit is calculated on Form 8801, *Credit for Prior Year Minimum Tax-Individuals, Estates, and Trusts.*

The AMT is caused by two types of adjustments and preferences: "exclusion" items and "deferral" items. Exclusion items are those that affect only a single tax year and therefore cause a permanent difference between regular taxable income and alternative minimum taxable income (AMTI).

For individual taxpayers, an example of an "exclusion item" is the deduction for state and local income taxes. These taxes are never deductible for AMT purposes, and they are added back into AGI in the calculation of AMTI in the year they are paid. Deferral items are adjustment and preference items, such as depreciation, that affect more than one tax year. Because they affect the difference between regular taxable income and AMTI in multiple tax years, they generally do not cause a permanent difference in taxable income over time. The minimum tax credit is allowed only for the portion of AMT caused by deferral items, which may generate credit for future years.

> **Example:** Tyson and Stacy are married and file jointly. They had an AMT liability in the previous year after they exercised some incentive stock options. They use Form 8801 to calculate how much of their AMT was related to that and other deferral items and discover they have a $1,500 credit carryforward. Their regular tax in 2018 is $4,000, and their tentative minimum tax is $3,000. They can use $1,000 of the minimum tax credit carryforward to reduce their regular tax, but they cannot reduce it below the tentative minimum tax amount. The credit balance of $500 can be carried forward to be used in a future year.

Kiddie Tax on Investment Income

Years ago, wealthy families could transfer investments to their minor children and save tax dollars because the investment income would be taxed at the children's lower rates. Congress closed this tax loophole, and now investment income earned by dependent children may be taxed at the parent's rate. This law became known as the "kiddie tax."

Starting in 2018, the Tax Cuts and Jobs Act modifies the Kiddie Tax. A child's investment income will no longer be taxed at their parents' income tax rates. Instead, it is taxed using the same tax rates applicable to trusts and estates.

The kiddie tax does not apply to earned income (such as wages); it applies only to investment income, such as interest, dividends, and capital gains distributions. Part of a child's investment income may be taxed at estate and trust tax rates if:

- The child's investment income is more than $2,100 (in 2018).
- The child is a dependent under age 18 or a full-time college student under age 24.
- The child is required to file a tax return for the tax year.
- At least one of the child's parents was alive at the end of the year.

Note: The kiddie tax does not apply to a child who is married and files a joint return with their spouse. This applies whether the child is a minor under age 18 or a full-time college student under age 24.

Remember: the kiddie tax *only* applies when a dependent child's investment income exceeds $2,100 in 2018. The first $1,050 in investment income is tax-free; the second $1,050 is taxed at the child's marginal rate.

All of the child's investment income in excess of $2,100 is then taxed at estate and trust tax rates. To report the kiddie tax, the child should file their own separate tax return and attach Form 8615, *Tax for Certain Children Who Have Unearned Income*.

A child's investment income may be subject to the net investment income tax, which is calculated using only the child's income. However, the NIIT applies only if the child's net investment income exceeds the $200,000 threshold for single filers (this scenario would be very rare, and would only apply if a dependent child had more than $200,000 in taxable income).

Example: Rochelle is 16 years old. She has a number of investments that she inherited when her parents died three years ago. Rochelle lived with her grandmother, Pearl, all year. Rochelle has $5,600 in investment income during the year. Rochelle is not subject to the kiddie tax rules because both of her parents are deceased (she does not have a living parent). In this case, Rochelle would not be required to file Form 8615, even if Pearl claims her granddaughter as a dependent on her tax return.

> **Example:** Alistair and Renee have a 15-year-old son named Robby. In 2018, Robby has $2,500 of interest income from a CD his grandfather gave him. Robbie does not have any other taxable income. The first $1,050 of investment income is not taxable. The next $1,050 is taxed at the 10% income tax rate, which is Robby's marginal rate. The remainder, $400, is taxed at estate and trust tax rates.

First-Time Homebuyer Credit Repayment

First-time homebuyers who claimed a special tax credit in 2008 are required to repay a portion of the funds received over a 15-year period. The First-Time Homebuyer Credit took the form of a loan in 2008. For example, a homebuyer who claimed the maximum credit of $7,500 must repay $500 per year as an additional tax. The amount is entered on line 60b on Schedule 4, Form 1040.

> **Example:** Melinda purchased her home in 2008 and claimed the full amount of the First-Time Homebuyer Credit. She still lives in the home and continues to use it as her main residence. She is required to pay back her credit in equal yearly installments of $500 over a period of 15 years. When she files her 2018 tax return, the repayment is listed on her Form 1040 (Schedule 4) as an additional tax.

A taxpayer who claimed the credit and sells the home (or converts it to a rental property) must complete Form 5405, *Repayment of the First-Time Homebuyer Credit*. In the case of a sale (including through foreclosure), the taxpayer must repay the credit with the tax return for the tax year in which the sale is completed.

The following are exceptions to the repayment rule:

- **Involuntary conversion:** If the home is destroyed or condemned, and the taxpayer does not acquire a new home within the 2-year replacement period, the repayment owed with the taxpayer's return for the year in which the 2-year period ends is limited to the gain on the disposition.[134] The amount of the credit in excess of the gain doesn't have to be repaid.

- **Transfers Incident to Divorce:** If the home was transferred to a spouse (or ex-spouse as part of a divorce settlement), the spouse who received the home is responsible for repaying the credit (regardless of whether he or she was the purchaser) if none of the other exceptions apply.

- **The person who claimed the credit dies:** If a person who claimed the credit dies, repayment of the remaining balance of the credit is not required unless the credit was claimed on a joint return. If the credit was claimed on a joint return, then the surviving spouse is required to continue repaying his or her half of the credit (regardless of whether he or she was the purchaser) if none of the other exceptions apply.

---

[134] If the taxpayer does not have a gain on the involuntary conversion, they do not have to repay any of the credit, unless they sold the home under threat of condemnation to a related party.

Example: Giuliana and Arturo purchased a home together in 2008, and claimed the full amount of the First-Time Homebuyer Credit. They use the home as their primary residence. On December 1, 2018, Arturo dies. Giuliana is required to continue repaying her half of the credit, but Arturo's portion of the credit does not have to be repaid (it is considered forgiven).

The repayment is limited to the amount of gain on the sale if the sale is to an unrelated taxpayer. The credit was also available in 2009 and 2010 but has since expired. A taxpayer who purchased his home and received the credit in either 2009 or 2010 does not have to repay the credit unless he sold the home within a three-year period following the purchase.

Nanny Tax (Tax on Household Employees)

A taxpayer who has household employees may need to pay employment taxes. This obligation is commonly referred to as the "nanny tax" or the tax on Household Employees.

Example: Monroe hires Luz to babysit his three children and do housework in his home. Monroe sets Luz's schedule and gives specific direction about household and childcare duties. Monroe also provides all the equipment and supplies Luz needs to do her work. Luz is Monroe's household employee and subject to the nanny tax rules.

If a taxpayer pays a household employee cash wages (including amounts paid by check, money order, etc.) of $2,100 or more in 2018, he must normally withhold the employee's share of Social Security and Medicare taxes and remit them along with the employer's matching share, for a total of 15.3%, unless he chooses to pay both the employer's and employee's shares. If the amount of wages paid to an employee during the year is less than this threshold, no Social Security or Medicare taxes are owed.

Note: An employer is not required to withhold *income* tax from a household employee's wages. However, income tax may be withheld at the employee's request. Even if the employer is not required to pay FICA (Social Security and Medicare) taxes, the employee's wages may be subject to income tax.

A worker is the taxpayer's employee if the taxpayer can control not only what work is done, but how it is done, regardless of whether the work is full-time or part-time; the employee is paid on an hourly, daily, weekly, or per-job basis; or the employee is hired through an agency. Examples of household employees include babysitters, housekeepers, private nurses, yard workers, and chauffeurs.

A self-employed worker, such as a daycare provider who cares for several children from different families in her own home, is not considered a household employee.

Example: Elon is a widowed single taxpayer with infant twin boys. Elon hires Hilda to take care of his twin boys while he is at work. Hilda usually works Monday through Friday, 9 AM to 6 PM. She is an experienced nanny, and she also cleans Elon's home during the day. Hilda is a household employee. Elon is required to file payroll returns as well as Schedule H with his Form 1040.

> **Example:** Leonard hires Jorge to do weekly yard maintenance and cut his grass. Jorge runs a lawn care business and provides gardening services to many other clients. Jorge also advertises his business in the local newspaper. Jorge provides his own tools and supplies. Jorge is self-employed and not considered Leonard's household employee.

A taxpayer who is required to pay Social Security and Medicare taxes or federal unemployment taxes for household employees, or who withholds income tax for them, must file Schedule H, *Household Employment Taxes,* with his Form 1040. The taxpayer will need an employer identification number (EIN) to file Schedule H. He also must file Form W-2, *Wage and Tax Statement,* and furnish a copy of the form to the employee.

A taxpayer who is an employer of household employees may need to increase the federal income tax withheld from his pay or pension or make estimated tax payments to avoid an estimated tax penalty resulting from his liability for employment taxes in connection with household employees, (as shown on Schedule H). The taxpayer has several options. He can:

- Increase federal income tax withheld by giving his employer a new Form W-4

- Increase his federal income tax withheld by giving the payor of his pension a new Form W4-P, *Withholding Certificate for Pension or Annuity Payments*

- Make estimated tax payments by filing Form 1040-ES, *Estimated Tax for Individuals*

Estimated taxes must be withheld or paid as the tax liability is incurred, so a taxpayer cannot wait until he files his tax return (and Schedule H) to pay household taxes owed.

Wages paid to a taxpayer's spouse, parent, or child under the age of 21 are exempt from the nanny tax rules. In that case, the taxpayer would not have to withhold FICA tax.

> **Example:** Geraldine hires her mother, Enola, to take care of her children during the week. In this case, since Geraldine has hired her mother, the payments are exempt from the nanny tax rules. No Social Security and Medicare taxes will be owed by either Geraldine or her mother. No Federal Unemployment Tax (FUTA) would be owed. However, Enola would owe income tax on the amounts that she earned, and she would need to report the income on her individual tax return.

A taxpayer cannot claim a household employee as a dependent, even if the employee lives with the taxpayer.

Section 199A Qualified Business Income Deduction

This new provision, also known as the "Section 199A Deduction" or the "QBI deduction,"[135] allows a deduction of up to 20% of qualified business income for owners of some businesses. Eligible taxpayers can claim it for the first time on their 2018 federal income tax returns. The deduction is available, regardless of whether an individual itemizes their deductions on Schedule A or takes the standard deduction. This deduction expires after 2025, unless Congress decides to extend it.

---

[135] The final regulations for 199A deduction were released in 2019, but this deduction is listed on the official Prometric test specs, so you may see a question on this topic on the exam. See T.D. 9847 (final regulations under section 199A), February 8, 2019.

The deduction only applies to pass-through entities. Individuals, sole proprietors, partners in partnerships, beneficial owners of trusts, estates, and shareholders in S corporations may be eligible for this new deduction. Income earned by a C corporation is not eligible for the 199A deduction. It is only available to pass-through entities and their owners. The deduction allows eligible taxpayers to deduct up to 20% of their qualified business income.

Income Limitations

For taxpayers with taxable income that exceeds $315,000 for a MFJ filers, or $157,500 for all other taxpayers, the deduction is subject to certain limitations such as: the type of trade or business, the taxpayer's taxable income, the amount of W-2 wages paid by the qualified trade or business and the unadjusted basis immediately after acquisition (UBIA) of qualified property held by the trade or business.

Example: Kylie is married and files jointly with her husband, Larry. Kylie operates a medical billing service as a sole proprietor. Her business has one employee, a secretary who is paid $50,000 during 2018. The business has no significant assets. After figuring her allowable deductions, Kylie's business generates $200,000 of taxable income. Larry earns $15,000 in wages during the year. Larry and Kylie's total taxable income is $215,000. Kylie is entitled to a QBI deduction of $40,000 ($200,000 business income x 20%QBI deduction). The wage and UBIA limitations do not apply because Kylie and Larry's joint taxable income is less than $315,000.

The 199A deduction only applies to domestic income (U.S. business activities). Only taxable income is counted. A taxpayer's "QBI component" is generally 20% of the taxpayer's QBI from qualifying trades or businesses. QBI is the net amount of qualified items of income, gain, deduction and loss from any qualified trade or business. Only items included in taxable income are counted. In addition, the items must be effectively connected with a U.S. trade or business. Items such as capital gains and losses, certain dividends and interest income are excluded.

In other words, the business income must be generated by domestic business activity. "Qualified Business Income, or QBI, does not include:

- Employee wages,
- Reasonable compensation of the taxpayer from an S corporation;
- Any guaranteed payment from a partnership for services rendered with respect to the trade or business;
- Investment income; such as capital gains or interest and dividend income,
- Hobby income,
- Non-taxable income, (such as muni bond interest)
- Rental income where the owner is not engaged in a bona-fide real estate "trade or business" is not QBI. This does not mean that the taxpayer has to be a "real estate professional" in order to get the QBI deduction. The rental of real property may constitute a trade or business, even if the rental activity is reported on Schedule E.

The QBI deduction is claimed by individuals, so S corporations and partnerships cannot take the deduction at the entity level. However, all S corporations and partnerships report each shareholder's or partner's share of QBI on Schedule K-1, so the shareholders or partners may claim the 199A deduction on their individual tax returns.

> **Note:** The determination of whether a business qualifies for the 199A QBI deduction occurs at the *entity* level. The deduction then "flows through" to the individual owners. The QBI deduction and entity limitations are covered more extensively in Part 2, *Businesses*.

Eligible individuals may also be entitled to a deduction of up to 20% of their combined qualified real estate investment trust (REIT) dividends and qualified publicly traded partnership (PTP) income. The deduction is the lesser of:

- 20% of qualified business income plus 20% of their qualified real estate investment (REIT) trust dividends and qualified publicly traded partnership (PTP) income, or

- 20% of taxable income minus net capital gains.

An overall qualified business loss results in no QBI deduction for the taxable year. The loss carries over to subsequent years and reduces the section 199A deduction for QBI for those years.

Foreign Income and Taxes

Generally, all income of U.S. citizens and U.S. resident aliens is subject to tax by the United States, regardless of where the individual lives and even if the income is earned outside the United States. "Foreign earned income" is income received for services performed in a foreign country while the taxpayer's tax home is also in a foreign country. It does not matter whether the income is paid by a U.S. employer or a foreign employer. The tax home of the taxpayer (where the taxpayer resides) is the determining factor.

> **Example:** Candice is a U.S. citizen living in Mexico. She works online for a U.S. company. She has lived continuously in Mexico for the last five years, only coming back to the U.S. on sporadic short visits of less than a few days. Her tax home is in Mexico, and therefore, her income is considered "foreign earned income." The *taxpayer's* tax home is what matters, not the physical location of the employer.

Foreign Earned Income Exclusion

If a taxpayer is eligible for the foreign earned income exclusion, his income up to a certain threshold is not taxed. For 2018, the maximum foreign earned income exclusion is $103,900. For married couples, the exclusion is applied on a per spouse basis, whether filing MFS or MFJ.

In other words, if married taxpayers file jointly (or separately) and both individuals live and work abroad, each can claim the foreign earned income exclusion, for a total exclusion amount of $207,800.

> **Example:** Clara and Arron are married and file jointly. In 2018, they were both employed in Peru, with Clara earning $80,000 and Arron earning $56,000. They lived in Peru the entire year. Each qualifies for the foreign earned income exclusion.

Nonresident aliens do not qualify for the foreign earned income exclusion.

A taxpayer must be either a U.S. citizen or a legal resident alien of the United States who lives and works abroad and must pass one of two tests to claim the exclusion:

- **Bona Fide Residence Test:** A U.S. citizen or U.S. resident alien who is a bona fide resident of a foreign country for an uninterrupted period that includes an entire tax year.

- **The Physical Presence Test:** A U.S. citizen or U.S. resident alien who is physically present in a foreign country or countries for at least 330 full days during twelve consecutive months. A taxpayer may qualify under the physical presence test, and the income may span a period of multiple tax years. If so, the taxpayer must prorate the foreign earned income exclusion based on the number of days spent in a foreign country.

Note: The foreign earned income exclusion generally does not apply to the wages and salaries of members of the Armed Forces and civilian employees of the U.S. government. However, in 2018, the IRS makes an exception for combat-zone contract workers. In 2018, citizens or residents of the U.S. serving in a combat zone qualify as having a tax home in a foreign country, even if the taxpayer retains a home in the U.S.

The foreign earned income exclusion is calculated using Form 2555, *Foreign Earned Income,* which must be attached to Form 1040. If a choice is made to exclude foreign earned income, the choice remains in effect for subsequent years, unless revoked.

Foreign Housing Exclusion or Deduction

In addition to the foreign earned income exclusion, a taxpayer can claim an exclusion (or a deduction) for foreign housing costs. The maximum foreign housing exclusion for 2018 is $14,546 (14% of the maximum foreign earned income exclusion at $103,900).

The foreign housing *exclusion* applies only to amounts paid by an employer, while the foreign housing *deduction* applies only to amounts paid with self-employment earnings.

Qualified housing expenses include reasonable expenses paid for housing in a foreign country. Only housing expenses for the part of the year that the taxpayer actually qualified for the foreign earned income exclusion are considered.

Example: Samuel is a U.S. citizen who lived in Hong Kong all of 2018 and was employed by a foreign company as an advertising consultant. He lived rent-free in an apartment provided by his employer. Samuel received a salary of $95,000, and the fair rental value of his housing was $12,000, for a total of $107,000 of earned income. He qualifies for the foreign earned income exclusion as well as the foreign housing exclusion.

Foreign Income Taxes: Generally, income taxes paid to a foreign country can be deducted as an itemized deduction on Schedule A or as a credit against U.S. income tax. A taxpayer can choose between a deduction or a credit and use whichever one results in the lowest tax.

Foreign Tax Credit

U.S. citizens and resident aliens are eligible for the Foreign Tax Credit, which is designed to relieve taxpayers of the double taxation burden that occurs when their foreign source income is taxed by both the U.S. and a foreign country. Nonresident aliens are not eligible for this credit. Four tests must be met to qualify for the credit:

- The tax must be imposed on the taxpayer.

- The taxpayer must have paid the tax.

- The tax must be a legal and actual foreign tax liability.

- The tax must be an income tax (not an excise tax, sales tax, etc.).

Although taxpayers can choose between taking the deduction or the credit for all foreign taxes paid, in most cases, it is to their advantage to take the Foreign Tax Credit, since a credit directly reduces tax liability.

Note: Individuals claim the Foreign Tax *deduction* on Schedule A (Form 1040) as an itemized deduction. The Foreign Tax *Credit* is claimed on Form 1116, *Foreign Tax Credit.* A taxpayer cannot claim both—the deduction and the tax credit—on the same return, but may alternate years, taking a credit in one year and a deduction in the next year.

Taxpayers cannot claim the Foreign Tax Credit for taxes paid on any income that has already been excluded using the foreign earned income exclusion or the foreign housing exclusion. Unlike the foreign earned income exclusion, which applies only to income that is earned while a taxpayer is living and working abroad, the Foreign Tax Credit applies to any type of foreign income, including investment income. Foreign tax paid may be reported to the taxpayer by a financial institution on Form 1099-INT or Form 1099-DIV.

If the amount of foreign tax that the taxpayers incur is small, then taxpayers can claim the credit directly on Form 1040 if, among other conditions, all foreign income is specified passive income and total taxes paid do not exceed $300 ($600 MFJ). If the foreign tax paid exceeds $300 ($600 MFJ), the taxpayer must file Form 1116, *Foreign Tax Credit*, in order to claim the credit.

Example: Astrid and Benedict are married and file jointly. They own a number of foreign stocks, and their Form 1099-DIV shows foreign tax paid of $590. The couple is not required to complete Form 1116 because their foreign taxes are less than $600 on their jointly-filed return.

Certain taxes do not qualify for the Foreign Tax Credit, including interest or penalties paid to a foreign country, taxes imposed by countries involved with international terrorism, and taxes on foreign oil or gas extraction income.

Note: Currently, the foreign tax credit does not apply to any tax paid to Iran, North Korea, Sudan, or Syria. These countries are sanctioned by the U.S.

Example: Arshad is a U.S. citizen. He lived and worked in Iran until May 2018, when he was transferred to Greece. Arshad paid taxes to each country on the wages earned in that country. Arshad cannot claim a foreign tax credit for the income taxes he paid in Iran. Because the income he earned in Iran is a disallowed category of foreign income, he must fill out a separate Form 1116 for that income. Further, he cannot take a credit for the taxes paid on the income earned in Iran, but all his income is taxable by the United States.

A taxpayer is allowed to switch between claiming the Foreign Tax Credit or an itemized deduction for foreign tax paid. If a taxpayer claimed an itemized deduction for a prior year for qualified foreign taxes, the taxpayer can also switch to claiming a credit by filing an amended return within *ten years* from the original due date of the return. This type of amended return has a much longer statute period than normal amended returns.

Fixed, Determinable, Annual, or Periodic (FDAP) Income

Fixed, Determinable, Annual, or Periodic (FDAP) income applies to foreign persons earning income in the U.S. FDAP income consists primarily of passive investment income, but can also include other types of income. The following items are examples of FDAP income:

- Compensation for personal services (such as proceeds from performances)
- Dividends and interest,
- Pensions and annuities
- Alimony
- Real property income, such as rents
- Royalties
- Taxable scholarships and fellowship grants
- Other grants, prizes and awards
- The distributable net income of an estate or trust that is FDAP income, and that must be distributed currently, or has been paid or credited during the tax year, to a nonresident alien beneficiary
- A distribution from a partnership that is FDAP income, or such an amount that, although not actually distributed, is includible in the gross income of a foreign partner
- Prizes or purses awarded to nonresident alien professional athletes, boxers, performers, or entertainers.

Compensation for personal services performed by a nonresident alien in the United States can also be FDAP income. This includes income such as commissions and proceeds from performances. If an individual qualifies as a nonresident alien, then they are taxed only on the income they earn or derive from the US.

> **Example:** Hudielle is a popular Brazilian singer that regularly performs all over the world. In 2018, she negotiates a contract for periodic performances in Las Vegas. The income she receives from the performances will be FDAP income. She must report the income she earns in the U.S. on Form 1040NR.

Deductions are not allowed against FDAP income, and it is taxed at a flat 30% rate (or a lower rate if there is a tax treaty between the U.S. and the taxpayer's country of residency).

This 30% or lower rate only applies if the FDAP income or gains from U.S. sources are not "effectively connected" with a taxpayer's U.S. trade or business. A nonresident alien who receives income that is effectively connected with his trade or business in the United States is taxed at the rates that apply to U.S. citizens and U.S. residents. The IRS definition of FDAP includes all passive investment income except:

- Gains derived from the sale of real or personal property
- Items of income excluded from gross income, regardless of the U.S. or foreign status of the income's owner, such as tax-exempt municipal bond interest and qualified scholarship income

If a nonresident alien receives income for personal services performed partly in the U.S. and partly outside the U.S., he must allocate the income based on the number of days where the services were performed.

> **Example:** Bryce, a citizen and resident of Canada, is employed as a professional hockey player by a U.S. hockey team. He received $200,000 in compensation for 120 days of play during 2018: 75 days in the U.S. and 45 days in Canada. The amount of U.S. source income is $125,000 ([75 days of play in the US ÷ 120 total days = .625] × $200,000). Bryce's compensation would be considered FDAP income. Canada has a favorable tax treaty with the U.S., so Bryce should consult with his tax advisor about how best to file his nonresident return.

GILTI Tax

GILTI stands for "Global Intangible Low-Taxed Income." This new tax law provision was added into the code by the Tax Cuts and Jobs Act.[136] This significantly broadens the scope of foreign earnings that, prior to tax reform, had been subject to U.S. tax. The GILTI tax affects individuals and partnerships that are shareholders of controlled foreign corporations (CFCs).

A "U.S. shareholder" is defined as a U.S. person who owns (directly or indirectly) 10% or more of the total combined voting power of all the classes of voting stock of a CFC or 10% or more of the total value of shares of all classes of stock of a CFC.

The GILTI rules obligates more-than-10% U.S. shareholders of a foreign corporation to include, as income, a deemed distribution equal to their allocable share of the earnings and profits that are considered GILTI earnings.

---

[136] The Internal Revenue Service (IRS) published proposed regulations on Oct. 10, 2018 that contain the proposed rules to implement the GILTI provisions of the TCJA.

Example: Francis is a legal U.S. resident. He owns 13% of an industrial plant located in Greece. The company distributes and sells its products only to foreign consumers. Francis is subject to the GILTI tax.

The GILTI tax is calculated on Form 8992, *U.S. Shareholder Calculation of Global Intangible Low-Taxed Income.*

Note: The rules governing the GILTI are extremely complex. The law is very broad and impacts all companies and all U.S. individuals that have ownership in overseas entities.

Unit 15: Study Questions

(Test yourself first; then check the correct answers at the end of this quiz.)

1. Abdiel is a citizen and resident of Iran, a country that does not have a tax treaty with the United States. Abdiel is not a U.S. citizen or U.S. resident, but he owns several rental properties and other investments in the U.S. that produce passive investment income. His FDAP income is taxable at a flat _____ rate.

A. 15%
B. 20%
C. 30%
D. 35%

2. Regina is a U.S. citizen who lives and works in France, which is her tax home. She does not maintain a residence in the U.S., although she does own a residential rental property in Florida. In 2018, she received the following income:
   - Rental income earned on the Florida rental: $12,500
   - Municipal bond interest: $2,000
   - Wages earned in Australia: $90,000

Regina wants to take the foreign earned income exclusion on her individual tax return. What is the total amount of qualifying foreign earned income that Regina can report on her Form 2555?

A. $102,100
B. $99,200
C. $92,000
D. $90,000

3. Bella hired a part-time nanny to work in her home. She paid the nanny $1,900 of wages in 2018. Which of the following statements is correct?

A. Bella is not required to issue a Form W-2 to the nanny and does not have to report or pay Social Security and Medicare taxes on the nanny's wages.
B. The income is not taxable to the nanny.
C. No reporting is required by either party if the wages are paid in cash.
D. Bella can deduct the nanny's wages as a business expense on Schedule C.

4. Colton is 22, a full-time college student, and is claimed as a dependent on his parents' tax return. He also has a part-time job at a local mall. Colton has $210 of dividend income in 2018. What is the maximum amount of wages Colton can earn in 2018 without triggering the kiddie tax?

A. $350
B. $2,100
C. $6,200
D. Not applicable.

5. All of the following statements are correct about the alternative minimum tax *except*:

A. Congress passed the alternative minimum tax to ensure that individuals and corporations that benefit from certain exclusions, deductions, or credits pay at least a minimum amount of tax.
B. The tentative minimum tax is figured in addition to a taxpayer's regular tax.
C. The AMT is the excess of the tentative minimum tax over the regular tax.
D. The AMT is permanently indexed for inflation.

6. In 2018, at which threshold does an employer have to withhold and pay Social Security and Medicare taxes for a household employee?

A. When a taxpayer pays an employee for household services, regardless of the dollar amount
B. When the taxpayer pays a household employee $1,000 or more of wages a year
C. When the taxpayer pays a household employee $2,100 or more of wages a year
D. When the taxpayer pays his 20-year-old daughter to care for her younger siblings

7. Which of the following taxpayers would not be eligible for the Credit for the Prior Year Minimum Tax by filing Form 8801?

A. An S corporation
B. A trust
C. An estate of a deceased taxpayer
D. An individual

8. Which of the following statements is correct regarding the Foreign Tax Credit?

A. The Foreign Tax Credit is a refundable credit.
B. The Foreign Tax Credit is available to U.S. citizens and nonresident aliens.
C. Taxpayers may choose to take a deduction for foreign taxes paid, rather than claim the Foreign Tax Credit.
D. Taxpayers can claim both a deduction and a tax credit for foreign taxes paid, provided the taxes were paid to different countries.

9. Victor and Alyssa filed their 2008 return as Married Filing Jointly and claimed $7,500 for the first-time homebuyer credit. The couple used their home as a primary residence. In 2018, Victor and Alyssa converted the home into rental property. What, if any, is the tax obligation of the taxpayers regarding the first-time homebuyer credit?

A. Since they used the home at least 2 of the last 5 years, there is no requirement to repay
B. They must pro-rate the credit received over 15 years and repay 50% of the original credit
C. They must reduce their depreciable basis in the property by 50% of the unpaid balance of the credit
D. They must pay the unpaid balance of the credit

10. The Foreign Tax Credit applies to:

A. Taxpayers who have paid foreign taxes to a foreign country on foreign-sourced income and are subject to U.S. tax on the same income
B. Taxpayers who have paid U.S. taxes while living and working abroad
C. Taxpayers who have paid U.S. taxes while living and working abroad and who are subject to U.S. tax on their worldwide income
D. Nonresident aliens who have paid foreign taxes to a foreign country on foreign-sourced income and are subject to U.S. tax on the same income

11. Salvador is a tax professional. Upon reviewing a new client's prior year tax return, Salvador sees taxes paid for the first-time homebuyer credit. The preparer should ask the taxpayer all of the following questions *except:*

A. What was the total amount of the original credit received?
B. How much of the original credit was repaid on prior years returns?
C. Was the entire credit used towards the purchase of their main home?
D. Are the taxpayers still using the home that generated the credit as their main home?

Unit 15: Quiz Answers

.1. The answer is C. Abdiel will be taxed at a flat 30% rate on his FDAP (Fixed, Determinable, Annual, or Periodical) income. A 30% (or lower treaty) tax rate applies to FDAP income or gains from U.S. sources, but only if they are not effectively connected with a taxpayer's U.S. trade or business. FDAP income consists primarily of passive investment income, including interest, dividends, rents, royalties, pensions, and annuities. FDAP income is all income except:

- Gains derived from the sale of real or personal property
- Items of income excluded from gross income, without regard to the U.S. or foreign status of the owner of the income, such as tax-exempt municipal bond interest and qualified scholarship income

2. The answer is D. Regina has $104,500 of gross income, but only her wages ($90,000) would qualify for the foreign earned income exclusion. U.S. citizens and U.S. resident aliens who live abroad are taxed on their worldwide income. However, they may qualify to exclude a portion of their foreign earnings (up to $103,900 for 2018). A qualifying individual with qualifying income may elect to exclude foreign earned income, and this exclusion applies only if a tax return is filed and the income is reported. The municipal bond interest would be nontaxable, so the only income which would potentially be subject to tax in this scenario would be the $12,500 in rental income.

3. The answer is A. Bella is not required to issue a Form W-2 to her nanny and does not have to report or pay Social Security and Medicare taxes on the nanny's wages. If an employer pays a household employee wages of less than $2,100 in 2018, the employer is not required to report or pay Social Security and Medicare taxes on that employee's wages. Regardless of whether Form W-2 is issued, the nanny must report the income on Form 1040.

4. The answer is D. Colton's wage income will not be subject to the kiddie tax. The kiddie tax *only* applies to investment income, not to wages. Under the provisions of the kiddie tax, unearned income that is in excess of $2,100 will be taxed at estate and trust tax rates. Since Colton's dividend income is way below this threshold, he will not be subject to the kiddie tax.

5. The answer is B. The tentative minimum tax is calculated separately from the regular tax (it is *not* figured *in addition* to the taxpayer's regular tax). The AMT is owed only if the tentative minimum tax is *greater* than the regular tax.

6. The answer is C. In 2018 the nanny tax applies when a taxpayer pays a household employee $2,100 or more of wages a year.

7. The answer is A. Only individuals, estates, and trusts are eligible to claim the Credit for the Prior Year Minimum Tax by filing Form 8801. The AMT credit is calculated differently for corporations, which use a different form and set of instructions to determine whether they are eligible for the credit.

8. The answer is C. Taxpayers have the option to claim an itemized deduction for foreign taxes paid on Schedule A. They may choose either the deduction or the credit, whichever gives them the lowest tax. Taxpayers cannot claim both the deduction and a tax credit on the same return.

9. The answer is D. Victor and Alyssa must pay the unpaid balance of the credit in 2018, the year of the rental conversion.

10. The answer is A. The Foreign Tax Credit applies to taxpayers who have paid *foreign* taxes to a foreign country on foreign-sourced income and are subject to U.S. tax on the same income.

11. The answer is C. Salvador does not need to ask if the entire credit used towards the purchase of their main home. From the instructions for Form 5405: To properly complete Form 5405, all of the questions should be asked *except* for the use of the proceeds of the credit. There was no stipulation as to how the credit would be used when the first-time homebuyer received it. (This question is modified from an actual exam question that the IRS released).

Unit 16: Individual Retirement Accounts

> **More Reading:**
> Publication 590, *Individual Retirement Arrangements (IRAs)*
> Publication 575, *Pension and Annuity Income*
> Publication 560, *Retirement Plans for Small Business*

There are a variety of retirement accounts individuals can establish for themselves and retirement plans that can be established by employers and self-employed individuals.

In this unit, we primarily cover traditional individual retirement arrangements (traditional IRAs) and Roth IRAs, as they are tested heavily on Part 1 of the EA exam. We will also briefly address other types of retirement plans. Form 1099-R, *Distributions from Pensions, Annuities, Retirement or Profit-Sharing Plans, IRAs, Insurance Contracts, etc.*, is used to report distributions of $10 or more from a retirement plan or an IRA.

Traditional IRA: Amounts in a traditional IRA, including contributions and earnings, are generally not taxed until they are distributed. Typically, a taxpayer can deduct his traditional IRA contributions as an adjustment to gross income. However, the deduction can be phased out at higher income levels, when the taxpayer (or the taxpayer's spouse) is also covered by a workplace retirement plan.

Roth IRA: Contributions to a Roth IRA are paid with after-tax income and are not deductible. In contrast to a traditional IRA, withdrawals from a Roth IRA are generally not taxed. Income limits apply in determining who is eligible to participate in a Roth IRA. However, there is no income limit for taxpayers who wish to convert their traditional IRA to a Roth.

Note: The rules regarding IRAs and retirement plans apply to same-sex spouses who are legally married in any state. A same-sex spouse is entitled to all spousal benefits and protections provided to heterosexual spouses from traditional IRAs, Roth IRAs, and qualified retirement plans. However, these rules do *not* apply to domestic partnerships and civil unions.

Traditional IRA Rules

To make contributions to a traditional IRA:

- The taxpayer must be under age 70½ at the end of the year.

- The taxpayer must have qualifying taxable compensation, such as wages, salaries, commissions, tips, bonuses, or self-employment income.

If either the taxpayer or his spouse is covered by an employer plan and his income is too high, his deductible IRA contribution will be phased out. However, as long as a taxpayer has qualifying compensation and is below 70½ years of age, he may contribute to a traditional IRA (although he may not be able to *deduct* the contribution).

Note: If the taxpayer (or their spouse) *does not* participate in a retirement plan at work, their traditional IRA contribution is fully deductible up to their allowable contribution limit.

For purposes of making an IRA contribution, taxable alimony (but not child support payments) counts as qualifying compensation. This allows taxpayers to build retirement savings in IRAs even if they rely on alimony income for support. Nontaxable combat pay also qualifies as compensation for this purpose.

> **Example:** Charlton is an Army medic serving in a combat zone for all of 2018. Although none of his combat pay is taxable, it is still considered qualifying compensation for purposes of an IRA contribution. He is allowed to contribute to a Roth or Traditional IRA if he wishes.

"Compensation" for purposes of contributing to an IRA does not include:

- Rental income
- Dividend and interest income
- Pension or annuity income
- Deferred compensation
- Prize winnings or gambling income
- Items that are excluded from income, such as foreign earned income and excludable foreign housing costs (except for nontaxable combat pay)

IRA Contribution Limits

The limits for contributions to an IRA in 2018 are the lesser of qualifying taxable compensation (as described below) or the following amounts:

- **$5,500** per taxpayer (**$6,500** if age 50 or older)
- Taxpayers filing MFJ (even if only one had compensation): **$11,000** (or **$13,000** if both spouses are age 50 or older)

This yearly IRA contribution limit does not apply to:

- Rollover contributions[137] (rolling over from one IRA account to another)
- Qualified reservist repayments[138]
- Repayments of qualified disaster distributions (covered later)

> **Example:** Dalton is 54 and wants to contribute to his traditional IRA. He received $15,000 of rental income; $8,000 of interest income; and $3,000 of wages from a part-time job. The rental and interest income are not considered for purposes of determining his IRA contribution. Therefore, the maximum he can contribute to his traditional IRA is $3,000, the amount of his wages.

> **Note:** A taxpayer can never contribute more than he has earned for the year. Minors who want to start contributing to an IRA must abide by limits based on their own taxable income, *not* the income of their parents.

---

[137] Trustee-to-trustee rollovers are not limited.
[138] If a taxpayer was a reservist in the Armed Forces and was called to active duty, the taxpayer can contribute (repay) any IRA amounts equal to any qualified reservist distributions received. The taxpayer can make these repayment contributions even if the payments would cause the total yearly contributions to exceed the general limit on IRA contributions.

Example: Connie is 17 years old and has a part-time job. She is claimed as a dependent on her parent's return. She earns $4,300 in wages during 2018. She also has $3,500 in dividend income from stocks that she inherited from her grandmother. Connie may contribute to an IRA in 2018 because she has qualifying earned income (her wages). Her IRA contribution would be limited to $4,300, the amount of her wages. The investment income is not qualifying compensation for IRA purposes. Connie would be allowed to take a deduction for her IRA contribution on her individual tax return, even if she is claimed as a dependent by her parents.

If married taxpayers choose to file separately, they must consider only their own qualifying compensation for IRA contribution purposes.

Example: Falco is 35, works full-time, and earned $55,000 in wages during the year. His wife, Danielle, is 34 and earned $3,600 in 2018. They choose to file MFS. Therefore, Danielle is limited to a $3,600 IRA contribution, the amount of her qualifying compensation. Falco may contribute the full $5,500 to his own IRA account.

IRAs cannot be owned jointly. Therefore, each spouse must have their own IRA account. However, a married couple filing jointly may contribute to each of their IRA accounts, even if only one taxpayer has qualifying compensation. This is also called a "spousal IRA contribution."

Example: Derrick, 49, and Elaine, 51, are married and file jointly. Derrick works as a paramedic and makes $46,000 per year. Elaine is a homemaker and has no taxable income. Even though Elaine has no qualifying compensation, they may contribute to her IRA account. Their combined maximum contribution for 2018 is $12,000. Derrick may contribute $5,500 to his IRA, and Elaine may contribute $6,500 to her IRA because she is over 50 years old. This special rule only applies if married taxpayers file jointly.

Contributions can be made to a traditional IRA at any time on or before the due date of the return (*not* including extensions). For the 2018 tax year, a taxpayer may make an IRA contribution up until April 15, 2019. This makes an IRA contribution a rare opportunity for late-stage tax planning because it can occur after the tax year has already ended. A taxpayer can even file his return claiming a traditional IRA contribution before the contribution is actually made. However, if a contribution is reported on the taxpayer's return, but it is not made by the deadline, the taxpayer must file an amended return.

Example: Felton timely files his 2018 tax return on March 5, 2019, and claims a $4,000 deduction for an IRA contribution on the return. Felton may wait as late as April 15, 2019, the due date of the return, to actually make the IRA contribution.

If a person's only qualifying compensation for the year is from self-employment and the self-employment activity generates a loss for that year, he would not be able to contribute to an IRA. However, if the taxpayer has wages *in addition* to self-employment income, a loss from self-employment would not be subtracted from the wages when figuring total "qualifying" compensation income for purposes of determining his IRA contribution.

Example: Florence is 45 and earns $10,000 of wages working part-time for a library. She also works as a self-employed photographer, but her photography business has a net loss of ($5,400) for the year. Even though Florence's *net* income for 2018 is only $4,600 ($10,000 wages - $5,400 loss from self-employment), her "qualifying compensation" for purposes of an IRA contribution is still $10,000, the amount of her wages. This means that Florence can make a full IRA contribution of $5,500 in 2018, assuming she has enough available funds to do so.

For married taxpayers filing a joint return, the combined IRA contributions cannot exceed their combined qualifying compensation.

Example: Gilbert and Doreen are both age 49 and married. Gilbert has $23,000 of passive rental income for the year. Doreen has $18,000 of pension income and $7,000 of wages. Only Doreen's wages count as qualifying compensation for purposes of an IRA contribution. If they file jointly, they can contribute a maximum of $7,000 to their IRAs. One of them can contribute up to the maximum annual amount ($5,500), and the other can contribute up to $1,500 (equal to the remaining amount of Doreen's qualifying compensation), or they could split the $7,000 in another manner.

Splitting IRA Contributions Between Multiple Accounts

A person may have IRA accounts with multiple financial institutions and may split his annual contributions between accounts; his aggregate contributions for the year are subject to the limits described above. In other words, a taxpayer can deposit into multiple IRA accounts, as long as he doesn't contribute more than the annual limit.

Further, a taxpayer may choose to split his contributions between a traditional IRA and a Roth IRA; again, his combined contributions are subject to the maximum annual contribution limits outlined before.

Example: Bartholomew is 52. He has a traditional IRA through his bank and a Roth IRA through his stockbroker. Bartholomew wants to contribute to both accounts. Bartholomew can contribute to both of his retirement accounts, but the combined contributions for 2018 cannot exceed $6,500, the annual maximum for his age (he is allowed a catch-up contribution because he is over 50). Bartholomew decides to contribute $3,000 to his Roth IRA and $3,500 to his traditional IRA.

Example: In 2018, Gaspar has $3,200 in wages and $45,000 in rental income. He does not have any other earnings during the year. His maximum IRA contribution is limited to $3,200 (the amount of his earned income). Gaspar decides to split his IRA contributions between a traditional IRA and a Roth IRA. He contributes $2,200 to a traditional IRA and $1,000 to a Roth IRA. The most Gaspar will be able to deduct as an adjustment to income is the $2,200 contribution to his traditional IRA. Roth IRA contributions are never deductible.

Example: Inez, 25, has $3,000 of interest income and no other income in 2018. Inez marries Isaac during the year. Isaac has taxable wages of $64,000, and he plans to contribute $5,500 to his traditional IRA. If he and Inez file a joint return, each can contribute $5,500 to a traditional IRA. Inez, who has no qualifying compensation, can use Isaac's compensation, reduced by the amount of his IRA contribution ($64,000 - $5,500 = $58,500), to determine her maximum contribution to a traditional IRA.

Deductibility of Traditional IRA Contributions

A taxpayer may not be able to deduct all of his traditional IRA contributions. Deductibility is based on income, filing status, and whether the taxpayer or his spouse is covered by an employer retirement plan at work. A taxpayer with qualifying compensation is permitted to contribute to a traditional IRA regardless of whether he or his spouse is covered by an employer retirement plan; however, the *deductibility* of the contribution may be limited. This section only applies to traditional IRA contributions, because Roth IRA contributions are never tax-deductible.

If a taxpayer exceeds the income limits for making a fully deductible contribution to a traditional IRA, the excess portion can still be made as a nondeductible or after-tax contribution. Regardless of whether a portion of the contribution is nondeductible, the related earnings will grow on a tax-deferred basis.

Taxpayer (and Spouse) Not Covered by an Employer Plan: If neither the taxpayer nor his spouse is covered by an employer plan, there is no limitation on the deductibility of either of their traditional IRA contributions, other than as stated above. Thus, either can deduct the smaller of:

- $5,500 ($6,500 if 50 or older) or $11,000 ($13,000 if 50 or older) if filing MFJ, or

- 100% of qualifying compensation.

If a taxpayer makes nondeductible contributions to a traditional IRA, he must attach Form 8606, *Nondeductible IRAs.* Form 8606 reflects a taxpayer's cumulative nondeductible contributions, which is his tax basis in the IRA. If a taxpayer does not report nondeductible contributions properly, all future withdrawals from the IRA will be taxable unless the taxpayer can prove, with satisfactory evidence, that nondeductible contributions were made.

Taxpayer (or Spouse) Covered by an Employer Retirement Plan: If neither spouse is a participant in an employer-sponsored retirement plan, their IRA contributions are fully deductible on Schedule 1 (Form 1040) as an adjustment to income.

Example: Henrietta, age 61, works full-time as a restaurant manager. Her employer does not offer a retirement plan. Henrietta's husband, Kirk, 62, is a welder who is also not covered by a retirement plan at work. Both spouses have a traditional IRA. Their joint AGI in 2018 is $105,000. Since they are over 50 years of age, they can contribute and deduct a traditional IRA contribution up to $6,500 each for 2018, no matter how much they earn.

However, if either a taxpayer or his spouse, or both, is covered by (participates in) an employer retirement plan, the tax-deductible contribution to a traditional IRA is phased out at the following levels of modified adjusted gross income (MAGI):

2018 Phaseouts when Taxpayer (or Spouse) is Covered by an Employer Plan		
Filing Status	**MAGI Range**	**Allowable Deduction**
Single, HOH, or MFS (did not live with spouse*)	$63,000 or less	A full deduction
	more than $63,000 but less than $73,000	A partial deduction
	$73,000 or more	No deduction
MFJ (for the covered spouse*), QW	$101,000 or less	A full deduction
	More than $101,000 but less than $121,000	A partial deduction
	$121,000 or more	No deduction
MFS (lived with spouse*)	less than $10,000	A partial deduction
	$10,000 or more	No deduction
If neither spouse is a participant in an employer retirement plan, their traditional IRA contributions are fully deductible.		
*Note #1: If the taxpayer files MFS but <u>did not live</u> with their spouse at all during the year, the IRA deduction is determined under the "Single" filing status.		
*Note #2: If filing as MFJ and only **one** spouse is covered by a retirement plan, for the *non-covered* spouse, in 2018, a full deduction is allowed at MAGI of $189,000 or less; a partial deduction for more than $189,000 but less than $199,000; and no deduction at $199,000 or more.		

Remember, taxpayers can have a traditional IRA whether or not they are covered by another retirement plan. However, they may not be able to *deduct* all of their traditional IRA contributions if they are also covered by an employer plan.

Example: Julie is single and earned $109,000 in 2018. She is covered by a 401(k) retirement plan at work, but she also wants to contribute to a traditional IRA. She is phased out for the deduction because her MAGI exceeds the threshold for single filers covered by an employer plan. If she contributes to a traditional IRA in 2018, she must file Form 8606 to report her nondeductible contribution. She is still allowed to contribute to a traditional IRA, but the amounts would not be deductible on her Form 1040.

> **Example:** Thomas and Araceli are married and file jointly. Thomas is a member of the U.S. House of Representatives and covered by a retirement plan at work. Araceli is not covered by a workplace retirement plan, because she is self-employed. Thomas' salary for the year is $174,000. Araceli earned $45,000 in taxable self-employment income. Araceli makes a $5,500 contribution to her traditional IRA during the year. Since Thomas is covered by a retirement plan at work, and their joint AGI exceeds the phaseout threshold, (The phase-out is $199,000 or more if one spouse is covered by a retirement plan at work) Araceli's IRA contribution is not deductible. She is still allowed to make a nondeductible contribution, and the earnings in her IRA account will grow tax-free.

Married taxpayers who file MFS generally have a much lower phaseout range than those with any other filing status. However, if a taxpayer files a separate return and *did not live* with his spouse at any time during the year, the taxpayer is treated as "single" for IRA contribution purposes.

> **Example:** Stefano, age 43, and his wife are not legally divorced, but they have lived in separate residences for the past three years. In 2017, Stefano earns $48,000 and files MFS. Stefano is covered by a 401(k) at work, but he has a traditional IRA, also. He is nevertheless allowed to deduct his full IRA contribution of $5,500. This is because he did not live with his spouse during the year, and therefore is not subject to the lower IRA phaseout limits that normally apply to MFS filers.

Required Minimum Distributions (RMDs)

A person cannot keep funds in a traditional IRA account indefinitely. When the account owner reaches 70½ years of age, the funds must be distributed in annual required minimum distributions (RMDs).

The first RMD payment can be delayed until April 1 of the year *following* the year the taxpayer turns 70½. The distribution for each subsequent year must be made by December 31. The amount of each RMD is based on IRS tables.[139]

Failure to take an RMD can result in a penalty tax equal to 50% of the amount the taxpayer should have withdrawn but did not. He must file Form 5329, *Additional Taxes on Qualified Plans*, to report the excise tax that applies as a result of the failure to take the RMD.

> **Example:** Lorena reaches age 70½ in 2018. Her first RMD must be distributed to her by April 1, 2019, to avoid the 50% excise tax. At the end of the year, her IRA account balance was $79,500. The applicable distribution period per the IRS tables for someone her age (71) on that date is 26.5 years. Her required minimum distribution for 2018 is $3,000 ($79,500 ÷ 26.5). She must withdraw this amount from her IRA no later than April 1, 2019.

Required Minimum Distributions also apply to inherited IRAs. With an inherited IRA, the beneficiary generally needs to take annual distributions no matter what age he is. The same rule about taking a Required Minimum Distribution still applies. The beneficiary of the

---

[139] An RMD is calculated by dividing the balance of the IRA account by a life expectancy factor that the IRS publishes in tables within Publication 590, *Individual Retirement Arrangements (IRAs)*.

inherited IRA must begin withdrawing no later than December 31 *following* year after the IRA owner died.

> **Example:** Leanne dies on May 1, 2018. Leanne's only son, Marlon, is the sole beneficiary of Leanne's traditional IRA account. Marlon must begin withdrawing an RMD no later than December 31, 2019, the year after his mother's death. This rule applies no matter how old Marlon is.

> **Note**: RMDs are not required if the beneficiary of an inherited IRA is a surviving spouse under 70½ years of age, and the spouse simply does a spousal rollover into his or her own IRA.

> **Example:** Montgomery, age 72, and Nanette, age 61, are married. Both spouses have traditional IRA accounts. Montgomery began taking required distributions from his traditional IRA in the previous year. However, in 2018, Montgomery dies, and his wife inherits his IRA account. Rather than take a distribution from her late husband's account, Nanette decides to do a spousal rollover of the entire account balance into her own IRA. The rollover is not a taxable event, and Nanette is not required to take any minimum distributions from the account until she reaches age 70½.

Taxability of IRA Distributions

Distributions from a traditional IRA are generally taxable in the year they are received, subject to the following exceptions:

- Rollovers to another retirement plan or account (other than conversions to a Roth IRA, as discussed below)
- Qualified charitable distributions directly to a qualified charity (must be a trustee-to-trustee transfer)
- Tax-free withdrawal of contributions
- Distributions of nondeductible contributions

Qualified Charitable Distributions (QCD)

A taxpayer who is 70½ or older may choose to make a qualified charitable distribution (QCD)[140] of up to $100,000 ($200,000 for MFJ) from his IRA to qualified charitable organizations. In order to qualify, the funds must come out of the taxpayer's IRA by the deadline for minimum distributions (generally December 31). Charitable distributions are reported on Form 1099-R for the calendar year the distribution is made.

> **Example:** Dineen is 72. Her required minimum distribution is $9,400 in 2018. She made a $15,000 qualified charitable distribution from her traditional IRA account directly to her church. She has satisfied her required minimum distribution for the year.

The IRA trustee must make the distribution directly to the qualified charity (the taxpayer cannot request a distribution and then donate the money later). Likewise, any tax withholdings on behalf of the owner from an IRA distribution cannot qualify as QCDs.

---

[140] The PATH Act made the QCD election permanent.

> **Example:** Patty regularly donates to the Red Cross, a qualified U.S. charity. In 2018, Patty turned 71. Instead of taking a minimum distribution from her IRA, she contacts her IRA trustee and requests to make a Qualified Charitable Contribution directly to the charity. The QCD counts toward her current year's RMD, as long as the funds are withdrawn from the IRA by December 31.

10% Penalty on Early Distributions and Penalty Exceptions

A taxpayer may withdraw funds at any time from a traditional IRA account. However, distributions before age 59½ will generally be subject to an extra 10% excise tax, in addition to normal income tax on the amount distributed. There are some exceptions to the general rule for early distributions. An individual may not have to pay the additional 10% tax in the following situations:

- To the extent the taxpayer has unreimbursed medical expenses that exceed 7.5% of adjusted gross income

- The distributions do not exceed the cost of the taxpayer's medical insurance while unemployed

- The taxpayer becomes disabled or dies

- The distributions are not more than qualified higher education expenses

- The distributions are used to buy, build, or rebuild a first home (up to $10,000)

- The distributions are used to pay the IRS due to a levy

- Made as part of a series of substantially equal periodic payments for the life of the taxpayer

- The distributions are made to a qualified reservist (an individual called up to active duty)

- Qualified disaster distributions (covered later)

Even though distributions in these situations will not be subject to the additional 10% tax, they will be subject to income tax at the taxpayer's normal rates. Distributions that are properly rolled over into another retirement plan or account (other than conversions to a Roth IRA) are generally not subject to either income tax or the 10% additional penalty.

> **Example:** Oksana, age 39, takes a $5,000 distribution from her traditional IRA account. She does not meet any of the exceptions to the 10% additional penalty tax, so the $5,000 is an early distribution. Oksana must include the $5,000 in her gross income and pay income tax on it. In addition, she must pay a 10% penalty tax of $500 (10% × $5,000).

Roth IRA vs. Traditional IRA

Roth IRAs and traditional IRAs have many differences, but they are both used for retirement planning. Unlike a traditional IRA, none of the contributions to a Roth IRA are deductible, but the entire balance is generally tax-free at the time of withdrawal. The major differences between a Roth IRA and a traditional IRA are as follows:

- Contributions to a Roth IRA are not deductible by the taxpayer, and participation in an employer plan has no effect on the taxpayer's contribution limits.

- There are no required minimum distributions from a Roth IRA. No distributions are required until a Roth IRA owner dies.

- Unlike traditional IRAs, contributions to a Roth IRA can be made by individuals of any age, even those who are over the age of 70½.

- Income limits apply, which means high-income earners may be prohibited from contributing to a Roth IRA.

Whether or not a taxpayer can make a Roth IRA contribution depends on his filing status and modified adjusted gross income (MAGI). In 2018, the following income limits apply to Roth IRAs:

Filing Status	2018 Roth IRA Phaseout Ranges
Single, HOH filers[141]	Phaseout begins at $120,000; ineligible at $135,000
MFJ and QW filers	Phaseout begins at $189,000; ineligible at $199,000
MFS (lived with spouse)	$0-$10,000

In general, a taxpayer cannot contribute to a Roth IRA if his income is above the phaseout thresholds. However, a "backdoor" Roth IRA is still possible in 2018. By this method, the taxpayer simply opens a traditional IRA, makes a contribution, and then converts the funds to a Roth in the same year. We will cover IRA conversions in more detail later.

IRA Rollovers

A rollover is a transfer from one retirement plan to another retirement plan or account. If executed properly, most rollovers are nontaxable events. A taxpayer can make only one rollover from an IRA to another IRA in any twelve-month period, regardless of the number of IRAs the taxpayer owns. There are two exceptions to this rule:

- Trustee-to-trustee transfers between IRAs are not limited.

- Rollovers from a traditional IRA to a Roth IRA are not limited (this is also commonly called a "backdoor conversion").

A rollover from a traditional IRA to a Roth IRA is more commonly called an "IRA conversion," but it is still a type of rollover. In this case, the conversion will result in taxation of any previously untaxed amounts in the traditional IRA that were rolled over into a Roth IRA.

Rollover Rules

If a taxpayer receives an IRA distribution and wishes to make a nontaxable rollover, he must complete the transaction by the 60th day following the day he receives the distribution.

---

[141] This phaseout range also applies to MFS taxpayers who did not live with their spouses at any time during the year.

The "60-day rollover rule" applies to indirect rollovers of a qualified retirement account, such as an IRA or 401(k). Once a taxpayer takes a distribution from their account, they won't owe any interest or penalties as long as the money is redeposited into another qualified retirement account within 60 days.[142]

It is not uncommon for employees to roll funds from one retirement plan to another, especially after a job change. With a *direct* rollover, the funds from the taxpayer's current retirement account are transferred directly to a new retirement plan. This is also called a "trustee-to-trustee" transfer. With an *indirect* rollover, it is up to the employee to redeposit the funds into the new IRA or other qualifying retirement account within the mandatory 60-day period to avoid penalty.

> **Example:** Sheldon quits his old job on September 1, 2018. On October 14, 2018, Sheldon begins a new job. He has an existing retirement account at his old employer. He decides to transfer the balance of his traditional IRA account to his new employer's retirement plan. Rather than disclose any information about his new workplace to his former boss, Sheldon decides to receive a direct distribution from his IRA of $60,000 in cash and $50,000 in stock. On October 30, 2018, Sheldon deposits the entire amount of $110,000 into his new employer's retirement plan. Because the transaction is completed within 60 days, it is completely non-taxable. However, the rollover must be reported on Form 1040.

If a taxpayer sells the distributed property (such as stocks or bonds distributed from an IRA) and rolls over all the proceeds into another traditional IRA or qualified retirement plan within the required time frame, no gain or loss is recognized. The sale proceeds (including any increase in value) are treated as part of the distribution and are not included in the taxpayer's gross income.

If a taxpayer receives both property and cash in a rollover distribution, he can roll over part or all of the property, part or all of the cash, or any combination of the two he chooses. He can also sell the property and roll over the proceeds into a traditional IRA. But he cannot keep the property and substitute his own funds for property he receives.

> **Example:** Todd receives a distribution from his employer's plan of $20,000 cash and $30,000 worth of stock. He decides to keep the distributed stock. He can roll over the $20,000 cash received, but he cannot substitute an additional $30,000 in cash in place of the stock and treat this amount as if it had also been rolled over.

A taxable distribution paid from an employer-sponsored retirement plan is subject to mandatory tax withholding of 20%, even if the taxpayer intends to roll it over. If the taxpayer does roll it over and wants to defer tax on the entire taxable portion, he will be forced to add funds from other sources equal to the amount of tax withheld.

In order to avoid this mandatory withholding, a taxpayer may request a "direct rollover." The distribution is then made directly from the custodian or trustee for the employer-

---

[142] IRS Revenue Procedure 2016-47 allows eligible taxpayers to now qualify for a waiver of the 60-day rollover limit and avoid possible early distribution taxes. Taxpayers will submit the self-certification to their plan administrator or an IRA trustee (NOT to the IRS). In the past, taxpayers who failed to meet the rollover time limit could only obtain a waiver by requesting a private letter ruling from the IRS.

sponsored plan to the custodian for the employee's IRA or his new employer's retirement plan. Under this option, the 20% mandatory withholding does not apply.

Rollover after the Death of an IRA Owner

Following the death of an IRA owner, the IRA usually passes to a beneficiary. There are very different rules if the beneficiary is a surviving spouse, versus any other type of beneficiary (such as a child or a sibling).

After the death of a traditional IRA's owner, a surviving spouse has two options: he or she can elect to treat the IRA as being his own by changing the ownership designation or roll over the IRA balance to his own IRA account or certain other types of retirement plans.

> **Example:** Tamika, 42, and Onassis, 53, are married. Tamika dies suddenly in 2018, and at the time of her death, she has $83,000 in her traditional IRA account. Onassis chooses to roll over the entire $83,000 into his own IRA account, thereby avoiding taxation on the income until he retires and starts taking distributions.

For any beneficiary other than a surviving spouse, there are a number of factors that determine the period over which amounts remaining in an IRA upon the owner's death would be payable. These include whether the owner died on or before the date he was required to begin taking distributions, whether the beneficiary is an individual (or the owner's estate), and the life expectancies of the owner and the beneficiary in the year of death. If a Roth IRA owner dies and the sole beneficiary is the spouse, he can delay distributions until the owner would have reached 70½ or treat the IRA as his own.

For other beneficiaries, the account balance must generally be fully distributed by the end of the fifth calendar year after the owner's death, or be paid as an annuity over the beneficiary's life expectancy beginning the year following the year of death.

> **Example:** Pauline, who was unmarried and had no children, died in 2018. At the time of her death, Pauline had a traditional IRA worth $102,000. The beneficiary of her IRA is her brother, Rudy, age 42. Although he cannot roll over the IRA since he is not Pauline's spouse, Rudy can choose how he receives the IRA proceeds. Rudy can choose a lump sum distribution, a five-year distribution, or a "stretch" IRA payout (an annuity paid over his lifetime). No matter what type of distribution Rudy selects, the amounts he withdraws from the IRA will be subject to income tax. However, the 10% early withdrawal penalty is waived for a beneficiary of an IRA when the original IRA owner has died, (regardless of how old the beneficiary is).

Conversion of a Traditional IRA to a Roth IRA

In the past, taxpayers in higher income brackets were unable to contribute to a Roth IRA. They were also unable to convert from a traditional IRA to a Roth IRA. The IRS rules changed several years ago, and there is no longer an income threshold on Roth IRA conversions.

High-income taxpayers can convert a traditional IRA to a Roth as long as they pay the appropriate tax on the conversion. This is frequently called a "backdoor Roth" or "backdoor conversion."

There is no 10% early withdrawal penalty if the funds from the traditional IRA are deposited into a Roth IRA within 60 days. If a taxpayer wishes to convert all or a portion of his traditional IRA to a Roth IRA, he is required to pay income taxes on the amount of pretax (deductible) contributions converted, as well as the growth in value resulting from earnings on those contributions. After the funds are converted to a Roth IRA, additional earnings are tax-free, and distributions are generally not subject to tax.

Example: Ruth converted her traditional IRA to a Roth IRA in 2018. The traditional IRA has a balance of $150,000. The entire balance represents deductible contributions and earnings that have not previously been taxed. She reports the amount of the balance that was converted to a Roth IRA as taxable income on her 2018 tax return.

A Roth conversion is reported on Form 8606, *Nondeductible IRAs*. An inherited traditional IRA is generally not eligible to be converted to a Roth IRA unless it is inherited directly from a spouse. Non-spousal beneficiaries (for example, a child who inherits a traditional IRA from a deceased parent) are not allowed to convert a traditional IRA to a Roth IRA.

Recharacterizations

A taxpayer may undo or reverse a rollover or conversion of one type of IRA to a different type of IRA through a *recharacterization.* Essentially, by recharacterizing an IRA, it is as if the conversion or rollover never occurred.

Note: Beginning in 2018, the Tax Cuts and Jobs Act eliminates the option to recharacterize, or "unwind" an earlier Roth conversion. The law also prohibits recharacterizing amounts rolled over to a Roth IRA from other retirement plans, such as 401(k) plans. However, if a taxpayer converted their traditional IRA to a Roth IRA in 2017, and later changes their mind about the conversion, a recharacterization will still be permitted through October 15, 2018. An election to recharacterize past this deadline is allowable (by an executor) if the taxpayer has died. The election must be made by an executor on behalf of a decedent on decedent's final return.

Example: Leon converted his traditional IRA to a Roth IRA on December 30, 2017. Leon dies one month later, on January 30, 2018. His daughter, Elektra, is Leon's sole heir and the executor of his estate. Since Leon completed the conversion in 2017, Elektra is permitted to reverse the conversion. Elektra decides to recharacterize Leon's earlier conversion and move all the converted funds back to a traditional IRA. Elektra instructs the trustee of her deceased father's IRA account to make a trustee-to-trustee transfer of the Roth conversion contribution *back* to a traditional IRA. This is a recharacterization. Elektra should report the recharacterization on her father's final form 1040, and sign the return as his executor.

Example: On June 1, 2018, Lawrence converts his traditional IRA to a Roth IRA. However, his investments perform poorly, and his account loses value after the conversion. He wants to go back and change his mind. However, since he converted his traditional IRA to a Roth in 2018, the conversion is permanent. He cannot recharacterize the conversion.

Some types of recharacterizations are still permitted under the TCJA. A client can use the recharacterization rules to fix the invalid rollover, for example. A taxpayer must report an IRA recharacterization on Form 8606, *Nondeductible IRAs.*[143]

Excise Tax on Excess IRA Contributions

If a taxpayer accidentally contributes more to his IRA than is allowed for the year, the excess contribution is subject to a 6% excise tax. Contributions made to a traditional IRA in the year a taxpayer reaches age 70½ are also considered excess contributions. However, the IRS will allow a taxpayer to correct an excess contribution if certain rules are followed.

If he makes a contribution that exceeds the annual maximum or his qualifying compensation, the excess contribution and all related earnings must be withdrawn from the IRA before the due date (*including* extensions) of the tax return for that year. If a taxpayer corrects the excess contribution within this period, the 6% penalty will apply only to the amounts earned on the excess contribution.

The taxpayer must also report the earnings on the excess contribution as taxable income for the year in which the withdrawal is made. For each year that the excess amounts remain in the IRA, the taxpayer must pay the 6% tax.

However, this tax can never exceed 6% of the value of the taxpayer's IRA at the end of the tax year.

Note: A taxpayer cannot apply an excess contribution to an earlier year even if the taxpayer contributed less than the maximum amount allowable for an earlier year. However, the taxpayer is allowed to apply an excess contribution to a *later* year if the contributions for that later year are less than the maximum allowable for that year. This is a type of recharacterization.

Example: In 2018, Torrey is 49 years old and single. His wages for the year are $52,000. He has two different IRA accounts in separate banks. He contributes $3,000 to each account in 2018. Torrey has accidentally made an excess contribution of $500 ($6,000 total IRA contributions - $5,500 contribution limit). The excess contributions earned $5 interest in 2018 and $6 interest in early 2019. Torrey does not realize his mistake, and he does not withdraw the $500 in excess contribution or the interest it earned by the due date of his return. Since he doesn't discover the error until after his filing deadline, now Torrey is liable for an excise tax on his excess contributions. He figures the additional tax on Form 5329. To avoid the excise tax for 2019, he can correct the excess amount by allocating the $500 to the next year, or he can withdraw it from the account.

---

[143] A Roth IRA conversion made in 2017 may still be recharacterized as a contribution to a traditional IRA if the recharacterization is made no later than October 15, 2018.

Example: Trisha, age 62, is self-employed and owns several rental properties. She contributes the maximum, $6,500, to her traditional IRA. She files for an extension to prepare her tax return. When she finally gives her records to her accountant, he discovers that Trisha's taxable income from self-employment is only $5,500 and her rental income is $78,000. Only the self-employment income counts as compensation for purposes of contributing to her IRA, so Trisha has inadvertently made an excess contribution of $1,000. Instead of withdrawing the excess contribution, Trisha chooses to recharacterize it, and she applies the excess IRA contribution to 2019. As long as she has qualifying compensation of at least $1,000 in 2019, then she will be allowed to keep the contribution in her traditional IRA.

Prohibited Transactions

Generally, a prohibited transaction is the "improper use" of an IRA by the owner, a beneficiary, or a disqualified person (typically a fiduciary or family member). Prohibited transactions related to an IRA include:

- Borrowing money from it[144]

- Using it as security for a loan

- Buying property for personal use with IRA funds

- Personally borrowing money from the IRA (i.e., there is no such thing as an "IRA loan," although some types of retirement plans do allow limited borrowing, traditional IRAs do not)

- Selling, leasing, or exchanging property to the IRA account

- Accepting unreasonable compensation for managing property or assets held by the IRA

- Granting account fiduciaries to obtain, use, or borrow against account assets for their own gain

- Transferring plan assets, lending money, or providing goods and services to "disqualified persons," usually a close family member, or a business that a close family member owns and controls.

Note: Prohibited transactions are rare occurrences, and they generally only occur when a taxpayer has a "self-directed" IRA. A self-directed IRA is a type of account that offers a taxpayer the ability to use his retirement funds to make almost any type of investment without requiring a financial institution or another custodian.

For the purposes of the prohibited transaction rules, "family members" includes the taxpayer's spouse, parents, grandparents, children; and grandchildren and spouses of the taxpayer's children and grandchildren. Family members do not include in-laws, cousins, friends, aunts, uncles, siblings, and stepsiblings.

---

[144] Do not confuse the borrowing restrictions for traditional IRAs and other types of retirement accounts. Loans are *not permitted* from IRAs or from other IRA-based plans such as SEP-IRAs and SIMPLE IRA plans. Loans are only possible from qualified plans, such as: 401(k) plans or 403(b) plans, and from governmental plans. Qualified retirement plans are covered in more detail in Book 2, *Businesses.*

Although occurrences of prohibited transactions are rare, the consequences can be catastrophic. If a prohibited transaction occurs at any time during the year, normally the account ceases to be treated as an IRA, and its assets are treated as if having been wholly distributed on the first day of the year.

However, in situations where an IRA account, or a portion of an IRA account, is used as a security for a loan, only the amount used as security for the loan is treated as a distribution from the IRA as of the first day of the year that the loan was made, but the IRA continues to exist. If the total fair market value as of that date is more than the taxpayer's basis in the IRA, the excess amount is reportable as taxable income. It may also be subject to the additional 10% penalty on early distributions.

Example: Zamir, age 40, has a self-directed IRA account. The fair market value of Zamir's traditional IRA was $300,000 as of January 1, 2018. He had previously made $200,000 of nondeductible contributions to his IRA, so that was his basis in the account. On January 10, 2018, Zamir borrowed $150,000 from his IRA to purchase a vacation home for himself. This is a prohibited transaction, and Zamir's entire IRA account will no longer be treated as an IRA from the date of the withdrawal. Since the FMV of the IRA on the first day of the year, $300,000, is greater than Zamir's basis, $200,000, the excess amount of $100,000 is reported as taxable income. Zamir would also be subject to the additional 10% penalty for withdrawing funds before the age of 59½.

Example: Wilbert is 52 and has $180,000 in his traditional IRA. His daughter, Teralynn, wants to buy a home for $140,000 but does not have sufficient funds. As a result, Wilbert lends his daughter $140,000 from his self-directed IRA to buy the home. This is a prohibited transaction. For Wilbert, the IRA is deemed immediately disqualified as of January 1, 2018 (the year in which the prohibited transaction occurred). The entire amount of the IRA is deemed distributed in 2018, and an early withdrawal penalty of 10% would also apply to the entire amount of the IRA ($180,000).

Prohibited IRA Investments

Almost any type of investment is permissible inside an IRA, including stocks, bonds, and real estate. However, there are some investments that are prohibited. For example, the law does not permit IRA funds to be invested in life insurance or collectibles. If the taxpayer invests in any of these using IRA funds, it is treated as a prohibited transaction. The following investments are prohibited:

- Collectibles and jewelry, such as: artwork, antiques, baseball cards, uncut gemstones, or comics
- Precious metals, coins, and gemstones (exceptions exist for U.S. coins and bullion)
- S corporation stock
- Life insurance contracts
- Real Estate for personal use

There is a narrow exception for investments in gold and silver coins minted by the U.S. Treasury Department. Investments in certain gold, silver, palladium, and platinum bullion are also allowable.

Retirement Plans for Businesses

Retirement plans for businesses include Simplified Employee Pension (SEP) plans, Savings Incentive Match Plan for Employees (SIMPLE) plans, and qualified plans. The term "qualified" refers to certain IRS requirements that the employer must adhere to in order to obtain a retirement plan's tax-favored status. SEP and SIMPLE plans must also meet certain requirements but are much less complex than those that apply to qualified plans.

Study Note: Business retirement plans are covered in greater detail, and from the *employer's* perspective, in *PassKey's EA Review Book 2: Businesses*, as much of the related information is tested on Part 2 of the EA exam. In Part 1 of the exam, you will need to understand the employee's perspective with regard to retirement plans. For Part 2, you must understand retirement plans from the employer's perspective.

If retirement plans are structured and administered properly, businesses can deduct contributions they make on behalf of their employees or, if self-employed, themselves. Both the contributions and the earnings are generally tax-free until distribution. Further, some plans also allow employees to make contributions, most commonly in pretax dollars (so that a portion of their salaries are not taxed until the amounts are later distributed to them by the plan).

SEP Plans: SEPs provide a simplified method for employers to make contributions to a retirement plan for themselves and their employees. Instead of setting up a profit-sharing plan with a trust, an employer can adopt a SEP agreement and make contributions directly to individual SEP-IRA accounts (similar to a traditional IRA as described previously) for himself and each eligible employee. A SEP plan is funded exclusively by employer contributions; employee contributions are not permitted. A self-employed taxpayer may set up a SEP and fund it, as long as he has earnings from his business.

SIMPLE Plans: An employer can generally set up a SIMPLE plan if the business has 100 or fewer employees who received at least $5,000 of compensation during the preceding year. Under a SIMPLE plan, employees can choose to make salary reduction contributions rather than receiving these amounts as part of their regular pay. An employer is allowed to contribute matching contributions or non-elective contributions.

A SIMPLE plan can be structured in one of two ways: using SIMPLE IRAs (again, similar to traditional IRAs as described previously) or as a SIMPLE 401(k) plan (similar to the qualified 401(k) plans described below).

Qualified Retirement Plans

There are two basic kinds of qualified retirement plans: defined contribution plans and defined benefit plans, and different rules apply to each. An employer is allowed to have more than one type of qualified plan, but contributions cannot exceed annual limits. Contributions for self-employed taxpayers are limited to 100% of compensation. If the business does not have any income for the year, no contribution can be made. All qualified plans are subject to federal regulation under the Employee Retirement Income Security Act (ERISA). The federal government does not require an employer to establish a retirement plan, but it provides minimum federal standards for qualified plans.

Defined Benefit Plans

A defined benefit plan, often called a traditional pension plan, promises a specified benefit amount or annuity for each participant after retirement. Benefits are typically based on formulas that consider the participant's years of service with the employer and his earnings history. The federal government and most state and local governments provide defined benefit plans for their employees. However, fewer and fewer private businesses offer defined benefit plans because they are costly to administer and inflexible.

The benefits promised by many defined benefit plans are protected by federal insurance. Contributions to a defined benefit plan are not optional. Contributions are typically based on actuarial calculations that estimate the amounts necessary to pay benefits in the future.

Defined Contribution Plans

A defined contribution plan provides an individual account for each participant in the plan depending upon how the plan is structured. It provides benefits to each participant based on the amounts contributed to the participant's account, along with subsequent investment income or losses, and, in some instances, allocations of forfeitures among participant accounts.

The participants, the employer, or both may contribute to the individual participant accounts. Examples of defined contribution plans include profit-sharing plans, 401(k) plans, 403(b) plans, and 457 plans.

Depending upon how a qualified plan is structured, salary reduction/elective deferral contributions are employee contributions based on a percentage of the employee's compensation and are generally made on a pretax basis.

This limitation applies to the aggregate amounts of contributions to any qualified plans, SEPs, and SIMPLE plans in which the individual participates during the year. However, the contribution cannot exceed the amount of the employee's compensation. Depending on the individual plan, the employer may provide matching contributions for employees who make elective deferrals.

> **Example:** Spencer earns $80,000 per year as an insurance executive. He participates in his company's profit-sharing 401(k) plan. He contributes 3% of his pretax wages to the plan in 2018, or $2,400 ($80,000 × .03). Spencer's company contributes a matching 3% to his individual 401(k) account.

Distributions: Distributions to participants may be made either on a periodic basis, such as annuity payments or as a lump sum. As is the case with distributions from traditional IRA accounts (as well as SEP and SIMPLE plans), distributions generally are not permitted prior to when the participant retires or otherwise terminates employment, dies, becomes disabled, or reaches age 59½. Earlier distributions are generally subject to an additional 10% penalty tax.

> **Note:** For purposes of the net investment income tax (NIIT), net investment income does not include distributions from a qualified retirement plan, such as a 401(k), or from traditional or Roth IRAs. However, these distributions are taken into account when determining the modified adjusted gross income threshold.

Required minimum distributions (RMDs) from defined contribution plans[145] must generally begin by April 1 of the year following the calendar year when the taxpayer retires, or the year in which the taxpayer reaches age 70½, whichever comes later.

> **Example:** In 2018, Spencer retires at age 63 after working 35 years at an auto manufacturer. He would have been required to take distributions by April 1 of the year following the calendar year in which he reaches age 70½. However, Spencer chooses to begin taking distributions from his 401(k) account in the same year he retires. The distributions would be taxed as retirement income on his individual tax return.

> **Example:** Esther is a secretary working for a large retail company. Esther turned 70 on February 15, 2018. Although she was eligible to retire years ago, she prefers to keep working. Esther is required to take her first RMD by April 1, 2019, regardless of whether or not she is still employed.

Restricted Loans from Qualified Plans

Unlike traditional IRAs and Roth IRAs, where withdrawals are permitted at any time, distributions from qualified plans are generally restricted. This means that a taxpayer cannot withdraw from the account whenever he chooses, (like he can from a traditional or Roth IRA). Generally, distributions of elective deferrals cannot be made until one of the following occurs:

- The taxpayer dies, becomes disabled, or has a severance from employment.
- The plan terminates, and no successor defined contribution plan is established or maintained by the employer.
- The taxpayer reaches age 59½ or
- The taxpayer incurs significant financial hardship.

Some limited borrowing from qualified plans is allowed. Loans are not dependent upon hardship, but some plans may provide for loans and hardship withdrawals (although the plan is not required to do so). A qualified plan may allow its participants to borrow specified portions of their individual account balances, subject to certain restrictions. A loan can generally be no more than the lesser of $50,000, or the greater of $10,000 or 50% of the vested portion of the participant's account balance.

> **Note:** Most qualified plans offer employees the ability to borrow from their own retirement account and repay that amount with interest to their own retirement account. IRS regulations permit qualified plans to offer loans to plan participants, but the plan is not *required* to.

---

[145] Defined contribution plans include 401(k) plans, profit-sharing, and 403(b) plans.

> **Example:** Harry has a vested account balance of $98,000 in his company's 401(k) Profit Sharing Plan. His retirement plan allows loans to its employee-participants. Harry may borrow up to $49,000 from his qualified plan, which is 50% of his vested balance and less than $50,000.

If a loan is not repaid according to the specified payment terms, it may be considered a taxable distribution. This may apply if a participant terminates employment with the employer that sponsors the plan.

Hardship Distributions and Qualified Disaster Distributions

A 401(k) plan may allow participants to receive hardship distributions because of an immediate and heavy financial need, such as sudden medical or funeral expenses. Hardship distributions are limited to the amount of the employee's elective deferrals and generally do not include any income earned on the deferred amounts. The amount of the distribution may include amounts necessary to pay taxes or penalties anticipated to result from the distribution, including the 10% penalty levied on early distributions.

> **Example:** Sharon's home is in foreclosure, and she is in immediate danger of being evicted. She requests a hardship distribution from her 401(k), which is granted. Since she is under age 59½, Sharon would likely have to pay the 10% early distribution penalty.

Qualified Disaster Distributions

The *Bipartisan Budget Act of 2018* (HR 1892, "Budget Act") included several tax provisions for disaster relief. In 2018, the law allows for an exception to the 10% early withdrawal penalty for taxpayers who are affected by presidentially declared disasters.[146] This is called a "qualified disaster distribution." Amounts distributed can also be *recontributed* over a three-year period, and the taxpayer is allowed to recoup any income tax paid on the distribution.

> **Note:** A "hardship distribution" is not the same as a "disaster distribution." A qualified disaster distribution gets special tax treatment and is only available to taxpayers who have incurred losses or hardship in a presidentially declared disaster area.

A "qualified disaster distribution" is an amount up to $100,000 taken by a participant whose main home was in the federally declared disaster area and the distribution was made between the following dates:

- Hurricane Harvey, after August 22, 2017, and before January 1, 2019;
- Hurricane Irma, after September 3, 2017, and before January 1, 2019;
- Hurricane Maria, after September 15, 2017, and before January 1, 2019;
- California wildfires, after October 7, 2017, and before January 1, 2019.

Other than a loan, a retirement plan distribution generally can't be repaid, unless it qualifies as an eligible rollover distribution. Hardship distributions are also generally not eligible for repayment, but qualified disaster distributions *can* be repaid.

---

[146] A "Qualified Disaster" is any presidentially declared disaster, or any natural disaster, military or terroristic act deemed by the Secretary of Treasury to be a Code Section 139(c) qualified disaster.

Example: Frederick is 32 years old and single. Frederick's main home was severely damaged by the California wildfires, a presidentially declared disaster. Frederick takes a $40,000 distribution from his traditional IRA on January 2, 2018,[147] to help him rebuild and also to pay living expenses. The distribution is subject to income tax, but not the 10% penalty. If Fredrick chooses to do so, he may repay the distribution within a 3-year period. The amount of the repayment is treated as a trustee-to-trustee transfer and is not included in income.

If a taxpayer's residence is in a qualified disaster area, disaster withdrawals from qualified plans and traditional IRAs are permitted, and not subject to the normal 10% early withdrawal penalty. The law also expands the availability of 401(k) plan loans and extends the normal repayment period for those loans.

With regard to qualified retirement plans (i.e., 401(k), 403(b) and 457(b) plans), the loan limit is increased to $100,000 or 100% for taxpayers in affected presidential disaster areas. Any repayment would be treated as a trustee-to-trustee transfer made within the 60-day time frame under applicable regulations.

Example: Lorelei is 42 and lives in Texas. Lorelei's apartment complex was destroyed by Hurricane Harvey on August 29, 2017, and she was left homeless. Four months after the disaster, on January 3, 2018, she withdrew $35,000 from her 401(k) plan to pay emergency expenses and housing costs. Her withdrawal is not subject to a 10% early withdrawal penalty, because it qualifies as a disaster distribution. If she wishes to repay the distribution a later date, she has three years to do so.

---

[147] For the California wildfires, a distribution made on or after October 8, 2017 and before January 1, 2019, is considered a "qualified disaster distribution" if the taxpayer's home was in the affected disaster zone.

Traditional IRA vs. Roth IRA Comparison

Issue	Traditional IRA	Roth IRA
Age limit	A person over 70½ cannot contribute.	No age limit for contributions
2018 Contribution limits	The lesser of $5,500 (or $6,500 if age 50 or older by the end of the year) and qualifying taxable compensation.	Same
Deductibility of contributions	Generally deductible.	No. Contributions to a Roth IRA are never deductible.
Filing requirements	No filing requirement unless nondeductible contributions are made. Nondeductible contributions must be reported on Form 8606.	Filing requirement related to a conversion of a traditional IRA to a Roth IRA. None related to contributions made directly to a Roth IRA.
Mandatory distributions	RMDs by April 1 of the year following the year a taxpayer reaches age 70½.	There are no required distributions unless the IRA owner dies.
How distributions are taxed	Distributions from a traditional IRA are taxed as ordinary income.	Distributions from a Roth IRA are generally not taxed.
Income limits	Anyone with qualifying compensation can contribute. Phaseout of deductibility is based upon AGI if the taxpayer and/or spouse are covered by an employer plan.	There are income limits for contributions, but conversions of a traditional IRA to a Roth IRA are still allowable.

Unit 16: Study Questions

(Test yourself first; then check the correct answers at the end of this quiz.)

1. When does the IRS require the owner of a Roth IRA to start taking withdrawals?

A. After the death of the IRA owner
B. At age 59½
C. At age 70½
D. Never

2. Enoch is 42 and unmarried. He has a Roth IRA and a traditional IRA with two different financial institutions. In 2018, he contributed $1,500 to his Roth IRA. He also wants to contribute to his traditional IRA account. What is the maximum he can contribute to a traditional IRA in 2018, assuming he had sufficient qualifying compensation?

A. $0
B. $3,000
C. $4,000
D. $5,000

3. Contributions to a traditional IRA can be deducted for a given tax year if they are made:

A. Any time during the year or by the due date of the return, not including extensions
B. Any time during the year or by the due date of the return, including extensions
C. By December 31
D. Any time during the year, but only while the taxpayer is employed

4. Which of the following statements is correct regarding loans from a qualified plan?

A. Loans from a qualified plan are never permitted.
B. Loans are permitted up to the full amount of the employee's contributions to the plan.
C. Loans are generally permitted, but generally cannot exceed $50,000, or the greater of $10,000 or 50% of the vested portion of the employee's account balance.
D. Loans are permitted, but only under specific and defined circumstances of hardship.

5. Elizabeth and Landon are both age 62, married, and lived together all year. They both work, and each has a traditional IRA. In 2019, Landon earned $4,000 of wages and received $11,000 of annuity income. Elizabeth earned $52,000 in wages. They prefer to file separately. If they file MFS, what is the maximum that Landon can contribute to his IRA?

A. $1,000
B. $4,000
C. $5,500
D. $6,500

6. Lucas, an unmarried college student working part-time, earns $3,500 in wages during 2018. He also receives $500 of interest income and $4,000 from his parents to help pay tuition. What is his maximum IRA contribution in 2018?

A. $0
B. $3,500
C. $5,500
D. $6,500

7. Penny, age 48, and William, age 49, are married and file jointly. Both are self-employed and report their business income on Schedule C. William's Schedule C business has $9,900 in profits during the year. His wife, Penny, has a net operating loss of ($5,100) on her Schedule C. Penny also earned $3,000 in wages from a part-time seasonal job. They also co-own a rental property that earned $23,000 in rental income during the year. What is their maximum allowable IRA contribution for 2018?

A. They are allowed to contribute $5,500 each.
B. William can contribute $5,500. Penny can only contribute $3,000.
C. William can contribute $5,500. Penny can only contribute $4,400.
D. William can contribute $5,500. Penny cannot contribute to her IRA because she has an overall loss for the year.

8. Kristina, 48, is a full-time graduate student with $1,200 of wages. She marries Omar, 50, during the year. Omar has taxable compensation of $66,000 in 2018. What is the maximum they can contribute to their traditional IRA accounts in 2018 if they file jointly?

A. $1,200
B. $6,700
C. $11,000
D. $12,000

9. Steven, age 36 and single, is in the Marines. He has the following income in 2018:

Nontaxable combat pay	$30,500
Regular wages	2,100
Interest income	4,600

What is the maximum amount that Steven can contribute to a traditional IRA?

A. $2,100
B. $4,600
C. $5,500
D. $6,500

10. Franklin, age 72, and Susie, age 50, are married and file jointly. In 2018, Franklin earned wages of $30,000, and Susie earned $5,000. If Franklin and Susie file jointly, how much can they contribute to their traditional IRAs?

A. Susie and Franklin can each contribute $5,500 to their respective IRA accounts.
B. Susie and Franklin can each contribute $6,500 to their respective IRA accounts.
C. Susie can contribute $5,500. Franklin can contribute $6,500.
D. Susie can contribute $6,500. Franklin cannot make an IRA contribution.

11. Rafael, 40, earns $26,000 in wages during the year. Although he is allowed to contribute up to $5,500 to his traditional IRA, he only has enough cash to contribute $2,500. On April 30, 2019, Rafael expects to receive a big commission bonus, and he wishes to make a catch-up contribution for 2018. Rafael filed an extension for his tax return, so his federal return isn't due until October 15, 2019. Which of the following statements is correct?

A. Rafael can contribute an additional $3,000 by April 30, 2019, and allocate the contribution for the 2018 tax year as long as he files his tax return by the extended due date.
B. Rafael cannot contribute an additional $3,000 for the 2018 tax year past the normal tax return filing deadline.
C. Rafael cannot make a 2018 contribution to his traditional IRA unless he files his return by April 15, 2019.
D. Rafael cannot make a 2018 contribution to his IRA after December 31, 2018.

12. Which of the following statements is correct?

A. A taxpayer can convert a traditional IRA to a Roth IRA. The transaction is tax-free.
B. A taxpayer can convert a traditional IRA to a Roth IRA. Any applicable tax must be paid on the conversion.
C. A taxpayer can rollover a traditional IRA to a Roth IRA only if his income is under $100,000 in 2018.
D. A taxpayer cannot convert a traditional IRA to a Roth IRA.

13. An excess contribution to an IRA is subject to an excise tax. Which of the following statements is correct?

A. The taxpayer will not have to pay the 6% tax on the excess contribution if he withdraws the excess contribution and any earnings on the excess contribution before the due date of the tax return for the applicable year, including extensions.
B. The 6% tax is due on both the excess contribution and any earnings on the excess contribution, even if the taxpayer withdraws the excess contribution from the account.
C. A taxpayer will not have to pay the 6% tax on the excess contribution if he withdraws the excess contribution and any earnings on the excess contribution before the due date of the tax return for the year, not including extensions.
D. A taxpayer will not have to pay the 6% on earnings on the excess contribution if he is disabled.

14. Undoing or reversing an earlier Roth conversion is called a:

A. Conversion
B. Marital Rollover
C. Recharacterization
D. Distribution

15. Ginger is single, age 63, and has the following taxable income in 2018:

Annuity income	$15,600
W-2 Wages	3,000
Alimony income	2,300
Interest income	2,800
Rental income from a residential rental	16,000

What is the maximum amount that Ginger can contribute to her traditional IRA in 2018?

A. $3,000
B. $5,300
C. $5,500
D. $6,500

16. Which of the following distributions from a traditional IRA is subject to an additional 10% penalty?

A. Distributions made prior to age 59½
B. Distributions made after age 70½
C. Distributions made to an unrelated beneficiary after the IRA owner's death
D. Distributions made due to an IRS levy

17. Shari received a distribution in 2018 from her IRA and wanted to roll it over to an IRA with another bank. How long does she have to complete the rollover to avoid income tax and penalties on the distribution?

A. 30 days
B. 60 days
C. Until the end of the year
D. Until the due date of her return

18. Which of the following is considered an excess contribution to an IRA?

A. A contribution to a traditional IRA by a taxpayer in the year he has reached age 70½
B. A rollover to a Roth IRA
C. A contribution to a Roth IRA by a taxpayer who is age 75
D. A contribution made by a taxpayer who only has alimony income

19. Gwendolyn, age 38, is single and has no dependents. She contributes $5,500 to a traditional IRA, and she also participates in her employer's 401(k) plan. She has a modified adjusted gross income of $209,000 in 2018. Which of the following is correct regarding her IRA contribution?

A. It is fully deductible.
B. It is partially deductible.
C. It is not deductible.
D. She would be subject to a 6% excise penalty if she contributed to an IRA.

1. The answer is A. Unlike traditional IRAs, Roth IRAs do not require withdrawals until after the death of the owner. This is why Roth IRAs are used as an estate-planning tool. Traditional IRAs require owners to begin taking required minimum distributions (RMDs) at age 70½, but a Roth IRA does not require any distributions until after the owner's death.

2. The answer is C. Assuming Enoch has sufficient qualifying compensation; he could contribute $4,000 to his traditional IRA. The 2018 maximum for contributions to *all types* of IRAs is $5,500 per taxpayer (for taxpayers under the age of 50). Taxpayers are allowed to have different types of IRA accounts, but the maximum contribution limits apply to their total contributions for the year.

3. The answer is A. A taxpayer cannot deduct a contribution to an IRA after the due date of his tax return, even if he files for an extension. IRA contributions for 2018 must be made by April 15, 2019.

4. The answer is C. Depending on its terms; a qualified plan (such as a 401(k)) may allow a participant to borrow funds from his account balance. A loan can be no more than the lesser of:
- $50,000, or
- The greater of $10,000 or 50% of the vested portion of the participant's account balance.

These amounts are increased if the participant lives in a qualified disaster area.

5. The answer is B. Since Landon is married and lived with his wife during the year but is filing separately, he can contribute no more than $4,000, the amount of his only qualifying compensation for IRA purposes.

6. The answer is B. Lucas' IRA contribution for 2018 is limited to $3,500, the total amount of his wages. The interest income and the gifted money from his parents are not qualifying compensation for IRA purposes.

7. The answer is A. On a jointly filed return; they are both allowed to contribute and deduct the maximum allowable for their age bracket ($5,500 each in 2018). The rental income is not qualifying compensation for IRA purposes, but William and Penny may use their combined self-employment income to figure their maximum allowable IRA contribution. Even though Penny's business had a net operating loss for the year, she is not required to "offset" her Schedule C losses from her wages when determining her allowable IRA contribution. The answer is figured as follows:

William: $9,900 self-employment income +
Penny: $3,000 wages = $12,900 in qualifying compensation

If they file jointly, they can each contribute $5,500 ($5,500 x 2 = $11,000, which is less than the amount of their qualifying compensation).

8. The answer is D. They can contribute $12,000 if they file jointly. Kristina can contribute $5,500, and Omar can contribute $6,500 because he is 50. Even though Kristina only has $1,200 of compensation, she can use her husband's compensation to determine her maximum contribution.

9. The answer is C. Steven may contribute $5,500, the maximum contribution allowed for his age, because a taxpayer may *elect* to treat nontaxable combat pay as qualifying compensation for IRA purposes. The interest income is not considered qualifying compensation, but his wages exceed the maximum contribution amount, so he is still allowed to make the maximum contribution for the year.

10. The answer is D. Only Susie can contribute to a traditional IRA. Franklin cannot contribute because he is over 70½ years old. However, Susie is age 50 and can utilize Franklin's qualifying compensation to contribute the maximum of $6,500 to her own traditional IRA.

11. The answer is B. Rafael cannot contribute an additional $3,000 after April 15, 2019, the due date for filing 2018 tax returns, regardless of whether he files an extension. If contributions to a traditional IRA for the year were less than the limit, a taxpayer cannot contribute more after the original due date of the tax return to make up the difference. If Rafael wants to make an additional contribution for 2018, he must do it by the *normal* filing deadline, regardless of whether he files an extension or not.

12. The answer is B. A taxpayer may convert a traditional IRA to a Roth IRA. If a taxpayer wishes to convert all or a portion of his traditional IRA to a Roth IRA, he is required to pay income taxes on the amount of pretax (deductible) contributions converted, as well as the growth in value resulting from earnings on those contributions. After the funds are converted to a Roth IRA, additional earnings are tax-free, and distributions are generally not subject to tax. However, penalties apply if the taxpayer withdraws from the Roth IRA within five years of the conversion. The conversion is reported on Form 8606, *Nondeductible IRAs*.

13. The answer is A. The taxpayer will not have to pay the 6% tax on the excess contribution if the excess contribution and any earnings are withdrawn by the due date of his return, including extensions. If a taxpayer corrects the excess contribution in time, the 6% penalty will apply only to the earnings on the excess contribution.

14. The answer is C. When a taxpayer *reverses* a previous rollover or conversion of one type of IRA to a different type of IRA, it is called a recharacterization. A recharacterization can only be done through an IRA trustee. Because of changes in the Tax Cuts and Jobs Act, a 2018 conversion from a traditional IRA, SEP or SIMPLE to a Roth IRA cannot be recharacterized. However, a Roth IRA conversion made in 2017 could still be recharacterized as a contribution to a traditional IRA if the recharacterization was made by October 15, 2018.

15. The answer is B. Ginger's maximum contribution for 2018 is $5,300. Only Ginger's wage income of $3,000 and the $2,300 of alimony qualify as compensation for purposes of an IRA contribution. The annuity income, rental income, and interest income do not qualify.

16. The answer is A. Distributions made prior to age 59½ are subject to a 10% early withdrawal penalty, (if no exception applies). Some exceptions that allow early distributions from an IRA, as well as from qualified retirement plans, include the following:
- Distributions made to a beneficiary or estate after death
- Distributions made because of permanent disability
- Distributions to the extent of medical expenses (medical expenses that exceed 7.5%-of-AGI in 2018), whether or not the taxpayer itemizes deductions for the year
- Distributions made due to an IRS levy
- Qualified disaster distributions

The distributions listed above are not subject to the early distribution penalty, but they are subject to income tax at the taxpayer's normal tax rates.

17. The answer is B. Shari has 60 days to complete the rollover. If she does not complete the rollover within 60 days, the distribution is subject to income tax in 2018.

18. The answer is A. A taxpayer's contributions to a traditional IRA in the year he reaches age 70½ (and any later years) are considered excess contributions. An excess contribution and any earnings on it are subject to an additional 6% tax if the taxpayer does not withdraw the contribution and the earnings by the due date of the tax return, including extensions.

19. The answer is C. Gwendolyn cannot deduct her IRA contribution. Contributions to a traditional IRA who participates in an employer-sponsored retirement plan are allowed, but their deductibility is phased out at higher income thresholds. When MAGI reaches a certain threshold, the taxpayer's traditional IRA contribution is not deductible. In 2018, unmarried filers who participate in an employer plan and make more than $73,000 are not allowed to make deductible IRA contributions. If Gwendolyn makes nondeductible contributions to her traditional IRA, she must attach Form 8606, *Nondeductible IRAs*, to her tax return.

Unit 17: Foreign Financial Reporting

In this chapter, we will discuss foreign financial reporting requirements for U.S. taxpayers. The *Bank Secrecy Act* is the law that imposes the reporting of foreign financial accounts. The subject of foreign financial reporting is extremely complex, and the IRS continues to issue guidance on how taxpayers and tax professionals should approach this difficult topic.

A person who holds a foreign financial account may have a reporting obligation even when the account produces no taxable income, and even if the person does not have an individual income tax filing requirement. For the purposes of foreign financial reporting requirements, a "United States person" includes U.S. citizens, U.S. residents, and U.S. entities. There are four major forms used for reporting foreign bank accounts, foreign assets, and foreign gifts. These are:

- The FBAR (Form 114, *Report of Foreign Bank and Financial Accounts*)

- Form 8938, *Statement of Specified Foreign Financial Assets*

- Schedule B, *Interest and Ordinary Dividends (Part III)*

- Form 3520, *Annual Return to Report Transactions with Foreign Trusts and Receipt of Certain Foreign Gifts*

Federal law requires that U.S. persons report all worldwide income, including income from foreign trusts and foreign bank accounts. In many cases, these taxpayers need to complete Schedule B and attach it to their tax return. Certain taxpayers may also have to fill out and attach Form 8938, *Statement of Foreign Financial Assets*. Form 3520 is used to report certain foreign gifts and bequests. Schedule B, Form 3520, and Form 8938 are filed with the Internal Revenue Service.

The FBAR filing requirement, however, is considered a separate filing requirement than filing a regular tax return. FBARs are not filed with the IRS. These forms are filed directly with the Financial Crimes Enforcement Network (FinCEN), which is a division of the U.S. Treasury Department.

Generally, records of accounts required to be reported on the FBAR should be kept for five years from the due date of the report, which is the year *following* the calendar year being reported.

FBARs in General

The term "FBAR" refers to Form 114, *Report of Foreign Bank and Financial Accounts*. The FBAR is a reporting requirement and does not directly impact tax liability. In 2003, the Department of the U.S. Treasury delegated enforcement authority regarding the FBAR to the Internal Revenue Service (IRS). This means that the IRS does not process the FBAR filings, but the IRS is responsible for FBAR *enforcement*. With regard to FBAR filings, the IRS is responsible for:

- Investigating possible civil violations,
- Assessing and collecting civil penalties, and
- Issuing administrative rulings.

The FBAR must be filed electronically and is only available online through the BSA E-Filing System.[148] Taxpayers cannot paper-file FBAR returns. A U.S. taxpayer is required to file an FBAR if:

- The person had a financial interest in, or *signature authority* over, at least one financial account located outside of the United States, and
- The *aggregate* value of all foreign financial accounts exceeded $10,000 (U.S. dollars) at any time during the calendar year reported.[149]

The IRS defines "signature authority" as the authority of an individual or individuals to control the disposition of assets held in a foreign financial account by direct communication with the bank or other financial institution. In other words, FBAR reporting requirements are not determined by ownership of the funds. "Foreign financial accounts" include the following types of accounts:

- Foreign bank accounts, such as savings accounts, checking accounts, and time deposits,
- Foreign securities accounts such as brokerage accounts and securities derivatives or other financial instruments accounts, commodity futures or stock options accounts,
- Insurance policies with a cash value (such as a whole life insurance policy),
- Foreign mutual funds or similar pooled funds (i.e., a fund that is available to the general public with a regular net asset value determination and regular redemptions),
- Any other accounts maintained in a foreign financial institution or with a person performing the services of a financial institution.

The FBAR is due by April 15th of the year following the year in which the account holder meets the $10,000 threshold. This threshold is the same for every filing status. Whether or not an account produces income does not affect the requirement to file an FBAR.

> **Note:** The due date for FBARs coincides with the tax return due date. The "official" FBAR due date is April 15. However, FinCEN grants filers an automatic extension to October 15 to file the FBAR. There is no requirement or form to request this extra time.

---

[148] The "BSA E-Filing System" is an official U.S. Treasury website and is used for online filing of FBAR returns. The website also supports electronic filing of Bank Secrecy Act (BSA) forms through a secure network.

[149] Accounts are converted to U.S. currency based on the exchange rate as of the end of the calendar year, applied to the highest balance in the account during the year, even if the highest balance in the foreign account was sometime before the end of the year.

Example: Carlos, a U.S. citizen, co-owns a foreign bank account in Costa Rica with his father, Aquilino, who is a Costa Rican citizen. The maximum value in the account is $15,000 USD. Half of the income in the account belongs to his father, and the account does not produce any income. Carlos is required to file an FBAR to report the account.

There is no minimum age requirement for filing an FBAR. The requirement includes minor children, as well. If a child holds $10,000 in a foreign financial account, even if the account is not earning revenues, the child will be required to file their own FBAR.

This is true even if the child would otherwise not have a U.S. filing requirement. If a child cannot file his or her own FBAR for any reason, such as age, the child's parent, guardian, or another legally responsible person must file it for the child.

Example: Gideon is six years old. He is a U.S. citizen. Gideon's grandmother, Aurelia, is a citizen of Italy. Aurelia sets up a savings account for her grandson in an Italian bank, and deposits 50,000 Euros into the account. Aurelia then names Gideon as the co-owner of the account. Using current currency conversion rates, the account balance is worth approximately $56,300 U.S. dollars. Gideon is required to file an FBAR to report the existence and value of the account, even if he does not withdraw the funds or personally receive any of the proceeds from the account.

U.S. partnerships, corporations, estates and trusts that meet the $10,000 threshold are also required to file an FBAR.

Example: Russell is a U.S. citizen. Russell's parents are citizens of Canada and live in Canada. Russell has signature authority on his elderly parents' accounts in Canada, but he has never written a check or made any withdrawals from his parents' bank account. The bank account balance reaches $10,000 for the first time in 2018. Russell is required to file an FBAR by April 15, 2019. Whether or not his signature authority is ever exercised is irrelevant to the FBAR filing requirement.

Note: U.S. law requires taxpayers to file a Report of Foreign Bank and Financial Accounts (FBAR) if they meet a threshold of $10,000 in a foreign bank account at **any time** during the calendar year. This includes all accounts which the taxpayer may own or have any financial interest in—this includes signature authority, power of attorney, or custodianship.

An FBAR can be filed jointly with a spouse. All FBAR forms are required to be filed electronically with the Treasury Department's Financial Crimes Enforcement Network (FinCEN). The FBAR is not considered part of the taxpayer's individual tax return.

Penalties for Nonfiling the FBAR

The Treasury Department reports that FBAR filings have surged in recent years, with current filings exceeding one million per year. The consequences of failure to timely file an FBAR can be extremely severe. Both civil penalties and criminal sanctions can be imposed. By law, civil penalties could exceed $10,000 per year for a "non-willful" failure to file.

A "willful" failure could result in the greater of $100,000 or 50% of the balance in an unreported foreign account per year for up to six years. This is in addition to criminal penalties. Criminal penalties may include a fine of up to $250,000 and five years in prison.

> **Note:** The potential penalties for willful failure to file an FBAR are huge. These penalties can include criminal prosecution as well as severe monetary civil penalties.

The most common FBAR reporting mistake is simply failing to file. The IRS has issued guidance on penalties for failing to file an FBAR that caps the maximum percentage of the penalty.[150]

FBAR penalties for inadvertent or "non-willful" failure to file are limited. In most cases, the total penalty amount for all years under examination will be limited to 50% of the highest aggregate balance of all unreported foreign financial accounts during the years under examination.

The guidance also establishes procedures and documentation requirements for IRS examiners conducting examinations related to FBAR penalties.

Offshore Voluntary Disclosure Program (OVDP)

The IRS' Offshore Voluntary Disclosure Program (OVDP) offers taxpayers with undisclosed income from offshore accounts a way to disclose foreign accounts and possibly face reduced penalties and avoid criminal prosecution. Streamlined compliance procedures are also in effect. The IRS has FBAR submission procedures for taxpayers who do not need to use either OVDP or the streamlined procedures to report undisclosed income from offshore accounts. A taxpayer may avoid penalties for filing a delinquent FBAR if he:

- Has not filed a required FinCEN Form 114, *Report of Foreign Bank and Financial Accounts* (FBAR),
- Is not under a civil examination or criminal investigation by the IRS, and
- Has not already been contacted by the IRS about the delinquent FBARs.

The taxpayer should file the delinquent FBAR reports electronically, including a statement explaining why he is filing late.

The IRS will not impose a penalty for failure to file the delinquent reports if the taxpayer properly reported and paid all tax on the income from the foreign financial accounts that are reported on the FBARs. The statute of limitations for civil or criminal violations of the FBAR is generally six years.

> **Example:** Andromeda is a citizen of Spain and a legal U.S. resident. She frequently travels to her home country and maintains a bank account there with an average balance of $20,000. She is required to file an FBAR to report this foreign account. For tax year 2018, Andromeda must file her FBAR by April 15, 2019, but she is allowed an automatic extension of time to file until October 15, 2019.

---

[150] May 13, 2015, *Interim Guidance for Report of Foreign Bank and Financial Accounts (FBAR) Penalties,* Department of the Treasury.

Because foreign financial institutions may not be subject to the same reporting requirements as financial institutions located within the United States, the FBAR is designed to help the U.S. government identify persons or entities that use offshore accounts to hide income or illicit funds.

> **Example:** Gustavo is a U.S. citizen who has a bank account in Mexico. In prior years, the value of his foreign bank account totaled approximately $7,500. Therefore, Gustavo did not have an FBAR requirement. However, in 2018, Gustavo decides that he wants to build a vacation home in Mexico. He transfers $18,000 to his Mexican bank account on January 10, 2018, to begin construction on his new residence. Although he later withdraws all the funds, he is still required to file an FBAR. Gustavo must file his FBAR by April 15, 2019, because the aggregate value of his foreign accounts reached $10,000 in 2018. However, he is not required to file Form 8938 (to be discussed later), because the value of his foreign assets is below the required threshold.

Foreign Financial Accounts

For FBAR purposes, a foreign financial account is a financial account located outside of the United States. A foreign "financial account" also includes a commodity futures or stock options account, an insurance policy with a cash value (such as a whole life insurance policy), an annuity policy with a cash value, and shares in a foreign mutual fund or similar pooled fund (i.e., a fund that is available to the general public with a regular net asset value determination and regular redemptions). The following accounts are not considered "foreign financial accounts":

- Foreign financial accounts owned by a governmental entity
- Foreign financial accounts owned by an international financial institution
- Foreign financial accounts maintained on a United States military banking facility (for example, a banking institution on a U.S. military base).

An owner or beneficiary of an IRA or another qualified retirement plan is also not required to report a foreign financial account that is held in the retirement plan.

> **Example:** Grady directly holds shares of a U.S. mutual fund. The mutual fund invests in foreign stocks as well as domestic stocks. Since the foreign stocks are held in a U.S.-based mutual fund, Grady does not need to report his ownership in the mutual fund or the holdings of the mutual fund. The mutual fund itself would be responsible for any foreign financial reporting that was required.

> **Note:** A safe deposit box at a foreign financial institution is not considered a "financial account" for tax reporting purposes. However, under the FBAR rules, if gold, bullion, or foreign currency is held inside a foreign financial institution, it is subject to FBAR reporting. Specified foreign financial assets do not include gold, bullion, or currency *held directly* by the taxpayer.

> **Example:** Ebner is a U.S. citizen who lives in Columbia. Ebner collects gold and silver coins. He keeps the coins in a wall safe inside his home. He does not trust banks, so he does not have a foreign bank account. He keeps all his cash inside the wall safe, too. Ebner does not have an FBAR filing requirement.

Form 3520: Reporting Foreign Gifts and Bequests

U.S. individuals who received large gifts or bequests from certain foreign persons may be required to file Form 3520, *Annual Return to Report Transactions with Foreign Trusts and Receipt of Certain Foreign Gifts.* Form 3520 is due at the same time as the U.S. person's income tax return (including extensions) but is filed separately from the income tax return.

A foreign person is defined as a nonresident alien individual or a foreign corporation, partnership, or estate. In 2018, a U.S. person must file Form 3520, *Annual Return to Report Transactions with Foreign Trusts and Receipt of Certain Foreign Gifts,* if he receives gifts or bequests valued at more than $100,000 from a nonresident alien individual or foreign estate. A taxpayer must aggregate gifts received from related parties.

> **Example:** Nehemiah is a U.S. citizen that has many relatives living in Canada. In 2018, Nehemiah received $60,000 from her Canadian grandfather and $52,000 from her Canadian brother. Nehemiah must report the gifts because the total is more than $100,000 in a single year. She is required to report them in Part IV of Form 3520.

Form 3520 is considered an "information return," not a tax return, because foreign gifts or bequests are not subject to income tax.

However, failure to file a required Form 3520 can result in steep penalties. The penalty for reporting a foreign gift late is $10,000 or 35% of the gift's value. However, no penalty applies if the failure to report was due to reasonable cause and not willful neglect. The taxpayer is required to report a gift or bequest on Form 3520 when he constructively receives it.

Two transferors or grantors of the same foreign trust, or two U.S. beneficiaries of the same foreign trust, may file a joint Form 3520, but only if they file a joint income tax return.

> **Note:** A "foreign gift" to a U.S. person does not include amounts paid for qualified tuition or medical payments made on behalf of the U.S. person.

> **Example:** Jason is a U.S. citizen attending college in the United States. His aunt, Sedona, is a citizen of Australia. Sedona offers to pay her nephew's tuition. She makes a payment directly to Jason's college. There are no filing requirements for this foreign gift.

> **Example:** Daniel is a U.S. citizen who lives and works in the United States. Daniel's grandmother, Claudette, is a French citizen. In January 2018, Claudette dies and leaves Daniel a large inheritance of $250,000. After his grandmother's estate is settled by the executor, Daniel receives the inheritance via wire transfer on March 1, 2018. Since Daniel constructively received the funds in 2018, his Form 3520 is due on April 15, 2019. The funds are not taxable to Daniel, but the inheritance must be reported, since it is a bequest from a foreign estate over the reporting threshold.

Form 8938: Statement of Specified Foreign Financial Assets

Generally, taxpayers who hold "specified foreign financial assets" must also file Form 8938, *Statement of Specified Foreign Financial Assets,* with their tax returns if the amount of their assets exceeds certain thresholds. This is a separate filing requirement in addition to the FBAR filing requirements. Form 8938 requires the taxpayer to provide detailed financial information about their foreign accounts. Specified foreign assets include:

- Foreign stock or securities

- Financial accounts maintained by a foreign financial institution

- Foreign pensions or deferred compensation plans[151]

- Interests in a foreign estate

A filing requirement is triggered if the aggregate value of specified foreign financial assets is more than the following reporting thresholds:

1. **Unmarried taxpayers living in the US:** The total value of specified foreign financial assets is more than $50,000 on the last day of the tax year or more than $75,000 at any time during the tax year

2. **Married taxpayers filing MFJ and living in the US:** The total value of specified foreign financial assets is more than $100,000 on the last day of the tax year or more than $150,000 at any time during the tax year

3. **Married taxpayers filing MFS and living in the US:** The total value of specified foreign financial assets is more than $50,000 on the last day of the tax year or more than $75,000 at any time during the tax year.

4. **Taxpayers living abroad:** Unmarried taxpayers (and taxpayers filing MFS) living abroad must file Form 8938 if the total value of their specified foreign assets is more than $200,000 on the last day of the tax year or more than $300,000 at any time during the year; or, for joint filers, the value of their specified foreign assets is more than $400,000 on the last day of the tax year or more than $600,000 at any time during the year.

Failure to report foreign financial assets on Form 8938 may result in a penalty of $10,000 (and a penalty up to $50,000 for continued failure after IRS notification). Further, underpayments of tax attributable to non-disclosed foreign financial assets will be subject to an additional substantial understatement penalty of 40%.

If a taxpayer accidentally omits Form 8938 when they file their income tax return, the taxpayer should file Form 1040X, *Amended U.S. Individual Income Tax Return*, with their Form 8938 attached. However, a taxpayer who is not required to file an income tax return for the year does not need to file Form 8938, even if the value of his specified foreign assets is greater than one of the reporting thresholds.

---

[151] Payments or the rights to receive the foreign equivalent of social security, social insurance benefits or another similar program of a foreign government are not specified foreign financial assets and do not have to be reported.

The filing of Form 8938 does not relieve a taxpayer of the separate requirement to file the FBAR if they are required to do so, and vice-versa. Depending on the situation, the taxpayer may be required to file both forms, and certain foreign accounts may be required to be reported on both forms.

This reporting requirement also applies to specified domestic entities, including a domestic trust if one or more of the trust's current beneficiaries is a U.S. citizen or U.S. resident alien and the asset value thresholds are surpassed.

> **Example:** Inga is a U.S. citizen and resident with funds deposited in three different foreign banks. As of December 31, 2018, bank account #1 had $5,000; bank account #2 had $3,000; and bank account #3 had $2,500. Inga is required to electronically file an FBAR by April 15, 2019, because the aggregate value of her accounts is more than $10,000. However, she is not required to file Form 8938, because the value of her offshore assets is below the required thresholds.

> **Example:** Darius is a U.S. expat living and working in Mexico. At the end of the year, Darius has $385,000 in a Mexican bank account, because he is saving up money to purchase a condo in Cancun. Darius must file an FBAR as well as a Form 8938.

> **Example:** Jocelyn has an uncle who is a Greek citizen. In 2018, her uncle died, and Jocelyn inherited $200,000 in foreign bearer bonds from her uncle. The bonds are held outside of a regular bank account. Jocelyn is required to report the value of the bonds on Form 8938, even if she did not cash them out.

> **Example:** Edward, a U.S. citizen, purchased securities of a French company through a professional securities brokerage firm located in New York. Edward is not required to report these securities because he purchased the securities through a financial institution located in the United States.

A taxpayer does not need to report a financial account maintained by a U.S. financial institution or U.S. brokerage firm, even if the financial institution or fund invests in foreign stock. This also includes U.S. affiliates of foreign financial institutions. Examples of financial accounts maintained by U.S. financial institutions include:

- U.S. Mutual fund accounts
- IRAs (traditional or Roth)
- 401 (k) retirement plans
- Qualified U.S. retirement plans
- Brokerage and investing accounts maintained by U.S. financial institutions

Foreign real estate is also not a "specified foreign financial asset." Therefore, a personal residence or a rental property in a foreign country does not have to be reported as a "foreign financial asset," unless the property is held by a foreign entity.[152] Directly-held tangible assets,

---

[152] If the real estate is held through a foreign entity, such as a corporation, partnership, trust or estate, then the interest in the entity is a specified foreign financial asset that is reported on Form 8938, if the total value of all the taxpayer's specified foreign financial assets is greater than the reporting threshold that applies.

such as art, gold, antiques, jewelry, cars and other collectibles, are also not specified foreign financial assets.

Foreign currency is not a specified "foreign financial asset" if it is directly-held by the taxpayer and not held in a financial institution.

Example: Phineas is a U.S. citizen living and working in Mexico. He owns a house in Mexico, and also some very valuable artwork. The value of the house is $370,000 USD and the value of the artwork is $125,000. He owns the house and the artwork outright. He is not required to report the value of these assets on Form 8938. He also has a foreign bank account in Mexico, with the equivalent of $9,000 USD. His foreign bank account balance has never exceeded $10,000 USD during the year, so he does not have to file an FBAR, either.

Example: Khloe is a U.S. citizen who lives and works in Brazil for an online tutoring company that is based in the United States. Khloe lives with her grandmother, who is a Brazilian citizen. Khloe does not have a bank account in Brazil. Instead, she has a bank account in the U.S. and she uses her ATM card and credit cards to withdraw money and make purchases. She keeps a fairly large amount of Brazilian currency inside her home, in a safe, with her jewelry. Since she does not have a foreign bank account or any other specified foreign assets, she does not have to file Form 8938 or the FBAR.

Schedule B, Reporting Foreign Accounts and Trusts

Schedule B is used to report interest and dividend income received during the tax year. However, the last part of Schedule B (Part III) is used by taxpayers who have financial accounts in foreign countries. This section of the form is where the taxpayer must disclose any foreign bank or investment accounts and whether or not the taxpayer received any distributions from a foreign trust.

The reporting requirements for these taxpayers have increased significantly in recent years as part of FATCA, which refers to the Foreign Account Tax Compliance Act. The law addresses tax noncompliance by U.S. taxpayers with foreign accounts by focusing on reporting by these taxpayers and by foreign financial institutions.

In general, federal law requires U.S. citizens and resident aliens to report any worldwide income, including income from foreign trusts and foreign bank and securities accounts. In most cases, affected taxpayers need to complete and attach Schedule B to their tax returns. Part III of Schedule B asks about the existence of foreign accounts, such as bank and securities accounts, and generally requires U.S. citizens to report the country in which each account is located.

On Part III, Schedule B, a taxpayer must check yes or no to the question of whether he had at any time during the year a financial interest in or signature authority over a financial account.

A taxpayer who had a financial interest in a foreign account should check the "yes" box even if he is not required to file FinCEN Form 114, *Report of Foreign Bank and Financial Accounts* (FBAR). There is no dollar threshold on the duty to report foreign accounts on Schedule B.

Note: If a taxpayer does not otherwise have a filing requirement, they are not required to file a tax return merely to report their foreign financial accounts on Schedule B.

For reporting purposes on Schedule B, a "foreign financial account" includes securities, brokerage, savings, checking, deposit, time deposit, or other accounts that are maintained within a financial institution. A financial account also includes a commodity futures or options account, an insurance policy with a cash value (such as a whole life insurance policy), an annuity policy with a cash value, and shares in a foreign mutual fund.

A financial account is considered to be located in a foreign country if the account is *physically located outside* of the United States. This includes accounts maintained with a branch of a U.S. bank if it is physically located outside the United States. However, a branch of a foreign bank is not a foreign account if it is physically located in the United States.

Differences Between the FBAR vs. Form 8938		
Data	**FBAR**	**Form 8938**
Who must file?	U.S. persons, which includes U.S. citizens, U.S. resident aliens, trusts, estates, and domestic entities	Specified individuals, which includes U.S. citizens, resident aliens, and certain nonresident aliens who elect to be treated as resident aliens for purposes of filing a joint income tax return. This form also applies to specified domestic entities.
Reporting thresholds	$10,000 held in any foreign bank at any time during the calendar year	$50,000 ($100,000 MFJ) on the last day of the tax year or $75,000 ($150,000 MFJ) at any time during the tax year (note that filling thresholds are higher for U.S. citizens and U.S. residents that have a foreign tax home)
When does the taxpayer have "an interest" in an account or asset?	Financial interest in an applicable foreign account, or signature authority on an applicable foreign account	Any income, gains, losses, deductions, credits, gross proceeds, or distributions from holding or disposing of the account or asset that are (or would be required to be) reported, included, or otherwise reflected on the taxpayer's return
What is reported?	The maximum value of financial accounts	The maximum value of specified foreign financial assets
How are values determined and reported?	Converted to U.S. dollars using the end of the calendar year exchange rate and reported in U.S. dollars.	The fair market value of the asset in U.S. dollars
Due date	Due by April 15 (an automatic extension is allowed to October 15)	The same due date as the taxpayer's individual return, including extensions
Filing procedures	File electronically through FinCEN's BSA E-Filing System. The FBAR is not filed with a federal tax return.	This form must be filed with the taxpayer's income tax return (Form 1040).
Penalties	Willful non-filing: up to the greater of $100,000 or 50% of account balances; "non-willful" violation civil penalties are up to $10,000 per violation. Criminal penalties may also apply.	Up to $10,000 for failure to disclose, and an additional $10,000 for every 30 days of non-filing after IRS notice of a failure to disclose; criminal penalties may also apply

(Test yourself first; then check the correct answers at the end of this quiz.)

1. Annabelle is unmarried and lives in Texas. She is a U.S. citizen and has ownership of specified foreign assets totaling $75,000. Which form is Annabelle required to submit to the IRS?

A. Form 8938
B. Form 1040 G
C. Schedule L
D. FBAR

2. Part _____ of Schedule B is completed by taxpayers who have financial accounts in foreign countries.

A. Part I
B. Part II
C. Part III
D. Schedule B is not used for this purpose

3. Which of the following documents is completed to report foreign bank and financial accounts?

A. Schedule B
B. Form 1116
C. Form 2555
D. FinCen 114

4. Generally, U.S. citizens, resident aliens, and certain nonresident aliens must report specified foreign financial assets ___ if the aggregate value of those assets exceeds certain thresholds.

A. Form 1040
B. FinCen 114
C. Form 8938
D. Form 9465

5. As a general rule, how long should taxpayers keep records related to an FBAR filing?

A. 3 years
B. 5 years
C. 7 years
D. 10 years

6. Regarding the FBAR reporting requirement, the IRS issued guidance on penalties for failing to file the FBAR that caps the maximum percentage of the penalty. In most cases, the total penalty amount for all years under examination will be limited to _____ of the highest aggregate balance of all unreported foreign financial accounts during the years under investigation.

A. 50%
B. 75%
C. 25%
D. 10%

7. Which of the following is a NOT considered United States person for the purposes of filing an FBAR?

A. A U.S. citizen who lives in Israel
B. A U.S. Resident who lives in Russia
C. A nonresident alien with $100,000 in U.S. investments
D. A U.S. consular officer that lives and works overseas in a U.S. embassy

8. Jim, a U.S. citizen who lives in Iowa, has a bank account located in Austria. He opened the account several years ago to send money to his mother, who is a citizen of Austria. He has signature authority on the account but does not withdraw money from it or collect any of the interest income on the account. On December 31, 2018, the account has a balance of $23,000. He receives Social Security and otherwise does not have a U.S. filing requirement or any tax liability for the year. What is Jim's reporting requirement for this account?

A. He is not required to file returns since he does not have a filing requirement or owe U.S. tax.
B. He must file Form 8938, *Statement of Specified Foreign Financial Assets*, with the IRS when he files his tax return.
C. He must file an FBAR, *Report of Foreign Bank and Financial Accounts*, with the Treasury Department.
D. He must file an FBAR, *Report of Foreign Bank and Financial Accounts*, with the Treasury Department, and file Form 8938, *Statement of Specified Foreign Financial Assets*, with the IRS when he files his tax return.

9. A U.S. person who receives a gift or bequest valued at more than _____ from a nonresident alien or foreign estate must file an information return with the IRS.

A. $10,000
B. $25,000
C. $50,000
D. $100,000

10. Which of the following is a "specified foreign asset" for reporting purposes?

A. Artwork displayed in a foreign museum.
B. Jewelry held in a foreign country.
C. Real estate held in a foreign trust
D. Foreign currency held at a taxpayer's primary residence.

11. When e-filing their federal return, a taxpayer who meets the requirements to file both Form 8938, *Statement of Specified Foreign Financial Assets,* and the FBAR (Form 114, *Report of Foreign Bank and Financial Accounts)*, should do which of the following?

A. Attach both forms to their federal return
B. Attach only the Form 8938 to their federal return and file the Form 114 through the Financial Crimes Enforcement Network's E-Filing system
C. Attach only the Form 114 to their federal return as it contains the 8938 information
D. Send both forms in separately to the Internal Revenue Service

Unit 17: Quiz Answers

1. The answer is A. Annabelle must file Form 8938. Generally, U.S.-based taxpayers who hold foreign financial assets with an aggregate value that exceeds $50,000 ($100,000 MFJ) on the last day of the tax year, or that exceeds $75,000 ($150,000 MFJ) at any time during the tax year, must file Form 8938. The thresholds are higher if the taxpayer has a foreign tax home.

2. The answer is C. Part III of Schedule B is completed by taxpayers who have financial accounts in foreign countries.

3. The answer is D. The FinCen 114 (FBAR) is the form used to report foreign bank accounts and foreign financial accounts.

4. The answer is C. U.S. citizens, resident aliens, and certain nonresident aliens must report specified foreign financial assets on Form 8938 if the aggregate value of those assets exceeds certain thresholds.

5. The answer is B. Generally, records of accounts required to be reported on the FBAR should be kept for five years from the due date of the report, which is the year *following* the calendar year being reported.

6. The answer is A. In most cases, the total penalty amount for all years under examination will be limited to 50% of the highest aggregate balance of all unreported foreign financial accounts during the years under investigation.

7. The answer is C. Nonresident aliens are not subject to the FBAR filing requirement. All of the following are subject to the FBAR filing requirement if they hold foreign bank accounts or applicable foreign assets.
- A citizen or resident of the United States
- A domestic entity
- A domestic corporation
- A domestic estate or trust

8. The answer is C. Jim is required to file an FBAR. There are two separate reporting requirements for taxpayers who hold certain types of foreign assets or who have certain amounts of funds in foreign bank accounts. An FBAR generally must be filed with the Treasury Department if a taxpayer has more than $10,000 in offshore bank accounts. Taxpayers also must file a statement with the IRS if they hold foreign financial assets with an aggregate value that exceeds $50,000 ($100,000 MFJ) on the last day of the tax year, or that exceeds $75,000 ($150,000 MFJ) at any time during the tax year. In Jim's case, since the funds in his foreign account total $23,000, he is only required to file an FBAR. He is required to file the FBAR, even if he earns no money from the account and owes no U.S. tax.

9. The answer is D. Form 3520, *Annual Return to Report Transactions with Foreign Trusts and Receipt of Certain Foreign Gifts*, is an information return, not a tax return because foreign gifts or bequests are not subject to income tax. In 2018, a U.S. person must file Form 3520 if he receives gifts or bequests valued at more than $100,000 from a nonresident alien individual or foreign estate.

10. The answer is C. Foreign real estate held in a trust would be a specified foreign asset. If the real estate is held through a foreign entity, such as a corporation, partnership, trust or estate, then the interest in the entity is a specified foreign financial asset that must be reported on Form 8938. Answers "A" and "B" are incorrect, because directly held tangible assets, such as art, antiques, jewelry, cars and other collectibles, are not specified foreign financial assets. Answer "D" is incorrect, because foreign currency is not automatically a specified foreign financial asset, unless it is held in a banking institution.

11. The answer is B. The taxpayer must only attach the Form 8938 to their federal return. The FBAR, Form 114, is not filed with a federal tax return or with the IRS. It is filed online with the Financial Crimes Enforcement Network e-filing system.

Unit 18: Estate and Gift Taxes

More Reading:
Publication 559, *Survivors, Executors, and Administrators*
Publication 950, *Introduction to Estate and Gift Taxes*
Instructions for Form 1041
Instructions for Form 706
Instructions for Form 709

Estates in General

An estate is a separate legal entity created when a taxpayer dies. The estate tax is a tax on the transfer of assets or property from an individual's estate to his beneficiaries after his death. The TCJA makes substantial changes to the estate tax exemption.

The TCJA doubles the estate tax exclusion to $11.18 million for single filers and $22.36 million for couples[153] and continues to index the exclusion levels for inflation through tax year 2025. The top estate and gift tax rate remains at 40%. A comparable increase applies to the generation-skipping transfer tax exemption (covered later). The portability election remains under the TCJA (also covered later). The 2018 annual gift exclusion is $15,000, increased from $14,000 in the prior year.

Note: For Part 1 of the EA exam, you will be required to understand how estate and gift taxes affect individual taxpayers, especially the surviving spouses and other beneficiaries of those estates. For Part 2 of the exam, you will be tested on the tax treatment of estates and trusts as legal entities. It is possible that questions will overlap, and therefore we cover the concept of estate taxation from various perspectives.

Personal Representative or Executor

After a person dies, a personal representative, (an executor or administrator appointed by a court), will typically manage the estate and settle the decedent's financial affairs. If there is no executor or administrator, another person with possession of the decedent's property may act as the personal representative. If a probate court proceeding is necessary, the judge will appoint an executor if one is not named in the decedent's will.

Note: Under state law, a "personal representative" is a living person appointed by the courts to administer an estate after a taxpayer has died. *Executors* are appointed when the decedent has a will, and *administrators* are appointed when the decedent dies without a will. The IRS also uses the term "personal representative" to refer to anyone filing a return on behalf of a decedent, regardless if that person has been appointed by the courts or formally named in the taxpayer's will.

The personal representative is also responsible for determining any estate tax liability before the estate's assets are distributed to beneficiaries. The tax liability for an estate attaches to the assets of the estate itself. If the assets are distributed to the beneficiaries before the taxes

---

[153] This exemption may be less in situations where the exemption has been reduced due to prior taxable gifts.

are paid, the beneficiaries or the executor may be held liable for the tax debt, up to the value of the assets distributed.

After a taxpayer dies, the following tax returns may need to be filed by the personal representative of the estate:

- **Form 1040:** Final income tax return for the decedent (for income received before death).

- **Form 1041**, *U.S. Income Tax Return for Estates and Trusts*: Fiduciary income tax returns for the estate for the period of its administration

- **Form 706**, *United States Estate (and Generation-Skipping Transfer) Tax Return*: If the gross estate, based on the fair market value of its assets, exceeds the applicable threshold. This return is used to report tax on the taxable estate (the gross estate minus certain deductions).

The personal representative or executor must sign each required return. A personal representative should sign the decedent's final return as "Personal Representative." If the taxpayer's final return is a joint return, then the surviving spouse would sign as a "Surviving Spouse."

Note: A personal representative or executor of an estate cannot be held liable if an insolvent estate does not have enough assets to cover any of the income taxes due or debts. *However*, the executor must be sure that any income taxes are paid before any assets are distributed to the beneficiaries of the estate; otherwise the executor might be held personally liable for the tax debt.

Example: Gabriel was named the executor of his late mother's estate. Gabriel has two younger sisters, who are beneficiaries of the estate, but are not executors or personal representatives of the estate. Gabriel distributes a large amount of stock and cash to both his sisters before he has had his mother's assets properly appraised. After the appraisal is done, Gabriel realizes that his mother's estate has a filing requirement and an estate tax liability. Since Gabriel distributed assets to the beneficiaries before determining the correct amount of tax due, he may be held personally responsible for paying the estate tax himself.

The executor or "personal representative" must include fees paid to them from an estate in their gross income. If the executor is not in the trade or business of being an executor (for instance, the executor is a friend or family member of the deceased), these fees are reported on the executor's individual Form 1040, as "other income." If the executor is in the "trade or business" of being an executor, (such as a self-employed estate attorney), the executor would report the fees received from the estate as self-employment income on Schedule C.

Final Income Tax Return (Form 1040)

The taxpayer's final income tax return is filed on the same form that would have been used if the taxpayer were still alive, but "deceased" is written after the taxpayer's name. The filing deadline is April 15 of the year following the taxpayer's death, the same deadline that applies for individual income tax returns.

The personal representative must file the final individual income tax return of the decedent for the year of death and any returns not filed for preceding years. If an individual died after the close of a tax year, but before the return for that year was filed, the return for that year will not be the final return. The return for that year will be a regular return, and the personal representative must file it.

> **Example:** Elaine dies on February 28, 2019. At the time of her death, she had not yet filed her prior year tax return. She earned $79,000 of wages in 2018. She also earned $16,000 of wages between January 1, 2019, and her death on February 28, 2019. Therefore, Elaine's 2018 and 2019 tax returns must be filed by her representative or executor. The 2019 return will be her final individual tax return.

> **Example:** Huxley was unmarried when he died on April 20, 2018. His daughter, Janna, is the executor of his estate. Huxley earned wages before his death, so a final tax return is required for 2018. Janna asks her accountant to help prepare her father's final Form 1040, which will include all the taxable income that Huxley received before his death. The accountant also helps Janna with the valuation of her father's estate. After determining the fair market value of all her father's assets, her accountant concludes that Huxley's gross estate is valued at approximately $12 million on the date of his death. As this exceeds the filing threshold for 2018, an estate tax return (Form 706) is also required to be filed, and Janna is responsible for filing both returns and signing them as the official representative of the estate.

On a decedent's final tax return, the rules for deductions are the same as those that apply for any individual taxpayer. The decedent's year of death is *not* treated as a short tax year. In other words, the full amount of the applicable standard deduction or any applicable credits may be claimed on the final tax return, regardless of how long the taxpayer was alive during the year. For example, a decedent who died in the middle of the year would still be eligible for EITC (the Earned Income Tax Credit), if they otherwise qualified, even though their final return covers less than twelve months.

> **Example:** Tonia, age 62, was unmarried when she passed away on January 30, 2018. Her adult son, Patrick, is named as the sole heir and executor of her estate. Tonia earned a small amount of wages, $5,300 in the month before she died. Her income is below the filing requirement, so a return does not have to be filed. However, taxes were withheld from Tonia's wages, so Patrick files an individual tax return in order to receive a refund. Tonia is allowed the full standard deduction in 2018, even though she was only alive for a single month during the tax year.

Income in Respect of a Decedent (IRD)

Income in respect of a decedent (IRD) is any taxable income that was *earned* but not *received* by the decedent by the time of death. IRD is not taxed on the final return of the deceased taxpayer. IRD is reported on the tax return of the person (or entity) that receives the income.

This could be the estate, in which case it would be reported on Form 1041, as described below. Otherwise, it could be the surviving spouse or another beneficiary, such as a child. If there is no designated beneficiary for the income, then the IRD items are reported on the estate's Form 1041.

IRD retains the same tax nature that would have applied if the deceased taxpayer were still alive. For example, if the income would have been short-term capital gain, it is taxed the same way to the beneficiary. IRD can come from various sources, including:

- Unpaid salary, wages, or bonuses

- Amounts distributed from retirement plans distributed by payor before the taxpayer's death, but not yet received by the decedent at the time of death.

- Deferred compensation benefits

- Accrued but unpaid interest, dividends, and rent

- Dividends declared *before* the decedent's death, but payable *after* death

- Accounts receivable of a sole proprietor

Example: Irving was owed $15,000 of wages when he died. The check for these wages was not remitted by his employer until three weeks later and was received by his daughter and sole beneficiary, Jolene. The wages are considered IRD, and Jolene must recognize the $15,000 as ordinary income, the same tax treatment that would have applied for Irving.

Example: Kathryn died on April 30. At the time of her death, she was owed (but had not yet received) $1,500 of interest on bonds and $2,000 of rental income from a residential rental that she owned. Kathryn's beneficiary will include $3,500 of IRD in gross income when the interest and rent are received. The income retains its character as interest income and passive activity rental income.

Example: Reginald decides to cash out his traditional IRA in order to take a nice vacation. He contacts his IRA trustee and requests a distribution of $12,000 on February 1, 2018. The trustee tells Reginald that the check will take 7-10 days to deliver to his home. Two days later, Reginald dies suddenly. The $12,000 check for the IRA distribution is received by Reginald's daughter, who is the executor of his estate. The distribution is treated as IRD.

IRD is included in the decedent's estate and may be subject to estate tax. If a beneficiary receives IRD and the income is subject to estate tax, the beneficiary can deduct the tax on Schedule A of their individual income tax return as a miscellaneous itemized deduction. The beneficiary must claim the IRD deduction in the same tax year in which they actually receive the income. The IRD deduction has not been suspended by the Tax Cuts and Jobs Act.

And if the value of the decedent's estate isn't subject to estate tax (because it falls within the estate tax exemption), the IRD deduction is not permitted.

The Estate Tax Return (Form 706)

An estate tax return is filed using Form 706, *United States Estate (and Generation-Skipping Transfer) Tax Return.* This return is due nine months after the death of the decedent. A six-month extension is allowed. After the taxable estate is computed, it is added to the value of lifetime taxable gifts. The applicable estate tax rate is applied to derive a tentative tax, from which any gift taxes paid or payable are subtracted to determine the gross estate tax. The maximum estate tax rate is 40% in 2018. However, all or a portion of the gross estate tax may be eliminated after applying the Basic Exclusion Amount. The estate tax exclusion is $11.18 million for single filers and $22.36 million for couples.[154] Less than 1% of taxpayers are affected by the estate tax.

> **Example:** Nelda died in 2018 and left an estate valued at $9 million. She had not previously used any of her basic exclusion amount to avoid paying gift taxes, so the entire exclusion amount of $11.18 million is available to her estate. As this amount exceeds the estate's value, no estate tax is owed, and an estate tax return (Form 706) does not need to be filed.

There is a special rule that applies to widows and widowers. A surviving spouse can add any unused exclusion of his deceased spouse who died most recently to his own estate tax return. This is also known as "portability," or the "DSUE," which we will cover later. The assessment period for estate tax is three years after the due date for a timely filed estate tax return. The assessment period is four years for transfers from an estate.

Form 1041, Annual Tax Return for Estates and Trusts

An estate is a taxable legal entity that exists from the time of an individual's death until all assets have been distributed to the decedent's beneficiaries.

> **Note:** Most estates are administered and distributed within 12-18 months, but sometimes, when the decedent was a very wealthy person, or if the estate is in litigation, the estate may not terminate for years, even decades.

As investment assets will usually continue to earn income after a taxpayer has died, this income, such as rents, dividends, and interest, must be reported. Form 1041 is a fiduciary return used to report the following items for a domestic decedent's estate, trust, or bankruptcy estate:

- Current income and deductions, including gains and losses from disposition of the entity's property, and excluding certain items such as tax-exempt interest (collectively, *distributable net income* or DNI)
- A deduction for income either held for future distribution or distributed currently to the beneficiaries (income distribution deduction) that are limited to DNI, and
- Any income tax liability

Current income would include IRD if it was received by the estate rather than by a specific beneficiary. Expenses of administering the estate can be deducted either from the estate's income on Form 1041 in determining its income tax, or from the gross estate on Form 706 in determining the estate tax liability but cannot be claimed for both purposes. Schedule K-1 is used to report any income that is distributed or distributable to each beneficiary and is filed with Form 1041, with a copy also given to the beneficiary.

---

[154] This threshold is much lower for nonresident aliens at $60,000 in 2018.

Example: Matthew owned three rental properties before his death, on June 1, 2018. The income from the rental properties that was received while he was alive would be reported on his final Form 1040, Schedule E. The rental income that was received by his estate after his death would be reportable on Form 1041, *Annual Tax Return for Estates and Trusts.*

Estates and trusts are allowed some of the same tax credits that are allowed to individuals. The credits are generally allocated between the estate and the beneficiaries. However, estates are not allowed the Child Tax Credit, or the Earned Income Tax Credit. However, the Earned Income Tax Credit, Child Tax Credit, and any other applicable credits can be claimed on the decedent's final return even if the return covers less than 12 months.

Note: Just like individual taxpayers, estates and certain trusts are subject to the Net Investment Income Tax (an additional tax of 3.8% on net investment income). The provisions for this tax are generally similar to those for individuals, and it must be reported on Form 8960, *Net Investment Tax: Individuals, Estates, and Trusts.*

The due date for Form 1041 is the fifteenth day of the fourth month following the end of the entity's tax year but is subject to an automatic extension of five-and-one-half months if Form 7004 is filed. The tax year may be either a calendar or a fiscal year for an estate, subject to the election made at the time the first return is filed. An election will be made on the first return as to the accounting method (cash, accrual, or other) of reporting the estate's income.

Form 1041 is required to be filed for any domestic estate that has gross income for the tax year of $600 or more or a beneficiary who is a nonresident alien (with any amount of income).

The Estate Tax

The estate tax may apply to the decedent's taxable estate, which is the gross estate minus any allowable deductions. In 2018, an estate valued at less than $11.18 million would generally not be taxable or have a filing requirement. However, this threshold is much lower for nonresident aliens at $60,000.

Example: Darren is a U.S. citizen who dies in 2018. The FMV of all his assets on the date of his death on March 1, 2018, totals 8 million dollars. His estate is not subject to estate tax. Form 706 does not need to be filed. His executor may be required to file a final Form 1040 for the income that Darren earned while he was alive (from January 1 to March 1, 2018). A Form 1041 may need to be filed if the estate earns gross income of $600 or more in 2018.

Example: Daeshim is a citizen and resident of South Korea. Daeshim is a popular Korean recording artist, and his travels bring him to the U.S. quite frequently. Daeshim owns a vacation home in Hollywood, CA, which he uses at least once a year to entertain guests. When he is not in the U.S., he uses a management company to rent out the home to short-term tenants. Daeshim dies on November 1, 2018. The Hollywood vacation home is the only U.S. asset that Daeshim owned. The house's FMV on the date of his death was approximately $450,000. Since Daeshim is a nonresident for U.S. tax purposes, his estate has a filing requirement. His executor must file Form 706-NA and report the value of the asset.

The Gross Estate

The gross estate is based upon the fair market value of the decedent's property, which is not necessarily equal to his cost, and includes:

- The FMV of all tangible and intangible property owned partially or outright by the decedent at the time of death
- Life insurance proceeds payable to the estate or, for policies owned by the decedent, payable to the heirs
- The value of certain annuities or survivor benefits payable to the heirs
- The value of certain property that was transferred within three years before the decedent's death

The gross estate does not include property owned solely by the decedent's spouse or other individuals. Lifetime gifts that are complete (so that no control over the gifts was retained) are not included in the gross estate.

Deductions from the Gross Estate

Once the gross estate has been calculated, certain deductions (and in special circumstances, reductions to value) are allowed to determine the taxable estate. Deductions may include:

- Funeral expenses paid out of the estate
- Estate administrative expenses, if not deducted on Form 1041
- Debts owed at the time of death
- The marital deduction (generally, the value of property that passes from the estate to a surviving spouse)
- The charitable deduction (generally, the value of property that passes from the estate to qualifying charities)
- The state death tax deduction (generally, any inheritance or estate taxes paid to any state)

The following items are not deductible from the gross estate:

- Federal estate taxes paid
- Alimony paid after the taxpayer's death; these payments are treated as distributions to a beneficiary

Property taxes are deductible only if they accrue under state law prior to the decedent's death.

Special Rule for Medical Expenses

Debts not paid before death, including medical expenses subsequently paid on behalf of the decedent, are liabilities that can be deducted from the gross estate on the estate tax return. Medical expenses are outstanding at the time of death are liabilities of the estate.

However, if medical expenses for the decedent are paid out of the estate during the one-year period beginning with the day after death, the personal representative can alternatively *elect* to treat all or part of the expenses as paid by the decedent at the time they were incurred, and deduct them on the decedent's final tax return (1040), if that gives the taxpayer a better tax result. This special election can be made on an amended return, as well.

> **Example:** Lauretta, age 76, died on March 1, 2018, after a long battle with cancer. She incurred $42,000 of medical expenses, half during 2017 (the prior year) and half during 2018. When she died in March, all of her medical bills remained unpaid. The estate's executor paid the entire outstanding $42,000 bill in December 2018. The executor elects to file an amended return (Form 1040X) for Lauretta for 2017, claiming $21,000 as a medical expense deduction. The remaining $21,000 will be deducted on Lauretta's final income tax return (her 2018 Form 1040), subject to the same limit.

The Marital Deduction

Transfers from one spouse to the other are typically tax-free. The marital deduction allows spouses to transfer an unlimited amount of property to one another during their lifetimes or at death without being subject to estate or gift taxes.

> **Note:** The marital deduction is NOT the same thing as the Deceased Spousal Unused Exclusion, or DSUE, which is covered in the next section. The DSUE is an *election* that is only available to U.S. spouses.

To receive an unlimited deduction, the spouse receiving the assets must be a U.S. citizen and a legal spouse and must have outright ownership of the assets. The unlimited marital deduction is generally not allowed if the transferee spouse is not a U.S. citizen (even if the spouse is a legal resident of the United States).

> **Example:** Loren and Margie are married, and both are U.S. citizens. Loren dies and leaves his wife, Margie, all his assets, which total $15 million on the date of his death. The transfer is tax-free to Margie because of the unlimited marital deduction. Margie's estate may or may not owe tax when she dies, but the transfer of assets to a surviving spouse is generally a nontaxable event, provided that the surviving spouse is a U.S. citizen.

> **Note:** If the receiving spouse is not a U.S. citizen, assets transferred tax-free are limited to an annual exclusion amount. Noncitizen spouses can only receive $152,000 in 2018. This is true even if the spouse is a legal U.S. resident (a green card holder); it is one of the rare instances where U.S. citizens are taxed differently than legal U.S. residents.

Deceased Spousal Unused Exclusion (DSUE)

This is the unused portion of the decedent's predeceased spouse's basic exclusion (the amount that was not used to offset gift or estate tax liabilities). A portability election must be made to claim the DSUE on behalf of the surviving spouse's estate. This election can be made automatically by timely completion and filing of Form 706 for the estate of the predeceased spouse. Portability is not automatic.

This means that the executor, usually a surviving spouse, will need to transfer the unused exclusion to the surviving spouse. This is done by filing an estate tax return. The estate tax return is required when the first spouse dies, even if no tax is owed. This return is due nine months after the death of the first spouse. A six-month extension is allowed.[155] The DSUE is not available to nonresident alien spouses.

> **Example:** Myron died on January 4, 2018, and left a gross estate valued at $19 million. His assets transferred to his wife, Polly (who is a U.S. citizen), and none of the estate was taxed because of the unlimited marital deduction. Thus, none of the $11.18 million basic exclusion amount available to Myron's estate was used (and none had been used to offset gift tax liabilities during his lifetime). Polly then died in the same year, on December 20, 2018. Assuming Form 706 was timely filed for Myron's estate, electing the DSUE, and Polly had not used any of her basic exclusion amount, Myron's unused basic exclusion is added to Polly's basic exclusion, for a total exclusion amount of $22.36 million between their two estates. If Polly's estate is valued at less than $22.36 million at her death, the full amount can be excluded, and no estate tax will be owed by Polly's heirs.

Inheritances

For federal income tax purposes, cash inheritances are generally not taxable to the beneficiary, although the beneficiary may be responsible if there is a related estate tax liability that has not been satisfied.

Distributions of retirement plan benefits or distributions from taxable IRA accounts to the decedent's beneficiaries are generally subject to income tax when received.

> **Example:** Bruce's aunt, Georgina, died and left him $175,000 cash in her will. Georgina's estate did not have a filing requirement, and no estate tax return was required. Bruce is a U.S. citizen. He does not owe any federal tax on this inheritance.

The decedent's surviving spouse may be able to defer taxation by rolling over the assets of a taxable IRA to another IRA or to a qualified plan. Qualified distributions from a Roth IRA[156] or of previously nondeductible contributions to a traditional IRA are generally not taxable.

> **Example:** Raquel dies and leaves her entire estate to her son, Atticus. At the time of her death, she had a significant cash balance in her bank account as well as several rental properties. The estate has a filing requirement, but Atticus ignores his accountant's advice and simply withdraws all the money from his late mother's bank account. He also sells all the rental properties and uses the money to take several lavish trips. Although inheritances are generally not taxable to the beneficiary, the fact that Atticus took possession of his mother's assets without filing her required estate tax return or satisfying the estate tax liability would make him directly responsible for the tax. The IRS can come after Atticus in order to satisfy the estate's tax liability.

---

[155] Revenue Procedure 2017-34 allows an executor up to two years to elect portability provided that no estate tax return is otherwise due.

[156] Inherited Roth IRAs are subject to a 5-year "inheritance" rule. Inherited Roth IRAs have a series of rules that mandate a five-year waiting period. As long as the Roth was held for more than 5 years by the decedent, the inheritance is tax-free.

The Basis of Estate Property

Although cash inheritances are not subject to federal income tax, money received from the sale of inherited property may be taxable. The basis of property inherited from a decedent is generally one of the following:

- The FMV of the property on the date of death

- The FMV on an alternate valuation date, if elected by the personal representative

- The value under a special-use valuation method for real property used in farming or another closely held business, if elected by the personal representative

- The decedent's adjusted basis in land to the extent of the value excluded from the taxable estate as a qualified conservation easement

Example: Easton is the executor of his late father's estate. His father owned a large collection of collectible figurines and rare comic books. His father's will directs that the estate be split equally between Easton and his four siblings. Their father dies on February 1, 2018, and Easton does not elect the alternate valuation date. The fair market value of his father's collectibles on the date of death is $500,000. The collectibles are the only valuable asset that the estate owns. On December 1, 2018, the siblings all agree to sell their late father's collection for $552,000. Collectively, they must report a capital gain of $52,000 ($552,000 sale price minus $500,000 adjusted basis).

Alternate Valuation Date: If elected, the alternate valuation date is six months after the date of death. The estate value and related estate tax must be less than they would have been on the date of the taxpayer's death. However, for any assets distributed to a beneficiary after death, but prior to six months after death, the basis for these assets is the fair market value as of the date of distribution.

Jointly Owned Property: Property that is jointly owned by a decedent and another person will be included in full in the decedent's gross estate unless it can be shown that the other person originally owned or otherwise contributed to the purchase price. The surviving owner's new basis of property that was jointly owned must be calculated. To do so, the surviving owner's original basis in the property is added to the value of the part of the property included in the decedent's estate. Any deductions for depreciation allowed to the surviving owner for his portion of the property are subtracted from the sum.

If a property is jointly held between a husband and wife as tenants by the entirety, or as joint tenants with the right of survivorship, one-half of the property's value is included in the gross estate, and there is a step-up in basis for that one-half. The other half is stated at the surviving spouse's cost basis, net of any deductions for depreciation allowed to the surviving spouse on that half. If the decedent holds property in a community property state, half of the value of the community property will be included in the gross estate of the decedent, but the entire value of the community property will receive a step-up in basis.

Example: George and Shauna, brother and sister, owned rental property they purchased for $60,000 as joint tenants with right of survivorship. George paid $30,000 of the purchase price (for 50% ownership), and Shauna also paid $30,000 (for 50% ownership). Under their state law, each had a half interest in the income from the property. When George died, the FMV of the property was $100,000. Depreciation deductions allowed before his death were $20,000. Shauna's original basis was $30,000. Upon George's death, she inherited his one-half share of the property and her basis in this portion of the property is "stepped-up" to $50,000 (.50 × $100,000), resulting in a basis of $80,000 ($50,000 + $30,000 = $80,000). After subtracting her half of the depreciation deductions taken, Shauna's adjusted basis in the property after George's death is $70,000 ($80,000 - $10,000).

Generation-Skipping Transfer Tax (GST)

In the past, wealthy families used various strategies to transfer wealth and assets to their grandchildren and other descendants. In response to this, Congress created the generation-skipping transfer tax, also known the GST, to close this tax loophole.

The generation-skipping transfer tax (GST) may apply to gifts during a taxpayer's lifetime or transfers occurring after his death, called bequests, made to "skip persons." A skip person is usually a grandchild, but it also applies to those who are more than 37½ years younger than the person making the gift or bequest. The most common scenario is when a taxpayer makes a gift to a grandchild.

The GST is assessed when the property transfer is made, including instances in which property is transferred from a trust. The GST is based on the amounts transferred to skip persons, after subtracting the allocated portions of the donor's available GST exemption. In 2018, the GST exemption is the same as the estate tax basic exclusion amount, and the GST tax rate is set at the maximum estate tax rate of 40%. The GST is imposed separately and in *addition* to the estate and gift taxes.

Example: Roosevelt sets up a trust that names his adult daughter, Nannette, as the sole beneficiary of the trust. In January 2018, Roosevelt dies, and the trust passes to Nannette. However, on June 1, 2018, Nannette also dies, and the trust passes to her children (Roosevelt's grandchildren). Roosevelt's grandchildren are skip persons for purposes of the GST, and the trust's property may now be subject to the GST.

Any payments for tuition or medical expenses on behalf of a skip person that are made directly to an educational or medical institution are exempt from gift tax and GST. There is no reporting requirement for this type of gift, regardless of the dollar amount.

Example: Melton wants to help support his grandchildren, but he tries to make sure that his gifts are not subject to gift tax, GST, or estate tax. In 2018, he pays his grandchild's college tuition in full and writes a check directly to the college for $25,000. Since the amounts were paid directly to the college, there is no tax consequence for this gift, and no additional reporting is required.

The Gift Tax

The gift tax may apply to the transfer of property by one individual to another, whether the donor intends the transfer to be a gift or not. Gift tax is imposed on the *donor*, not the *receiver*, of the property. The recipient of a gift typically owes no taxes and does have to report the gift unless it comes from a foreign donor. However, under special arrangements, the donee may agree to pay the tax instead of the donor.

As discussed previously, an individual taxpayer's liability for estate tax and gift tax is subject to a combined basic exclusion amount ($11.18 million for single filers and $22.36 million for couples in 2018), and the use of any portion of this exclusion amount to reduce payment of gift taxes during the taxpayer's lifetime will reduce the amount available upon death to reduce applicable estate taxes. The following gifts are not taxable:

- Gifts to an individual that do not exceed the annual exclusion amount. In 2018, the gift exclusion amount is $15,000 per donee.

- Tuition or medical expenses paid directly to the educational or medical institution for someone else

- Unlimited gifts to a spouse, as long as the spouse is a U.S. citizen

- Gifts to a political organization for its use

- Gifts to a qualifying charity

- A parent's support for a minor child. This may include support required as part of a legal obligation, such as by a divorce decree.

Gift taxes are reported on Form 709, *United States Gift (and Generation-Skipping Transfer) Tax Return*. Form 709 must be filed if:

- A taxpayer gives more than the annual exclusion amount to at least one individual (except to a U.S. citizen spouse)

- A taxpayer "splits gifts" with a spouse

- A taxpayer gives a future interest to anyone other than a U.S. citizen spouse

If a gift tax return is required to be filed, Form 709 is generally due by April 15 of the following year. However, if the donor dies during the year, the filing deadline may be the due date for his estate tax return. Taxpayers who extend the filing of Form 1040 for six months using Form 4868 are deemed to have extended their gift tax returns, if no gift tax is due with the extension.

If the taxpayer does not extend their individual return, the gift tax return can be extended separately by using Form 8892, *Application for Automatic Extension of Time to File Form 709 and/or Payment of Gift/Generation-Skipping Transfer Tax.*

Note: A gift is considered a **present interest** if the donee has all immediate rights to the use, possession, and enjoyment of the property or income from the property. A gift is considered a **future interest** if the donee's rights to the use, possession, and enjoyment of the property or income from the property will not begin until some future date. Future interests include reversions, remainders, and other similar interests or estates. A gift of a future interest cannot be excluded under the annual exclusion ($15,000 per donee in 2018). With a "future interest" the beneficiary typically does not become the owner of the property until the donor's death.

Example: Mack is 26, and Lynette is his mother. Lynette gives her son, Mack, a gift of $15,000 of cash during the year. She also pays his college tuition, totaling $21,000, and writes the check directly to the college. Lynette also pays for Mack's medical bills by issuing an $18,000 check directly to his doctor's office. None of these gifts are taxable, and no gift tax return is required.

Example: Andrew is single. In 2018, Andrew gives his nephew, Jimmy, $19,000 to help start his first business. The money is intended as a gift, not a loan, so Andrew is required to file a gift tax return since the amount exceeds the $15,000 annual exclusion amount.

Applying the Applicable Credit to Gift Tax: After a taxpayer determines which of his gifts are taxable, he must calculate the amount of gift tax on the total taxable gifts and apply the applicable credit for the year.

Gift Splitting by Married Couples

Both the basic exclusion amount and the annual exclusion amount apply separately to each spouse, and each spouse must separately file a gift tax return if he or she made reportable gifts during the year. However, if either spouse makes a gift to another person, the gift can be considered as being one-half from one spouse and one-half from the other spouse. This concept is known as *gift splitting.*

Gift splitting allows a married couple to give up to $30,000 (in 2018) to a single individual without making a taxable gift. Both spouses must consent to split the gift.

Example: Ignacio and his wife, Elinda, agree to split gifts of cash. Ignacio gives a friend $21,000, and Elinda gives her niece $18,000. Although each gift is more than the annual exclusion amount of $15,000, they can use gift splitting to avoid making a taxable gift to each donee. In each case, because one-half of the split gift is not more than the annual exclusion amount, it is not taxable. A gift tax return is required.

Example: Gertrude gives her favorite cousin, Freddie, $25,000. Gertrude elects to split the gift with her husband, Maurizio, and Maurizio is treated as if he gave Freddie half the amount, or $12,500. Assuming they make no other gifts to Freddie during the year, the entire $25,000 gift is tax-free. However, a gift tax return is required in order to report the "split gift."

If a married couple splits a gift, each spouse must generally file his or her own individual gift tax return. However, certain exceptions may apply that allow for only one spouse to file a return if the other spouse signifies consent on the donor spouse's Form 709. Note that if gifts are made by a spouse from community property funds, the gift is deemed to have been made 50% by each spouse.

The Basis of Property Received as a Gift

For purposes of determining gain or loss on a subsequent disposition of property received as a gift, a taxpayer must consider:

- The gift's adjusted basis to the donor just before it was given to the taxpayer,

- The gift's FMV at the time it was given to the taxpayer, and

- Any gift tax actually paid on the appreciation of the property's value while held by the donor (as opposed to gift tax offset by the donor's applicable credit amount).

If the FMV of the gift was equal to or greater than the donor's adjusted basis in the gift right before the transfer, the donee's basis will be the donor's basis (transferred basis), adjusted for any gift tax paid on the donor's appreciation. If the FMV of the gift was less than the donor's adjusted basis in the gift right before the transfer:

- When the donee sells the property received as a gift, he calculates gain based upon the donor's adjusted basis.

- If the donee sells the property at a loss, the taxpayer's basis would be the FMV at the time of the gift.

- If the donee sells the property at a price higher than the FMV at the time of the gift, but lower than the donor's adjusted basis at the time of the gift, the basis at the time of the sale will be the sales price, resulting in no gain or loss on the sale.

> **Example:** Manuela receives an acre of land as a gift from her brother. Her brother's adjusted basis in the land is $50,000, and its FMV on the date of the gift is $40,000. A couple of years later, Manuela sells the gifted land for $35,000. Since she sold the property at a loss, her basis in the land is $40,000, because it is the lower of her brother's adjusted basis and the FMV at the date of the gift.

> **Example:** Donovan's father gives him 20 shares of stock that are currently worth $900. Donovan's father has an adjusted basis in the stock of $500. Donovan's basis in the stock is also $500.

Generally, the value of a gift is its fair market value on the date of the gift. However, the value of the gift may be less than its fair market value to the extent that the donee gives the donor something in return.

> **Example:** Abraham sells his son, Brandon, a house well below market value. Brandon only pays $10,000 for the house. In 2018, the fair market value of the house is $90,000. Therefore, Abraham has made a gift to his son of $80,000 ($90,000 - $10,000 = $80,000). Abraham is required to file a gift tax return because the gift exceeds the $15,000 threshold for 2018.

The Unified Credit (the Applicable Credit)

A taxpayer's gross estate tax is reduced by the *applicable credit*, also referred to as the *unified credit*. The unified credit is the combination of the lifetime gift tax exclusion and estate tax exclusion. For the 2018 tax year, the estate tax exclusion is $11.18 million for single filers.

The annual gift tax exclusion is $15,000. Just as with the basic exclusion amount, any portion of the applicable credit amount used to avoid payment of gift taxes reduces the amount of credit available in later years that can be used to offset gift or estate taxes.

For example, if a taxpayer exceeds the annual gift tax exclusion amount in any year, the taxpayer can choose to either pay the gift tax on the excess or take advantage of the unified credit to avoid paying the tax in the current year.

Note: For taxable gifts, each taxpayer has an aggregate lifetime exemption before any out-of-pocket gift tax is due. For example, a taxpayer can give away up to $11.18 million during their lifetime *above* the annual $15,000 exclusion and still avoid paying any gift tax.

Example: Adelle, who was single, died in 2018 and left an estate valued at $20 million. During her lifetime, she had used $1 million of her basic exclusion to offset payments of gift tax. That reduces the amount her estate may exclude to $10.18 million, which is then subtracted from her $20 million taxable estate.

(Test yourself first; then check the correct answers at the end of this quiz.)

1. Which of the following is not income in respect of a decedent (IRD)?

A. Wages earned before death but still unpaid at the time of death
B. Vacation time paid after death
C. IRA funds that were distributed before the taxpayer's death, but not received until after death.
D. A royalty check that was received before death but not cashed

2. In 2018, Jeffrey gives $26,000 to his girlfriend, Rachel. Which of the following statements is correct?

A. The first $15,000 of the gift is not subject to the gift tax, but the remainder is subject to gift tax, and Rachel is responsible for paying it.
B. Rachel is required to file a gift tax return and pay tax on the entire gift.
C. Jeffrey is required to file a gift tax return, Form 709.
D. Jeffrey may choose to report the gift on his individual Form 1040, Schedule A.

3. Eileen's aunt gives her a gift of a future interest on her estate. Eileen will have full use of the estate after her aunt dies. Which is the correct statement about this gift?

A. Eileen's aunt can use the annual gift tax exclusion for this gift in 2018.
B. The gift is considered a present interest.
C. Eileen must pay estate tax on the gift in 2018.
D. Eileen's aunt cannot use the annual gift tax exclusion for this gift.

4. Shawn, a single taxpayer, has never been required to file a gift tax return. In 2018, Shawn gave the following gifts:

- Tuition paid directly to a state university for an unrelated person: $18,000
- Payment to General Hospital for his brother's medical bills: $15,500
- Cash donations paid to his city's homeless shelter, a qualified 501(c)(3) organization: $50,000
- Gift paid to the Libertarian Party (not a qualified 501(c)(3) charity): $25,000

Is Shawn required to file a gift tax return for 2018?

A. No
B. Yes, because the donation to the political party is not an excludable gift
C. Yes, because each of the gifts exceeded $15,000
D. Yes, because the political gift is a reportable transaction

5. Maximo dies on May 1, 2018, and leaves his entire estate to his wife, Jeanne, a U.S. citizen. The estate is valued at $50 million on the date of his death. What amount of tax must Jeanne pay on her husband's estate in 2018?

A. $0
B. $15.52 million
C. $20 million
D. $38.82 million

6. Cash inheritances are generally:

A. Taxable to the beneficiary
B. Taxable for federal tax purposes, but not for state tax purposes
C. Taxable in amounts over $5 million
D. Not taxable to the beneficiary

7. When is an estate tax return due?

A. Four months after the close of the taxable year
B. Six months after the close of the calendar year
C. Nine months after the date of death
D. Twelve months after the date of death

8. Phil is unmarried and died in 2018. At the time of his death, he had assets of $10 million and owed debts of $500,000. He also had a life insurance policy in place that paid $1 million to his only child. He had not used any of his basic exclusion amount during his lifetime. Based upon the information provided, what is the taxable amount of Phil's estate that must be reported on Form 706?

A. $0
B. $4 million
C. $4.5 million
D. $5 million

9. Delia's estate has funeral expenses for the cost of her burial. How should the executor deduct these costs?

A. Funeral expenses are an itemized deduction on Form 1040.
B. Funeral expenses are deducted on Form 1041.
C. Funeral expenses are deducted on Form 706.
D. Funeral expenses cannot be deducted as an expense.

10. In general, who is responsible for paying gift tax?

A. The estate
B. The donor
C. The receiver of the gift
D. The executor

11. Duncan died in 2018. Following his death, the executor of his estate paid the following bills. Which of these is not an allowable deduction in determining Duncan's taxable estate?

A. Administration expenses
B. State inheritance taxes
C. Charitable contributions
D. Alimony paid after the taxpayer's death

12. Alana had gifts totaling $48,000 in 2018 that were subject to gift tax. When is her gift tax return due?

A. March 15, 2019
B. April 15, 2019
C. October 15, 2019
D. September 15, 2019

13. Which of the following statements concerning the deceased spousal unused exclusion (DSUE) is correct?

A. The DSUE allows an unlimited estate tax deduction for a surviving spouse and his or her children.
B. The predeceased spouse must have died from natural causes.
C. The maximum DSUE available for a spouse who dies in 2018 is $15,000.
D. A portability election can only be made by filing Form 706.

14. Leighton received 100 shares of stock as an inheritance from her brother, who died on January 6, 2018. Her brother's adjusted basis in the stock was $14,750. The stock's fair market value on the date of her brother's death was $26,200. The executor of the estate elects the alternate valuation date for valuing the gross estate. Six months later, on July 6, 2018, the stock's fair market value had dropped to $23,100. Leighton finally received the stock on August 26, 2018, when its fair market value was $23,500. She sold the stock a week later for $23,450. What is Leighton's basis in the inherited stock, in order to determine her taxable gain on the sale?

A. $23,100
B. $23,450
C. $22,200
D. $26,200

15. Emma's father dies during the year. Emma is the sole beneficiary of her father's traditional IRA. Emma is 46 years old when she takes possession of her father's IRA. Which of the following statements is correct about the distributions from the inherited IRA account?

A. Emma can avoid taxation by rolling over the IRA to another IRA or to a qualified plan.
B. The distributions are taxable to Emma but not subject to an early withdrawal penalty.
C. Any tax on the distributions must be paid from her father's estate.
D. The distributions are taxable to Emma, and also subject to an early withdrawal penalty because Emma is younger than 59½.

16. Sandy and Matthew are married and have combined assets of $13 million. They are both U.S. citizens. On May 10, 2018, Sandy dies. The FMV of Sandy's estate is $5 million on the date of her death. Matthew is the executor of his wife's estate and her sole beneficiary. Since the value of Sandy's estate was below $11.18 million threshold, Matthew decides not to file an estate tax return, and he declines to take the portability election. What future impact does this have on Matthew, the surviving spouse?

A. There is no taxable effect on Matthew in this scenario.
B. Since Matthew declined to file an estate tax return, he did not elect portability. There will be estate tax due upon Matthew's death, assuming that the value of his assets does not decline, and there will be no deductions for estate tax purposes.
C. Matthew will owe estate tax in 2018 on his inheritance.
D. Sandy's estate will owe estate tax in 2018. Her estate tax return must be filed by the executor.

17. The executor of Ophelia's estate is her sister, Elise. Elise decides to make a distribution of 100% of the estate's assets before paying the estate's income tax liability. Which of the following statements is correct?

A. The beneficiaries of the estate can be held liable for the payment of the liability, even if the liability exceeds the value of the estate assets.
B. No one can be held liable for the tax if the assets have been distributed.
C. Elise and the beneficiaries can be held liable for the tax debt, up to the value of the assets distributed.
D. None of the above

18. Bruno pays $19,000 of college tuition for his niece, Delia, directly to her college. Which of the following statements is correct?

A. The gift is taxable, and Delia must report the gift tax on her individual tax return.
B. The gift is not taxable, but Bruno must file a gift tax return.
C. The gift is taxable, and Bruno must file a gift tax return.
D. The gift is not taxable, and no gift tax return is required.

19. Which of the following items is not an allowable deduction from the gross estate?

A. Debts owed at the time of death
B. Medical expenses
C. Funeral expenses
D. Federal estate tax

20. Roberto and Sybil owned business property that they purchased for $100,000. They were joint tenants with right of survivorship. Each paid one-half of the purchase price. They took depreciation deductions prior to Sybil's death of $40,000. Under local law, each had a one-half interest in the income from the property. At the time of Sybil's death, the fair market value of the property was $200,000, one-half of which is includible in Sybil's estate. What is Roberto's basis in the property after Sybil's death?

A. $80,000
B. $100,000
C. $130,000
D. $200,000

21. In which case must a gift tax return be filed?

A. A married couple gives a gift of $15,000 to an unrelated person
B. A married couple gives a gift of $25,000 to a related person
C. A single individual gives a gift of $14,000 to an unrelated person
D. A wife gives a gift of $20,000 to her husband who is a U.S. citizen

22. All of the following gifts are excluded from the determination of the gift tax except:

A. A gift made to a political organization for its own use
B. A cash gift given to a nonresident alien spouse of a U.S. citizen
C. A medical bill paid directly to a hospital on behalf of a relative
D. A gift made to a qualifying charity

23. Janna is the executor for her father's estate. He died on November 5, 2018. Which of the following dates may she elect to use as an alternate valuation date for his estate?

A. December 31, 2018
B. April 15, 2019
C. May 5, 2019
D. October 15, 2019

24. Which of the following statements is incorrect regarding a married couple that uses gift splitting?

A. They must file a joint gift tax return along with their annual return (Form 1040).
B. They can give a gift of up to $30,000 in 2018 to a single individual without using any of their basic exclusion amounts to avoid paying gift tax.
C. They must file gift tax returns even if no gift tax is owed.
D. Each must consent to split gifts.

25. Karlotta died in 2018. Which of the following assets would not be included in the calculation of her gross estate?

A. Life insurance proceeds payable to Karlotta's children
B. The value of property transferred to Karlotta's son five years before her death
C. The value of property owned jointly by Karlotta and her spouse
D. The value of Karlotta's traditional IRA

26. A taxpayer dies on May 4, 2018. Assuming that Form 706 needs to be filed for his estate, when is his estate tax return due?

A. November 4, 2019
B. January 1, 2019
C. February 4, 2019
D. April 15, 2019

27. All of the following tax returns may include income in respect of a decedent (IRD) *except*:

A. The final Form 1040 for the decedent
B. The decedent's estate, Form 1041, if the decedent's estate receives right to the income
C. The Form 1040 of any person to whom the estate properly distributes the income
D. A beneficiary's Form 1040, if the right to income arising out of the decedent's death is passed directly to the beneficiary and is never acquired by the decedent's estate

Unit 18: Quiz Answers

1. The answer is D. Since the royalty check was received before the taxpayer died, it is not considered IRD income. Income in respect of a decedent is taxable income earned but not received by the decedent by the time of death. The fact that the royalty check was not cashed has no bearing on the nature of the income, and it should be reported as taxable income on the decedent's final income tax return (Form 1040).

2. The answer is C. Jeffrey is required to file a gift tax return. Gift tax is paid by the donor, not the recipient, of the gift. The first $15,000 of the gift is not subject to gift tax because of the annual exclusion. The remaining $11,000 must be reported on Form 709.

3. The answer is D. A gift of a future interest cannot be excluded under the annual exclusion ($15,000 per person in 2018). A gift is considered a present interest if the donee has all immediate rights to the use, possession, and enjoyment of the property or income from the property. A gift is considered a future interest if the donee's rights to the use, possession, and enjoyment of the property or income from the property will not begin until some future date. "Future interests" include: reversions, remainders, and other similar interests or estates.

4. The answer is A. Shawn is not required to file a gift tax return. None of the gifts are taxable gifts, and therefore, no reporting is required. Tuition or medical expenses paid for someone directly to an educational or medical institution are not counted as taxable gifts. Nor are gifts to a political organization for its own use or gifts to a qualified charity.

5. The answer is A. Jeanne will owe no estate taxes related to the value of Maximo's estate. The marital deduction allows for the transfer of an unlimited value of property from one spouse to another during his lifetime or from his estate after death without being subject to gift or estate taxes. To qualify for this unlimited deduction, the spouse receiving the assets must be a U.S. citizen and a legal spouse and must have outright ownership of the assets.

6. The answer is D. For federal income tax purposes, cash inheritances are generally not taxable to the beneficiary, although the beneficiary may be responsible for a related estate tax liability that has not been satisfied.

7. The answer is C. Estate tax returns are due nine months from the date of death, although the executor may request an extension of time to file.

8. The answer is A. After calculating allowable deductions from the gross estate, Phil's net estate is valued at $10.5 million. This amount is less than the basic exclusion amount of $11.18 million for 2018, so no estate tax is applicable in this case. Also, because the gross value of the estate was less than $11.18 million an estate tax return is not required to be filed.

FMV of Assets	$10,000,000
Minus liabilities	(500,000)
Life insurance proceeds	1,000,000
Net Estate	**$10,500,000**

9. The answer is C. No deduction for Delia's funeral expenses can be taken on Form 1041 or Form 1040. Funeral expenses may be claimed only as a deduction from the gross estate on Form 706. If an estate tax return is not filed, then the funeral expenses are not deductible.

10. The answer is B. The donor is generally responsible for paying gift tax.

11. The answer is D. Alimony paid after a taxpayer's death is not deductible from the gross estate. It is considered a distribution to a beneficiary. Deductions from the gross estate are allowed for:
- Funeral expenses paid out of the estate and administration expenses for the estate
- Debts owed at the time of death
- The marital deduction, charitable deduction, and state death tax deduction

12. The answer is B. Alana would be required to file her gift tax return by April 15, 2019, the filing deadline for individual returns. Gift tax returns are typically due on April 15 of the following calendar year (the filing deadline), and payment of the tax is also due then, although the filing may be subject to a six-month extension. If the donor died during the year, the filing deadline is the due date for his estate tax return.

13. The answer is D. The portability election allows a surviving spouse's estate the right to use a deceased spousal unused exclusion (DSUE), which is the remaining unused portion of the previously deceased spouse's basic exclusion amount. The portability election must be made by filing an estate tax return for the deceased spouse, even if no estate tax is owed.

14. The answer is A. The basis of property received from a decedent is generally the fair market value of the property on the date of the decedent's death. However, an executor has the option of choosing an alternate valuation date, which is six months after the date of death for valuing the gross estate. Since the alternate valuation date was elected by the executor, Leighton's basis is the fair market value on the alternate valuation date, or $23,100. This is the basis that she must use in order to calculate her gain or loss on the sale of the stock.

15. The answer is B. The IRA distributions are taxable to Emma, but not subject to a penalty. Distributions of retirement plan benefits or distributions from taxable IRA accounts to a decedent's beneficiaries are generally subject to income tax when received. The decedent's surviving spouse may be able to defer taxation by rolling over the assets of a taxable IRA to another IRA or to a qualified plan. However, a child or other beneficiary is not allowed this same treatment. Qualified distributions from a Roth IRA or of previously nondeductible contributions to a traditional IRA are generally not taxable.

16. The answer is B. Since Matthew declined to file an estate tax return, he did not elect portability. No estate tax is due after Sandy's death because the value of her estate is below the exclusion amount. However, all her assets passed to her surviving spouse. Matthew's estate is now in excess of the annual exclusion amount. Assuming there is no change in the value of Matthew's assets and no applicable deductions upon his passing, there will be estate tax due upon his death. He could have avoided this scenario if he had filed an estate tax return and elected portability.

17. The answer is C. Elise and the beneficiaries can be held liable for the tax debt, up to the value of the assets distributed. The tax liability for an estate attaches to the assets of the estate itself. If the assets are distributed to the beneficiaries before the taxes are paid, the executor and the beneficiaries can be held liable for the tax debt, up to the value of the assets distributed.

18. The answer is D. Bruno does not have a gift tax return requirement. Tuition or medical expenses paid directly to a medical or educational institution for someone else are not included in the calculation of taxable gifts, and there is no reporting requirement.

19. The answer is D. Federal estate tax is not deductible from the gross estate. The other items listed are allowable deductions from the gross estate. The decedent's unpaid medical expenses represent liabilities that can be deducted from the gross estate. Alternatively, if the expenses are paid by the estate during the one-year period beginning with the day after death, the personal representative can elect to treat all or part of the expenses as paid by the decedent at the time they were incurred and deduct them on the decedent's final tax return (1040).

20. The answer is C. When they purchased the property, Roberto's basis was $50,000 ($100,000 × .50. He was allowed half of the depreciation ($40,000 ÷ 2 = $20,000), which decreased his basis to $30,000. When Roberto acquired the property in its entirety after Sybil's death, the fair market value of the portion owned by Sybil was included, based on the stepped-up basis of $200,000. The one-half portion representing Sybil's interest ($200,000 × .50 = $100,000) is added to Roberto's basis for a final basis of $130,000.

21. The answer is B. In order to make a gift to one individual in excess of the annual exclusion of $15,000 and avoid using any of their basic exclusion amounts; a married couple can use gift splitting. Gift splitting allows married couples to give up to $30,000 to a single person in 2018 without making a taxable gift, but they each must consent to the gift, and each may be required to file a gift tax return. Gifts to a spouse generally do not require a return to be filed, unless the spouse is not a U.S. citizen.

22. The answer is B. Although a full marital deduction is allowed for a spouse who is a U.S. citizen, a transfer of property to a noncitizen spouse is limited, and the excess amount would be subject to gift tax. Noncitizen spouses can only receive $152,000 in 2018. This is true even if the spouse is a legal U.S. resident (a green card holder).

23. The answer is C. Janna can choose an alternate valuation date of May 5, 2019. An estate is normally valued on the date of the decedent's death. However, an executor may elect, under certain requirements, an alternate valuation date for an estate, which would be six months after the date of death.

24. The answer is A. If a married couple splits a gift, each spouse must generally file his or her own individual gift tax return. Couples cannot file a joint gift return. However, certain exceptions allow for only one spouse to file a return if the other spouse signifies consent on the donor spouse's Form 709.

25. The answer is B. The value of property transferred to Karlotta's son five years before her death would not be included in her gross estate. A taxpayer's gross estate includes the following:
- The FMV of all tangible and intangible property owned partially or outright by the decedent at the time of death
- Life insurance proceeds payable to the estate or, for policies owned by the decedent, payable to the heirs or beneficiaries
- The value of certain annuities or survivor benefits payable to the heirs or beneficiaries
- The value of certain property transferred within three years before the taxpayer's death (not five years, as stated in answer B)

26. The answer is C. If required to be filed, Form 706, *United States Estate (and Generation-Skipping Transfer) Tax Return,* must be filed nine months after the date of a decedent's death. The estate tax would be owed at this time. An executor may request a six-month extension to file Form 706, but the tax would still be owed on the earlier date.

27. The answer is A. The final Form 1040 for the decedent would not include IRD.

INDEX

About the Authors

Richard Gramkow, EA, MST

Richard Gramkow is an Enrolled Agent with over twenty years of experience in various areas of taxation. He holds a master's degree in taxation from Rutgers University and is currently an Assistant Director of State and Local Tax for a publicly held Fortune 500 company in the New York metropolitan area.

Kolleen Wells, EA

Kolleen Wells is an Enrolled Agent and a Certified Bookkeeper who specializes in tax preparation for individuals and small businesses. She has worked in the accounting field for many years, including positions at a CPA office and at the county assessor's office.

Christy Pinheiro, EA, ABA®

Christy Pinheiro is an Enrolled Agent and an Accredited Business Accountant. Christy was an accountant for two private CPA firms and for the State of California before going into private practice.

Joel Busch, CPA, JD

Joel Busch is a tax professor at San Jose State University, where he teaches courses at both the graduate and undergraduate levels. Previously, he was in charge of tax audits, research, and planning for one of the largest civil construction and mining companies in the United States.

See more information and online webinars at: *www.PassKeyPublications.com*

13433430R00243